THE LESBIAN HISTORY SOURCEBOOK

This groundbreaking critical anthology gathers together a wide range of primary source material on lesbian lives in the past. The extracts are drawn from a diverse range of sources, including court records, newspaper reports, literary sources, writings on lesbianism from psychologists, doctors and anthropologists, as well as personal letters and journals.

The sources are arranged into themed chapters, covering topics such as lesbian archetypes – cross-dressing women and romantic friends – professional discourses on lesbians, the making of lesbianism in culture, public perceptions of lesbianism and women's own experiences. This book will be a milestone in the publishing of lesbian history, and is set to provoke the impetus for fresh research.

Alison Oram is Reader in Women's Studies at University College Northampton. **Annmarie Turnbull** works for a national charity.

20

THE LESBIAN HISTORY SOURCEBOOK

Love and sex between women in Britain
from 1780 to 1970

*Alison Oram and
Annmarie Turnbull*

London and New York

First published 2001
by Routledge
11 New Fetter Lane, London EC4P 4EE

Simultaneously published in the USA and Canada
by Routledge
29 West 35th Street, New York, NY 10001

Routledge is an imprint of the Taylor & Francis Group

© 2001 Alison Oram and Annmarie Turnbull

Typeset in Garamond by Taylor & Francis Books Ltd
Printed and bound in Great Britain by MPG Books Ltd, Bodmin

British Library Cataloguing in Publication Data
A catalogue record for this book is available from the British Library

Library of Congress Cataloging in Publication Data
The lesbian history sourcebook: love and sex between women in
Britain from 1780 to 1970 / [compiled by] Alison Oram and Annmarie
Turnbull.
p. cm.
Includes bibliographical references and index.
1. Lesbians–Great Britain–History–Sources. 2. Lesbianism–Great
Britain–History–Sources. I. Oram, Alison. II. Turnbull, Annmarie.
HQ75.6.G7 L47 2001
306.76'63'0941–dc21
2001019315

ISBN: 0–415–11484–5 (hbk)
ISBN 0–415–11485–3 (pbk)

For Annabel Faraday, who began
lesbian history in Britain

CONTENTS

ACKNOWLEDGEMENTS

Alison Oram would like to thank: Anna Clark, Lesley Hall, Wendy Petchey, Wren Sidhe, and Chris Willis and everyone else who helped with finding sources and discussing the context of this book.

Annmarie Turnbull thanks everyone who helped her with this project.

The author and publishers wish to thank the following for their permission to reproduce copyright material:

Extract from *The Diaries of Virginia Woolf* by Virginia Woolf, originally published by Hogarth Press. Used by permission of the Estate of Virginia Woolf and the Random House Group Limited; extract from *The Collected Letters of Virginia Woolf* edited by Quentin Bell and Angelica Garnett, originally published by the Hogarth Press. Used by permission of the Executors of the Virginia Woolf Estate and the Random House Group Limited; letter from 'Monday 22 December 1925' in *The Diary of Virginia Woolf*, Vol. III: 1925–30, by Virginia Woolf, © 1980 Quentin Bell and Angelica Garnett, reprinted by permission of Harcourt, Inc.; extract from *I Know My Own Heart: The Diaries of Anne Lister, 1791–1840*, reprinted by permission of Helena Whitbread; extract from the diary of Edith Simcox, reprinted by permission of the Bodleian Library, University of Oxford, Department of Special Collections and Western Manuscripts; extracts from *Problems of Adolescent Girls* by J. Hemming, Heinemann, 1960 and from *Sex Problems in Women* by A.C. Magian, William Heinemann Medical Books, 1922, reprinted by permission of Heinemann Educational Publishers, a division of Reed Educational & Professional Publishing Ltd; extracts from the *Daily Express* and the *Sunday Express* reprinted by permission of Express Newspapers; extract from *Inventing Ourselves: Lesbian Life Stories*, published by the Hall Carpenter Archives Oral History Project. The interview tapes are in the British Library National Sound Archive; extract from *Rootless in the City* by N. Timms, reproduced by kind permission of the National Council for Voluntary Organisations; extract from *The Woman's Side* by Winifred Ashton, Herbert Jenkins Ltd, 1926, reproduced by permission of Laurence Pollinger Limited; extract from *The Telegraph*, reproduced by permission of the Telegraph Group Ltd; D. Bussy's *Olivia*, pp. 13–17, originally published by

Hogarth Press, reproduced by permission of the Random House Group; material from Vera Brittain's *Testament of Friendship* is included with the permission of Mark Bostridge and Rebecca Williams, her literary executors; extract from *One in Twenty: A Study of Homosexuality in Men and Women* by Brian Magee (copyright Bryan Magee 1966), reprinted by permission of PFD on behalf of Bryan Magee; extracts from Sigmund Freud, Copyrights, the Institute of Psycho-Analysis and the Hogarth Press for permission to quote from *The Standard Edition of the Complete Psychological Works of Sigmund Freud* translated and edited by James Strachey; extracts from *Homosexuality and Prostitution, A Memorandum of Evidence*, BMA 1955, reproduced by kind permission of the British Medical Association; extracts from *Enduring Passion* and *Sex and the Young* by Marie Stopes, copyright the Galton Institute, London, and reproduced by permission of the Galton Institute; extracts from the *Manchester Guardian* reproduced by permission of the Guardian Media Group Plc; extract from *Despised and Rejected* by A.T. Fitzroy, [1918], published by GMP Publishers Ltd, 1988, reproduced by permission of The C.W. Daniel Company Ltd; R. O'Rouke's *Reflecting on the Well of Loneliness*, pp. 117–43, Routledge, 1989, reproduced with permission of Taylor & Francis Books Ltd; Simone de Beauvoir's *The Second Sex*, Jonathan Cape, 1972, pp. 441–4, reproduced by permission of the Random House Group Ltd; *Towards a Quaker View of Sex*, pp. 37–40, copyright Quaker Home Service of the Society of Friends in Britain; extract from Makeda Silvera, 'Man Royals and Sodomites: Some Thoughts on the Invisibility of Afro-Caribbean Lesbians' originally published in *Feminist Studies*, Vol. 18, No. 3 (Fall 1992), pp. 521–32, reproduced by permission of the publisher, Feminist Studies, Inc; *Hidden Agendas, Theory, Politics and Experience in the Women's Movement* by E. Wilson, pp. 139–47, Routledge, 1986, reproduced by permission of Taylor & Francis Books Ltd; *Five on a Treasure Island*, Hodder and Stoughton, 1942, reproduced by kind permission of the Enid Blyton Company Ltd, copyright Enid Blyton Limited, London; extracts from *Truth, Dare or Promise* by Liz Heron, Virago Press, 1985, reproduced by permission of Little, Brown and Company; 'Colonel Barker in the Dock at the Old Bailey' from the *Daily Herald* reproduced by permission of the News International Syndication; 'A Pernicious Book' and 'Condemned Novel: Appeal to Sessions' published in *The Times*, reproduced by permission of the News International Syndication; *The Sexual Perversions and Abnormalities* by C. Allen, pp. 124–6, Oxford University Press, 1940, reproduced by permission of Oxford University Press; extracts from Havelock Ellis, *Studies in the Psychology of Sex, Vol. II, Sexual Inversion*, Philadelphia, F.A. Davies, 1915, reproduced by kind permission of François Lafitte.

Every effort has been made to obtain permission to reproduce copyright material. If any proper acknowledgement has not been made, we would invite copyright holders to inform us of the oversight.

LIST OF SOURCES

16   M. Gordon, *Penal Discipline*, 1922, London: George Routledge and Sons Ltd, pp. 71–2
17   'Col. Barker's Tears', *Daily Express*, 28 March 1929, p. 1
18   ' "Col. Barker" in Dock at The Old Bailey', *Daily Herald*, 25 April 1929, p. 5
19   'Servant Dresses as a Man', *Daily Herald*, 25 April 1929, p. 1
20   'Woman Who Lived as a Man', *Daily Herald*, 10 May 1929, p. 1
21   'Woman's 20 Years' Pose as a Husband', *Daily Herald*, 29 August 1932
22   'Girl Witness in Male Attire', *The Times of India*, 22 July 1932, p. 9
23   'Married Girl Poses as Boy', *The Daily Telegraph*, 30 July 1932, p. 12
24   Lady V. de Frece, *Recollections of Vesta Tilley*, 1934, London: Hutchinson, pp. 233–5
25   T. Parker, *Five Women*, 1965, London: Hutchinson, pp. 87–8, 95–6

2 Romantic friends and lesbian couples

1   Letters and journal entries concerning the flight of Butler and Ponsonby, 1778 in G.H. Bell (ed.), *The Hamwood Papers of the Ladies of Llangollen and Caroline Hamilton*, 1930, London: Macmillan and Co. Limited, pp. 27, 32–3, 38–9
2   A. Seward, from 'Llangollen Vale', and 'Sonnet 32. To the Departing Spirit of an Alienated Friend' in S. Coote (ed.), *The Penguin Book of Homosexual Verse*, 1983, Harmondsworth: Penguin
3   *Thraliana. The Diary of Mrs Hester Lynch Thrale (Later Mrs Piozzi) 1776–1809*, 1942, Oxford: Clarendon Press, Vol. II, 1784–1809, pp. 740, 770, 868, 949
4   W. Wordsworth, 'To Lady Eleanor Butler and the Honble Miss Ponsonby. Composed in the grounds of Plas-Newydd, Llangollen', 1827, in G.H. Bell (ed.), *The Hamwood Papers of the Ladies of Llangollen and Caroline Hamilton*, 1930, London: Macmillan and Co. Limited, p. 354
5   C. Brontë letters to Ellen Nussey, 1836, T.J. Wise and J.A. Symington (eds), *The Brontës: Their Lives, Friendships, and Correspondence in Four Volumes*, 1932, Oxford: Shakespeare Head
6   H. Whitbread (ed.), *I Know My Own Heart. The Diaries of Anne Lister, 1791–1840*, 1988, London: Virago, pp. 177–9
7   D.M. Craik, *A Woman's Thoughts About Women*, 1858, Hurst and Blackett, p. 174
8   T. Hardy, *Desperate Remedies*, 1986 [1871], London: Macmillan
9   C.L. Maynard, diary and autobiography extracts in M. Vicinus, *Independent Women*, 1985, Virago, pp. 160, 332

10   L.T. Mallet, Reviews, *Shafts*, 21 January 1893, p. 183

11   'Olivia' (Dorothy Bussy), introduction to *Olivia*, 1949, The
     Hogarth Press, pp. 13–17

12   M. Field (Katherine Bradley and Edith Cooper), 'Maids, not to
     you my mind doth change'

13   A. Levy, 'To Vernon Lee', *A London Plane – Tree and Other Verse*,
     1889, T. Fisher Unwin

14   E. Smyth, *What Happened Next*, 1940, Longmans and Co., pp. 26–8

15   M. Stopes, *A Journal from Japan: A Daily Record of Life as Seen by a
     Scientist*, 1910, Blackie and Sons, pp. 106–12 *passim*

16   S. Cole, *Blue Grey Magic*, 1910, Mills and Boon, pp. 181–9

17   K. Mansfield, 'Friendship' in S. Coote (ed.), *The Penguin Book of
     Homosexual Verse*, 1983, Harmondsworth: Penguin, pp. 292–3

18   V. Trefusis, letter to Vita Sackville-West, March 1919, in M.A.
     Leaska and J. Phillips (eds), *Violet to Vita. The Letters of Violet
     Trefusis to Vita Sackville-West, 1910–1921*, 1989, London:
     Methuen, pp. 117–18

19   V. Woolf, diary entry Monday 21 December 1925 in A.O. Bell *The
     Diary of Virginia Woolf*, vol. 3: 1925–30, Harmondsworth:
     Penguin, pp. 51–3

20   E. J. Oxenham, *The Abbey Girls Win Through*, 1928, Collins, p. 9

21   C. Chesterton, *Women of the Underworld*, 1928, Stanley Paul and
     Co. Ltd, p. 199

22   E. Roper, biographical introduction to the *Poems of Eva Gore-
     Booth*, 1929, Longmans and Co., pp. 9–49 *passim*

23   E. Hodge, *A Woman Oriented Woman*, 1989 [1920s], West Sussex:
     Gooday Publishers, pp. 26–8

24   C. Harman (ed.), *The Diaries of Sylvia Townsend Warner*, 1995,
     London: Virago Press, pp. 69–70

25   V. Brittain, *Testament of Friendship: The Story of Winifred Holtby*,
     1980 [1940], London: Virago, pp. 166–9

26   M. Stocks, *Eleanor Rathbone*, 1949, Victor Gollanz Ltd, pp. 7–8,
     57–8

27   N. Spain, *Why I'm Not a Millionaire*, 1959, Hutchinson, pp. 133–5

28. B. Magee, *One in Twenty. A Study of Homosexuality in Men and Women*,
     1966, Martin Secker and Warburg, pp. 134–6, 143, 162, 169–71

29   S. Pinney (ed.), *I'll Stand By You. The Letters of Sylvia Townsend
     Warner and Valentine Ackland*, 1998, Pimlico, p. 386

PART II: PROFESSIONAL COMMENTARIES

3 Medicine

1   M. Ryan, *Prostitution in London*, 1839, London: H. Balliere, pp.
     178–9

2   T. Laycock, *A Treatise on the Nervous Disorders of Women*, 1840, London: Longmans and Co., pp. 141, 210

3   D. Hack Tuke (ed.), *A Dictionary of Psychological Medicine*, 1892, Vol. II, London: J. & A. Churchill, pp. 1156–7

4   H. Ellis, *Studies in the Psychology of Sex. Vol. 1. Sexual Inversion, 1897*, London: The University Press, pp. 83–100 *passim*

5   C.G. Seligmann, 'Sexual Inversion Among Primitive Races', *The Alienist and Neurologist*, Vol. 23, No. 1, 1902, pp. 11–13

6   S. Freud, 'Female Sexuality', in *On Sexuality, Freud Library Vol. 7*, 1979 [1905], Harmondsworth: Penguin, pp. 374–6.

7   E. Carpenter, *Love's Coming-of-Age*, 1915 [1906], London: Methuen, pp. 114–34 *passim*

8   F.W.S. Browne, *The Sexual Variety and Variability Among Women*, 1917, British Society for the Study of Sex Psychology

9   B. Hollander, *The Psychology of Misconduct, Vice and Crime*, 1922, London: George Allen and Unwin Ltd, pp. 141, 144

10 A.C. Magian, *Sex Problems in Women*, 1922, London: William Heinemann (Medical Books) Ltd, pp. 4, 105–10

11 M. Stopes, *Enduring Passion*, 1928, Hogarth Press, pp. 29–31

12 L. Hutton, *The Single Woman and her Emotional Problems*, 1935, London: Bailliere, Tindall and Cox, pp. 40–3, 86–7, 91–2, 101–4, 105–6

13 C. Allen, *The Sexual Perversions and Abnormalities*, 1940, Oxford University Press, pp. 124–6

14 K. Walker, *The Physiology of Sex*, 1940, Harmondsworth: Penguin, pp. 144–5

15 A.L. Winner, 'Homosexuality in Women', *The Medical Press*, Vol. 218, No. 10 (No. 5652), 3 September 1947, pp. 219–220.

16 E. Chesser, *Sexual Behaviour, Normal and Abnormal*, 1949, London: Medical Publications Ltd, pp. ix, 164

17 British Medical Association, *Homosexuality and Prostitution, A Memorandum of Evidence Prepared by a Special Committee of the Council of the British Medical Association for Submission to the Departmental Committee on Homosexuality and Prostitution*, 1955, British Medical Association, pp. 18–19, 48–9

18 M. Schmideberg, 'Reality Therapy With Offenders', *British Journal of Delinquency*, Vol. 5, No. 2, April 1965, pp. 179–80

19 E. Bene, 'On the Genesis of Female Homosexuality', *The British Journal of Psychiatry*, Vol. 111, No. 478, September 1965, pp. 815–21

20 M.J. MacCulloch and M.P. Feldman, 'Aversion Therapy in Management of 43 Homosexuals', *British Medical Journal*, Vol. 2, 3 June 1967, pp. 594–7

21 F.E. Kenyon, 'Physique and Physical Health of Female

Homosexuals', *Journal of Neurology, Neurosurgery and Psychiatry*, Vol. 31, 1968, pp. 487–9

22   J. Hopkins, ' The Lesbian Personality', *The British Journal of Psychiatry*, Vol. 115, No. 529, December 1969, pp. 1433–6

4 Education

1   L.H.M. Soulsby, *Stray Thoughts for Girls*, 1893, James Parker & Co., pp. 164–8

2   H. Ellis, *Studies in the Psychology Of Sex, Vol. 1, Sexual Inversion*, London: The University Press, 1897, pp. 82–5

3   K.Tynan, *Twenty-five Years: Reminiscences*, 1913, Smith, Elder & Co., p. 57

4   P. Blanchard, *The Case of the Adolescent Girl, A Book for Teachers, Parents and Guardians*, Kegan Paul, Trench, Trubner & Co., 1921, pp. 136–9

5   C. Dane, *The Woman's Side*,1926, Herbert Jenkins Ltd, pp. 53–65

6   M. Stopes, *Sex and the Young*, 1926, Gill Publishing Co. pp. 45, 48–9, 53–6

7   L.M. Faithfull, *You And I, Saturday Talks at Cheltenham*, 1927, Chatto & Windus, pp. 118–21

8   *The Manchester Guardian*, 7 September 1932, p. 3

9   M. Chadwick, *Adolescent Girlhood*, 1932, George Allen & Unwin, pp. 223, 243–6, 250–7

10   *Daily Herald*, 5 September 1935

11   R.K. Davies, *Four Miss Pinkertons*,1936, Williams & Norgate Ltd, pp. 35–6, 72–5, 78–80

12   A.S. Neill, *Hearts Not Heads in the School*, 1945, Herbert Jenkins Ltd, pp. 78–9

13   J. Macalister Brew, 'How The Mind Works', *Club News*, January 1945, p. 2

14   J. Newsom, *The Education of Girls*, 1948, Faber & Faber, p. 149

15   M. Fleming, *Adolescence, Its Social Psychology*,1948, Routledge & Kegan Paul (2nd edition 1963), p. 235

16   J. Hemming, *Problems of Adolescent Girls*, 1960, Heinemann, pp. 76–9

17   H. Richardson, *Adolescent Girls in Approved Schools*, 1969, Routledge & Kegan Paul, p. 50

5 Law

1   Miss Marianne Woods and Miss Jane Pirie against Dame Helen Cumming Gordon, 1975 [1810], New York: Arno Press

2   'Not Fit to Marry', *The News of the World*, 24 January 1915, p. 5

3   'Vision of Salome', *The News of the World*, 2 June 1918, pp. 3–4

4   A.T. Fitzroy, *Despised and Rejected*, 1988 [1918], GMP Publishers Ltd, pp. 217–21

5   'A Pernicious Book', *The Times*, 27 September 1918

6   Parliamentary Debates (House of Commons), Criminal Law Amendment Bill, 4 August 1921, para. 1799–1806

7   'Douglas-Pennant Case', *The Manchester Guardian*, 3 July 1931

8   Kerr v Kennedy, 1 All ER (1942) 412

9   P. Epps, 'A Preliminary Survey of 300 Female Delinquents in Borstal Institutions', *British Journal of Delinquency*, Vol. 1 No. 3, 1951, pp. 187–97

10   'The Case of Margaret Allen' in R. Huggett and P. Berry, *Daughters of Cain*, 1956, George Allen and Unwin, pp. 191–2, 209

11   Letter to *Arena Three*, Vol. 5, Nos 5/6, March 1968, p. 13

12   Spicer v Spicer (Ryan intervening), 3 All ER (1954) 208

13   *Report of the Royal Commission on Marriage and Divorce*, 1951–55, 1956, HMSO, pp. 30–31

14   J. Buxton and M. Turner, *Gate Fever*, 1962, The Cresset Press, pp. 114–16

15   Lord Chamberlain's Papers, Correspondence, Memorandum of 26 March 1965 from the Assistant Comptroller to the Lord Chamberlain concerning *The Killing of Sister George*

PART III: MAKING LESBIANISM IN CULTURE

6 *The Well of Loneliness*

1   V. Brittain, 'New Fiction. Facing Facts', *Time and Tide*, Vol. 9, No. 32, 10 August 1928, pp. 765–6

2   'A Book that must be Suppressed', *The Sunday Express*, 19 August 1928

3   Letter from Vita Sackville-West to Virginia Woolf, 31 August 1928, in L. DeSalvo and M. Leaska (eds), *The Letters of Vita Sackville-West to Virginia Woolf*, 1992, London: Virago, pp. 296–7

4   'The Well of Loneliness Decision', *Time and Tide*, Vol. 9, No. 27, 23 November 1928, pp. 1124–5

5   Letter from Virginia Woolf to Roger Fry, 16 October 1928, in N. Nicolson and J. Trautmann (eds), *Leave the Letters Till We're Dead. The Letters of Virginia Woolf*, 1980, London: The Hogarth Press, Vol. VI: 1936–1941, pp. 523–4.

6   'Condemned Novel. Appeal to Sessions', *The Times*, 15 December 1928, p. 4

7   'Miss Radclyffe Hall's Appeal', *The Woman's Leader*, 21 December 1928, p. 354

8   M. Royden, 'Well of Loneliness', *The Guildhouse Monthly*, Vol. 3,
     No. 26, April 1929, pp. 94–5, 98–101
9   Letter from Radclyffe Hall to Maude Royden, 3 January 1930,
     Agnes Maude Royden Papers, Fawcett Library
10   E. Mannin, *Impressions and Confessions*, 1936, Penguin, pp. 231–5
11   M. Renault, Afterword to *Friendly Young Ladies*, 1984 [1938],
     London: Virago, p. 281
12   G. Holmes, *In Love with Life*, 1944, Hollis & Carter, p. 136
13   A. Jivani, *It's Not Unusual. A History of Lesbian and Gay Britain in
     the Twentieth Century*, 1997, London: Michael O'Mara Books Ltd,
     p. 40
14   Hall Carpenter Archives Lesbian Oral History Group, *Inventing
     Ourselves. Lesbian Life Stories*, 1989, London: Routledge, pp.
     49–50
15   S. Neild and R. Pearson, *Women Like Us*, 1992, The Women's
     Press, pp. 127–39 *passim*
16   R. O'Rourke, *Reflecting on the Well Of Loneliness*, 1989, London:
     Routledge, pp. 117–42

7 Social perceptions

1   S. Hicks, *Difficulties: [An Attempt to Help]*, 1922, London:
     Duckworth and Co., p. 260–1
2   T. Croft, *The Cloven Hoof. A Study of Contemporary London Vices*,
     1932, London: Denis Archer, pp. 79–84
3   Mrs C. Chesterton, *Women of the London Underworld*, 1938,
     London: Readers Library Publishing Co. Ltd, pp. 72–4
4   'London's Night Club Pests Fear Police Clean Up', *The People*, 9
     July 1939, p. 17
5   E. Blyton, *Five on a Treasure Island*, 1942, Hodder and
     Stoughton, pp. 15–16
6   Mass Observation, *The Pub and People. A Worktown Study*, 1943,
     London: Victor Gollancz Ltd, pp. 184–5
7   J. McCrindle and S. Rowbotham (eds), *Dutiful Daughters: Women
     Talk about Their Lives*, 1979, Harmondsworth: Penguin, pp.
     142–3
8   L. Fairfield, 'Homosexuality in Women', *Medico-Legal Journal*,
     Vol. 15 No. 1, 1947, pp. 18–20, 22–3
9   S. de Beauvoir, *The Second Sex*, 1972 [1953], Harmondsworth:
     Penguin, pp. 441–4
10   V. Musgrave, 'Women Outside the Law', *The Twentieth Century*,
     Vol. 164, No. 978, August 1958, pp. 178–84
11   D. Rowe, 'A Quick Look at Lesbians', *The Twentieth Century*,
     Winter 1962–3, pp. 67–72 *passim*.

12   *Towards A Quaker View Of Sex*,1964, Revised Edition, London: Friends Home Service Committee, pp. 37–40

13   M. McIntosh, 'Bent or Straight Mates – A Sociologist's Views', *Arena Three*, Vol. 1, No. 6, June 1964, pp. 4–6

14   N. Dunn, *Talking to Women*, 1965, London: Pan, pp. 43–4

15   'Lesbian London' in H. Davies (ed.), *The London Spy: a Discreet Guide to the City's Pleasures*, 1966, London: Anthony Bond, pp. 231–8

16   N. Timms, *Rootless in the City*, 1968, London: The Bedford Square Press, pp. 36–8

17   S. McDermott, *Studies in Female Sexuality*, 1970, Odyssey Press, pp. 63–4, 66–70 *passim*

8 Identities and networks

1   H. Whitbread (ed.), *I Know My Own Heart. The Diaries of Anne Lister, 1791–1840*, 1988, London: Virago, pp. 268–71

2   Minnie Benson, 1871, retrospective diary quoted in B. Askwith, *Two Victorian Families*, 1971, Chatto and Windus, p. 138

3   E. Simcox, 'Autobiography of a Shirtmaker', quoted by P. Johnson, 'Edith Simcox and Heterosexism: A Lesbian-Feminist Exploration' in Lesbian History Group, *Not a Passing Phase*, 1989, London: The Women's Press, pp. 55–76

4   D. Campbell, 'The Woman Offender', *The Freewoman*, Vol. 1, No. 21, 11 April 1912, pp. 408–5

5   'The Human Complex', *The Freewoman*, Vol. 1, No. 22, 18 April 1912, pp. 437–8

6   'Frances Wilder' to Edward Carpenter, 25 October 1915, Carpenter Collection MS 386/262, Sheffield Public Library, Sheffield, South Yorkshire

7   E. Smyth, *Streaks of Life*, 1921, Longmans and Co., pp. 173–4

8   M. Silvera, 'Man Royals And Sodomites: Some Thoughts on the Invisibility of Afro-Caribbean Lesbians', *Feminist Studies*, Vol. 18, No. 3, Fall 1992, pp. 521–32 *passim*

9   *Urania*, No. 21, May–June 1920, p. 8

10   *Urania*, Nos 51 and 52, May–August, 1925, p. 3

11   *Urania*, Nos 101 and 102, September–December 1933, p.1

12   *Urania*, Nos 115 and 116, January–April 1936, p. 8

13   P. Noble, *Profiles and Personalities*, 1946, Brownlee, pp. 68–72

14   L. Heron (ed.), *Truth Dare or Promise. Girls Growing Up in the Fifties*, 1985, London: Virago, pp. 146–7, 219

15   'How It Started', *Arena Three*, Vol. 1, No. 9, September 1964, p. 2

16   *Arena Three*, Vol. 2, No. 2, February 1965, p. 13

17   *Arena Three*, Vol. 2, No. 6, June 1965, p. 11

18   *Arena Three*, Vol. 2, No. 1, January 1965, p. 4

19   *Arena Three*, Vol. 2, No. 10, October 1965, p. 14

20   *Arena Three*, Vol. 5, No. 5, May 1968, pp. 4–5

21   *Arena Three*, Vol. 5, No. 10, October 1968, pp. 4–5

22   *Arena Three*, Vol. 6, No. 5, May 1969, p. 3

23   A. Jivani, *It's Not Unusual. A History of Lesbian and Gay Britain in the Twentieth Century*, 1997, London: Michael O'Mara Books Ltd, p. 50

24   Brighton Ourstory Project, *Daring Hearts, Lesbian and Gay Lives of 50s and 60s Brighton*, 1992, Brighton, QueenSpark Books, *passim*

25   R. Manning, *A Time and a Tide*, 1971, Marion Boyers, pp. 136–7

26   E. Wilson, 'Gayness and Liberalism' in *Hidden Agendas. Theory, Politics and Experience in the Women's Movement*, 1986, London: Tavistock, pp. 139–47, *passim*

INTRODUCTION

WHO IS THE LESBIAN?

This is a book about British lesbian history which reaches across two centuries from the late eighteenth century to the mid twentieth century, ending just as the gay liberation and women's liberation movements were beginning. In the process of seeking out original sources over this period, we have asked ourselves – what are we looking for? What counts as sufficiently 'lesbian' for inclusion? The term 'lesbian' is a commonly understood and recognisable word, but it nevertheless carries many meanings. Inevitably our own sense of ourselves as lesbians today shapes what we think we're looking for in the past. But in the 1980s and 1990s the idea of 'lesbianism' encompassed a range of identities from the feminist woman-identified-woman (emphasising community and politics) to a specifically sexual definition (emphasising powerful eroticism and transgression).

Nor can we simply apply our categories to the past. Until the mid twentieth century lesbians rarely identified themselves as such. 'Lesbian identity' is a late-twentieth-century concept and the historical past was a very different sexual place. In the past women who loved and/or had sex with other women, or who cross-dressed, or who resisted heterosexuality, did not necessarily have a language to describe themselves as lovers of women, or to claim any particular identity based on their sexuality. They could only understand their desires, behaviour and experiences within the social context of their own times.

We cannot escape from our own time, and we are inevitably drawn towards evidence about behaviour in the past which has some parallels with that which signals same-sex desire today. Historians must enter into the culture of the past as best we can, and understand the social and economic constraints within which women could express or act out love and desire for other women, while at the same time recognising that our questions, concerns and interests, and the inter-pretations we make of women in the past, have arisen in our specific historical circumstances.

So what do we look for? Our own working definition of 'lesbian-like' cultures and behaviour (Vicinus 1994, Bennett 2000) ideally includes some evidence of eroticism, of sexual feeling in love relationships between women, as important in

1

the past; eroticism being broadly, and inevitably rather subjectively defined! Indications of passionate desire, sexual activity, erotic possibilities between women, committed love relationships, or a sense of self as transgressing hetero-sexual assumptions are all included. What emerges in the search for lesbianism and the lesbian is evidence centring around three components of women's behaviour: sexual practices, deviance from gender role norms of femininity, and women's consciousness of their feelings.

Evidence of sexual activities with other women, whether cuddling, kissing, cunnilingus or use of dildoes, is one starting point, and sometimes the end point in defining lesbianism. We should bear in mind Faderman's observation that what counts as 'sexual' in society is male-defined, and this, in certain periods, might give women considerable freedom. If certain behaviours were not interpreted as sexual, they might be indulged in with impunity (Faderman 1981). Once sexu-alised they could be stigmatised. The second sort of behaviour we have come to see as somehow related to lesbianism is the transgressing of gender roles. This might mean renouncing some aspects of 'femininity' (the apostrophes denote the historical specificity of the word) and/or embracing aspects of 'masculinity'. But gender role deviance and sexual practices with women cannot necessarily be elided. A masculine woman is no easier to label a lesbian than a woman who chooses at times to engage in sex with other women. The strength of sex role deviance as a focus in lesbian history is of course its greater visibility and there-fore its amenity to investigation. Discussing the depiction of the mannish Stephen in Radclyffe Hall's famous lesbian novel, *The Well of Loneliness* (1928), Newton contrasts the invisibility of the conventionally feminine Mary: 'Mary's real story has yet to be told' (Newton 1991: 293). While the Marys remain invisible so will their lesbianism. It is also important to make some distinction between behaviour (whether sexual activities or social roles) and consciousness, our third area. If women leave evidence that they are conscious of the power of their feelings for and attractions to other women, we can be more confident in our attempts to identify, albeit partially, their lives as lesbian lives.

To date – and we think usefully – the outcome of attempts to define lesbianism historically has not been to clarify or solidify the image of the lesbian in history but to underline the diversity and ephemerality of historical evidence of desire between women.

STRUCTURE AND AIMS

The sources in this book have been organised as follows. Part I illustrates two key archetypes of lesbianism in modern British history – cross-dressing women and romantic friends. Part II presents various kinds of public commentaries on sex between women. These include the dominant and powerful discourses of medicine, education and law. The final part looks more broadly at the making of lesbianism in culture. It opens with a twentieth-century case study. The trial of *The Well of Loneliness* for obscenity in 1928 and its aftermath demonstrates the interplay of representations and reality, of professional discourses with private practices in the forming of ideas about lesbianism. The next chapter explores the wider public perceptions of lesbianism across the twentieth century. The final chapter returns us to women's own voices and experiences in tracing the various ways of creating lesbian identity.

The first sources are from the late eighteenth century, a time of early industrialisation, social dislocation and changing gender relations. Concepts of 'lesbian-like' behaviour for much of the nineteenth century were muted, but historians have looked at romantic friendship, at networks of independent women (perhaps associated with the women's movement), and at women who partly or wholly dressed and passed as men as potential sources of evidence. Terms such as sapphist, tribade or lesbian were only rarely used. At the beginning of the nineteenth century romantic friendship was an acceptable relationship and cross-dressing was a significant theme in popular culture. New shifts and influences occurred with the emergence of the women's movement in mid century. The end of the century is associated with a more scientific delineation of sexualities, especially deviant practices such as homosexuality, presenting the opportunity for clearer social and self-defined identities to emerge. There was an increasingly full and explicit discussion of female homosexuality in the twentieth century; however it was not until after World War II that the (still shameful) concept of lesbianism appears to have been widely acknowledged as a sexual identity. More lesbian meeting places (although still only a handful and in urban areas) and political organising from the early 1960s paved the way for the emergence of the radical gay liberation and women's liberation movements in 1968–1970, the moment at which our book ends.

There is a great richness of material here, bursting out of the chapter boundaries; a mixture of chronologies, issues and models of lesbianism. We encourage readers to look across the various chapters to make links between themes and historical changes. These might include women's economic independence, the censure or acceptance of love between women, religious beliefs and views, the significance of feminist politics and networks and the ways that wartime disruption creates opportunities for lesbian lifestyles.

We aim to show how history is constructed according to present-day concerns as much as past ones; to encourage readers to look at the evidence behind different perspectives in lesbian history and to think about the theoretical and political standpoints on which our history is based. We believe there are many resonances in the past for today's experiences and political concerns. We hope to inspire others to research lesbian history, whether in community groups, as local historians, or in oral history projects, or more formally in academic institutions as part of undergraduate or postgraduate studies in history, women's studies or other disciplines.

LESBIAN HISTORY

Part of our intention was to illustrate some of the current issues and debates in lesbian history. Lesbian history in Britain can be found in a variety of different genres. History has always been important for political movements, especially in their beginning stages. Lesbian activists in the 1970s and 1980s felt it was vital to trace a heritage of lesbian sexuality in the past, to feel part of a long, powerful and transgressive lesbian/feminist/queer history. It was also important to try to understand mechanisms of oppression – why and how had lesbians been an invisible, stigmatised or persecuted minority, and how this had been challenged? Thus a major part of early work was the process of bearing witness, of making visible our lesbian past.

With its origins in the politics of the 1970s and 1980s, lesbian-feminist history, in Britain as in the USA, emphasised two issues; the political importance of love between women irrespective of its sexual expression, and the patriarchal control of lesbian sexuality (Rich 1980, Faderman 1981, Jeffreys 1985, Lesbian History Group 1989). Later, in the 1980s and 1990s, these initial approaches were challenged by histories that aimed to reinstate sexuality as key for lesbian existence and to stress women's agency in constructing lesbian identities. This process was aided by the rediscovery, decoding and publication of the secret diaries of the early-nineteenth-century English landowner Anne Lister, who wrote frankly about her sexual relationships with other women (Whitbread 1988). Lesbian history has become more complex as historians have traced same-sex erotic themes and cultural reference points in novels, medical texts and court records in the nineteenth and twentieth centuries (Oram 1997).

The 1990s found lesbian history in Britain in both popular and academic forms. A key task was to document lesbian lives and to assert the long history of lesbianism through oral history and biography. Oral history projects have included the Hall Carpenter project published as *Inventing Ourselves* and oral interviews by the Lesbian Archive (Cassidy and Stewart-Park 1977, Hall Carpenter Archives 1989, Neild and Pearson 1992). Community histories of particular areas have been carried out, notably of the longstanding gay resort of Brighton (Brighton Ourstory Project 1992). A number of biographies of lesbian writers, for example Vita Sackville-West, Sylvia Townsend Warner and Mary Renault signalled a new willingness of biographers to engage more directly with sexual orientation (Glendinning 1984, Mulford 1988, Harman 1989, Sweetman 1993). In addition there have been biographies informed by developments in feminist and lesbian history such as studies of Cicely Hamilton, Emily Wilding Davison, Nancy Spain and Winifred Holtby (Whitelaw 1990, Stanley and Morley 1988, Collis 1997, Shaw 1999).

Popular histories continue to be produced (Hamer 1996). On television, in the early 1990s, there was the brief appearance of lesbian costume drama in *Portrait of a Marriage*. More recently we have seen BBC2's documentary of lesbian and gay life and politics since 1918 (Jivani 1997) as well as history items in magazine programmes like *Gaytime* and *Out*. Lesbian historical fiction has begun to emerge as a genre in its own right. Novels such as Sarah Waters' *Tipping the Velvet* (1998) and Jay Taverner's *Rebellion* (1997) not only illustrate the attraction of recreating a lesbian past which suits our desires in the present – the projection back of our current identities – but also enable an exploration of what lesbian lives might have been like in the past in the frustrating absence of historical evidence.

Lesbian history is also about creating new questions and pursuing important themes. In the USA, lesbian history has moved on to document the formation of urban bar culture, the creation of lesbian and gay resorts, the various sexual nuances of nineteenth-century romantic friendship, and the shifts in identity and location created by World War II (Bérubé 1990, Kennedy and Davis 1993, Newton 1993). But in Britain there has been relatively less work done to expand the analysis and complexities of lesbian history – the hard slog of social history in both archives and oral sources. American scholarship has addressed the ways in which race and class divisions structured post-war bar culture and examined intimate relationships (and the language in which they were expressed) between professional African-American women in the mid nineteenth century (Kennedy and Davis 1993, Hansen 1995). Research on black lesbian history in Britain has barely begun, and has been confined to oral history of the recent past, reflecting the excellent but still limited work on black women's history here generally (Alexander 1990, Grant 1996, Heron 1985, Hall Carpenter Archives 1989, Cant 1997).

Articles on lesbian history can now be found in academic journals such as *Gender and History* and *Women's History Review*. Some women's and gender historians have taken on the insights and research findings of lesbian history, but we believe that most feminist historians do not yet question their heterosexual assumptions. The teaching of lesbian history in universities, even in history departments, continues to be patchy. The extent to which the study of lesbians has academic credibility may be significant here. The issue of academic respectability seems to be less of a barrier in women's studies, cultural studies and English. Higher education is an important site for the teaching and produc-tion of lesbian history especially as its presence in community groups and adult education remains limited. We hope this book will help to make it easier to teach a lesbian element in all women's history courses.

Much of the current academic work in lesbian history is not being conducted within the discipline of history at all, but in the related fields of English literature and cultural studies. This can teach historians much about the close reading of texts, and how signifiers of lesbian desire can be understood. But some of this type of work uses only the most accessible sources from the past – published novels, letters and diaries. It is important to identify a lesbian culture among the canon of Western literature, but this is not an adequate substitute for history. Both work in literary studies and biography privilege the lives and work of middle- and upper-class women (and within this a select group of those who were cultural producers). In the new century we need more large-scale work to deepen and widen the analysis of lesbian lives.

UNDERSTANDING THE EVIDENCE

Our sources are typical of the evidence available to historians and range from official government publications, professional journals and newspapers to fiction, poetry, personal papers and ephemera. Almost all are printed sources and have been found in university libraries, specialist libraries, the British Library, the newspaper library at Colindale, and in published collections of letters and diaries. Some were found through tedious searches in the indexes to professional journals, others discovered by serendipitous explorations in likely sounding titles. But of course we have also built on the excellent work of other scholars and have chosen some key sources that they have previously unearthed.

As in all social history investigations, the sources are fragmented and partial and of particular types. Some indicate a general perspective, other than the experience of an individual. Because the male homosexual is a firm legal actor, there is far more evidence in legal records for men than there is for the homosexual woman. In contrast, there is a rich literature of unconstrained romantic expression between women, which has no parallel for homosexual men.

Explicit evidence of women's sexual lives with each other is rarely found. Very unusually the twentieth-century novelist and poet Sylvia Townsend Warner knew the preciousness of her lesbian life and wanted to share it with others in some way. Her long life of writing poems, short stories and novels for publication also produced the voluminous private diaries and personal letters where she set out the sadnesses, joys, and every emotion in between, of her relationship with her lover Valentine Ackland. In 1972, in her late seventies, Sylvia wrote to the two friends to whom she had entrusted her correspondence with Valentine. 'We had no agreement about keeping them. We kept them I suppose, because we loved too much to throw them away – it would have seemed a slight. They were preserved not hoarded' (Maxwell 1982: 256). Two weeks later she wrote to them again: 'I am so glad you have read those letters – for now you know us' (ibid.: 257). It is much more usual that women have left no traces of their love for their own sex, burning letters and diaries, hiding information or writing in code, thus avoiding the risk of homophobic censure (Auchmuty 1989, Whitelaw 1990).

It is only possible at certain times, in certain ways and for certain women to write of their feelings for other women. The sources are particularly limited in relation to the lives of ordinary working-class or middle-class women. Records of working-class women's lives tend to be more indirect; they are more often represented by others than by themselves, for example in newspaper articles about odd or cross-dressing women, or by patronising social investigators. But there are also sources that have not yet been thoroughly explored, such as newspaper reports, and records of institutions like workhouses and reformatories. We were pleased to find some sporadic evidence of black women, another under-researched group. Here there are additional problems; the lack of recognition by historians that there were sizeable ethnic minority communities in parts of Britain and also that in the records the 'race' or ethnicity of individuals is rarely specified.

There is also another and far more voluminous literature, where others, men and women, have commented upon the 'lesbian'. We can identify many of these as professional commentaries from scientists, doctors, clerics, legislators or educators. They can be conceptualised as sets of discourses, which from their respective positions of social power contribute to the framing of dominant under-standings of the 'lesbian' in different periods. While many of these have been considered significant, the discourses were neither homogenous nor hegemonic. For example medical opinion was divided on the causes of lesbianism throughout the twentieth century, while it is a moot point how influential these sets of ideas were in creating meanings for ordinary women.

Contemporary intellectual fashions, knowledge and professional practices inevitably mediated the ways in which sex between women could be understood. Religious ideas about middle-class women's moral purity moulded the interpreta-tions of the judges in the Pirie and Woods case of 1811–19, leading them to dismiss the possibility of sexual intimacy between women as virtually unthinkable by respectable middle-class Scottish women. But at the same time the case came about because of the gossip of servants, schoolgirls, and their alternative notions of sexual possibilities, which also had credibility. No discourse was omnipotent. Indeed each was only representative of the concerns of those who produced it.

Marginal female sexualities have been represented in particular ways by domi-nant cultures, from eighteenth-century popular ballads to twentieth-century sexology. In this sense, lesbian history is all about representation. According to this approach there is no pure 'reality' of lesbian lives in the past; women who loved women have had to create an identity from the knowledge and meanings available to them (Scott 1991). To understand their lives we have to look at how these constructions of femininity and deviance were negotiated and how they intersected with class, ethnicity and occupation.

The sources also indicate the material parameters within which lesbian lives could be lived. Economic possibilities and constraints, the geographical location of women's homes, their possibilities for employment, their class position and social freedom, and family attitudes were all important. Power relations have lived outcomes. Physical experiences might include not only enjoying the body and physical sex, but also facing exclusion from the family, violence and assault, and psychiatric or medical control. Historians continue to discuss whether lesbian history should use the theoretical tools and approaches of cultural history or social history (Vicinus 1994, Freedman 1998, Duggan 1998).

READING THE SOURCES

How can we read these difficult and fragmentary sources in a creative yet careful way? We have to ask who produced these sources, for what purposes – ranging from the moralising to the sensationalist – and to what extent they are likely to indicate the perspective of the author rather than the subject. What kinds of people were the assumed or actual readers? As commercial, official or private documents, these sources had different methods of circulation, from the single recipient, through narrow and specialised readerships to large popular markets.

There is plenty of scope for differing interpretations of these sources. For example, can we read the passionate love poetry written by middle-class Victorian poets to other women as evidence of lesbian feelings? Or was it simply an exercise in taking the male voice, and understood by contemporaries as refer-ring to heterosexual love? Again, were nineteenth-century women seen as so desexualised that passionate romantic declarations could be viewed only as a convention of women's writing? Vicinus and other historians have emphasised the importance of 'reading the gaps' when researching lesbian history and of weighing the importance of the 'not said' and the 'not seen' (Vicinus 1994, 1997). How should we read silences? Should we see all spinster couples living together as potentially lesbian? How do we distinguish between those New Women who wore neckties and severely cut clothes as sexual signifiers, and those who dressed this way for comfort or to make feminist points about independence?

This collection of sources will provoke controversy about lesbian lives in the past. But it will also provide the impetus for the fresh investigations and writing of a lesbian history which celebrates women's passions and desires for each other.

EDITORIAL POLICY ON SOURCES

The spelling and punctuation of the original sources, as given in the List of sources, have been followed.

I

ARCHETYPES OF LOVE BETWEEN WOMEN

1

CROSS-DRESSING WOMEN

INTRODUCTION

By the late twentieth century lesbian historiography had come to regard the mannish woman of the past as an archetypal lesbian, whether she was simply adopting elements of male clothing, or successfully passing as a man in everyday life. This latter, more extreme form of cross-dressing, could sometimes deceive a 'wife' as well as neighbours and workmates. Cross-dressing has been viewed as a working-class version of lesbianism in the past; romantic friendship being its equivalent in the middle and upper classes. But this assumption bears scrutiny. While the majority of passing women for whom we present sources were indeed working class, there were nevertheless some from higher social class backgrounds. For example Dr James Barry, a successful army doctor in the first half of the nineteenth century was discovered to be a woman on her death (Rose 1977).

Evidence of cross-dressing women comes to light in very specific ways, often when the passing woman comes into contact with an official or regulatory body. One common type of unmasking was by the police, law courts, or prison authorities after the woman was arrested for a criminal activity (often unconnected with cross-dressing). Another was as a consequence of wounds and illness, if the woman was a soldier or sailor in battle, or a civilian ill in the workhouse or after an accident. Here the sources follow particular formats such as the newspaper report of a crime and the revelation of the sex of the criminal. Disguise might persist until death, the reports of inquests finally revealing the deception.

The stories of cross-dressing women, especially those who had engaged in military exploits, had a significant place in popular culture in the eighteenth and early nineteenth centuries, appearing in the broadsheet ballads that were printed commercially and very widely distributed, sold on the streets and sung in pubs, set to traditional tunes (Dugaw 1989). Ballads were used to report gossip and opinion about news, current affairs, politics, royal scandals, crimes and murders as well as human-interest stories. From the late nineteenth century, different media, the working-class Sunday papers and the mass-market popular press, took over this role of reporting oddities such as female husbands, as newsworthy entertainment.

We know little about most of the cross-dressing women represented in these sources. Sometimes the survival of more than one type of account (e.g. a ballad plus a newspaper report) gives us a fuller picture of their activities and the responses of others to their disguise. Women's own accounts are comparatively few. When we hear the voices of passing women, they are often shaped by the requirements of the court-room, or if they have written or reported their stories for publication this may be for a particular purpose, for example to raise money. The accounts of wives and female companions, too, must be regarded critically. They would have been under pressure to represent themselves only as innocent, duped victims.

The sources invariably emphasise that passing women exploited all possible symbols of masculinity; posture and mannerisms, voice, aggression and domestic violence, male pastimes like drinking and, of course, male attire. Dress was the most consistently recorded signifier of these women. But did it necessarily indicate same-sex desire? There is little consistency in historians' understandings of women's cross-dressing, and its links or not with lesbian sexuality.

Women's own explanations for their actions have tended to be framed by the genres of ballads and sensational stories, but have usually focussed on two issues, economic necessity and personal freedom. Working-class women were used to doing rough, dirty and heavy work in the eighteenth and nineteenth centuries. As women, however, they were excluded from most skilled work and earned a half or less of the typical male wage, sometimes barely enough to survive on without recourse to prostitution or the workhouse (Rendall 1990). By passing as men and working as sailors, publicans, carpenters, doctors, or labourers, they could live more comfortably.

Women also cross-dressed to gain physical freedom, particularly the freedom to travel and seek adventure, to go to sea or to war. At the beginning of this period, Britain was heavily involved in the Napoleonic Wars (1793–1815) and was also considerably expanding her commercial and imperial interests overseas. Ideals of femininity increasingly circumscribed women's opportunities to be patri-otic, heroic or start a new life. Passing as a man might enable certain kinds of crimes to be carried out, or escape from a situation such as indebtedness or an unhappy marriage. Some cross-dressing soldiers and sailors joined up to seek their husbands or male lovers; others sought to escape them. Women who passed as men could avoid both the economic pressures to marry, and unwanted sex with men. Economic motives to pass as men may have overlapped with sexual ones, and our generalisations about the subjectivity of cross-dressing women can only be speculative.

To determine which cross-dressing women might be included as lesbians we have to look for hints of relationships with other women. Many of the stories of cross-dressing soldiers and sailors, for example, describe them flirting with, or being pursued by other women. But historians interpret these women's actions differently. Wheelwright downplays this evidence, suggesting that passing women were obliged to behave like men in every way they could, including in their sexual behaviour (Wheelwright 1989). Donoghue, however, argues that this interpretation denies same-sex desire and calls for a more strongly lesbian reading of these erotic encounters between women (Donoghue 1993).

The female husbands are the most obvious category of passing women whom we might include as lesbians. Having a wife immediately suggests a sexual relationship. Historians of cross-dressing in the Netherlands and Germany have argued that female husbands dressed as men because they could only conceive of their love and desire for another woman in terms of the existing heterosexual paradigm (Dekker and van de Pol 1989). However, Donoghue has challenged this interpretation for British women, arguing that there were many other models of sexual desire between women circulating in the eighteenth century. Instead, she sees female husbands choosing marriage for practical reasons as it gave a female couple security, privacy and social status (Donoghue 1993).

Historians have tended to concentrate on the women who themselves cross-dressed as potential lesbians, but the wives, sweethearts and constant companions of passing women are as significant as their partners, although their presence in the sources is more muted. In expressing desire for the ambiguously gendered man-woman, and in acting as willing, if secret, partners over many years, we can trace more strongly expressed lesbian desires in some of these 'wives' than in the passing women themselves.

Theatre and performance have a long tradition of female cross-dressing. We might see the wives of passing women as on a continuum with the idolising female audiences for cross-dressed performers on the stage. This recurring theme in popular and high culture indicates that expressions of female desire for women can occur in the fantasy space of entertainment. A continuing practice of male impersonation from eighteenth-century theatre to nineteenth-century music hall to twentieth-century cinema has disrupted heterosexuality and opened up complex sexual ambiguities and possibilities for women audiences (Straub 1991, Bratton 1992, Weiss 1993).

Some cross-dressing women may have desired not lesbian relationships but simply to be men. Some theorists argue that much cross-dressing was indeed about gender inversion rather than sexuality, in a way that today would be called transgender or transsexuality (Prosser 1998a). Alternatively, Halberstam (1998) has suggested that conceptualising a range of female masculinities, to indicate the multiple meanings of gender as well as sexual desire, would enable greater historical specificity than the blanket use of the term lesbian.

Much of the period covered in this chapter has only begun to be researched. Historians have tended to concentrate on the eighteenth and early nineteenth centuries, and then on prominent individual cases in subsequent years. There have been debates about how female cross-dressing was represented in contemporary discourses and in what ways attitudes to passing women and the use by women of masculine styles of dress changed over the period from the late eighteenth century to the 1960s.

Considering popular representations at the beginning of the period, a distinction can be drawn between warrior women and civilian female husbands. Dugaw describes the powerful tradition of the female warrior as a preoccupation at every cultural level. She appeared in ballads and the theatre, and was represented as brave and heroic, especially if she had fought in battle (Dugaw 1989, Clark 1995). Her qualities enabled her to transcend normal feminine fears and weaknesses. It is argued that as exceptional heroines, these women did not pose a threat to the natural order, and their exploits could be celebrated. Female husbands might be treated differently, however. In the ballads, and to a lesser extent in the newspaper reports, they were seen as curiosities, sometimes ridiculed for being neither men nor women, and their wives were pitied. Whether or not there was a widespread notion of the possibility of sex between women in the late eighteenth century is much debated (Hitchcock 1997, Trumbach 1991, Donoghue 1993). Female husbands were sometimes described using the older term hermaphrodite, indicating they were incomplete sexual subjects. Whatever passed between this type of husband and wife was thus not regarded as a real sexual relationship. Some historians have argued that female husbands were treated with a degree of tolerance (Hitchcock 1997, Dugaw 1989). There were no laws against women's cross-dressing and they were not perceived as a great threat to social stability. But being laughed at was nevertheless a form of social control of their behaviour and served as a warning to others. Behind the jokes in the ballads, the female husband might be seen a challenge to the institution of marriage and heterosexuality, to the gender order, and to the nation itself. The disruptive potential of cross-dressing (Garber 1992) therefore varied according to context and over time.

A number of historians have argued that after the early nineteenth century the incidence of female cross-dressing – and popular representations of the practice – declined as new ideals of female domesticity took hold (Dekker and van de Pol 1989, Dugaw 1989, Hitchcock 1997). While this may have been the case for women passing as men in military contexts, the evidence suggests that in Britain, civilian female husbands continued to exist through the nineteenth and twentieth centuries. In the 1830s and 1840s stories about women who dressed as men for work continued to circulate in popular culture (Clark 1987). Townsend (1996) identifies a number of cases in the 1860s and argues that while gender roles were becoming stricter for middle-class women, working-class communities still had sympathy for women who needed to survive and avoid the Poor Law, even by means of gender transgression.

Meanwhile, in middle-class circles some women were beginning to challenge prevailing conceptions of femininity in behaviour and dress. From the late nineteenth century, a plainer, more masculine style of dress was adopted by some middle-class women – students, teachers, office workers, writers and other 'New Women' – to signal their economic independence, feminist principles and, for some, a sexual affinity with women rather than men. Attacks on these women's 'male impersonation' sometimes hinted at lesbianism, increasingly so by the

1900s when the suffrage movement was at its height (Rolley 1991, Vicinus 1996). Historians debate the extent to which cross-dressing women in the theatre (such as the music hall star Vesta Tilley) inspired early-twentieth-century lesbians to develop this style (Vicinus 1996, Bratton 1992).

The English sexologist Havelock Ellis, writing at the turn of the century, strongly associated lesbianism with some degree of transvestism. For him, a masculine appearance signified the true invert with her active – and thus necessarily masculine – desire for other women, while her (psuedo-) lesbian lover might retain a feminine style of dress. Historians disagree over whether the sexologists actually created the idea of the 'butch' lesbian or simply described already existing forms of dress code among some lesbians (Stanley 1992, Jackson 1994, Jeffreys 1985), but this description of sexual identity through dress and appearance as 'butch and femme' became a common stereotype of lesbianism from the middle decades of the twentieth century.

In the interwar years, tailor-made suits with simple lines were part of a highly fashionable, 'modernist' style for women. Prominent lesbians, including Radclyffe Hall, could wear severely cut clothes such as dark tweed suits, cropped hair and monocles, yet be praised as ultra fashionable rather than condemned for their masculine presentation. But as this style fell out of fashion, so masculine clothing became more clearly a badge of lesbian sexual identity in the 1930s and 1940s (Rolley 1990, Doan 1998a, Summerscale 1998). In the post World War II period, the masculine butch look, complemented by the more conventionally dressed femme, shifted from being an upper-class or middle-class lesbian fashion to become more of a working-class style. By this time, trousers (or slacks) had become more acceptable as women's wear, and therefore lesbians had to work harder to look masculine and indicate their identity (Wilson 1990).

While elements of masculine style became a lesbian signifier in the twentieth century, women also continued to seek to pass as men. Little research has been done on this period but it is likely that cross-dressing women were still represented as heroic if discovered in wartime. Sexological ideas did not appear to influence perceptions of female husbands, who continued to be reported regularly in the popular press as eccentric curiosities rather than sexual deviants. In the prominent 1929 trial of Colonel Barker, for example, lesbianism was not mentioned, despite the fact that this followed just a few months after the prosecution of *The Well of Loneliness* (Vernon 2000).

Wearing masculine clothes – along a continuum which stretches from completely passing as a man to adding a few masculine touches to their dress – has provided an important means of survival or identification for many lesbians over the centuries.

1 *The Annual Register*, 19 June 1773, p. 111

A young woman dressed in man's cloaths was carried before the Lord Mayor, for marrying an old woman. The old woman was possessed of 100£ and the design was to get possession of the money, and then to make off; but the old lady proved too knowing.

2 *The Annual Register*, 5 July 1777, pp. 191–2

July 5th. A woman was convicted at the Guildhall, Westminster, for going in men's cloaths, and being married to three different women by a fictitious name, and for defrauding them of their money and cloaths: She was sentenced to stand in the pillory at Charing-cross, and to be imprisoned six months.

3 Mary Anne Talbot, 'The Intrepid Female or Surprising Life and Adventures of Mary Anne Talbot, otherwise John Taylor' in *Kirby's Wonderful and Scientific Museum*, Vol. II, 1804

Mary Anne Talbot (1778–1808) was the illegitimate daughter of Earl Talbot. Between the ages of 5 and 14 she was sent to boarding school in Chester. In 1792 her guardian gave her into the care of a Captain Bowen.

In consequence of an order from the regiment to which Captain Bowen belonged he was obliged to embark for St. Domingo, and conceiving me properly subjugated to his purpose, and remarking that my figure was extremely well calculated for the situation he had projected for me, he produced a complete suit of male attire, and for the first time made me acquainted with the unmanly design he had formed of taking me with him to the West Indies in the menial capacity of his foot-boy.

I had not much time to deliberate how to act; and by this time knowing his peremptory disposition, in a fit of frenzy and despair I yielded to the base proposal and assumed the character he had thought fit to assign me, together with the name of John Taylor, which I ever after retained.

After the trip to the West Indies, the regiment was ordered back to Europe. Mary Talbot took part in the siege of Valenciennes (1793) as a drummer boy and was injured. She described the scenes of battle graphically.

Towards the end of this memorable siege I received two wounds, though fortunately neither deep nor dangerous: the first from a musket ball, which, glancing between my breast and collar-bone, struck my rib, and the other on the small of my back from the broadsword of an Austrian trooper, which, I imagine, rather proceeded from accident than design, the marks of which two wounds I still bear. I carefully concealed them, from the dread of their discovering my sex, and effected a perfect cure by the assistance of a little basilicon, lint, and a few Dutch drops.

Having left the army, in 1796 she worked as a senior officer on an American merchant ship sailing to New York.

The only circumstance of an unpleasant nature that occurred during my stay in America arose from the strong partiality which the captain's niece conceived to my company, and which proceeded to such an extent as to induce her to make me an offer of her hand in marriage. I made several excuses, but could not divert her attention from what she proposed. Mrs. Field at length becoming acquainted with the circumstance, made great objection to my youth and inexperience of the world; but neither my excuses nor Mrs. Field's remonstrances had any weight, opposed to the young lady's inclination, which she fondly cherished to the last hour of my residence at Rhode Island. She requested before Mrs. Field that I would make her a present of my picture; for which purpose I sat for a miniature at New York, in the full uniform of an American officer – for this picture I paid eighteen dollars. The time of our departure for England being arrived, I took my leave, not without regret, of Mrs. Field and family, but had scarcely proceeded two miles on my way to New York before I was summoned back, being overtaken by a servant, who informed the captain and myself that we must return, as the young lady was in strong fits. We returned and found her still in a fit, out of which, with great difficulty, we recovered her; and by making her a promise of a speedy return from England, she very reluctantly allowed me to depart.

Back in London Mary Anne Talbot revealed her sex when press-ganged into the British navy.

But while about to land at St. Catharine's we were attacked by a press-gang, whom we resolutely opposed; I in my defence taking up one of the scullers of the boat, with which I struck one or two who attempted to secure me. In this contest I received a wound on my head by a cutlass, a large seam from which remains to the present hour. After a long struggle, during which I was tumbled out of the boat up to my armpits in water, the mate and I were both secured. ... Finding I had nothing to prevent [impressment into the navy] but a disclosure of what I had so long kept within my own breast, I accosted the inspecting officers, and told them I was unfit to serve his Majesty ... being a female. On this assertion they both appeared greatly surprised, and at first thought I had fabricated a story to be discharged, and sent me to the surgeon, whom I soon convinced of the truth of my assertion. The officers upbraided each other with ignorance at not discovering before that I was a woman, and readily gave me a discharge.

Mary Talbot then applied for the back pay and prize-money due to her for her military service.

Having undergone a long private examination [by the magistrates], the consequence was a subscription was immediately made, and by the recommendation of some gentlemen present I was placed in a lodging at the house of Mrs. Jones, Falcon Court, Shoe Lane, with a strict injunction, if possible, to break me of the masculine habit to which I was so much used. I received twelve shillings a week for my support till I could obtain the money due to me from Government. ...

I had not yet changed my seaman's attire, but during the stay I made with Mrs. Jones I resumed the dress of my own sex, though at times I could not entirely forget my seafaring habits, but frequently dressed myself and took excursions as a sailor. Whenever I dressed myself as a sailor, I sought the company of some messmates I had known on board the *Brunswick*, and, as long as my money lasted, spent it in company with the brave fellows at the 'Coach and Horses', opposite Somerset House, a place where they mostly frequented.

Though awarded an army pension for her war service, Mary Talbot was impoverished. After failing to pay her bills in 1801–2 she was taken to court by her landlady and thrown into Newgate (the debtors' prison). She was imprisoned in the women's wing, but still sometimes wore men's clothing.

My time in Newgate was rendered more comfortable than I had any reason to expect, from the constant attention of a female who lived with me some time previous to my being arrested; for when no longer in my power to support her in the way I had been accustomed, instead of quitting me she remained in the prison, and by needlework which she obtained contributed greatly to my support. She has remained a constant friend in every change that I have since experienced.

This account was first published in 1804, to raise money. In 1807 Mary Anne Talbot fell into a decline as a result of her injuries and died in early 1808, at the age of 30.

4 'Extraordinary Female Affection', *General Evening Post*, 24 July 1790

The description of Miss Butler as masculine, in an article on the Ladies of Llangollen, did have the power to connote perversion in the late eighteenth century. The Ladies called on their friend Edmund Burke to give them legal advice to protect their reputations. At the time this piece was published, Miss Butler was fifty-one, short and plump.

Extraordinary female affection

Miss Butler and Miss Ponsonby have retired from society into a certain Welch Vale. Both Ladies are daughters of the great Irish families whose names they retain. Miss Butler, who is of the Ormonde family had several offers of marriage, all of which she rejected. Miss Ponsonby, her particular friend and companion, was supposed to be the bar to all matrimonial union, it was thought proper to separate them, and Miss Butler was confined. The two Ladies, however found means to elope together. ...

The beautiful above-mentioned vale is the spot they fixed on where they have resided for several years unknown to the neighbouring villagers by any other appellation than *the Ladies of the Vale*! ... [N]o entreaties could prevail on the Ladies to quit their sweet retreat.

Miss Butler is tall and masculine, she wears always a riding habit, hangs her hat with the air of a sportsman in the hall, and appears in all respects as a young man, if we except the petticoats which she still retains. Miss Ponsonby, on the contrary, is polite and effeminate, fair and beautiful. ... They live in neatness, elegance and taste. Two females are their only servants. Miss Ponsonby does the duties and honours of the house, while Miss Butler superintends the gardens and the rest of the grounds.

5 *The Annual Register*, 1 September 1815, p. 64

An early example of a black woman who cross-dressed, William Brown was clearly a skilled and experienced seaman. Like other passing women, her claim that her disguise had heterosexual origins is countered by her evident relish of a masculine role.

Amongst the crew of the Queen Charlotte, 110 guns, recently paid off, it is now discovered, was a female African, who had served as a seaman in the royal navy for upwards of eleven years, several of which she has been rated able on the books of the above ship by the name of William Brown, and has served for some time as the captain of the fore-top, highly to the satisfaction of the officers. She is a smart well formed figure, about five feet four inches in height, possessed of considerable strength and great activity; her features are rather handsome for a black, and she appears to be about 26 years of age. Her share of prize money is said to be considerable, respecting which she has been several times within the last few days at Somerset-place. In her manner she exhibits all the traits of a British tar, and takes her grog with her late messmates with the greatest gaiety. She says she is a married woman, and went to sea in consequence of a quarrel with her husband, who, it is said, has entered a caveat against her receiving her prize money. She declares her intention of again entering the service as a volunteer.

6 M. Ryan, *A Manual of Medical Jurisprudence*, 1836, London: Sherwood, Gilbert and Piper, pp. 227–9, quoting *The Times*, 1829

The sources documenting the case of James Allen include this inquest report and the next extract, one of at least two extant street ballads. At the formal judicial inquest, speculation on her life is limited, while the ballad defuses the threat she posed to heterosexuality and the nation by poking fun at both Allen and her wife.

An inquest of a singular and mysterious nature took place at St Thomas's Hospital, before Mr. Thomas Shelton, Coroner, relating to a person named James Allen, aged forty-two. The deceased expired on the way to the hospital, and on examination by the medical gentlemen was found to be of the female sex. The utmost curiosity was excited, and the whole of the hospital pupils crowded into the Jury-room.

Evidence commenced. – William Shrieve, a sawyer in the employment of Mr. Crisp, of Dockhead, had known the deceased for two years. On Monday he was at work with him at a saw-pit in Mill-street, Dockhead, and a piece of timber falling on his head occasioned his death; he was quite sober at the time. Deceased had a weakly voice, and neither beard nor whiskers; always understood he was a married man, and had been so upwards of twenty-one years. Within the last six months his sex had been doubted, and he was considered an hermaphrodite. The wife is a hard-working woman, but believes they did not live on good terms together; it was said that he sometimes used her ill. The deceased and his wife parted two or three times on account of the former being jealous. They never had any children.

Jane Daley deposed, that she had known the deceased a number of years. Witness never doubted the sex of the deceased till lately, when his wife said, 'She was sure her Jemmy was not a proper man;' he, the woman-husband, treated his wife very ill at times, and witness often advised her to leave him as a worthless, good-for-nothing thing, who was not the quarter of a man. I am sure they were married, I have seen the certificate; the ceremony took place at Camberwell church. I can swear that the wife is a real woman; I am firmly of opinion that she never knew man, and is as innocent as my granddaughter. I am certain she did not find out her mistake till lately, how she had been imposed upon! She is a woman of ten thousand.

Mr. John Martin, dresser to Mr. Key, testified the body to be that of a female, perfect in every respect.

The Jury expressed a wish to have the widow examined, but the Coroner said, they had only to inquire into the cause of deceased's death, which had been satisfactorily accounted for, and their duty was at an end.

The Foreman of the Jury said, he should certainly wish to inquire fully into so extraordinary an occurrance; there is no doubt something in the back ground which they have not arrived at. The Coroner observed, that the circumstance was one of an extraordinary description, but still they had not to develope it.

After further discussion, a verdict was returned, 'That the deceased was accidently killed.' The wife of the deceased was present in the inquest-room.

The wife swore positively, that she did not know the sex of her husband, but considered him an imperfect man or a hermaphrodite. He never caressed her, and when she declared her doubts of his manhood, he became angry and jealous. The body was examined, and found to be that of a woman. The parties were married at Camberwell church, on the 13th of December, 1808.

7 'The Female Husband', *c.*1838, street ballad

The female husband

If you want to hear a bit of fun
Oh listen unto me,
About a Female Husband,
The like you never see,
Such a singular thing you never knew
No not in all your life,
As two Females to be wed,
And live as Man and Wife.

Chorus

So young women all a warning take,
And mark what I do say,
Before you wed, your husbands try,
Or else you'll rue the day.

The Female Husband lived
In service as a Groom
'Twas there that she got wed,
To the housemaid in her bloom,
At Camberwell the truth I tell,
The Wedding was, it's true,
You'll laugh till all is blue.

The parties they were shown to bed,
The bride sir, thought of that,
But the bridegroom he was taken ill,
Made everything look flat,
From his bride he turn'd and twisted,
Then she to herself did say,

21

My Husband is a Hermaphrodite,
A wager I would lay.

Time passed on for many years,
A virgin she was still,
But her husband would for jealousy,
Oft use her very ill,
At Dockhead, it was asserted,
You may believe now what I may,
By her husband it was thought
She was in the family way.

But when she turn'd herself in bed,
Dear Jemmy, she would say,
We have been married many years,
Remember this, I pray,
But what a disappointment,
Now when she thought of that,
But what she never got,
Why, it could not make her fat.

Sometime he was a Publican,
And dwelt in Baldock town,
With good ale and beer, his customers
He did supply around.
Then to the Docks he went to work,
As we had often heard,
Where the men would often joke
About his whiskers and his beard.

Sometime he was a Sawyer,
Done his duty like a man,
'Twas there his days were ended,
As you shall understand.
There was not one as we could hear,
Did of his manhood doubt,
But now its o'er he is no more,
And the secret is found out.

Now for Twenty years they lived,
As man and wife so clever,
Both eat and drank, and slept,
And just these things together;
If women all could do the same,

And keep their virgin knot,
Why the King and all his subjects,
Would quickly go to pot.

So now my song is ended,
I hope it's pleased you all,
This poor woman had a husband,
That had nothing at all.
Twenty years she lived a married life.
Still a maid she may remain,
But we trust she'll find a difference,
If she ever weds again.

So I do advise young woman all,
To look before you wed,
For if you should be so deceived,
You will rue your marriage bed.

8 Anon., *The Sinks of London Laid Open: A Pocket Companion for the Uninitiated*, 1848 [1835], London: J. Duncombe, pp. 65–71

This is a journalistic account of a cheap lodging house in Seven Dials, London (Covent Garden). In this period it was a disreputable slum area with a poor, racially mixed, semi-criminal community, many of whom made a living on the streets of the city. The source illustrates the lack of legal penalties for women who cross-dressed and, unusually, we hear the assertive voice of the wife.

Chapter X

The return; – and a little unknown

The kitchen was again getting crowded. The fire once more gave notice that it was busy with chops and steaks; and as for the gambling-table, it had literally become thronged. The bawlers of catch-penny papers, or 'book-sellers,' as they styled themselves, were now beginning to make their appearance, in parties of three or four; every one having a copy of the news he had been so loudly proclaiming stuck in the front of his hat, with that awful word, 'murder,' printed in large letters as the head-line; or the more melancholy announcement of the dying speech of one John So-and-so. They busied themselves in arranging their papers and dividing the gains. ...

A singular being now entered the kitchen ...

The man, (for the creature was in masculine garb,) was between four and five feet high; he was long armed, and one leg was rather longer than the other, which caused one of his shoulders to rise a little when he walked or stood, and which gave his shoulders, which were naturally broad, a very square appearance.

He was dressed in one of those flash coats already described whose full make, too, by no means diminished his breadth. A kind of shawl crossed his neck, or rather bosom, for his neck, was bare, in a style as if arranged by the hand of a female; and underneath of which peeped two corners of his shirt. His features were of that kind, that carried precisely the expression of those of a masculine woman; and when he spoke, it was a perfect puzzle to the stranger, to know whether he heard the voice of a man or a woman.

The creature himself (as if conscious of those singularities) affected a superior degree of manliness. Swaggered around the room, his hat half pulled over his brows, and slouched a little on one side; assuming the scowling look of a bully, and at times the flashy air of a gallant.

He had a wife; and, as if that was not enough for any man, likewise had a mistress; and, to show that he was a professed admirer of the kind of Eve, took hold of his mistress when he entered with one hand, and waving the other above his head, sung 'My love is like the red, red rose,' in a voice at once powerful and sweet. Then taking her upon his knee struck up 'the light, the light guitar,' in a style so exquisitely musical and rich, as fairly to disturb the card-table, and draw from the whole company a thundering round of applause, with 'Bravo, Bill!'

He appeared to be a creature of great spirit and vivacity, dashed about, throwing himself into pugilistic attitudes, and striking out, right and left, at his cronies, in sportive play, using at the same time the true slang of low, blackguard life; as, with great emphasis, 'I'll — into you, your — pall!' with a vast deal more of such high-toned language so appropriate for the gallant of a cadging house. He fell a capering, singing all the while with great animation, and beating time most elegantly with heel and toe, and giving vent to the fulness of his spirits in shouts, as 'He hows,' 'the Cadger Lad,' 'A roving life for me,' &c., and, catching hold of his wench again, thrust his hand into his bosom – pulled out a handful of silver; swore, bravadoed – squirted tobacco juice in the grate, and boasted of always being able to earn his ten shillings a day, and thought nothing of picking up a guinea in the same time at a race or fair.

This money-making man, it may be supposed, was a street singer; and was reported to be a native of that country – the land of leeks and cheese; that place where goats are said to abound – Wales.

The landlord opened the door, and gave orders for the card players to cease; it was twelve o'clock. The gamblers were loth, but the master was peremptory.

This portrait, with the whole of the work, was written, and given to the

24

publisher of one of the first magazines of the day, in November 1834, and the following report appeared in the papers in February 1835, and which, we think, authenticates pretty clearly the correctness of our statement. The reader will perceive a likeness.

Hatton Garden. Extraordinary case – a man-woman

A creature in the garb of a man, who at the station-house had given the name of Bill Chapman, was placed at the bar with one Isabella Watson, and complained of for being a common cheat and imposter, and creating a disturbance.

Oakley, inspector of the E division, stated that although the thing before them, that called itself Bill Chapman, was attired in man's apparel, he had ascertained that it was a woman.

Mr. Bennett [magistrate], who was very much surprised, looked steadfastly at the prisoner and asked her name.

PRISONER:	(*speaking in a rough manner.*) It is Mary Chapman.
MR. BENNETT:	I never saw a figure more like a man, and the voice is manly.
OAKLEY:	I have known her at least ten years, and she always appears in a dress similar to the one she now wears, namely, a hat, smock-frock, trousers or knee-breeches, and until last night I always supposed her to be a man. She is known all over England as a ballad-singer and a crier of 'The last dying speeches,' &c.
MR. BENNETT:	She may be a disorderly and disreputable character, which, in fact, her dressing as a man clearly shows, but I know of no law to punish her for wearing male attire.
OAKLEY:	She travels the country with a woman named Isabella Watson, and they are both known at every race-course and fair as ballad-singers, and considered to be man and wife.
MR. BENNETT:	She may have more than one reason for dressing in that manner, and passing as the husband of the woman Watson, and I wish it was in my power to imprison her.
OAKLEY:	For upwards of seven years she has occasionally lodged with Watson, at Mr. — in — street, St. Giles's, and they always passed as man and wife; and, moreover, Chapman smokes; and whenever Watson gives her any offence, she beats her and blackens her

	eyes, though Watson is so much taller and apparently stronger.
MR. BENNETT:	It is a very extraordinary case. What have you to say, prisoner?
PRISONER:	Isabella has lived with me as my companion for many years.
MR. BENNETT:	Why do you dress as a man?
PRISONER:	I own I am disguised, and it was owing to the cruelty of a father-in-law that I first dressed in this manner. I never did harm to any person. I have been all over the kingdom, and never was in prison in my life before.
MR. BENNETT:	Well I should advise you to be careful: if I could punish you I would.
ISABELLA WATSON:	The poor fellow has been with me hundreds of miles as my companion, and he never got into a scrape before.
MR. BENNETT:	It is a case that puzzels me, but I must discharge the prisoner.

The prisoner, who was chewing tobacco, then bowed his head, and walked out of the office with Isabella, who exclaimed, 'Never mind, my lad, if we live a hundred years it will be in this manner.'

Watson is about five feet seven inches in height, with rather an intelligent countenance; and Chapman is not more than five feet high. Her hair is light brown, and cut short, the same as a man's; and she has the gait of a man, and looks like a costermonger.

We agree with this account in every thing except the height of the individuals. The reporter, we think, is a little man, who always sees inches through a magnifier. The man-woman is the height we have stated, or rather less, and his wife is five feet two inches, instead of five feet seven. It is curious but nevertheless a fact, that, although this strange being had lodged for a number of years at the house alluded to, it was never known it was a woman, though at the same time it was never supposed that the creature was a man.

9 'A Female Husband in Manchester', *The Weekly Dispatch*, 15 April 1838, p. 175

A female husband in Manchester

A few days ago a respectable female waited upon an attorney in this town, and asked his advice in a case of a very peculiar nature. It seems that her husband, a master bricklayer, who had been in the habit of trusting her implicitly in his business, even leaving to her management the book-keeping requisite in his trade, had of late, for some cause or other, refused to allow her the usual weekly sum for housekeeping. Having also, in other respects, treated her, as she conceived, in an unkind manner, she came to take advice as to how she should proceed, under the circumstances, against her husband, whom, to the no small astonishment of the professional gentleman she was then consulting, she declared to be not a man, but a woman. The attorney thought it his duty, under such singular circumstances, to bring the matter under the notice of Mr. Foster, the Magistrate, who directed that Mr. Thomas should take the case under his management, and bring the parties for private examination before him (Mr. Foster), at the police-office. Mr. Thomas took the necessary steps, and on Thursday the parties were brought before Mr. Foster in the deputy constable's room at the police office, when the truth of the wife's averment to the attorney was corroborated in the most distinct and unqualified manner, by Mr. Ollier, surgeon to the police, who gave a certificate declaring the individual in question was a woman. The woman-husband, we believe, did not make the least attempt to deny her sex, but contented herself with stating that her wife had been only led to make this exposure because she had withheld from her the weekly allowance of money for housekeeping expenses. The wife replied, that this was not the only cause she had of complaint against her spouse; for that she (the husband) was occasionally intoxicated, and that, when in that state, the husband treated her very ill. The wife has also stated that she accidentally made the discovery of the sex of her husband as much as two or three days back, but that she had kept the secret until the present time. From what could be gleaned of the history of this female husband, it would seem that she assumed the garb and character of a boy at an early age, and that, in that character, she was apprenticed, at the age of 16 or 17, to a master builder, in one of the large towns of Yorkshire. Being of good exterior, with prepossessing appearance and manners, and of features rather handsome, the supposed young man attracted the attention of many females in the same condition of life; and amongst others was the one who afterwards became the wife. The attentions of the young bricklayer were acceptable and accepted, and the union took place shortly after the expiration of the apprenticeship. Soon afterwards this couple came to Manchester, we are told, about the year 1829, where the husband commenced the business of a builder, and by considerable skill, ability, and attention to business, was tolerably successful. Amongst other branches of the business, this builder became remarkable, indeed almost to celebrity, for skill and success in the erection of flues, ovens, &c., and, we believe, is at this moment in very good business, employing several hands, and giving very general satisfaction to those for whom any work has been executed. The wife had the entire management of the books and accounts in the business, and, as far as we have heard, there was not the slightest imputation on her character. We believe that nothing was done in the way of legal proceedings. Several articles, claimed by the wife as her property, have been sent to the police-office by the husband, who, so far as we have heard, has not offered any reparation to the wife for the cruel and painful situation in which she is now placed. One thing is tolerably certain, that after the exposure which has taken place, and the affair was currently talked of as early as Thursday and Friday last, the woman who has ventured to assume the character of a man will no longer be able to continue to carry on business in this town, and that she must either lay aside her disguise, and resume the appearance which most befits her sex, or if she still retain her unfeminine appearance and character, she must seek to hide her imposture in some place where she is not known, and where she may hope for awhile to escape detection. We believe that many persons who have employed her join in declaring that they had not the slightest suspicion that she was other than she seemed.

10 D. Hudson, *Munby: Man of Two Worlds. The Life and Diaries of Arthur J. Munby 1828–1910*, 1972, London: John Murray, p. 110

Arthur Munby, civil servant and minor poet, had an obsessive interest in working-class women, especially those who did heavy manual labour. He wrote about his many encounters with such women in his diaries and made a series of photographs of women in their working clothes. He was particularly interested in trouser-wearing women, passing or not. Mary Newall's story was also commemorated in street ballad form.

Tuesday, 19 November *{1861}*

Went out to the Westminster Police Court, to the examination of Mary Newell, the maid of all work who robbed her master last week, went off in man's clothes, travelled down to Yarmouth, took lodgings there, smoked cigars, & made love to her landlady. Assuming that she had as I was told done it only for a lark, I admired her pluck skill and humour, and wished to observe her person & character. But the inspector who helped to catch her showed me that she was probably a practised thief and a dissolute girl. ...

At noon the court opened, with a great rush of people to see the prisoner. As a barrister, I had a reserved seat in front of her. She was led in and placed on high in the dock: a sullen but fairly good looking girl, of moderate height, and not unfeminine. Drest in shabby finery: her hair, which she had cut short, hanging over her forehead. Her hat, coat, trousers, and the rest of her male clothing were exhibited on a table. ... After she had been committed for trial at the Sessions, I walked away with her master – a surveyor – and his pupil, the young man whose name & garments she assumed. She was a dirty and untidy servant, they said; was in the habit (they now found) of stealing out to low theatres alone, hiring cabs to go in and smoking cigars with the cabmen.

11 'Mary Newall, The Artful Girl of Pimlico', reprinted in C. Hindley, *Curiosities of Street Literature*, 1966 [1871], London: Reeves and Turner

Mary Newall, The Artful Girl of Pimlico

Come all you ladies list to me,
　　And give me every attention,
It's all about a servant girl,
　　That I am going to mention,
Mary Ann Newall is her name,
　　She possessed herself of riches,
She collar'd all her master's tin,
　　And swore she'd wear the breeches

Mary Newall is a nice young girl,
　　She possessed herself of riches,
In the Vauxhall Road she crack'd the crib
　　And put on the pegtop breeches.

Her master went out for a walk,
　　And as he abroad did roam,
I will tell you what Miss Newall did,
　　While her master was from home;
She turned the house near inside out,
　　Indeed I am no joker,
She cut the hair from off her head,
　　And stuck it on the poker.

She got a lot of bullock's blood,
　　And mixed up in a pail, Sir,
So to think that I am murdered, now
　　Master will not fail, Sir;
She smashed the poker right in two,
　　That no one should doubt it,
With a bit of glue, now this is true,
　　She stuck the hair about it.

She in the wainscoat cut a hole,
　　Just the size of a man, sir,
She smashed a window from the inside,

Saying, I'm the girl that can, sir,
Crack a crib with any chap,
  And back up all the riches,
Then she pulled off her crinoline,
  And put on the pegtop breeches.

With new spring boots, & fine cloth vest
  And overcoat to match, sir,
With the lodger's hat & nice gold guard,
  She was up to the scratch, sir,
She had the cheek to call a cab,
  With boxes in rotation,
Saying, Cabby, old boy, as quick as you like,
  Drive off to Shoreditch Station.

Now her master soon returned home,
  The truth I do declare, sir,
Saying the house is rob'd and Mary's dead,
  Here's the poker cover'd with hair, sir
To the station-house he quick did send,
  Murder and robbery, who could doubt it,
But Detective Sheen, a clever chap,
  Soon told them all about it.

The telegraph was set to work,
  The best thing for to track her,
It was soon found she at Yarmouth was
  A smoking of her tobacco;
Drest up in slap togs, you're sure,
  Like the greatest swells of the day,
She got dead nuts on her landlady,
  And took her to the play.

Sheen, the detective, soon found her out
  And the place where she dwelt, sir,
The landlady told him, her nice young man
  Was walking with the girls, sir
But she was nabbed, cigar in hand,
  She swore she fight a duel,
Sheen says, where is your petticoats?
  I know you Mary Newall.

She sold her togs, both stays and shift,
  Hair bag, dresses, and bustle,

> She had bought a pair of pegtop tights,
>> To go off in a bustle;
> To the Magistrate she was brought up,
>> And stripped of all her riches,
> The Magistrate said, take her away,
>> And pull off this lady's breeches.

12 'A Woman as a Cabdriver for Ten Years', *The Liverpool Mercury*, 13 February 1875

A woman as a cabdriver for ten years

A romance of the rank

On Thursday (as will be seen by our police report of that day) William Seymour, who appeared to be about 25 years of age, was committed for trial at the sessions, on a charge of stealing two pieces of meat from the shop of Mr. H. Moorby, butcher, Leece-street. The prisoner was removed to Walton goal in the usual course, and it was then discovered that 'William' was a woman. She was consequently removed to the female side of the gaol, where she afterwards related the following particulars relative to her early life and her adoption of men's habits: –

She was born at Taunton, Somerset, where her father was land agent to a nobleman. She had a great liking for 'handling the ribbons,' and learned to drive horses while very young. When little more than 14 years of age she was married to an army surgeon of the name of Honeywell, and her name, as a married woman, is Margaret Honeywell. The two lived together so unhappily that at length she ran away from home and went to London. She there met with a woman who had formerly been farm-servant to her father, and who had married a cabman, and, from what she heard in regard to the cabdriving business, she resolved to earn an independent living in that branch of industry. By wearing her hair short, and by a judicious use of clothing, she managed to present the appearance of a short stout man. Her face being of a masculine type, her complexion florid, and she having an impediment in her speech, caused by a defective palate, conspired to render the illusion perfect. For three years in London and six in Liverpool she plied the whip as a cab 'man,' her sex being unknown and unsuspected by all, with one exception. During that period she was on several occasions placed in a peculiar and delicate position, but came out from each ordeal without even suspicion of her sex being aroused. On one occasion a noted bone-setter in Liverpool examined her knee, which she thought had been injured, but which turned out to be only affected with rheumatism. Although he treated the complaint successfully, he seems to have noticed nothing peculiar in the formation of the limb. Mrs. Honeywell states that during the time she acted as a 'cabby' she saw a notice in the newspaper that her husband had failed in business. The one exception referred to is a woman, who has been known as 'Bill Seymour's wife' for some years, and who has also been in the habit of taking her 'husband's' dinner to the cabstand daily. In all probability the public would not have heard for some time of this female cabdriver had it not been for the unfortunate transaction in Leece-street. When the prisoner was taken into the detective office, it was noticed by one of the officers that, although the 'man' seemed to be getting on for 30 years of age, there was sign neither of beard nor of the use of the razor.

Yesterday, at the borough quarter sessions, before Mr. J. B. Aspinall, Q.C., recorder, the prisoner was indicted, in the name of William Seymour, alias Mary Seymour, alias Mary Honeywell, for stealing 30lbs. of meat, the property of Henry Moorby. ...

Upon being called upon for her defence, the prisoner strongly protested that she was innocent.

The jury at once found the prisoner guilty, and, in reply to the recorder, Mr. Robinson (the chief warder) said nothing was known against her.

THE RECORDER:	(to the prisoner) How do you account for the way in which you are going about in male clothes and as a car driver? What is the meaning of it? Of course, that is not an offence, but one wishes to know something about you.
THE PRISONER:	I have done it ten years – ever since I have been·away from home.
THE CLERK OF THE PEACE:	She is a widow, I think. (Laughter)
PRISONER:	No, sir, not that I know of. (Renewed laughter)
THE RECORDER:	I don't know that there is any reason why I should treat you differently from any other prisoner. This is your first offence?
PRISONER:	I am innocent. The boy (the witness) has made a mistake, I am sure.
THE RECORDER:	He cannot be mistaken. There are two or three things which make it difficult to believe he is mistaken, and I don't see how anybody could have an interest in putting the meat into the box of the cab but you. I have no doubt the boy is speaking the truth; but, as I have said, I don't see why I should treat you differently from any other person. You seem, although in an odd way, to have been obtaining an honest livelihood and

in such a case I always deal with a prisoner with the utmost possible leniency.

The learned recorder then sentenced the prisoner to two months hard labour.

13 H. Ellis, *Studies in the Psychology of Sex. Vol 1. Sexual Inversion*, 1897, London: The University Press, pp. 94–7

Ellis was not the first observer to assume a link between masculine appearance and lesbianism, but he integrated it into sexological theory, creating the category of the invert, the true 'butch' lesbian.

The chief characteristic of the sexually inverted woman is a certain degree of masculinity. As I have already pointed out, a woman who is inclined to adopt the ways and garments of men is by no means necessarily inverted. In the volume of *Women Adventurers*, edited by Mrs. Norman for the Adventure Series, there is no trace of inversion; in most of these cases, indeed, love for a man was precisely the motive for adopting male garments and manners. Again, Colley Cibber's daughter, Charlotte Charke, a boyish and vivacious woman, who spent much of her life in men's clothes, and ultimately wrote a lively volume of memoirs, appears never to have been attracted to women, though women were often attracted to her, believing her to be a man; it is, indeed, noteworthy that women seem, with special frequency, to fall in love with disguised persons of their own sex. There is, however, a very pronounced tendency among sexually inverted women to adopt male attire when practicable. In such cases male garments are not usually regarded as desirable chiefly on account of practical convenience, nor even in order to make an impression on other women, but because the wearer feels more at home in them. Thus Moll mentions the case of a young governess of sixteen who, while still unconscious of her sexual perversion, used to find pleasure when everyone was out of the house in putting on the clothes of a youth belonging to the family. And when they still retain female garments these usually show some traits of masculine simplicity, and there is nearly always a disdain for the petty feminine artifices of the toilet. Even when this is not obvious there are all sorts of instinctive gestures and habits which may suggest to female acquaintances the remark that such a person 'ought to have been a man'. The brusque, energetic movements, the attitude of the arms, the direct speech, the inflexions of the voice, the masculine straightforwardness and sense of honour, and especially the attitude towards men, free from any suggestion either of shyness or audacity, will often suggest the underlying psychic abnormality to a keen observer. Although there is sometimes a certain general coarseness of physical texture, we do not find any trace of a beard or moustache.

It is probable, however, that there are more genuine approximations to the masculine type. The muscles are everywhere firm with a comparative absence of soft connective tissue, so that an inverted woman may give an unfeminine impression to the sense of touch. Not only is the tone of the voice often different, but there is reason to suppose that this rests on a basis of anatomical modification. At Moll's suggestion, Flateau examined the larynx in twenty-three inverted women, and found in several a very decided masculine type of larynx, especially in cases of distinctly congenital origin. In the habits not only is there frequently a pronounced taste for smoking (sometimes found in quite feminine women), but there is also a dislike and sometimes incapacity for needlework and other domestic occupations, while there is often some capacity for athletics.

14 'Woman's Attempt to Join the Army', *The Hornsey Journal*, 18 August 1916, p. 7

Woman's attempt to join the army

A surprise for the tribunal.

A remarkable story of a Hornsey woman's success in passing herself off as a man, and her failure when she attempted to enlist at Mill Hill, is told in 'The Illustrated Sunday Herald.'

A slightly-built, fair-haired, and smooth-faced 'conscript,' dressed in a neat navy-blue suit, brown cap, and patent-leather boots, presented a yellow form, which bore the name of Albert – 32 years and four months old, a native of Clerkenwell, and – although this last item has been found to be incorrect – a geographer by trade. These statements were transcribed in the books at the depot, but they have since been ruled through in red ink. Immediately after entering the barracks, 'Albert' asked that she might be medically examined in private.

'No,' replied the sergeant, 'I don't think so. Why do you ask?'

'I have some cardiac trouble,' was the answer, 'and would much prefer to see the doctor alone.'

Further to induce the sergeant to grant the request she produced a National Health Insurance form bearing the words 'Cardiac trouble.' No doctor's name appeared, but this omission not infrequently occurs. The request was refused, and not one of the large number of soldiers and recruits who stood by guessed that the disappointed applicant was a woman.

'The voice was soft and rather gentle,' it was stated, 'but no notice was taken of that. Plenty of young fellows – and she looked like a young man of twenty-four – have effeminate voices, and when a great many men are being dealt with practically together, individual characteristics like that are passed without comment.'

'Albert' took a seat, and in due course underwent the eyesight and other tests before her sex was discovered.

A soldier who saw her said, 'She was the most perfect male impersonator I have ever seen. Not one of the women who wear men's attire on the stage – and I have seen all the best of them – could approach her. We were absolutely deceived, and I can tell you that when the truth came out there was something like consternation in the barracks. "Albert" is about 5ft. 4ins. in height, and, at a guess, has a chest measurement of something like 44 inches – which is greater than a man of that height would be expected to have, but not so much as a normal woman would possess. The woman was well-spoken, and I noticed that her manner was rather on the polite side. She didn't seem in the least degree nervous, even when she was found out. She was detained and handed to the civil police, who took her away in a motor-car.'

'The Illustrated Sunday Herald' has ascertained that the woman was closely questioned by the police, and told a story which entitles her to sympathy and the shielding of her identity.

Four years ago, she said, she left her husband, and with her two children went to live with her sister at Hornsey. There she passed as her sister's husband, and dressed as a man. She obtained work in Hornsey as a printer, but feared all the time that her husband would find her. When the National Registration Act was passed she maintained the fiction that she was a man by allowing herself to be registered as 'Albert.'

'Then came the yellow form, calling me up,' she has since told someone interested in her. 'I looked upon it as a godsend, and felt that here was a chance, at any rate, of getting where my husband would never find me. I knew there was a risk, although I was not aware of the kind of examination that would have to be undergone, and I was prepared to take the risk.'

It transpires that the masquerade has been kept up without exciting suspicion for four years. Six or seven years ago the woman was married in a northern seaport, but the union turned out unhappily, and within a year or two she left her husband. Her two children died in infancy, and the woman, who was then about 25, had no friends to whom she could turn. For a time, it is alleged, she lived in an apartment-house where a number of men were staying, after she had adopted male dress, and after a time the new lodger imparted the secret of her masquerade to another woman. The two started life afresh as husband and wife. F— had adopted male dress partly as an additional precaution against discovery by her husband, and partly to make it easier to gain a livelihood. They resembled any other couple except that the 'husband' appeared to be far from robust. The name F— was her maiden name.

The employer, in an interview, said the man-woman had always been a worker of more than average ability. 'She was engaged first in outdoor advertising work, but it was really not a good enough job, as I soon realised. I offered to teach her the process of aerographing, which is rather technical, and requires to some extent the possession of an artistic temperament. I have had to weed out a good many whom I have tried to teach because they find it impossible to carry through the work successfully. But she learned the process readily, and in a very little while was able to earn very high wages even for a man. As a matter of fact, five of my men have joined up, and I preferred to lose the whole five rather than her.

'I have heard all her story, and I am satisfied that she is a high-minded woman who has sacrificed herself to shield another woman's good name – and a woman who is not related in any way. It has been said that it was her widowed sister that she was living with, but that is not true. She has gone away from here now, but she will, I hope, find it possible to return. There is nothing disgraceful in her conduct, and the publication of her name, or the name of this business, would only make it more difficult for her to resume her position. She was in charge of the work in my absence, and the men were under her direction. She always exercised her authority properly, and I knew that I could leave things with every confidence to her control.

'So far from there being any suspicion here that she was anything but a rather short and slight man with a high-pitched voice, I can assure you that when the certificate, of the Mill Hill Medical Board was produced, I combated the idea that she was a woman as strenuously as I could. It seemed to me incredible, and I was convinced that there was a great mistake somewhere.'

15 'Why Women Masquerade as Men', *Illustrated Sunday Herald*, 27 August 1916, p. 15

Why women masquerade as men: the craving they endure in this day of big things

by Berta Ruck

Scene: Any home in England
Time: Now
Persons: Any two women of opposing types. Take, for instance, a mild, diffident and feminine Blonde, and a contrasting Brunette, full of character and independent ways.

THE BLONDE:	(*putting down a newspaper that she has been studying*) Fancy! Here's an account of a woman who has been masquerading as a man for four years, and who has only just been discovered!
THE BRUNETTE:	Another of them? Only lately I heard about that girl who ran away from home, dressed as a boy, to earn her living as a plumber's mate. Then there was that doctor-'man' in America. There was the woman who

served in the ranks and became a Chelsea pensioner. Quite often these cases seem to crop up.

THE BLONDE: I suppose it's because, as men, the women get better jobs and earn better money than they would do as members of their own sex.

THE BRUNETTE: Sometimes, perhaps; not always. Every now and then a woman is born who feels she's only a woman by mistake. She has the character, the strength, the capabilities of a man. Her male individuality is clothed in a feminine body; but it seems to her an oversight, just as if pickles had been packed into a labelled jam-jar. So she 'puts on male attire,' like the bailiff's daughter in the song, simply because she feels it dresses her true character. And she takes up male work.

A woman in war-time

THE BLONDE (*wonderingly*) This woman in the paper says that it was her dearest wish to be passed through as a soldier; she was grieved, actually grieved because she was stopped!

THE BRUNETTE: Well, my dear, can't you understand that? Nowadays any woman would wish she could possibly become a soldier, help her country, 'do her bit', avenge the friend she's lost by killing a few brutes of Germans with her own hands! Isn't it a deadly job to be a woman in wartime?

16 M. Gordon, *Penal Discipline*, 1922, London: George Routledge and Sons Ltd, pp. 71–2

Mary Gordon was a feminist, and a leading prison doctor and reformer. She lived with a woman partner, and in later life wrote a biography of the Ladies of Llangollen, *Chase of the Wild Goose* (1937). In this memoir of her prison career and argument for prison reform, she described several individual women. It is interesting that she personally helped this young prisoner, something she usually left to the prison's Lady Visitors.

I came across another young woman who was continually in prison for stealing men's clothes. She had several long sentences. I asked her what would keep her out of prison, and she replied: 'If I could go to sea.' On investigation I found that she felt it impossible to live as a woman, but could live as a man, and enjoyed men's work.

I told her that there was no law against her wearing men's clothing decently, if she did not steal it. After she had had two more convictions, I fitted her out with the clothes she wanted, and paid her fare to South Wales. She got work in a night shift, and lay on her back in a coal-pit hewing coal. All the year she did well, and wrote that she was living respectably. In her letter she said: 'This is the first Easter for ten years that I have spent out of prison.' She suffered many severe vicissitudes, including a mental attack, but came to prison very little in after years. To make useful citizens out of lost vagabonds cannot be done on prejudice of any kind.

17 'Col. Barker's Tears', *Daily Express*, 28 March 1929, p. 1

The case of 'Colonel Barker' was the most prominent and widely reported of several interwar examples of passing women who appeared in the press. She was sentenced to nine months imprisonment for perjury. She had later brushes with the law, when continuing to pass as a man, and appeared in a Blackpool freak show in 1937.

'Col. Barker's' tears

Swooning woman sent for trial

'Marriage' charge

'COLONEL BARKER' was the most embarrassed woman in London, when she had to make a public appearance at Marylebone Police Court yesterday. She was in mental anguish every moment she was on view in the stuffy, over-crowded court.

This extraordinary woman, who for five years had successfully posed as a man who had held the rank of colonel and won the D.S.O. in the war, crumpled up and burst into a flood of tears before she was committed to stand her trial at the Old Bailey.

Public curiosity unnerved 'Colonel Barker' from the moment she set foot inside the court. She shrunk back and hid her face in a grey fox fur that was draped round her neck, and when she took her seat she bent her head so low that little could be seen but the crown of her mannish black felt hat, the brim of which she had pulled down over her eyes.

She was a strangely incongruous figure in the rough tweed coat and skirt that hung shapelessly on her massive frame. She is the size of a Falstaff. The policemen who led her into court looked almost puny by comparison.

Obvious agitation

Her agitation was obvious enough while she was listening to the evidence in support of the charge that she had committed perjury in swearing a false statement in connection with a High Court action. She never once raised her head. Her breath came in gasps, and her great shoulders heaved under the stress of suppressed emotion.

It was the addition of a second charge of perjury for causing a false statement to be made in the register of marriages, and the appearance in the witness-box of the young woman who had been her 'wife', that made 'Colonel Barker' abandon any semblance of composure.

Mrs. Lillias Irma Valerie Arkell-Smith, to give 'Colonel Barker' her true name, was a picture of dejection when Miss Alfreda Haward, the 'wife' of the Brighton wedding ceremony, took the oath. Miss Haward looked straight at the shrinking figure wedged sideways in the narrow space in front of the dock.

'Do you recognise her?' Miss Haward was asked.

'I cannot see her,' replied Miss Haward.

A low moan came from 'Colonel Barker,' and her head sank lower and lower until she was doubled up in her chair.

She was almost in a swoon when the magistrate committed her for trial, and two policemen had to help her to her feet and half carry her out of court.

18 ' "Col. Barker" in Dock at the Old Bailey', *Daily Herald*, 25 April 1929, p. 5

'Col. Barker' in dock at the Old Bailey

New revelations in remarkable life of adventures

Sentence to-day

The woman who for several years posed as a man passing as 'Colonel Barker' – Lilias Irma Valerie Arkell-Smith, aged 34 – appeared in the dock at the Old Bailey yesterday.

She pleaded 'Not guilty' to committing perjury in an affidavit, but pleaded 'Guilty' to a charge of having caused a false statement to be entered in a marriage registry.

The second plea was accepted by the prosecution, and the Recorder (Sir Ernest Wild, K.C.) postponed sentence on this charge until to-day, the accused meantime remaining in custody.

The details of the first charge alleged that Mrs. Arkell-Smith committed perjury in an affidavit sworn by her on June 29, 1928, in which she stated that she was truly named Leslie Ivor Gauntlett Bligh Barker, that she was a retired Colonel in His Majesty's Army and had been an officer in a cavalry regiment during the late war and had acted as messing officer to various officers' messes during the war.

The second charge alleged that she caused a false statement to be entered in a register of marriage on November 14, 1923, in the name of Victor Barker, bachelor, when she went through the form of marriage with Alfreda Emma Hayward at the parish church, Brighton.

The accused, a tall, upstanding figure, with complexion deeply bronzed, wore a raincoat over a light grey costume, golfing stockings, and a soft black felt hat, pulled down over her closely cropped hair. In the button-hole of her coat was a bright red rose.

Mr. Percival Clarke (for the prosecution) explained that in 1922 Mrs. Arkell-Smith was passing as Mrs. Pearch Crouch. She was the wife of an Australian soldier, and was married in 1918 at Milford Parish Church, Surrey, to Lieutenant Harold Arkell-Smith, of the Australian force.

They lived together for about six months, and at the termination of the war defendant joined a woman friend in running a teashop at Warminster, Wiltshire.

Australian soldier

While there she met an Australian soldier, called Pearce Crouch, and they lived together as man and wife, she being known as Mrs. Pearce Crouch. By him she has two children, a boy aged nine, and a girl aged seven.

In 1922, passing as Mrs. Pearce Crouch, she became a customer at a chemist's shop kept by a Mr. Haward at Littlehampton. Though she was Mrs. Pearce Crouch in name, she dressed as what was then known as a 'land girl,' in riding breeches and open-neck shirt and coat. She explained to Mr. Haward, who had a daughter, that she was really Sir Victor Barker, Bart.

Masquerading as Sir Victor Barker, she proposed marriage to Mr. Haward's daughter and went through a form of marriage with her at Brighton, describing herself in the certificate as Sir Victor Barker, and a bachelor.

During the masquerade as a man, Barker passed as a captain in the Army, as a colonel in the Army, as a member of the Distinguished Service Order, and by the use of that name, rank and title, obtained credit from various persons, among others for clothing, and in May, 1926, was sued by a firm to whom she owed about £40 for clothing.

The action was brought in the High Court against Sir Victor Barker, Baronet, and in June, 1926, in opposition to an application in Court, an affidavit was sworn by Victor Barker, Baronet. The action however was not pursued.

About two years ago 'Lady Barker,' who was really Miss Haward, returned to her father at Littlehampton, and as far as counsel knew had lived with him ever since.

Lived as man and wife

The Recorder: Do I understand these two women were living together as man and wife from 1923 for about four years?

Mr. Clarke: Yes.

At the beginning of 1927, continued counsel, Captain Victor Barker, D.S.O., became associated with the National Fascisti Movement, and was summoned for an offence against the Firearms Act.

He had a pistol and produced a firearms certificate which was supposed to authorise the carrying and possession of that pistol, but on examination the certificate was found to be a forgery.

Barker, therefore, was prosecuted for, among other things, uttering a forged document, being a public document, with intent to deceive. The judge held that it was not a public document, and she was acquitted.

'On that occasion this masquerade as a man was used and the prisoner came into court with eyes bandaged, led into the dock by a friend. It was explained to the court that 'Barker' had previously suffered temporary blindness owing to war wounds, and the strain on his nerves had brought on the trouble again.'

The Recorder: This woman stood her trial in this court as a man?

Mr. Clarke: Yes; not a soul in court – and I think I prosecuted her on that occasion – was aware that it was other than a man in the dock.

On October 13 last year, a receiving order in bankruptcy was made against Victor Barker, who made no appearance.

A warrant which was issued was executed on February 28 at the Regent Palace Hotel, where the court tipstaff found Barker dressed as a man, acting as a reception clerk. She was taken to Brixton Jail, where it was found that Barker was a woman.

The Recorder: Were there any banns of this marriage?

Mr. Clarke: No, it was by licence. You will realise how important it is that marriage registers should not be falsified.

The Recorder intimated that the maximum penalty for that was one of seven years' imprisonment.

'Wife's' evidence

Alfreda Emma Haward, aged 33, a slight woman, who appeared somewhat nervous, said she lived with the defendant for three years after going through the form of marriage with her at Brighton. When she first knew the defendant she was living as Mrs. Pearce Crouch. She understood that Crouch treated her very badly, knocking her about.

Sir H. Curtis-Bennett, K.C. (for the defence): Did you stay at Brighton with the defendant in October, 1923, up to the date of your marriage? – Yes.

Living there as apparently husband and wife? – Yes.

Did you sleep in the same room and bed? – Yes.

The Recorder: You first met this person apparently as a woman, and he told you he was a man? – Yes.

Courted as a man

Did you believe that? – Yes.

In reply to further questions, Miss Haward said that Barker courted her as a man and she believed he was a man.

When did you discover she was a woman? – I never discovered it until I saw it in the papers.

How did he keep up the deception with you? – I do not know.

In his speech for the defence Sir H. Curtis-Bennett said that Miss Haward knew the defendant was living with Pearce Crouch and knew her as a woman. She knew her as the mother, according to his instructions, of two children.

The Recorder: Assuming Miss Haward knew all along that defendant was a woman, do you say it makes any difference to the offence? If two women, knowing themselves to be two women, conspire together to falsify the marriage register, is the gravity of the offence affected?

Sir Henry: I think so.

The Recorder: Your contention is that Miss Haward knew all along that she was living with a woman?

Sir Henry said that Miss Haward would know there could be no normal relations because she believed the defendant had been wounded in the war.

The Recorder: But I understand your argument to be based on common sense that she must have known defendant was a woman.

Sir Henry: Yes.

'More sinned against'

'I do submit,' said Sir Henry, 'that for many years this woman was more sinned against than sinning. She took the very stupid course of believing she could obtain more money and get employment easier to support her children as a man than as a woman.

'An abnormal interest has been taken in this case, as is shown here to-day, when she is going through the greatest ordeal of her life.'

The Recorder: You might almost use the word prurient.

Sir Henry: Has this woman not been punished enough? Is the publicity and the finish of her career and the difficulties of the future not enough punishment for her? I ask your lordship earnestly to say it is a case where you can stay your hand.

The Recorder: If I pass no sentence, would it not be an example to others to do the same sort of thing? I desire to take a little time before I pass sentence, and I shall, therefore, postpone sentence until tomorrow.

19 'Servant Dresses as a Man', *Daily Herald*, 25 April 1929, p. 1

Servant dresses as a man

Masquerade that ended in charge of theft

A pretty 16-year-old servant, Elsie Carter, who has been masquerading in the Boston and Skegness district dressed as a man, appeared at North Holland Police Court, Boston, yesterday, charged with stealing a man's suit and bicycle.

Three nights ago she was stopped near Boston Dock, when dressed as a man, and a policeman took her to the workhouse, but she escaped.

Next night her employer's father missed his coat, and it appeared that she had dressed in his clothes and ridden on his bicycle to Skegness; but her return was delayed.

It was stated that two years ago the girl was in a serious accident and received a head injury.

The magistrate remanded her to Nottingham Jail with a view to Borstal treatment, and directed that her mental condition should be inquired into.

20 'Woman Who Lived as a Man', *Daily Herald*, 10 May 1929, p. 1

Woman who lived as a man

Another surprising case of deception

'Wife's' story

Discovery made when illness came

Another case of a woman posing as a man and deceiving, amongst others, a woman as to her sex was reported yesterday from the Midlands.

The discovery was made when a person, giving the name of William Sidney Holton, aged 42, timber carter, of Merstow green, Evesham, was admitted to Evesham Poor Law Infirmary, where she now lies dangerously ill.

Holton refused to give particulars of her career when questioned, but it is stated that for four and a half years she has lived with another woman, and posed as this woman's husband.

This statement is corroborated by the supposed wife, a single woman, aged 31, of Birmingham, who told a reporter yesterday that she met Holton when 'he' was working at her brother's coal wharf in Birmingham. 'He' was then living with a woman.

Great strength

'Holton never aroused my suspicions in any way,' said the woman. 'I always believed Holton to be a man, and I cannot believe otherwise. 'His' voice was that of a normal man, and 'he' always had great strength, and 'he' smoked from two to three ounces of tobacco weekly in a clay pipe.'

In March, 1927, 'he' was a witness at the inquest on a foreman haulier who was killed, and since then 'his' nerves had given way and 'he' had been under treatment, but 'his' sex was never suspected until just before 'he' was removed to the infirmary.

Dr. Duncan, whose suspicions had been aroused on the previous Saturday, communicated with the medical officer of the institution, and Holton was transferred from the male to the female wing of the building. Holton is now critically ill with enteric fever and is not expected to recover.

Holton is 5ft. 3in. in height, and slightly built, and has noticeably small hands. She had the appearance of a man, and seemed entirely normal, said a man who worked with her.

'He' had great strength and handled horses very well.

21 'Woman's 20 Years' Pose as a Husband', *Daily Herald*, 29 August 1932

Woman's 20 years' pose as a husband

Masquerade for a girl's sake

Navvy who was noted for her strength

A woman's 20-years' masquerade as a married man, so that she might earn enough to support a girl friend and her child has been ended by her death.

Before she died, at the age of 46, at her mother's house at Aston Magna, near Blockley, Gloucestershire, her real identity as Mrs. Sarah Holtom had become known.

It was at Aston Magna that she married, at the age of 19, a villager named William Holtom.

The couple migrated to Essex, but two years later the woman left her husband and returned to the Midlands.

Unable to find work as a woman, she donned men's clothing and assumed the name of 'William Sidney Holtom.' Thereafter, for 20 years, she passed as a man.

She worked as a timber-haulier or navvy, and was noted for her strength. Part of her leisure she spent in the local inn with a mug of ale, smoking a short clay pipe.

While working on a coal wharf at Ledbury, Holtom befriended a girl with a child, and they settled as a married couple at Evesham.

There another child was born to the girl, and Holtom was described on the birth certificate as the father. No other person, not even the doctor who attended the supposed husband for 15 months, suspected 'his' real sex.

The secret was revealed in hospital, however, three years ago, and the 'wife' was bound over at the Assizes for having made a false declaration on the birth certificate that Holtom was the father of the child.

At the trial it was stated Holtom wore feminine garments for the first time in the 20 years.

22 'Girl Witness in Male Attire', *The Times of India*, 22 July 1932, p. 9

Girl witness in male attire

Nasik sensation

Brought up as a boy and knows wrestling

(from our own correspondent) Nasik, July 19

Seldom has a woman been found with such masculine traits as the one who appeared in the court of Mr. K. B. Wassoodev, Sessions Judge, Nasik, today as a prosecution witness in a sensational murder trial, in which five persons are involved. The accused are Khandu Narayan, Gumpya, Ramkrisha, Narayan and Nana, of whom the first is charged under Section 302, I.P.C., for killing his son, Dada, (about 25), by shooting him dead with his double-barrel 12-bore gun of Belgium make, while the rest are alleged to have assisted him in the crime.

Quite a surprise was sprung on the crowded court when a good-looking Hindu 'youth', responding to the call of the crier for the prosecution witness – a girl named Mumti, – stepped into the witness box. However, all speculations were shortly put to rest when the witness declared 'himself' to be Mumti – a girl with hair closely cropped and wearing a 'dhoti,' turban, and shirt, all complete.

Giving evidence she said that ever since her childhood she had been brought up in male dress and manners and was attending the 'talin' (gymnasium) and also knew how to wrestle. She said that she was neither married nor desirous of entering the matrimonial market in future. She mainly corroborated the evidence given by her mother the previous day.

... The girl Mumti, is known in her place by the name of Mahomed and she herself wishes to be known as such.

23 'Married Girl Poses as Boy', *The Daily Telegraph*, 30 July 1932, p. 12

Married girl poses as boy

Joined a men's club

How admiral was deceived

A 17-year-old married girl who masqueraded as a boy and deceived an admiral, Church Army officials, a doctor, hotel proprietor, and others, was bound over at Feltham police-court yesterday and ordered to go to a home.

In the name of Jack McDonald she was charged with theft from a Teddington hotel, where she was employed as a kitchen 'boy.'

At the last hearing McDonald, whose correct name was stated to be Madeline Dixon, of Grangemouth, Stirlingshire, appeared in male attire, but she now wore woman's clothes. She pleaded guilty.

Detective-sergeant H. Gimblett said that he saw the girl walking over Richmond Bridge dressed as a man. Nobody had suspected her identity at the hotel, and she also belonged to a men's club at Twickenham. She was 'keeping company' with a local girl.

She was married last year, but left her husband after two days. Her mother and father emigrated to America when she was a child, and she had been brought up by foster parents. In June she decided to cycle to London from Scotland, and on reaching Berkhampsted she met Rear-Admiral Smith-Dorrien, who took compassion on her. He arranged lodgings for her, and recommended her to the Church Army, who found her a job at the hotel.

Played billiards

'A delightful boy'

'I was completely deceived,' Admiral Smith-Dorrien said in an interview. 'I met this smart-looking boy on a country road near Berkhampsted. He told me he had cycled from Scotland, that he had lost his father and mother, and that he had come to try and find a job. He struck me as a straightforward kind of boy.

'The "boy" had a charming manner and was very polite. He didn't moan, and I thought I would try and help him.

'I paid his bill at a local inn, where he stayed for about a week, and put him in touch with the Church Army people, who found him a job at Teddington within a day.'

Church Army officials were equally surprised to find McDonald was a girl. 'Two of us interviewed McDonald twice,' an official said, 'and neither of us had the faintest suspicion that McDonald was a girl. Admiral Smith-Dorrien christened her "Jack Tar", and that was what we called her. We regarded "her" as a really delightful boy.'

The kitchen 'boy' smoked cigarettes, took a keen interest in football and played billiards. She told the police she masqueraded as a boy to get and retain a job.

24 Lady V. de Frece, *Recollections of Vesta Tilley*, 1934, London: Hutchinson, pp. 233–5

Vesta Tilley (1864–1952) was one of the most celebrated and successful music hall stars of her day, retiring in 1920. Most famous for her male impersonation, she was the epitome of respectability off stage.

It may be because I generally appeared on the stage as a young man that the big percentage of my admirers were women. Girls of all ages would wait in crowds to see me enter or leave the theatre, and each post brought piles of letters, varying from an impassioned declaration of undying love to a request for an autograph, or a photograph, or a simple flower, or a piece of ribbon I had worn. To illustrate the impression I made upon at least one of my girl admirers, I have in my possession now a complete diary of a young girl, covering a period of some ten years, in which she records the first time she saw me, her journeys to see me in the various towns at which I appeared, her opinions of the many new songs I had introduced during the time, all punctuated with expressions of lasting love and devotion. *A Diary of my most loved Artiste Miss Vesta Tilley* is the title. This diary was sent to me by the writer in 1920. It is now 1933, and even to-day I receive frequent letters from my now grown-up admirer, and I see her often when I go to England. Clearly it is not a case of girlish infatuation, and I hope I have not offended her by mentioning the diary in my book. In any case none but herself and myself know her identity.

During one of my tours I received masses of most beautiful flowers from a girl who apparently followed me from town to town during the whole trip. Every night, when I appeared on the stage, I invariably saw the same girl in a box, gazing down at me, until at last it began to get slightly on my nerves. As she had made repeated requests to be received in my dressing-room, I at last said she might come and visit me. I took off my wig, undid all my little plaits and left my hair in a fuzzy bush without even bothering to put a comb through it, partially removed my make-up, and smothered my face with cream. As anyone who has ever worked behind the scenes knows full well, an artiste is not at her best when removing grease-paint! I then threw round me the wrapper which I kept for making up only, and said she could come in. She entered, stood still and gazed at me. I let her have a good look and then said: 'There, now you see what you have been following round for so long. Perhaps that will cure you!' But she only said: 'Oh no! I know you have only made yourself look like that on purpose, and I love the real you more than ever!' Now, what can you do with people like that?

25 T. Parker, *Five Women*, 1965, London: Hutchinson, pp. 87–8, 95–6

This book is a collection of journalistic studies of five women who had been involved in crime. The first paragraph here consists of Parker's description of Joe; the rest of the extract is in her own voice.

Fifteen minutes, forty minutes, once even an hour late the figure would appear, coming slowly along the street: duffle-bag over shoulder, head down, feet splayed out. A round fleshy face, big nose, thin lips, grey eyes always avoiding the direct glance, short cropped hair chopped in a ragged black fringe on the forehead. Short nail-bitten nicotined fingers cupping a cigarette, long arms dangling out of the sleeves of a rough navy-serge leather-on-the-shoulders workman's jacket; bulky body top-heavy over thick legs in tight concertina-wrinkled jeans; heavy black crepe-soled lace-up shoes. ... At a glance, a rather aggressive-looking young labourer in his early twenties, perhaps.

* * *

I do get to thinking sometimes I ought to make a bit more effort about the way I look, really. You know, not go quite so far with it as I do. I start thinking I ought to, well, at least wear women's slacks instead of men's trousers like these with zip flies, and women's casual shoes instead of real heavy men's. I mean it's to my own advantage, isn't it? Otherwise women who might like the idea of going with another woman, they can't even tell that you *are* a woman, so they're not interested because they think you're a man.

Mind you, I only think about it: I never get round to doing anything. For one reason, I've never got the money to buy a new set of clothes, and I don't suppose I ever shall. If I had that much money, it wouldn't go on clothes, that's one thing certain. So you see it's hopeless, I can never make the effort to tone it down, not one little bit. There's a lot of the girls don't like it you know; they don't mind you wearing drag in private, but they don't think you ought to be as butch as I am, not in public anyway.

People look at you in the street, you can tell what they're thinking, Is that a man or a woman? To me there's no such thing as a division like that: I'm just a person, I've never known what it's like to be any different, to me it's just ordinary, it's me, it's not anything extraordinary. ...

I took my case down to the left luggage at Victoria, and went up the West End, Wardour Street and Berwick Street, wandering round there, looking at the clubs I'd heard about.

There was one coffee bar I went in, I was just sitting there drinking, and I noticed girls kept coming in and going downstairs one after another, so I thought I'd see what was going on. I went to the top of the stairs and the man at a counter behind the espresso machine called out at me 'It's ladies only down there, mate.' I just gave him a cold look and said 'Well what do you think I am, then?' He sort of looks at me hard for a minute, and then he says 'Oh': so down I went.

That's a thing I get quite a lot of, you know, in toilets and that sort of place. At first the attendant very often tries to stop me going in until I tell them. Or a landlady'll say, if I go about a room, 'I'm sorry, it's for females only.' Mind you, some can tell straight off without having to be told: the more intelligent ones.

Anyway I went downstairs at this coffee bar, and underneath is a big room with a jukebox and subdued lighting and little tables and chairs. And it's all women, dancing with each other, necking with each other, and nobody bothering about it, it was fabulous. I stayed there all night, it seemed the most marvellous place in the world. The girls were all taking pills and smoking reefers, and some of them were 'popping', it was terrific. After a bit one of them came up to me and she said 'What's your name, then?' I said 'Joe Bishop,' and she said 'Hello Joe, nice to meet you.'

Why 'Joe'?

I don't know, I just fancied it. My name's really 'Jean', so at least it begins with the same letter, doesn't it? But 'Hello Joe' – that sounds really nice, I think. When she said it like that the first time, it was just as though I was being christened or baptised, it felt absolutely right. I've never used any other name since, I even make them put it on my record in prison. 'That's my name' I say, and they can't do anything about it.

2

ROMANTIC FRIENDS
AND LESBIAN COUPLES

INTRODUCTION

Historically paralleling cross-dressing, the other archetype of lesbianism has been the romantic friendship – a close, loving relationship between two women. This has nearly always been associated with middle-class and upper-class women, reflecting both the material possibilities and the types of records that survive to document it. The sources presented here are of a type that historians must regard critically. They are often some form of special pleading such as an enthusiastic book review in a feminist publication or the vivid stereotyping of popular journalism. They include the fiction of poetry and novel, albeit often the fictionalised reality of the author's experiences, and the personal reflections of autobiography, private papers, correspondence and diaries. The guarded commentaries of protective biographers require particularly careful reading.

These were all forms of communication only available to educated, literate women. The different genres reveal various facets of passionate friendship. Private letters could be used to convey the strength of loving feelings, to discuss plans and fantasies. Poetry was a more public form, and could also allow the writer to distance herself from the subject – love poetry could be written using unspecified genders, for example. This type of evidence privileges middle-class women, especially women who had a public profile, as their writing is more likely to have been preserved. There are few sources for working-class romantic friends or lesbian lovers. Despite these limitations, the extracts together comprise a rich collage illustrating women's love for each other and the responses of others to that love.

Romantic friendship was a form of love between women established in the eighteenth and nineteenth centuries. The extracts in this chapter document the changes in this model into the twentieth century, as lesbian identity is constructed.

Throughout most of the nineteenth century, dominant beliefs that respectable middle-class women were without sexual passion meant that romantic friendship was largely acceptable within the framework of female virtue; after all, it had nothing to do with men. But domestic ideology, which attached women to the home and family, and assumed their economic dependence on and passive obedience to male relatives, gave most women few opportunities for free choice in relation to life partners, or the creation of households (Davidoff and Hall 1987). Women had little official place or power in the public world of politics and employment, and only a small number of women could be truly independent via inheritance or professional work until the later part of the nineteenth century (Rendall 1990). Expressions of deeply felt love between women, therefore, often had to exist alongside marriage, and without the possibility of a joint domestic life. The growth in the proportion of single women from the mid nineteenth century, continuing into the mid twentieth century, led to debates over the role of 'surplus' women, while the growth of the women's movement in the late nineteenth century led to new ideas about and opportunities for love between women.

As with cross-dressing women, the sources offer a variety of perspectives into how women in romantic friendships or lesbian relationships saw themselves, and how they were seen by others. The power and intensity of love between women comes through very strongly in these sources, whether written about or to the beloved. There are varying emotional styles of love between women, which sometimes include expressions of sensual and physical affection. The extracts also demonstrate how other women are fascinated by expressions of love between women. Another issue is that of the domestic lives of women lovers; in particular whether they can compete with other family demands on each other's time, and whether they are financially and socially able to fulfil any dream of living together. Support for each other's professional work, perhaps as writers and artists, can be an important characteristic of relationships between women. Sometimes marriage destroys an intense friendship, causing unhappiness to one or both women. Conversely some women, Vita Sackville-West and Katherine Mansfield for example, maintained lesbian relationships despite marriage.

The direct and unselfconscious representation of intense feeling between women in some of these sources might lead us to hypothesise that openness about their love was easier for nineteenth-century than twentieth-century women, when awareness of lesbianism as a stigmatised sexual identity increased. But not all twentieth-century women were guarded in writing about their love for other women, even when they hid their sexuality publicly.

The sources also reveal how some contemporaries saw women in couples. Being women-centred in a heterosexual world could give women respectability rather than otherwise, certainly in the nineteenth century, but the acceptability of romantic friendship was not unbounded – it depended on the behaviour and circumstances of the women. Contemporaries could sometimes read 'sapphism' into female friendship in the nineteenth century, while female couples could still be seen as perfectly innocent well into the more sexually knowing mid twentieth century. Class and professional status, family acceptance (or conversely membership of an artistic bohemian world) could protect women from criticism.

Romantic friendship has been a major focus of lesbian historiography since the 1970s. Historians have documented the powerful evidence of love between women, while grappling with the relevance of sexual expression to the definition of lesbianism. In early work on lesbian and gay history, Weeks, for example, was unwilling to use the word lesbian to describe relationships between women before the twentieth century. The difficulties facing him are encapsulated in his response to Charlotte Brontë's declaration of love to her friend Ellen Nussey. In 1836 Charlotte had written to Ellen Nussey, 'If we had a cottage and a competency of our own I do think we might love until Death without being dependent on any third person for happiness.' Weeks writes of this powerful assertion of love and commitment: 'It is almost meaningless to attempt to analyse this along the modern polarity of lesbian/heterosexual, because for very few women up till the present century was such a polarity even conceivable' (Weeks 1977: 95).

Lesbian-feminist historical work from the late 1970s gradually began to theorise new ways of conceptualising relationships between women. The first work to examine romantic friendships in detail was Smith-Rosenburg's essay 'The Female World of Love and Ritual' (1975). Her conception of female closeness was valorised within the women's movement when in 1980 Rich published an article that was later to become a foundation text for lesbian studies. In 'Compulsory Heterosexuality and Lesbian Existence' she presented a vision of a rich world of female bonding. 'Lesbian existence', she explained, 'suggests both the fact of the historical presence of lesbians and our continuing creation of the meaning of that existence' (Rich 1980: 239). Significantly for historians, Rich also posited the idea of a lesbian continuum, broadening the view of lesbianism to separate it from what she saw as the clinical patriarchal definitions of sexual contact that had constrained earlier historians, and seeking to re-eroticise female friendship, comradeship and shared joy between women.

> But as we deepen and broaden the range of what we define as lesbian existence, we begin to discover the erotic in female terms: as that which is unconfined to any single part of the body or solely to the body itself.
>
> (1980: 240)

By accepting the widening of the definition of lesbian and lesbian eroticism to include all women-identified women, lesbian-feminist historians began to extend their exploration of same-sex loyalties. Faderman's *Surpassing the Love of Men* (1981) presented an archetype of the pre-twentieth century lesbian, grounded in the intense female friendships nurtured in a middle and upper-class milieu and moulded during the eighteenth and nineteenth centuries by romanticism and changes in schooling, religion and social roles for women.

Historians mapped networks of women that had been forged by shared political, educational and vocational concerns. For example Vicinus (1985) examined the many nineteenth-century and early-twentieth-century women's communities that allowed women to escape the restrictions of middle-class family life. Stanley and Morley's (1988) work on the life of the suffragette Emily Wilding Davison showed the love and communality between women in suffragette networks. Auchmuty (1989) charted the network of professional women living, working and supporting each other emotionally in one London locality, Lambeth.

Different elements of women's intense relationships have been examined by other historians. Rizzo researched women living as paid and unpaid companions among the eighteenth-century gentry and aristocracy. She argued that the emotional depth and importance of these economic relationships was often more significant than that of contemporary heterosexual marriage (Rizzo 1994).

While Faderman's work had espoused and encouraged a diffuse focus on love between women it simultaneously, if unintentionally, championed the lesbian couple as the ideal type of lesbian existence. Faderman's definition of lesbianism as 'an all consuming emotional relationship in which two women are devoted to each other above anyone else' (1981: 19) might admit Brontë and Nussey, but such a definition inevitably moves the historical study of lesbianism to the study of pairs of women. This is fruitful; exploration of the female lifelong friends, inseparable companions and life partners of the past has provided the biographers of these women with the opportunity (not always grasped) to explore the domestic lives of women without men. Eleanor Butler and Sarah Ponsonby's 53-year relationship, in which they never spent a night apart, stands at some sort of pinnacle of women's partnerships. As their biographer Mavor puts it, it was 'what we in modern terms would consider a marriage' (1973: xvii). Without a more sophisticated language to understand women's lives together it is perhaps inevitable that these relationships have been crudely conceptualised either as that most fundamental of heterosexual institutions, the marriage, or as mere friendship (Johnson 1989).

But the acknowledgement of the woman couple as a model for lesbian history has also provoked criticism. Taking issue with Faderman's conception of lesbianism, Donoghue has argued:

> This reduces the rich variety of lesbian culture to its most privileged form, the exclusive bond. So many of us have been left out of such history; celibate women, lesbian friends, women who have more than one lover at a time, and all of us who experience lesbian culture not just as a nation of couples but as many communities.
>
> (1993: 223)

Faderman's work has been challenged from another direction. The absence of historical sources (other than pornography) explicitly discussing erotic activity between women had, along with contemporary lesbian-feminism, led Faderman to see pre-twentieth-century lesbianism as largely desexualised. Elevating the emotional lives of women could potentially denigrate or deny the importance of their physical desires and relationships. Whitbread's publication of selections from the diaries of Anne Lister, *I Know My Own Heart* (1988), brought physical sexuality between women firmly into focus. Anne Lister was an upper-middle-class Yorkshirewoman whose explicit descriptions in her diaries of her sexual activities with other women in the early nineteenth century were so unprecedented as source material that they were rumoured to be forgeries. The diaries confound the previous historiography and have encouraged historians to emphasise sexual passion in women's same-sex relationships in the eighteenth and nineteenth centuries (Moore 1992, Donoghue 1993).

Vicinus (1985) has termed relationships where women felt passionately for each other homoerotic and this historiographical characterisation can be seen as some sort of middle path between the romantic friend of the eighteenth century and the lesbian partner of the twentieth. It is however illusory to assert a move from non-sexualised nineteenth-century intimacy to twentieth-century sexual activity. Such a crude periodisation falls apart in the face of a source such as Anne Lister's diaries. Some relationships warrant consideration by historians of lesbianism on the grounds that the women lived their private lives in partnership for many years, sharing homes until separated by the death of one woman. We can speculate that the women's relationships with each other ranged from intimate friendship to homoerotic attraction to explicitly sexual partnerships. But it is impossible to say which women who shared beds also shared physical passions.

From early in the twentieth century, when 'lesbian' had begun to be regarded as a pathological sexual condition, the expression of loving feelings between women, whether physically or in writing, was increasingly liable to pejorative interpretation. A number of social changes altered women's lives and the context for female friendship, lesbian sexuality and love between women. Gender boundaries delimiting women's and men's social worlds became increasingly flexible. Opportunities for middle-class women's education, employment and economic independence increased considerably (Bruley 1999, Rowbotham 1999). Bodies of professionals, including doctors, psychologists, clergy, educationalists and welfare workers, involved themselves in categorising and commenting on human relationships. Jeffreys and Jackson have argued that the writings of late-nineteenth-century sexologists were a particularly powerful influence here (Jeffreys 1985, Jackson 1994).

Lesbian research on the twentieth century has been much more bold in tracing and assuming lesbian sexual identities and activities. But despite the inevitable paucity of historical evidence on whether or not 'they did it', the recent historiography has been in danger of asserting the sexual at the expense of an investigation into the rich complexity of women's relationships with other women (Collis 1994, Hamer 1996).

1 Letters and journal entries concerning the flight of Butler and Ponsonby, 1778 in G.H. Bell (ed.), *The Hamwood Papers of the Ladies of Llangollen and Caroline Hamilton*, 1930, London: Macmillan and Co. Limited, pp. 27, 32–3, 38–9

In the spring of 1778 two aristocratic spinsters, 39-year-old Eleanor Butler and 23-year-old Sarah Ponsonby, left their homes in Ireland with the intention of fleeing the country and living together in North Wales. The extracts below are from letters and journal entries in the papers of Sarah Ponsonby and her descendants and concern this first, unsuccessful attempt at elopement. Finally, their determination to be together prevailed and with their families' consents they settled in Llangollen Vale where they lived together in Plas Newydd for over fifty years.

Woodstock, 2nd April 1778

My dear Mrs. Goddard

The Runaways are caught and we shall soon see our amiable friend again whose conduct, though it has an appearance of imprudence, is I am sure void of serious impropriety. There were no gentlemen concerned, nor does it appear to be anything more than a scheme of Romantic Friendship. My Mother is gone to Waterford for Miss Butler and her, and we expect to see them to-night. I am happy at having this opportunity of giving my dear Mrs. Goddard pleasure and of assuring her I am her

affectionate Friend and servant

S. TIGHE

9th

My dear G.

Sally is much better, but weak, low and dejected. She made me watch the windows all day yesterday, she was so sure you will lose no time. She was most anxious to see your letter to me. I did not read it all, as anything against Miss P. is death to her. Be very cautious till we meet. Storys to be sure there must be in plenty. I cant help giving credit to Sarah Ponsonby's which is that they were to live together. A convent, I used to think, – but she now sais that is what she flew from and that we are all much mistaken, and that if we knew Miss P. we would love her as well as she did. All together it is a most extraordinary affair. I sometimes can hardly think the cause is known by anyone but themselves. God knows how it is, or how it will end. I know she is very ill. I am sure nothing could be of so much use to her as seeing you and having you talk to her.

Ever yours
E. FOWNES

Thursday, 30th April

The ladies did not comedown to dinner for fear Mr. Park should be questioned about Miss P.

Saturday, 2nd May

I talked again to Miss Pons. not to dissuade her from her purpose but to discharge my conscience of the duty I owed her as a friend by letting her know my opinion of Miss Butler and the certainty I had they never would agree living together. I spoke of her with harshness and freedom, said she had a debauch'd mind, no ingredients for friendship that ought to be founded on Virtue, whereas hers every day more and more show'd me was acting in direct opposition to it, as well as to the interest, happiness and reputation of the one she professed to love. Sir W. join'd us, kneel'd, implored, swore twice on the Bible how much he loved her, would never more offend, was sorry for his past folly that was not meant as she understood it, offer'd to double her allowance of £30 a year, or add what more she pleased to it even tho' she did go. She thanked him for his past kindness but nothing cd hurt her more, or wd she ever be under other obligation to him. Said if the whole world was kneeling at her feet it should not make her forsake her purpose, she would live and die with Miss Butler, was her own mistress, and if any force was used to detain her she knew her own temper so well it would provoke her to an act that would give her friends more trouble than anything she had yet done. She, however, haughtily, and as it were to get rid of him, made Sir W. happy by telling him if ever she was in distress for money he should be the first she would apply to. They dined with us and I never saw anything so confident as their behaviour.

2 A. Seward, from 'Llangollen Vale', and 'Sonnet 32. To the Departing Spirit of an Alienated Friend' in S. Coote (ed.), *The Penguin Book of Homosexual Verse*, 1983, Harmondsworth: Penguin

The critic and poet Anna Seward (1747–1809) 'Queen Muse of England' memorialised her love for her foster-sister Honoria Snyd in a series of passionate poems. She first met the Ladies of Llangollen in 1895 and in *Llangollen Vale*, pays tribute to their 'Davidion friendship'.

Anna Seward from Llangollen Vale, inscribed to the Right Honourable Lady Eleanor Butler and Miss Ponsonby, lines 84–101

Now with a vestal lustre glows the Vale,
  Thine, sacred Friendship, permanent as pure;
In vain the stern authorities assail,
  In vain persuasion spreads her silken lure,
High-born, and high-endow'd, the peerless twain,
Pant for coy Nature's charms 'mid silent dale, and plain.

Thro' ELEANORA, and her ZARA's mind,
  Early tho' genius, taste, and fancy flow'd,
Tho' all the graceful arts their powers combin'd,
  and her last polish brilliant life bestow'd,
The lavish promiser, in youth's soft morn,
Pride, pomp, and love, her friends, the sweet enthusiasts scorn.

Then rose the fairy place of the Vale,
  Then bloom'd around it the Arcadian bowers;
Screen'd from the storms of Winter, cold and pale,
  Screen'd from the fervours of the sultry hours,
Circling the lawny crescent, soon they rose,
To letter'd ease devote, and Friendship's blest repose.

Anna Seward, Sonnet 32. To the Departing Spirit of an Alienated Friend

Behold him now his genuine colours wear,
  That specious false-one, by whose cruel wiles
  I lost thy amity; saw thy dear smiles
  Eclips'd; those smiles, that used my heart to cheer,
Wak'd by the grateful sense of many a year
  When rose they youth, by Friendship's pleasing toils
  Cultured; – but Dying! – O! For ever fade
  The angry fires. – Each though, that might upbraid
Thy broken faith, which yet my soul deplores,
  Now as eternally is past and gone
  As are the interesting, the happy hours,
Days, years, we shared together. They are flown!
  Yet long must I lament thy hapless doom,
  Thy lavish'd life and early hasten'd tomb.

3 *Thraliana. The Diary of Mrs Hester Lynch Thrale (Later Mrs Piozzi) 1776–1809*, 1942, Oxford: Clarendon Press, Vol. II, 1784–1809, pp. 740, 770, 868, 949

Hester Lynch Thrale née Salusbury (1741–1821) was married, against her will, to Henry Thrale. She was a friend of Samuel Johnson, touring France with him in 1775 and publishing her correspondence with him in 1788. Her diaries provide a lively record of contemporary social mores amongst her peers.

Notes: Anne Damer was a sculptress whose husband committed suicide in 1776, Racoux is Françoise Marie Antoinette Saucertotte, called Raucourt, a French tragedi-ennne.

p. 740 1 April 1789

Nature does get strangely out of Fashion sure enough: One hears of Things now, fit for the Pens of Petronious only, or Juvenal to record and satyrize: The Queen of France is at the Head of a set of Monsters call'd by each other *Sapphists*, who boast her Example; and deserve to be thrown with the *He* Demons that haunt each other likewise, into Mount Versuvius.

p. 770 17 June 1790

There is a strange Propensity now in England for these unspeakable Sins. Mrs *Damor* a Lady much suspected for liking her own Sex in a criminal Way, had Miss Farren the fine comic Actress often about her last Year; and Mrs Siddons's Husband made the following Verses on them.

> Her little Stock of private Fame
> Will fall a Wreck to public Clamour,
> If Farren leagues with one whose Name
> Comes near – Aye very near – to Damn her

p. 868 23 January 1794

Tis my scourge to think better both of the World & of all the Individuals in it than they deserve: that House of Miss Rathbone's is now supposed to have been but a Cage of unclean Birds,[*] living in a sinful Celibat. Mercy on us! Colonel Barry is with Lord Moyra; he had a good Escape of Miss Trefusis if all be true.[†]

Footnotes

[*] Jonson, *The Alchemist*, v,iii, 47
[†] Why was Miss Weston so averse to *any Marriage* I am wondering; – and why did Miss Trefusis call Colonel Barry *Hylas* of all names? And why did

Miss Weston make such an *Ado* about little Sally Siddons's Wit & Beauty & Stuff? The Girl is just like every *other* Girl – but Miss Weston did use to like *every Girl* so. *Mrs. Piozzi.*

p. 949 9 December 1795

The Advent Sermon at St Asaph was very good today – very good *indeed*: Mr Butler Clough of Eriviatte one of the Canons preached it – he is an escellent man they say, and I doubt it not: he said how Christianity had mended the World in general; & how the Vices of the Ancients were *unknown* to Modern Times excepting as they are preserved by Poets & Historians. – poor dear Man!! I read Juvenal's satires when I came home, and found that *Insatiability* was the worst thing he could urge against the Roman Ladies – except their unnatural Passion for Eunuchs; – of those two Brutal & detestable Vices I'll swear Christianity has not cured them – Witness Caecilia Tron & Principessa Belmonte – and hundreds, *hundreds* more: while French and English Women are now publicly said to practise Atrocities of which He – Juvenal was igno-rant, for he says in His Satire against men's horrible Propensity for their own Sex – 'that even Women are more virtuous than they –' because tho' Flavia does hire herself out to Fellows – She goes home to Bed at last, and lies chastly by the Side of Catulla.' Whereas 'tis now grown common to suspect Impossibilities – (such I think 'em) – whenever two ladies live too much together;* the Queen of France was all along accused, so was Raucoux the famous Actress on the Paris Stage; & 'tis a Joke in London now to say such a one visits *Mrs Damer.* Lord Derby certainly insisted on Miss Farren's keeping her at Distance & there was a droll but bitter Epigram made while they used to see one another often.

> Her little Stock of private Fame
> Will fall a Wreck to public Clamour
> If Farren herds with her whose Name
> Approaches very near to *Damn her.*

Footnotes

* Its odd that ye Roman Women did not borrow that horrible Vice from Greece – it has a greek name now & is call'd sapphism, but I never did hear if it in Italy where the Ladies are today exactly what juvenal described them in his time – neither better nor worse than I can find. Mrs Siddons has told me that her sister was in personal Danger once from a female Fiend of the Sort; & I have no reason to disbelieve the Assertion. Bath is a Cage of these unclean birds I have a Notion, and London is a Sink for every Sin. Gibbon blames Justinian for making no difference between the Guilt of active &

passive Paederasty. Justininan was right, were there none of ye 1st the last wd dye away. *Mrs Piozzi.*

4 W. Wordsworth, 'To Lady Eleanor Butler and the Honble Miss Ponsonby. Composed in the grounds of Plas-Newydd, Llangollen', 1827, in G.H. Bell (ed.), *The Hamwood Papers of the Ladies of Llangollen and Caroline Hamilton*,1930, London: Macmillan and Co. Limited, p. 354

William Wordsworth joined the idolatrous voices of many contemporaries in celebrating Eleanor Butler and Sarah Ponsonby's life together in a sonnet published in 1827.

To Lady Eleanor Butler and the Honble Miss Ponsonby

Composed in the grounds of Plas-Newydd, Llangollen

A Stream to mingle with your favorite Dee
Along the Vale of Meditation flows;
So styled by those fierce Britons, pleased to see
In Nature's face the expression of repose,
Or, haply there some pious Hermit chose
To live and die – the peace of Heaven his aim,
To whom the wild sequestered region owes
At this late day, its sancifying name,
Glyn Cyfaillgaroch, in the Cambrian tongue,
In ours the Vale of Friendship, let this spot
Be nam'd where faithful to a low roof'd Cot
On Deva's banks, ye have abode so long,
Sisters in love, a love allowed to climb
Ev'n on this earth, above the reach of time.

5 C. Brontë (1816–1855) letters to Ellen Nussey, 1836 in T.J. Wise and J.A. Symington (eds), *The Brontës: Their Lives, Friendships, and Correspondence in Four Volumes,* 1932, Oxford: Shakespeare Head

Charlotte Brontë and Ellen Nussey met at school in 1831 and were close friends thereafter. Ellen claimed she had received 500 letters from Charlotte of which about 300 survive. They met for the last time in the autumn before Charlotte's death in the spring of 1855.

Sep. 26, 1836

... Ellen I wish I could live with you always, I begin to cling to you more fondly than ever I did. If we had but a cottage and competency of our own I do think we might live and love on till Death without being dependent on any third person for happiness. – Farewell my own dear Ellen.

Feb. 20, 1837

I read your letter with dismay, Ellen – what shall I do without you? Why are we so to be denied each other's society? It is an inscrutable fatality. I long to be with you because it seems as if two or three days or weeks spent in your company would beyond measure strengthen me in the enjoyment of those feeling which I have so lately begun to cherish. You first pointed out to me that way in which I am so feebly endeavouring to travel, and now I cannot keep you by my side, I must proceed sorrowfully alone.

Why are we to be divided? Surely, Ellen, it must be because we are in danger of loving each other too well – of losing sight of the *Creator* in idolatry of the *creature*. At first I could not say, 'Thy will be done'. I felt rebellious; but I know it was wrong to feel so. Being left a moment alone this morning, I prayed fervently to be enabled to resign myself to *every* decree of God's will – though it should be dealt forth with a far severer hand than the present disappointment. Since then, I have felt calmer and humbler – and consequently happier.

6 H. Whitbread (ed.), *I Know My Own Heart. The Diaries of Anne Lister, 1791–1840,* 1988, London: Virago, pp. 177–9

No source on women's love for each other is as explicit in its celebration of physical love as are the coded diaries of Anne Lister. Lister was an upper-class woman who lived at Shibden Hall near Halifax in West Yorkshire and her diaries give a detailed and intimate portrait of her adult life. In these extracts she writes of her relationship with 'M—', Marianne or Mary Lawton née Belcombe whom she had loved since meeting her in 1812. Although Marianne married they continued their relationship. At this point Anne is sexually involved with Tib, Isabella Northcliffe, but tiring of her.

Sunday, 6 January 1822

M— very low tonight. We sat up talking & consoling each other & latterly in playful dalliance & gentle excitement. Our hearts are mutually & entirely attached. We never loved & trusted each other so well & have promised ourselves to be together in six years from this time. Heaven grant it may be so.

Monday, 7 January 1822

The carriage at the door at 9.10. ... Went with M— as far as a couple of miles beyond Ripponden, where they drove us in 40 minutes, then meeting the Highflier coach, left M—, got into it & reached Halifax in an hour ... M— & I had parted tolerably but the sight of my room was melancholy. I sighed & said to myself, 'She is gone & it is as tho' she has never been.' I was getting very low & therefore sat down to write my journal. ... Then obliged to while away my time talking to my aunt & doing nothing. How dull without M—, my wife & all I love. ... Felt very low & dull. Oh, that M— & I were together. Had a fire at night contrary to my usual custom. It cheered the room a little but everything looked & I felt, desolate.

Monday, 21 January 1822

Walked to Halifax. Was there just before the mail arrived &, after waiting some time for a chaise at the Union Cross, brought Isabella with me & we got in at 5½. She is looking well but has got bad cold. ... Came upstairs at 11. Melancholy enough at the thought of going to bed with Tib. I cannot even affect any warmth towards her.

Monday, 28 January 1822

Did nothing in the afternoon & evening, til 9, when I came upstairs. ... Talking of my sleeping with Eliza Belcombe, said I should not like it, & that I was much altered of late in all these matters. Tib laughed, looked incredulous, bade me not say so, & added, 'it would be unnatural in you not to like sleeping with a pretty girl.' I thought of M—, as I do perpetually & that for her I could & would do anything. Tib is affectionate, seems happy here & is quieter than she used to be. She appears to have no suspicion of my living [with] & loving seriously, any other than herself. Poor soul, I know how she will take it when the truth comes out.

7 D.M. Craik, *A Woman's Thoughts About Women*, 1858, Hurst and Blackett, p. 174

Craik's book is one of the large number of volumes promulgating advice to the women of Britain's growing middle class.

For two women, past earliest girlhood, to be completely absorbed in one another and make public demonstration of the fact, by caresses or quarrels, is so repugnant to common sense, that where it ceases to be silly it becomes actually wrong. But, to see two women, whom Providence has denied nearer ties, by a wide substitution making the best of fate, loving, sustaining, and comforting one another, with a tenderness often closer than that of sisters, because it has all the novelty of election which belongs to the conjugal tie itself – this, I say, is an honourable and lovely sight.

8 T. Hardy, *Desperate Remedies*, 1986 [1871], London: Macmillan

Desperate Remedies was Hardy's first published novel. This scene has had an interesting literary history. The novel was read and at first rejected by Macmillan in part because of the 'highly extravagant' bed scene. The novel was published, but later editions saw the subtle bowdlerisation of this scene. The extract is from Chapter 6, 'The Events of Twelve Hours'. Cytherea Graye, the heroine, is the new lady's maid of Cytheria Aldclyffe. On the first night at her new employer's home she is unable to sleep.

A minute later, and she fancied she could distinguish a soft rustle in the passage outside her room. To bury her head in the sheets was her first impulse; then to uncover it, raise herself on her elbow, and stretch her eyes wide open in the darkness; her lips being parted with the intentness of her listening. Whatever the noise was, it had ceased for the time.

It began again and came close to her door, lightly touching the panels. Then there was another stillness; Cytherea made a movement which caused a faint rustling of the bed-clothes.

Before she had time to think another thought a light tap was given. Cytherea breathed: the person outside was evidently bent upon finding her awake, and the rustle she had made had encouraged the hope. The maiden's physical condition shifted from one pole to its opposite. The cold sweat of terror forsook her, and modesty took the alarm. She became hot and red; her door was not locked.

A distinct woman's whisper came to her through the keyhole: 'Cytherea!'

Only one being in the house knew her Christian name, and that was Miss Aldclyffe. Cytherea stepped out of bed, went to the door, and whispered back 'Yes?'

'Let me come in, darling.'

The young woman paused in a conflict between judgment and emotion. It was now mistress and maid no longer; woman and woman only. Yes; she must let her come in, poor thing.

She got a light in an instant, opened the door, and raising her eyes and the candle, saw Miss Aldclyffe standing outside in her dressing gown.

'Now you see that it is really myself; put out the light,' said the visitor. 'I want to stay here with you, Cythie. I came to ask you to come down into my bed, but it is snugger here. But remember that you are mistress in this room, and that I have no business here, and that you may send me away if you choose. Shall I go?'

'O no; you shan't indeed if you don't want to,' said Cythie generously.

The instant they were in bed Miss Aldclyffe freed herself from the last remnant of restraint. She flung her arms round the young girl, and pressed her gently to her heart.

'Now kiss me,' she said. 'You seem as if you were my own, own child!'

Cytherea, upon the whole, was rather discomposed at this change of treatment; and, discomposed or no, her passions were not so impetuous as Miss Aldclyffe's. She could not bring her soul to her lips for a moment, try how she would.

'Come, kiss me,' repeated Miss Aldclyffe.

Cytherea gave her a very small one, as soft in touch and in sound as the bursting of a bubble.

'More earnestly than that – come.'

She gave another, a little but not much more expressively.

'I don't deserve a more feeling one, I suppose,' said Miss Aldclyffe, with an emphasis of sad bitterness in her tone. 'I am an ill-tempered woman, you think; half out of my mind. Well, perhaps I am; but I have had grief more than you can think or dream of. But I am a lonely woman, and I want the sympathy of a pure girl like you, and so I can't help loving you – your name is the same as mine – isn't it strange?'

Cytherea was inclined to say no, but remained silent.

'Now, don't you think I must love you?' continued the other.

'Yes,' said Cytherea absently ...

'Why can't you kiss me as I can kiss you? Why can't you!' She impressed upon Cytherea's lips a warm motherly salute, given as if in the outburst of strong feeling, long checked, and yearning for something to care for and be cared for by in return.

'Do you think badly of me for my behaviour this evening, child? I don't know why I am so foolish as to speak to you in this way. I am a very fool, I believe. Yes. How old are you?'

'Eighteen.'

'Eighteen! ... Well, why don't you ask me how old I am?'

'Because I don't want to know.'

'Never mind if you don't. I am forty-six; and it gives me greater pleasure to tell you this than it does to you to listen. I have not told my age truly for the last twenty years till now.'

'Why haven't you?'

'I have met deceit by deceit, till I am weary of it – weary, weary – and I long to be what I shall never be again – artless and innocent, like you. But I suppose that you, too, will prove to be not worth a thought, as every new friend does on more intimate knowledge. Come, why don't you talk to me, child? Have you said your prayers?'

In saying her prayers aloud Cytherea mentions her sweetheart Edward. Miss Aldclyffe presses her to find out who he is.

Miss Aldclyffe shifted her ground. 'Were you ever in love?' she inquired suddenly.

Cytherea was surprised to hear how quickly the voice had altered from tenderness to harshness, vexation, and disappointment.

'Yes – I think I was – once,' she murmured.

'Aha! And were you ever kissed by a man?'

A pause.

'Well, were you?' said Miss Aldclyffe, rather sharply.

'Don't press me to tell – I can't – indeed, I won't, madam!'

Miss Aldclyffe removed her arms from Cytherea's neck. ''Tis now with you as it is always with all girls,' she said, in jealous and gloomy accents. 'You are not, after all, the innocent I took you for. No, no.' She then changed her tone with fitful rapidity.

'Cytherea, try to love me more than you love him – do. I love you more sincerely than any man can. Do, Cythie: don't let any man stand between us. O, I can't bear that!' She clasped Cytherea's neck again.

'I must love him now I have begun,' replied the other.

'Must – yes – must,' said the elder lady reproachfully. 'Yes, women are all alike. I thought I had at last found an artless woman who had not been sullied by a man's lips, and who had not practised or been practised upon by the arts which ruin all the truth and sweetness and goodness in us. Find a girl, if you can, whose mouth and ears have not been made a regular highway of by some man or another! Leave the admittedly notorious spots – the drawing-rooms of society – and look in the villages – leave the villages and search in the schools – and you can hardly find a girl whose heart has not been had – is not an old thing half worn out by some He or another! If men only knew the staleness of the freshest of us! that nine times out of ten the "first love" they think they are winning from a woman is but the hulk of an old wrecked affection, fitted with new sails and re-used. O Cytherea, can it be that you, too, are like the rest?'

'No, no, no,' urged Cytherea, awed by the storm she had raised in the impetuous woman's mind. 'He only kissed me once – twice I mean.'

'He might have done it a thousand times if he had cared to, there's no doubt about that, whoever his lordship is. You are as bad as I – we are all alike; and I – an old fool – have been sipping at your mouth as if it were honey, because I fancied no wasting lover knew the spot. But a minute ago, and you seemed to me like a fresh spring meadow – now you seem a dusty highway.'

'O no, no!' Cytherea was not weak enough to shed tears except on extraordinary occasions but she was fain to begin sobbing now. She wished Miss Aldclyffe would go to her own room, and leave her and her treasured dreams alone. This vehement imperious affection was in one sense soothing, but yet it was not of the kind that Cytherea's instincts desired. Though it was generous, it seemed somewhat too rank and capricious[*] for endurance.

[*] In the first edition this read 'too rank, sensuous and capricious'. The word sensuous was first omitted in the 1896 edition of the novel.

9 C.L. Maynard, diary and autobiography extracts in M. Vicinus, *Independent Women*, 1985, London: Virago, pp. 160, 332

The educationalist Constance Louisa Maynard dedicated herself to the development of women's education. She founded Westfield College in London. Her personal life was characterised by her search for close relationships with other women and her diaries and unpublished autobiography reveal the intensity of these friendships.

{1887}

It's all very well to call [my] loneliness 'sex feeling,' but I can honestly say my thoughts never strayed to a man. I wanted to live thus with my flock in a happy community, but I wanted one life to stand beside me, one heart to pour its fullness into mine, and then I should be amply content.

{1891}

[Ralph] was not well, and I went up to see that she was rightly attended to. As I left she said with gentle hesitation, 'You never bite my fingers now, as you used to do.' 'Oh no, never,' I replied lightly. 'And you never snarl and growl like a jaguar when you can't express yourself. I never heard anyone growl as well as you.' 'No', I said, 'it's useless. I've been cured of that.' The sweet low voice went on, 'And you never rock me in your arms and call me your baby.' 'No,' I said in the same even tone, 'I've been cured of that too.' 'Oh!,' she said, with quite a new meaning, 'oh, I see.' Here was a spot too painful to be touched, and I said, 'Goodbye, dear,' and left the room. I will not go into the desolation I felt when alone again. I was like a pot-bound root all curled in upon itself, like an iron-bound bud that has lost the spring, and now no rain and no sunshine can open it.

10 L.T. Mallet, Reviews, *Shafts*, 21 January 1893, p. 183

Shafts was a short-lived feminist journal. This book review of the letters of Geraldine Jewsbury, who was single, and Jane Welsh Carlyle (1801–1866), who was married to the writer Thomas Carlyle, emphasises the intensity of Jewsbury's feelings for Carlyle. They were close friends for over twenty-five years.

The letters of Miss Geraldine Jewsbury to Mrs. Carlyle are such as rarely meet the eye of an indifferent public. They are the outpourings of the heart of one woman to another whom she loved as her own soul. The book is very fragmentary, the letters are most of them incomplete, the subjects to which they allude are frequently most provokingly hidden from the reader, and can only be conjectured, and they supply one of the delights which is usually found in literary gossip. The reader of these letters has none of the comfortable satisfaction which is afforded by feeling oneself on terms of intimate acquaintance with the distinguished personages of the day, nor do they satisfy the deeper and worthier sentiment of human interest in people of whom one has heard and read. On the contrary, the perusal of these letters is accompanied with a tantalising sense of disappointment; you are constantly checked and pulled up short with a sense of frustration which sometimes tempts you to fling down the book in a rage. And yet with all these drawbacks the perusal of these letters is entrancing. That study of unrivalled interest – the innermost presentment of a human soul – is unfolded before you – a woman's heart stands there revealed.
...

Miss Geraldine Jewsbury writes to Mrs. Carlyle

'I want to see you very much, more than I have any chance of making you understand. I am tired to death of writing letters into space; the best of letters are fractions of fragments, and deceive one by pretending to do away with the inconveniences of absence, whereas one only writes, after a long separation, to oneself instead of to one's friend. ... . I want to see you so much that I can write about nothing, tell you nothing, for what on earth do I know about you at this blessed moment? Nothing. I might just as well be writing a supposititious letter for the new edition of the COMPLETE LETTER WRITER from a lady to a female friend whom she has not seen for a long time! Next Monday I shall be thinking of you all the day. Heaven send you safe without accident!'
...

'Dearest Jane, this is only a hasty kiss on your safe arrival, for you will be too tired for more, dear love: how glad I feel to know that you are so near!

11 'Olivia' (Dorothy Bussy), introduction to *Olivia*, 1949, The Hogarth Press, pp. 13–17

A world of adolescent love is represented in Dorothy Bussy's autobiographical novel, *Olivia*. It recounts her experiences in a French boarding school in the early 1880s and this extract from the introduction demonstrates the importance to Dorothy of the relationships she describes. How far the fictionalised plot bears any relation to actual events at the school is not known.

Love has always been the chief business of my life, the only thing I have thought – no, felt – supremely worth while, and I don't pretend that this experience was not succeeded by others. But at that time, I was innocent, with the innocence of ignorance. I didn't know what was happening to me. I didn't know what had happened to anybody. I was without consciousness, that is to say, more utterly absorbed than was ever possible again. For after that first time there was always part of me standing aside, comparing, analysing, objecting: 'Is this real? Is this sincere?' All the world of my predecessors was there before me, taking, as it were, the bread out of my mouth. Was this stab in my heart, this rapture, really mine or had I merely read about it? For every feeling, every vicissitude of my passion, there would spring into my mind a quotation from the poets. Shakespeare or Donne or Heine had the exact phrase for it. Comforting, perhaps, but enraging too. Nothing ever seemed spontaneously my own. As the blood dripped from the wound, there was always part of me to watch with a smile and a sneer: 'Literature! Mere literature! Nothing to make a fuss about!' And then I would add, 'But so Mercutio jested as he died!'

And there were not only the poets to poison the sources of emotion, there were the psychologists, the physiologists, the psycho-analysts, the Prousts and the Frauds. It was deeply interesting, this withdrawal of oneself from the scene of action, this lying in ambush, waiting and watching for the prowling beasts, the nocturnal vermin, to come creeping out of their lairs, to recognise this one and that, to give it its name, to be acquainted with its habits – but what was left of oneself after this relinquishing of one's property? Wasn't one a mere field where these irresponsible animals carried on their antics at their own free will? Irritation, disgust, cynicism and scepticism are bred of such thoughts – the poisonous antidotes of the poison of passion. But the poison that works in a girl of sixteen – at any rate in the romantic, sentimental girl I then was – has no such antidote, and no previous inoculation mitigates the severity of the disease. Virgin soil, she takes it as the South Sea islanders took measles – a matter of life and death.

How should I have known indeed, what was the matter with me? There was no instruction anywhere. The poets, it is true (for even then I frequented the poets), had a way of talking sometimes which seemed strangely to illuminate the situation. But this, I thought, must be an illusion or an accident. What could these grown-up men and women with their mutual love-affairs have in common with a little girl like me? My case was so different, so unheard of. Really no one had ever heard of such a thing, except as a joke. Yes, people used to make joking allusions to 'schoolgirl crushes'. But I knew well enough that my 'crush' was not a joke. And yet I had an uneasy feeling that, if not a joke, it was something to be ashamed of, something to hide desperately. This, I suppose, was not so much a matter of reflection (I did not think my passion was reprehensible, I was far too ignorant for that) as of instinct – a deep-rooted instinct, which all my life has kept me from any form of unveiling, which has forbidden me many of the purest physical pleasures and all literary expression. How can one bathe without undressing, or write without laying bare one's soul?

But now, after many years, the urgency of confession is upon me. Let me indulge it. Let me make my offering on the altar of – absence. The eyes that would have understood are closed. And besides, it is not my soul but that of a far away little girl of sixteen.

One more oblation to the gods! May they grant me not to have profaned a rare and beautiful memory!

12 M. Field (Katherine Bradley and Edith Cooper), 'Maids, not to you my mind doth change'

Michael Field was the name under which Katherine Harris Bradley (1846–1914) and Edith Emma Cooper (1862–1913), who were aunt and niece, wrote poetry and drama. Their first joint volume *Bellerophon* came out in 1881 under the names of Arran and Isla Leigh. *Long Ago* (1889) rewrote the legend of Sappho and was influenced by Henry Thornton Wharton's controversial translation, which indicated that Sappho loved women.

Maids, not to you my mind doth change

(Greek quotation ' To ye, fair maids, my mind changes not')

> Maids, not to you my mind doth change;
> Men I defy, allure, estrange,
> Prostrate, make bond or free:
> Soft as the stream beneath the plane
> To you I sing my love's refrain;

Between us is no thought of pain, peril, satiety.

Soon doth a lover's patience tire,
But ye to manifold desire
Can yield response, ye know
When for long, museful days I pine,
The presage at my heart divine;
To you I never breathe a sign
Of inward want or woe.

When injuries my spirit bruise,
Allaying virtue ye infuse
With unobtrusive skill:
And if care frets ye come to me
As fresh as nymph from stream or tree,
And with your soft vitality
my wary bosom fill.

13 A. Levy, 'To Vernon Lee', *A London Plane – tree and Other Verse*, 1889, T. Fisher Unwin

During the 1880s Amy Levy (1861–1889), the first Jewish woman to matriculate at Newnham College, Cambridge, was quite well known as a poet and novelist. In 1889, at the age of 27 she took her own life at her family home in London. She was a friend of Olive Shreiner and after her suicide there were intimations in the press that Shreiner was implicated. The brilliant Englishwoman, Vernon Lee (Violet Paget (1856–1935)), lived in Italy and had a series of intense relationships with women.

On Bellosguardo, when the year was young,
We wandered, seeking for the daffodil
And dark anemone, whose purples fill
The peasant's plot, between the corn-shoots sprung.

Over the grey, low wall the olive flung
Her deeper greyness; far off, hill on hill
Sloped to the sky, which, pearly-pale and still,
Above the large and luminous landscape hung.

A snowy blackthorn flowered beyond my reach;
You broke a branch and gave it to me there;
I found for you a scarlet blossom rare.

Thereby ran on Art and Life our speech;
And of the gifts of gods had given to each –
Hope unto you, and unto me Despair.

14 E. Smyth, *What Happened Next*, 1940, Longmans and Co., pp. 26–8

Ethel Smyth (1858–1944), composer and feminist, had a series of intense relationships with women. When travelling in Europe in 1896 she visited the writer Vernon Lee. Here she writes her impressions of Lee's *cultes* of women who included Mary Robinson, whose marriage devastated Lee, Kit Anstruther-Thomson and a Mme Bulteau.

On the way home I paid a first and memorable visit to Il Palmerino, Vernon Lee's charming villa outside Florence, but I cannot say I wholly enjoyed it. For one thing, though I am certain that Vernon's intentions were of the most hospitable, it was only by secretly invoking the aid of her then resident friend, Miss Anstruther-Thomson, that I eventually got *two* pats of butter and *two* rolls for breakfast. Also the speciality of Vernon's cook was said to be real old Italian dishes seldom met with to-day. One, I remember, was tongue stewed in chocolate; another the claws of birds of prey (but I suspected they were song-birds shot by Vernon's gardener) cunningly concealed in an omelette.

But hardest to bear was the tone of the house, in which every afternoon a symposium raged. Kit Anstruther-Thomson, as I knew her in former years, was just a nice strapping handsome girl who went well to hounds. But if Vernon was seized with one of her *cultes* for anyone, that person was firmly manipulated into an expert on art, and incidentally into Vernon's slave and familiar friend. When no symposium was on, Kit spent her time stroking Vernon's hand; and, symposium or no symposium, in stroking her vanity. ...

The story of Vernon's many *cultes*, which succeeded each other all down her life, was always the same. Each of them was at first deeply flattered at finding herself treated as an authority on aesthetics; asked to pronounce on some bust in the Vatican that in Vernon's opinion was wrongly deemed a Greek original by the authorities; told to look steadily at the hind-legs of two different chairs and judge by her physical reactions – *tiraillements* they called them – which had the more beautiful curve. But Vernon was a tyrannical taskmaster, and the *culte* gradually discovered she was being lovingly but tightly bound by unbreakable cords to 'OUR WORK'. In the end of course there came a moment of violent disruption, and Vernon suffered deeply. ...

Myself, I believe the tragedy of her life was that without knowing it she loved the *cultes* humanely and with passion; but being the stateliest and chastest of beings she refused to face the fact, or indulge in the most innocent demonstrations of affection, preferring to create a fiction that to her these friends were merely *intellectual* necessities. One of them once said – but

71

this was after the friendship had come to grief: 'Her kisses – very rare – were of the sacramental kind; you felt you had been to your first communion'. I myself can testify to the killing accuracy of this description, but always thought a warmer style was probably reserved for those she was *really* fond of. I am sure, now, that it was not so.

15 M. Stopes, *A Journal from Japan: A Daily Record of Life as Seen by a Scientist*, 1910, Blackie and Sons, pp. 106–12 *passim*

Marie Stopes was known as a sex reformer, birth control campaigner and author of popular marriage manuals. In the first decade of the new century Stopes gained her doctorate and then spent about eighteen months researching fossils in Tokyo.

February 25 {1908}

... A ball at the British Embassy in the evening, very pleasant ... Captain van L— introduced me to the loveliest of women there – an American (sad to hear their awful accent coming out of such patrician lips!), the one who at a previous dance had so entranced me and my young partner that we spent our sitting-out time following her around to see her eat ices and laugh; her manner was perfection – calm, still, and gracious, honey-sweet looks in eyes that never smiled while one was speaking to her, and that just broke into little curls of smiles as she answered – a suggestion of humility while waiting to hear another's banalities, yet with it a commanding dignity that forbade any one else to interrupt the person who was speaking to her. Her name is Mrs. D—, and I am going to see her, as she very graciously invited me to do. I wonder if she included thought-reading among her other charms and read my admiration? Her high-heeled pink satin slippers twinkled gaily in the dance; she did not hesitate to lift the Worth frock very high – with such ankles I wouldn't! On her white soft neck were the loveliest little blue veins, I never saw anything so suggestive of living marble. She was like white marble, with an underflush of rose and violet. The little wrinkles at the corners of her eyes added to her charm rather than detracted from it. She is the only woman in Tokio who has bewitched me. ...

February 28

I visited the Charmer to-day, and stayed an unconscionably long time. No one has bewitched me in this way since my school-days. She had a lovely gown of blue-and-white chiffon. ... I had about half-an-hour of the Charmer to myself – her husband is the Naval Attaché. She is simply alluring. ...

March 5

Fossils till 4 – then I went to tea with Mrs. D— Mrs. D had another lovely frock, and was a dream of sweetness and beauty. Why do I always fall in love with women!

16 S. Cole, *Blue Grey Magic*, 1910, Mills and Boon, pp. 181–9

In the first decade of the new century Sophie Cole's novel, *Blue Grey Magic* explored many issues facing the New Woman. Even in this short extract three issues concerning women's relationships are explored. First there is the androgyny of passionate writing, second, a belief in the possibility of women-to-women relationships as an alternative to those of women and men, and thirdly the association of emotional involvement with women as sexual perversion when Stella is told 'There's a kink in your brain'.

The heroine, Hester, is poor and treated as a servant/nursemaid to her relative's children. Stella is rich and Bohemian, an artist living on family money.

Hester looked at the self-possessed figure seated beside her; at the masculine ease of attitude coupled with the feminine perfection of detail in dress... 'It never occurred to me for one moment that a – that you – '

She paused, her pale face suddenly aflame at the realisation of the direction in which her words were tending.

Stella caught the suggestion of the pause and the blush, and a look of comprehension dawned in her eyes. 'I believe,' she began deliberately, 'I really believe,' and there was a veiled scorn in her lowered voice, 'you thought it was a man!'

Hester shrank visibly from the contemptuous epithet in which she was involved and the other went on with increasing excitement. 'And you, whom I had always thought so sweet and refined, wrote letters – *those* letters – to a strange man!' Hester, stung by the taunt, roused herself to a feeble effort at retaliation. 'I certainly did not write them to *you*,' she answered, with a touch of spirit.

'No – you jumped at the usual vulgar interpretation, and preferred to feed the vanity of some unknown man by verbally throwing yourself into his arms.'

The shot sped home, and Hester received it with a shudder. 'Oh, why did you mislead me by writing me love letters?' she wailed.

'Because I took you for something better than the average coarse-minded girl who has no conception of any love but that which ends in marriage.'

'You were just to me then; you are not so now. You are unreasonable ... You hadn't sufficient imagination to put yourself in my place and foresee the possibility of a misunderstanding. I deny – I deny that it's coarse-minded to – to think what I did. It's you, rather, who are unnatural in your ideas.'

Stella Chase threw back her head with a gesture of rather exaggerated indifference. 'We can't prolong the discussion here,' she said, 'people are beginning to notice us. It has all been a ridiculous mistake.' There was an interval of depressed silence betwen the two girls, then Stella exclaimed with an air of cynical resignation, 'Well, there's another friendship died a violent death!'

Hester offers friendship.

Stella laughed ironically. 'No thank you,' she returned. 'I know what it means to be friends with a girl who has a lover. One exists only to be the recipient of confidences about the beloved.'

'I shouldn't bore you in that way', answered Hester, in a low, shamed voice. 'I have no lover'.

Barbara arrives, Hester leaves and Stella explains to Barbara

'You need not be spiteful, Barbara. I've just found out that I've made a fool of myself, which is quite sufficient punishment for thinking a girl of Hester's stamp capable of more than the usual One Idea!'

[Barbara] 'There's a kink in your brain, Stella. ... Of course I know a woman ought to have interests outside those of sex; but I can't understand your violent antagonism to ordinary healthy instincts. Why shouldn't Hester improve her mind to please a lover?'

'A woman should care for knowledge for itself, and not use it in the same way they wear showy clothes – to attract a man.' Stella delivered the remark oracularly, and with a scorn augmented by the particular application in her mind. ... I was bored... and it made a little break. Also I had theories about the girl which I wanted to put to the test. And, I began to get really fond of her. I contemplated asking her to come and live with me. ... She wrote such charming letters. ... And to think – to think – they were meant for a *man*! That I, of all persons, should have brought such a thing to pass!'

17 K. Mansfield, 'Friendship' in S. Coote (ed.), *The Penguin Book of Homosexual Verse*, 1983, Harmondsworth: Penguin, pp. 292–3

Katherine Mansfield (1888–1923) is best known for her short stories. She was brought up in New Zealand where as a young woman she had her first lesbian relationship. Her personal life was usually turbulent and at one time she shared a home with her husband, John Middleton Murray, and her lover, Ida Baker.

Friendship

When we were charming *Backfisch**

With curls and velvet bows
We shared a charming kitten
With tiny velvet toes.

It was so gay and playful;
It flew like a woolly ball
From my lap to your shoulder –
And, oh, it was so small,

So warm – and so obedient
If we cried; 'That's enough'
It lay and slept between us,
A purring ball of fluff.

But now that I am thirty
And she is thirty-one,
I shudder to discover
How wild our cat has run.

It's bigger than a Tiger,
Its eyes are jets of flame,
Its claws are gleaming daggers,
Could it have once been tame?

Take it away; I'm frightened!
But she, with placid brow,
Cries: 'This is our Kitty-witty!
Why don't you love her now?'

* teenagers

18 V. Trefusis, letter to Vita Sackville-West, March 1919 in M.A. Leaska and J. Phillips (eds), *Violet to Vita. The Letters of Violet Trefusis to Vita Sackville-West, 1910–1921,* 1989, London: Methuen, pp. 117–18

Vita Sackville-West's passionate affair with Violet Trefusis was first revealed by her son, Nigel Nicolson, in *Portrait of a Marriage* (1973). Her brief elopement to Paris with Violet he described as 'the only crisis of her marriage'. In 1920 Vita recalled of the summer of 1918 'Well, the whole of that summer she was mine – a mad and irresponsible summer of moonlight nights, and infinite escapades, and passionate letters, and music, and poetry.' For Violet too the affair was all-consuming, as her letters to Vita reveal.

My own sweet love, I am writing this at 2 o'clock in the morning at the conclusion of the most cruelly ironical day I have spent in my life.

This evening I was taken to a ball of some good people. Chinday had previously told all her friends I was engaged so I was congratulated by everyone I knew there. I could have screamed aloud. Mitya, I can't face this existence. I shall see you once again on Monday and it depends on you whether we shall ever see each other again.

It is really wicked and horrible. I am losing every atom of self-respect I ever possessed. I *hate* myself. O Mitya, what *have* you done to me? O my darling, precious love, what is going to become of us?

I want you every second and every hour of the day, yet I am being slowly and inexorably tied to somebody else. ... Sometimes I am flooded by an agony of physical longing for you ... a craving for your nearness and your touch. At other times I feel I should be quite content if I could only hear the sound of your voice. I try so hard to imagine your lips on mine. Never was there such a pitiful imagining. ... Darling, whatever it may cost us, tiri chinday* won't be cross with you any more. I suppose this ridiculous engagement will set her mind at rest. ...

Nothing and no one in the world could kill the love I have for you. I have surrendered my whole individuality, the very essence of my being to you. I have given you my body time after time to treat as you pleased, to tear to pieces if such had been your will. All the hoardings of my imagination I have laid bare to you. There isn't a recess in my brain into which you haven't penetrated. I have clung to you and caressed you and slept with you and I would like to tell the whole world I clamour for you. ... You are my lover and I am your mistress, and kingdoms and empires and governments have tottered and succumbed before now to that mighty combination – the most powerful in the world.

* your mother

19 V. Woolf, 1926, diary entry Monday 21 December 1925 in A.O. Bell *The Diary of Virginia Woolf*, Vol. 3: 1925–30, Harmondsworth: Penguin, pp. 51–3

The novelist Virginia Woolf (1882–1941) was entranced by the aristocratic Vita Sackville-West from their first meeting in December 1922, when she noted in her diary 'knows everyone – But could I ever know her?' Vita was equally fascinated, writing to her husband of Virginia, 'Darling, I have quite lost my heart.' While their relationship did not retain the intensity of this early account in Virginia's diary, they remained devoted to each other over two decades, until Virginia's suicide in 1941.

But no Vita! But Vita for 3 days at Long Barn, from which L. & I returned yesterday. These Sapphists love women; friendship is never untinged with amorosity. In short, my fears & refrainings, my 'impertinence' my usual self-

consciousness in intercourse with people who mayn't want me & so on –
were all, as L. said, sheer fudge; &, thanks to him (he made me write) I
wound up this wounded & stricken year in great style. I like her & being
with her, & the splendour – she shines in the grocers shop in Sevenoaks with
a candle lit radiance, stalking on legs like beech trees, pink glowing, grape
clustered, pearl hung. That is the secret of her glamour, I suppose. Anyhow
she found me incredibly dowdy, no woman cared less for personal appearance
no one put on things in the way I did. Yet so beautiful, &c. What is the
effect of all this on me? Very mixed. There is her maturity & full breasted-
ness: her being so much in full sail on the high tides, where I am coasting
down backwaters; her capacity I mean to take the floor in any company, to
represent her country, to visit Chatsworth, to control silver, servants, chow
dogs; her motherhood (but she is a little cold & offhand with her boys) her
being in short (what I have never been) a real woman. Then there is some
voluptuousness about her; the grapes are ripe; & not reflective. No. In brain
& insight she is not as highly organised as I am.

But then she is aware of this, & so lavishes on me the maternal protection
which, for some reason, is what I have always most wished from everyone.
What L. gives me, & Nessa gives me, & Vita, in her more clumsy external
way, tries to give me. For of course, mingled with all this glamour, grape
clusters & pearl necklaces, there is something loose fitting. How much, for
example, shall I really miss her when she is motoring across the desert? I
will make a note on that next year. Anyhow, I am very glad that she is
coming to tea today, & I shall ask her, whether she minds my dressing so
badly? I think she does. I read her poem; which is more compact, better seen
& felt than anything yet of hers.

... We go down to Charleston tomorrow, not without some trepidation
on my part, partly because I shall be hung about with trailing clouds of
glory from Long Barn which always disorientates me & makes me more than
usually nervous: then I am altogether so queer in some ways. One emotion
succeeds another.

20 E.J. Oxenham, *The Abbey Girls Win Through*, 1928, Collins, p. 9

The genre of the schoolgirl story had its greatest popularity in the 1920s and 1930s.
Elsie Jeanette Oxenham (1885–1960) was one of a group of popular women authors
who wrote series of books in which the same characters reappear. She wrote over thirty
'Abbey' books for young women. The stories repeatedly present a female-focused world
of support and love.

They were a recognised couple. Con, who sold gloves in a big West-End
establishment, was the wife and home-maker; Norah, the typist, was the

husband, who planned little pleasure trips and kept the accounts and took Con to the pictures.

21 C. Chesterton, *Women of the Underworld*, 1928, Stanley Paul and Co. Ltd, p. 199

Mrs Cecil Chesterton (Ada Jones) was founder of the Cecil Homes for homeless women and girls in London. This vignette from Chesterton's book is a rare glimpse of a loving relationship between two older working-class women.

There are two friends in poverty who live in and about Bayswater Road. During the day they sell matches or do a bit of begging, and at night they sleep in doorways, or behind a friendly dustbin, anywhere they can find a shelter. Annie and Nellie are over sixty; clad in rags and generally hungry, they still keep a curiosity and a cheerfulness towards life, waiting for the great day when Annie, the elder of the two, will be able to claim the old age pension and thus provide, they hope, a permanent home.

The two friends, active as sparrows, welcomed the coffee-stall and drank large draughts of boiling tea. Annie was out of luck. She had been warned by a policeman who suspected her of begging, and was seriously contemplating moving her pitch. Some of the other night-birds agreed it would be safer for her to move on now she'd been spotted by a copper, but Nellie insisted that she didn't want to go.

'Besides, we should miss the Welcome,' she explained. 'We're sure of a meal two or three times a week, and that means a lot. Here's your very good health, miss,' and she lifted her mug to the dispenser of the good cheer.

22 E. Roper, biographical introduction to the *Poems of Eva Gore-Booth*, 1929, Longmans and Co., pp. 9–49 *passim*

Eva Gore Booth (1870–1926) and Esther Roper (1868–1938) met in 1896 and lived together in Manchester and London until Eva's death. They worked together in the suffrage, trade union and peace movements. In the biographical introduction to the volume of Eva's poems published after her death Esther writes lovingly of their first meeting and subsequent relationship.

In 1896, in the House of George Macdonald, at Bordighera, where both were staying, she met the writer of this sketch, who for two years after leaving college had been working in Manchester for the political and economic enfranchisement of women. For months illness kept us in the south and we spent the days walking and talking on the hillside by the sea. Each was attracted to the work and thoughts of the other, and we became friends and companions for life. Very soon she made up her mind to join me in the work in Manchester. Her family had owned land in Salford for genera-tions, and a cousin held the family living there, but she herself did not know Lancashire. By 1897 she was settled in Manchester and was giving the greater part of her time to work for women. ...

Esther and Eva spent 1920–1921 travelling in Italy.

Soon after our return from Italy we settled in Hampstead. She cared as keenly as ever for every cause for which she had toiled in the past; the welfare of the women workers was always very near her heart. Her health made it impossible that her work should be of the same kind as formerly; but it was not for that reason any less vigorous or effective. ...

Eva Gore-Booth's sensitive and loving nature made her a perfect friend. No words of mine could ever tell the beauty of her friendship, but I can say of it truly, 'Love never faileth'. Through the years of difficult and trying work, through periods of terrible strain and grief, through ever-recurring times of intense pain, this was true. To the hard work which we did together for thirty years she brought a spirit of adventure and gaiety which nothing daunted. Of a gallant courage and a gentle courtesy she made life together a gracious thing. Even simple everyday pleasures when shared with her became touched with magic – wandering through the woods of her old home, or seeking the 'blue gentians and frail columbines' of a Swiss moun-tain, or finding 'beauty and life and light' in Italy. ...

Esther describes her death.

At the end she looked up with that exquisite smile that always lighted up her face when she saw one she loved, then closed her eyes and was at peace.

23 E. Hodge, *A Woman Oriented Woman*, 1989 [1920s], West Sussex: Gooday Publishers, pp. 26–8

Born in the first decade of the twentieth century Esther Hodge was a history graduate and secondary school teacher. Her autobiography shows a life strongly focussed on women. She worked for the Open Door Council, the Women's International League for Peace and Freedom and for the ordination of women. In these extracts she reflects on her sexuality.

I never thought of myself as lesbian. Indeed when my friend, Margery, said to me, with an air of tolerance, 'Of course I don't mind, but I've thought of you as lesbian from the way you go on about these friends of yours,' I was furious. This was sometime in 1960 or '61. Today, any two women who live companionably together are likely to be dubbed lesbian, a fact which angers another friend who cared devotedly for years for such a partner who fell into ill-health. It is ludicrous to suppose that two devoted churchwomen of my acquaintance, aged seventy-six and eighty now, are lesbian, but one of them felt she had to assure the new vicar that they were not, explaining to him on their first meeting the exact arrangement of their house in which each has a bedroom and a sitting room. However, if homosexuality in women means (more often than in men?) simply an orientation towards one's own sex, covering a longstanding commitment to one individual with whom love is freely expressed in hugging and kissing but not in any genital sexual stimulation (in or out of bed) then, yes, the word lesbian can pass. Lillian Faderman's book, *Surpassing the Love of Men*, details most interestingly the attitudes towards romantic friendship and love between women from the Renaissance to the present (Junction Books Ltd., 1981). I was (and remain) fascinated with the story of the Ladies of Llangollen, as told by Elizabeth Mavor (1971) after seeing their house during a cycling holiday in Wales with Margery, to whom they made no particular appeal.

My first experience of a passionate relationship with a woman had nothing to do with all this – indeed, she was a person whom, before I fell for her advances to me, I wrote off as someone of no importance on the staff of my school. Some people will condemn the single-sex institution, but such blame is equally applicable to the same thing when it happens in the single-sex institution for boys. The blame, supposing any to be attributable, lies in my case in the social circumstances of the time. The lesson that I learnt from it (and can claim to have followed) is that in any relationship between an older woman and a younger, the former must be very careful not to overlay the life of the latter.

Circumstances must always be understood. Places in the universities of Oxford and Cambridge were in the late 20s still so few that sitting for the Scholarship and Entrance examination was usually delayed until one's third year in the VIth form. Girls then might leave school in December or March, when successful, but the Headmistress wanted me to stay on as head girl to lead the cheering when the Duchess of Atholl came to open the new science block in July. I was therefore the only one of my age group during that summer term. So I came to revel in the companionship of two members of the staff, the senior French and the junior Latin mistress. The former was a perfectly well-balanced woman of whom I remember nothing but good; it was with the latter that emotion took over inordinately. The running was certainly made by her but I soon responded ardently, going frequently to her flat, while she came out to Ampthill a few times. My mother tried to break up the friendship (ineffectually of course). Her suspicions were aroused as much, I suspect, by the guest's silly revelation of her dislike of our headmistress, whom my mother respected, as of any dark thoughts of Lesbianism although these she may have had. I went to Germany during those summer holidays and wrote to Bronwen every other day. She came several times to visit me in Oxford during my first term. Then there was a busting row, I haven't the slightest recollection what about. She took up with another girl in the school, and then a few years later, at forty or so, she married.

24 C. Harman (ed.), *The Diaries of Sylvia Townsend Warner*, 1995, London: Virago Press, pp. 69–70

The poet and novelist Sylvia Townsend Warner (1893–1978) met Valentine Ackland (1906–1969) in 1930 and they lived together in Dorset until Valentine's death. During the day of 11 October 1930, in the week after they first set up residence together, they had visited the local Vicarage to confront a Miss Stevenson with allegations that she was mistreating her servant. Sylvia's diary for that day and the following, documents the beginning of their sexual relationship.

11 October 1930

... And then we went to bed. Just as I blew out the candle the wind began to rise. I thought I heard her speak, and listened, and at last she said through the door that this would frighten them up at the Vicarage. How the Vicarage led to love I have forgotten (oh, it was an eiderdown). I said, sitting on my side of the wall, that love was easier than liking, so I should specialise in that. 'I think I am utterly loveless'. The forsaken grave wail of her voice smote me, and had me up, and through the door, and at her bedside. There I stayed, till I got into her bed, and found love there, and a confidence that could twit me how rude I had been the first time we met. We heard a screech-owl wing up the valley to the vicarage, and after a while it came back to tell us with a few contemptuous hoots, of its errand there. And we remembered the light in the field, that I had been so wrong about, she so right.

12 October 1930

My last day, and our first. It was a bridal of earth and sky, and we spent the morning lying in the hollowed tump of the Five Maries, listening to the wind blowing over our happiness, and talking about torpedoes, and starting up at footsteps. It is so natural to be hunted and intuitive. Feeling safe and respectable is much more of a strain. A final tea at B.C. was called for, and it took three quarters of an hour to go there, owing to there being so many regrets and expostulations to rehearse. We stayed interminably, Francis walked back with us, and I shall never forget Valentine, ginless, standing with her back to the fire, keeping her eye on us lest we should dare to sit down, while Francis sipped with his stick propped on the table, and I weakly made conversation about the poltergeist. It is a fierce creature I have released, though so kind to me. 'Won't you sit down' it said, rather severely, after he had gone. And I sat with relief, as if a permission were given. Dinner was briskly through, and William was allowed once round the green, and my loving leopard took me off to bed.

25 V. Brittain, *Testament of Friendship: The Story of Winifred Holtby*, 1980 [1940], London: Virago, pp. 166–9

Vera Brittain (1896–1970) and Winifred Holtby (1898–1935) met in 1919 and shared homes together in London until Vera's marriage in 1925. Thereafter Winifred's permanent home was with Vera and her husband, George Catlin, who worked in the United States for part of each year. In *Testament of Friendship* Vera castigates the 'scandalmongers who invented for her (Winifred) a lurid series of homosexual relationships, usually associated with Lady Rhondda or myself'.

That night, when all the festivities were over and she returned home to the realisation that I was actually married and gone, she told me later that she became violently conscious of the ticking of the clocks in the empty flat. ... Too tired to go to bed immediately, she sat down at the large sitting-room table which we had shared for our work, and wrote a short poem called The Foolish Clocks. ...

> Now she is gone, but all her clocks are ticking
> With gentle voices, punctual and polite,
> Their thrifty hands the scattered moments picking
> Tossed from the careless bounty of the night.
>
> Oh, foolish clocks, who had no wit for hoarding
> The precious moments when my love was here,
> Be silent now, and cease this vain recording
> Of worthless hours, since she is not near.

...

For some days the aftermath of my wedding was so strenuous that Winifred had no time to fall again into the mood of sentimental reminiscence in which she wrote The Foolish Clocks. ...

When she arrived the following week for her work on Time and Tide, 'somewhat hot and dishevelled and in exceedingly dirty gloves,' Lady Rhondda, correctly deducing from these unusual symptoms a condition of strain, fatigue and loneliness, whirled her off to lunch in a Soho restaurant with Cicely Hamilton and Olga Lindo.

From a letter by Winifred written two or three weeks later to Vera Brittain.

'I am happy. In a way I suppose I miss you but that does not make me less happy. ... I find you in all small and lovely things; in the little fishes like flames in the green water, in the furred and stupid softness of bumble-bees fat as laughter, in all the chiming radiance of warmth and light and scent in the summer garden. ... When a person that one loves is in the world and alive and well, and pleased to be in the world, then to miss them is only a new flavour, a salt sharpness in experience. It is when the beloved is unhappy or maimed or troubled that one misses with pain.'

26 M. Stocks, *Eleanor Rathbone*, 1949, Victor Gollanz Ltd, pp. 7–8, 57–8

Eleanor Rathbone (1872–1946) met Elizabeth Macadam, a Scottish social worker employed as the warden of the Victoria Women's Settlement in Liverpool and they lived together until Eleanor's death. Until the last years of her life Eleanor always adopted causes and worked on issues challenging what she saw as 'male values'. At their request the two women's correspondence was burned after their deaths. Here their friend, Mary Stocks, explains how Eleanor's biography came to be written and the circumstances of the friends' first meeting.

Preface

It was a terrifying privilege to be entrusted with the writing of Eleanor Rathbone's life, and I was so bold as to undertake it because of the certainty that I should be greatly helped. First and foremost among those who helped is Elizabeth Macadam, Eleanor's best-loved friend, who survived her just long enough to read the typescript of this book. She provided a constructive and critical commentary from chapter to chapter. Elizabeth will say: 'You have been deliberately disobedient. When you showed me the manuscript of your book, I told you to keep me out of it. Yet as soon as my back was turned, you not only reinserted references which I had asked you to delete, but added others. I have not desired this publicity.' ... And to Elizabeth I shall say: 'Yes, indeed, I have disobeyed your orders – but on second thoughts and at a higher level you must surely see that they were unreasonable. Dear Elizabeth, you are part and parcel of the whole pattern of Eleanor's life and cannot be disentangled from it. So scold me – as you often did in the old days, but forgive me as you always did in the end. Believing that you will, I dedicate this book to you, because you told me that you liked it, and because I am grateful beyond measure for your own friendship and for a share of Eleanor's.'

Chapter V Apprenticeship

... Elizabeth Macadam became in due course the friend and companion of Eleanor's existence until death did them part, and at no subsequent period was Eleanor lonely. This momentous development bears no date. Hilda Oakeley recalls a phrase in a long-lost letter addressed to Canada: 'I am deriving much enjoyment from a new friendship ... ' So, like the biographer in John Masefield's poem, who has to confess that the external record of his life, 'reduced to dates and facts,' can tell us little of its really significant moments, we must be content with the knowledge that some time after the withdrawal of William Rathbone from Eleanor's personal life, Elizabeth Macadam came into it:

> 'And none will know the gleam there used to be
> About the feast days freshly kept by me,
> But men will call the hour of golden bliss
> "About this time" or "shortly after this".'

27 N. Spain, *Why I'm Not a Millionaire*, 1959, Hutchinson, pp. 133–5

By the late 1950s Nancy Spain (1917–1974) was a successful popular novelist and critic, and a press, radio and television personality. She lived with Joan (Jonnie) Werner Laurie, founder and editor of *She* magazine and Jonnie's children, Nicky and Tommy. In this extract from one of her three comic autobiographies she writes of their relationship.

What a difficult thing to write objectively of a relationship in which I have been happily bound up for five years, and which is still going on! Jonnie is, I think, one of the most remarkable people I have ever met: remarkable in her potential greatness and past achievement, but even more remarkable in being the only person I have ever met (except Lord Beaverbrook) who has never bored me. She is certainly the only person who has ever let me be myself ... therefore the only person with whom I can cheerfully live in close disharmony.

... You must have noticed that, although I have only written about the funny bits, until I met Jonnie I was a miserable sort of creature, a failure, hating everybody, living in a sort of ivory tower of work, refusing to allow Real Life in the shape of Family Life to intrude on me at all. I had become a terrible cynic, chiefly because all my boy-friends had darted off and married someone else.

On the day that I began to make judgments with Jonnie's hot beautifully controlled mind assisting me, the whole pattern of my behaviour changed. I began to make a little sense. Instead of doing and saying something from blind instinct and then discovering some weeks later what an ass I had made of myself, I quite often proceeded upon a basis of Jonnie's sound common sense. The result was spectacular. Pieces that I wrote for magazines succeeded. Things that I said to Editors began to make sense. Instead of leaning forward dramatically and asking, 'Where is your heart?' (as one Editor once did to me) they actually began to think I had a heart already.

... It is easy enough to talk or write about casual acquaintances, friends even. But it is impossible for me to take a step without consulting Jonnie, it is inevitable that she will shape my behaviour, read everything I write, tell me what other people will think of it, and I cannot write lightly of her, for she saved my life. She brought me back from the angry little garret when I sat, writing angry little books, lonely and bitter, despising the world and the good people in it who were bringing up families. By her example and her faith in me she has taught me things I could never have learnt in books. Her faith in the fact that I am doing my best is worth a hundred paragraphs of praise from other people. Oh, how difficult it is to write of gratitude. Of real goodness of heart. My pen dries and my heart spills over and cannot express itself when I think of everything that Jonnie and Nicky have done for me.

Jonnie, who uses her nervous energy in so many other directions, dislikes the unnecessary wear and tear of emotional scenes. But perhaps she will forgive this written demonstration, so sincerely meant.

Why, she has even taught me, by precept, how to love little children and animals. Quite *beastly* little children with dirty faces.

28 B. Magee, *One in Twenty. A Study of Homosexuality in Men and Women*, 1966, Martin Secker and Warburg, pp. 134–6, 143, 162, 169–71

Bryan Magee's book was developed from the two television programmes he prepared on homosexuality in 1964 and 1965.

What lesbians do

... Penis substitutes are not the only things about lesbian lovemaking which are the subject of almost universal ignorance. Another is the degree of sexual satisfaction achieved. Most people seem to take it for granted that this must be less than is gained by heterosexual women from heterosexual intercourse, but again this is not so. On the contrary, more specifically *sexual* satisfaction accrues to homosexual women than to heterosexual women. By this I mean more in quantity, not more in quality – virtually every act of homosexual intercourse between lesbians culminates in orgasm for both, whereas only a minority of heterosexual acts do likewise. All authorities, be they doctors, marriage guidance counsellors, social workers, sociologists, or whatever, seem to agree that most acts of sexual intercourse consist in the husband gratifying himself with his wife in such a way that the amount of gratification received by her is largely a matter of chance. Camille Mauclair's words that 'the ignorance of woman's physiology which prevails among most men is boundless and incredible' are still true. Many women go through their whole lives without experiencing orgasm in intercourse, and some without even knowing that such a thing is possible for a woman. And if they do not know, it is not surprising that a lot of men do not know either. Between lesbians none of this holds. Each knows the other's physiology in detail – what the erogenous zones are, how they are stimulated, indeed how they react to different kinds of stimulus. Being deviants they are almost certainly more physically and sexually conscious than most women, and, for the same reasons as those already explained in the case of men, more frank with themselves. From their own masturbatory techniques they know what excites, and how, and in what way, and they use these practices on each other.* I have heard of a lesbian doctor who, if one of her women patients complained of the sexual unsatisfactoriness of her marriage, would ask to see the husband, and would then give him advice on how to satisfy his wife which, unrealized by him, was the distillation of her lesbian experience.

Yet another myth about lesbian lovemaking that needs to be exploded is that there is always a 'masculine' partner and a 'feminine' one. This is true sometimes but not generally. The distinction between the masculine ('butch') and the feminine ('fem') types of lesbian, which will be the subject of a later chapter, is one which applies chiefly to behaviour outside the bed – to clothes, vocabulary, hair style, cosmetics, voice, stance, handshake, interests, occupation and the rest. Once in bed the majority of lesbians can assume, and at different times do assume, both an active and a passive role. Whether they take the initiative or not on a particular occasion depends on mood and circumstance. In many an act of lovemaking the distinction cannot be made anyway: it is an equal coming together.

* There is a strong suggestion of narcissism in this transfer of auto-erotic responses and practices to another person who is physically like oneself. In fact there is a narcissistic element in homosexuality as such, in that it consists in loving only people who are like oneself.

Lesbians and normal sex

... Some marriages are entered into by women who are incapable of falling in love with a man at all. Although these women may remain married all their lives, and perhaps never consider homosexual activity, the marriage suffers cruelly. Indeed the whole family suffers from what appears to be a coldness in the woman. The results may include not only ordinary unhappiness but neurosis in the children, even tragedy. For these reasons I think women who know themselves to be lesbian ought not to marry unless there are exceptional reasons for doing so. What they have always to bear in mind is that marriage is not just a partnership between themselves and their husbands. There are also children, and for children to grow up in a home where love is lacking between the parents can create psycho-emotional disturbances or personality disorders for which they may pay a terrible price in later life. Married lesbians with children who come out in their thirties or forties have the task of breaking it to the children, by their actions if not in words. Sometimes out of, say, three young but grown-up children, two will appear to accept it in a calm and sophisticated way, but one will withdraw emotionally to such a degree that it is obvious that serious damage has been done. It is harder for sons than for daughters, and not surprisingly: the relationship of every child to its parent of the opposite sex is known to be sexual in a deeply significant degree. (It is an old adage that 'mothers prefer sons, fathers prefer daughters'.) For a mother to go lesbian is felt as an extreme form of rejection by the son. ...

Lesbians at work

... The other fear – that lesbians will seduce and corrupt people with whom they come in contact in the course of their work – I find it hard to take seriously. Every large organization employing men and women is a hive of heterosexual activity. The number of people having affairs with other people in the same office or factory – one thinks for example of secretaries and their bosses – must run into hundreds of thousands. It is an utter commonplace of life, and no realistic person would expect to eliminate it. I simply do not see that there is anything worse, or for that matter better, if a small proportion of these people are having affairs with others of the same sex instead of the opposite sex. One may disapprove of sexual liaisons and affairs in places of work, but it is plainly absurd to disapprove more of one lesbian than of twenty adulterers. There is no case here for treating lesbians differently from others.

One aspect of the question remains in a separate category, and that is when children are involved. The sexual exploitation of children is wicked. The only profession in which one might expect it to be a danger is the teaching profession. Even here, fears are exaggerated. ...

Lesbians at home

... All over the country there are what must run into dozens of thousands of lesbian households where couples live happily together. I myself know of a large number not only in cities but also in villages, small country towns, all . kinds of out-of-the-way places. It could even be that these are the typical lesbians – that the majority of lesbians are like this. There is no way of telling. Obviously no statistics exist. There is always a danger that a reporter like me will see disproportionately much of the urban world, disproportionately much of the kaleidoscopic sex life of the big cities, with their clubs and so on. After all, there are hundreds of heterosexual clubs in London, and they are packed every night of the week, yet nevertheless the life of these clubs is completely alien to the life of most Londoners. Heterosexual mores in general in the heart of the big city are untypical of the population as a whole. And the same sort of gap exists between homosexual life in the metropolitan world and that in the population as a whole.

When I have visited what may well be a typical lesbian household I have often found the emotional atmosphere stifling. Even in a heterosexual household the weight of motherly and wifely concern is often burdensome to the other members of the family, and in lesbian relationships it frequently seems that there is double the amount, and only half the number of people to lavish it on. Each seems concerned about every detail of the other's health, appearance, what she eats, how she feels, what she enjoys, what she has been doing and what she is going to do, so that the atmosphere is one of obsessional concern for the details of behaviour and the trivialities of everyday life. To me, as a third party, it seems claustrophobic. But this criticism, if it is a criticism, is irrelevant, because such households are not set up for my benefit: they are made by and for the people who live in them, who seem on the whole to be neither more nor less happy than so-called happily married couples in the heterosexual world. ...

In their social lives a lesbian couple will present the familiar spectacle of two unmarried women sharing house. No reference to their sexual relationship will be made in front of any third party, and this will not even enter the heads of most of the people who know them. This particular aspect of the concealment is not very difficult after all, most heterosexual married couples also keep their sexual relationship private to such an extent that their behaviour in front of other people is compatible with their not having one. But lesbians do have to be careful about quite a number of small things – taking each other's hands, or in any way fondling each other in public, or the too frequent use of verbal endearments – and perhaps that aspect of domestic arrangements which is the biggest source of potential embarrassment, the double bed. As one partner in a lifelong lesbian partnership said to me: 'In normal circumstances if one has guests in the house one thinks nothing of taking the women into the bedroom, or asking guests to leave their coats on the bed; but I have to be always careful to keep guests out of the bedroom.' Because their whole life centres so much more on the home than does that of male homosexuals, there is comparatively little for them outside the home that corresponds to the 'world' of the male homosexual. For instance, in London there are scores of gay bars and clubs for men, but those for women can be counted on the fingers. For male homosexuals, as for male heterosexuals, prostitution amounts to a social institution, but for lesbians there is scarcely any such thing. Lesbian brothels exist, and occasionally a street walker will solicit a woman – or more often a woman, seeing an obvious street walker, will solicit her.

29 S. Pinney (ed.), *I'll Stand By You. The Letters of Sylvia Townsend Warner and Valentine Ackland*, 1998, Pimlico, p. 386

In December 1968, when Valentine Ackland was dying from cancer in Guy's Hospital, London, Sylvia wrote her a final love letter.

My Love,

Thirty-eight years ago I brought you a little bunch of herbs when you lay ill in a large bed with Sir Walter Raleigh and a tortoise. In all those years, my dearest, I have never doubted your love, nor my own. Much of what's to come is still unsure; but that glorious span of thirty-eight years of love and trust and happiness – care and courage too – will shine on us and protect us. I have always believed in you. Even when you gave me scented shells, I believed in them. You are my faith, I will live and die in it. If I have to live on alone, I will live and die in it, and because you believe there is a life after death, I will believe in that too. Our love is the one thing I can never question.

Now in return you must believe that I will be sensible, take care of myself, use Palfrey and the Goring amenities for all they are worth, eat an orange a day, and take care of your possession, your Tib.

My love, my Love. And my heart's thanks for all you have given me, all your understanding, your support, your tenderness, your courage, your trust. And your Beauty, outside and in, and your delightfulness.

Never has any woman been so well and truly loved as I.

Sylvia

Written on the back.

18.12.1968 6.45 p.m. This letter is my greatest treasure and must be carefully preserved and given back to Sylvia if I die.

Valentine

II

PROFESSIONAL COMMENTARIES

3

MEDICINE

INTRODUCTION

The nineteenth and twentieth centuries saw the growth of the professions, their increased social power, and their capacity to shape perceptions of social behaviour and relationships between women specifically. The next three chapters examine these developments in medicine, education and law. All the extracts from these professional discourses should be read against the background of the wider social context and other debates about gender roles. Perceptions of the lesbian and the degree of liberality shown towards her lifestyle were bound up with wider social anxieties. At the beginning of the twentieth century, for example, inverted, homosexual and 'masculine' women were often negatively associated with the educated, independent, unmarried New Woman figure, and with the movements for women's higher education and for women's suffrage (Faderman 1981, Newton 1991).

This chapter brings together sources on lesbianism that can broadly be described as medical. There is considerable change over time in the type and amount of material that was available, either to doctors and other professionals, or to the general public. British medical writers wrote little in the nineteenth century on what we would now term lesbian sexuality. Legitimate medical discussion of any aspect of female sexuality, including marital heterosexuality, was extremely limited throughout that century (Hall 1997). Historians have recently challenged the assumption that there was a dominant mid-Victorian discourse of women's asexuality, however, pointing to continuing knowledge of the function of the clitoris and populist beliefs that orgasm was necessary for conception (Mason 1995, Moscucci 1996, Laqueur 1989). However mainstream medical texts in any speciality, including gynaecology and psychiatry, rarely addressed female sexual desire directly and sexual practices between women almost never. Censorship by the courts of published material on birth control and sexuality restricted general access to information, compounding doctors' unwillingness to address these issues (Porter and Hall 1995, Hall 1994). While it has been suggested that some of the late-nineteenth-century anxiety about female masturbation was linked with homosexuality (Moscucci 1996), this area is still under-researched. When the subject was considered at all, it was generally with reference to sexual practices that were known on the continent (especially in Paris) but thought hardly to exist in Britain. Lesbianism was sometimes associated with prostitution, another category of non-respectable female sexuality, and both these connections can be traced into the twentieth century.

While there is a paucity of evidence for the nineteenth century, historians have invested medical literature, especially turn-of-the-century sexology, with immense power as a discourse on homosexuality, which categorised and pathologised the female invert or lesbian and aided the creation of a modern lesbian identity (Weeks 1977, Faderman 1981, Newton 1991). Sexology was an important turning point in theories of sexuality, and was gradually taken up in medical and popular discourses. The first translations of European sexologists (for instance Krafft-Ebing's *Psychopathia Sexualis*, first published in English in 1889) began a slow process of knowledge creation, at least among the few medical practitioners and writers who were concerned with the subject, mainly psychologists. Homosexuality was still, however, associated with perversion, masturbation and lack of self-control. To this aetiology was added a strand concerned with poor heredity and degeneration, but it took some time for the idea of congenital (innate) sexual inversion to emerge.

Havelock Ellis was the most important British sexologist, but his work (and that of French and German sexologists translated into English, such as Bloch, Forel, Weininger and Hirschfeld) was not easily available to lay members of the public before World War I, being restricted to medical practitioners, lawyers and bona fide sex researchers. Nor indeed was it widely read by doctors. The publications of another English socialist and sex reformer, Edward Carpenter, were rather more popular and more easily available, although his work on the intermediate sex was condemned by medical journals, unlike that of Ellis (Hall 1994). But the new study of sexuality was seen as politically radical by a small group of socialists, feminists and social scientists, and as opening up a vital area of personal experience for public debate (Bland and Doan 1998a and b).

One of the most important points made by the sexologists was the division of homosexual men and women into those who were congenitally inverted (born with the condition) and those whose homosexuality was acquired. While liberal opinion slowly began to support tolerance for the former group, the latter could often be seen as deviant, led astray and potentially recuperable for heterosexuality. According to most sexology of this period, inversion was as much about gender identity as about choice of sexual partner. Thus sexologists looked for and identified elements of masculinity – physical and psychological – in the lesbian. Ellis in particular elaborated a scenario whereby the masculine female invert actively sought a more feminine sexual partner (whose own homosexuality was acquired, not innate), thereby constructing, or reifying, the stereotypes of butch and femme.

It has been strongly argued by many historians that the construction of cate-gories and labels of deviance serve a regulatory purpose. Hence the authoritative discourse of the *science* of sex in relation to women and to marginal sexualities not only pathologised love between women, offering very limited versions of lesbian identity, but also emphasised the dangers inherent in female friendship and in celibacy, thus enforcing patriarchal heterosexuality. Furthermore, it is suggested that the scare figure of the lesbian produced by sexology was mobilised to undermine the feminist movement and its critique of male sexuality (Faderman 1981, Jeffreys 1985, Jackson 1994). In contrast, more recent work has interpreted the evidence differently, arguing that Ellis described already existing self-identified lesbian networks and sub-cultures. From this perspective it is claimed that the work of the sexologists, especially that of Edward Carpenter, was welcomed and taken up by some women, since it enabled them to describe their emerging and varied lesbian identities (Stanley 1992, Bland 1995).

At the same time as these turn-of-the-century sexologists were searching for, or assuming, biologistic explanations for lesbianism, Sigmund Freud was constructing a very different paradigm for accounting for the various forms of human sexual desire and practice. The development of psychoanalytic theories of lesbian sexuality progressed in the interwar period (O'Connor and Ryan 1993), but doctors in Britain only slowly took these on.

These early-twentieth-century investigations sought to classify the different types of sexual subjects and sexual behaviours, and to put forward accounts of their causation. Some also suggested treatment regimes. From the 1920s and 1930s, published medical or quasi-medical material on lesbianism began to increase. The rationale for publication of these medical texts and their intended audience varied. Some were addressed only to doctors and lawyers, others were intended to inform and educate the general public or promote a particular view-point. In the popularly available literature, discussions of lesbianism might be found in marriage manuals, especially those dealing with problems in marriage. There was also a genre of more salacious types of marriage manuals and sex information books, but it is unclear how widely sold these were or who read them.

In the interwar years, a number of different threads can be identified in medical accounts of lesbianism. Those following the biologistic approach of the sexologists (a variation of which was the British school of 'new psychology') incor-porated the new theories of endocrinology – the effects of (sexed) hormones – into their accounts (Oudshoorn 1994). Shifts in explanatory frameworks can also be traced in this period. Psychoanalytic explanations (often in a very simplistic and negative form) were clearly in evidence among British medical commentators by the 1940s, alongside a continuing dual model of inherent and acquired homo-sexuality, which often had some reference to glandular abnormality. The approaches of mainstream psychiatry to female homosexuality between the 1930s and the 1960s have yet to be explored thoroughly.

Alongside the diversity in their theoretical premises, there was also great variety in the extent to which doctors condemned, tolerated or condoned female homosexuality in the middle decades of the twentieth century. While the most common approach may have been the assumption of neurosis or mental illness, this was by no means ubiquitous. Before and after World War I, the awareness of a large number of single women who were unlikely to find husbands stimulated some discussion and advice by doctors about their appropriate lifestyles and friendships. Much of this was strongly positive in validating female friendships – countering the assumption made by some historians that sexology's invention of the lesbian served to stigmatise close female friendships (Oram 1992). Some authors warned of the dangers of obsessive friendships, but others were much more tolerant, even supportive, of sex between women. But demographic shifts and anxiety about low birth rates in the 1930s and 1940s also meant that lesbians could be associated with that most gross form of feminine deviance, refusing motherhood.

The various research methodologies that are apparent in these medical extracts are related to each writer's particular theoretical framework, and also to contemporary assumptions about correct scientific practices in the different periods. After the occasional references in the nineteenth century, early-twentieth-century work began to describe and classify lesbians and, in the case of Ellis, to build an argument around lists of examples culled from personal experience, history and anthropology. These lists accumulated and lengthened in later editions of *Sexual Inversion*. Psychoanalytic theories were built on individual case studies of patients, and only verified by internal reference to the assumptions of those theories. The case histories quoted here illustrate different theories of causation, and sometimes indicate treatment methods. By the 1960s we see in Britain a shift in research methods and a new interest in lesbianism (perhaps stimulated by the political debates about legalising gay male sex, and concurrent discussion of the social position of women). This followed earlier American work in developing 'scientific' quantitative investigations of lesbians who were not psychiatric patients, comparing them with control groups of 'normal' heterosexual women.

It is relatively straightforward to trace the dominant medical discourses on lesbianism in the twentieth century because they took place in a public professional domain where doctors published books and papers and others responded to them. However an issue that is crucial, but difficult to measure historically, is how widely known these different theories were, and how quickly they were taken up, either in actual medical practice or in common-sense understandings of who the lesbian was and what she did.

1 M. Ryan, *Prostitution in London*, 1839, London: H. Balliere, pp. 178–9

Michael Ryan, a prominent London physician, wrote several books on medico-legal topics. In this book he compared prostitution in London with the situation described in Paris by M. Duchatelet, who estimated that up to one-quarter of Parisian prostitutes had same-sex lovers. In London, Ryan depended largely on information from Mr Talbot, Secretary of the Society for the Prevention of Juvenile Prostitution. Most of this passage is translated from the original Latin.

Tribades. – Mr. Talbot has no information to give on this head such as that offered by M. Duchatelet. Tribades rarely present themselves in our society – from (Gr.) tribade, a woman who exercises her desires on her own sex; 'tribade' means the same as I rub, I smooth down. So tribades can be termed in Latin 'rubbers'. Juvenal, Martial, Horace etc speak about them. Nevertheless, by whatever means, our shameless prostitutes come together in the secret depraved pleasures of lust. 'Examples are rare,' says Mr. Talbot but there are a few new instances and Mr. Pritchard agrees.

2 T. Laycock, *A Treatise on the Nervous Disorders of Women*, 1840, London: Longman and Co., pp. 141, 210

A renowned professor of medicine, Thomas Laycock (1812–1876) had a particular interest in medical psychology and mental diseases. This book, a nineteenth-century classic on female hysteria, was mentioned by Ellis as referring to lesbianism among young women who worked together in confined workshops.

Young females of the same age, and influenced by the same novel feelings towards the opposite sex cannot associate together in public schools without serious risk of exciting the passions, and of being led to indulge in practices injurious to both body and mind. Dr Copland observes that 'whenever numbers associate previous to or about the period of puberty, and especially where several use the same sleeping apartment, and are submitted to a luxurious and over-refined mode of education, some will manifest a precocious developement of both mind and body; but in proportion to precocity will tone and energy be deficient, and susceptibility and sensibility increased.' Frequently, too, the daily exercise is little more than a lounging walk in two and two file, and consequently the sensory system becomes charged (as it were) with excitability, for nothing diminishes the affectability of this system so much as labour, or exalts it so much as indolence.

The consequence of all this is, that the young female returns from school to her home a hysterical, wayward, capricious girl; imbecile in mind, habits, and pursuits; prone to hysteric paroxysms upon any unusual mental excitement. ...

Hysteria is often seen amongst sempstresses, lace-workers, and others of the female population of large towns, confined for many hours daily at sedentary employments, or in heated manufactories; and who, from associating in numbers, excite each other's passions.

3 D. Hack Tuke (ed.), *A Dictionary of Psychological Medicine*, 1892, Vol. II, London: J. & A. Churchill, pp. 1156–7

Tuke (1827–1895) was co-author of *A Manual of Psychological Medicine* (1858), a standard work for decades. Although this later dictionary does not mention women or lesbianism in particular, the entry refers to sexual perversion as a condition that could be experienced by either sex, and indicates the contemporary mainstream medical approach.

SEXUAL PERVERSION – The term 'perverse sexual feeling' (*contrare Sexualempfindung*) was first used by Westphal (in *Archiv f. Psych.*) to express a condition which had already received attention from Casper and others, and which is described as consisting of an innate perversion or 'inversion' of the sexual feelings with consciousness of its morbid nature. It is maintained that in this condition a passion for the sex to which the sufferer belongs, instead of the normal inclination to the opposite sex, exists; and that this is a state which is innate – *i.e.*, appears as early as the dawn of sexual feelings, and remains constant; is in fact, *qua* the individual, a physiological state. The evidence to prove this view, which seems at a first glance so untenable, is derived in part from the statements of persons who have exhibited the symptoms of sexual perversion. These unhappy creatures, for whom the term 'Urnings' was invented by a certain German lawyer who wrote on the subject from personal experience, claim that a large number of the human race are born with this abnormal appetite, and that they have the power throughout life of recognising each other when they meet. Now it is to be observed that the reminiscences and confessions of persons exhibiting sexual disturbance of any kind are notoriously untrustworthy ...

... A more solid argument is derived from the fact that such persons often spring from neurotic families – are themselves neurasthenic, and frequently exhibit temporary or permanent conditions of degenerative mental disturbance. ... The sexual passion at its first appearance is always indefinite, and is very easily turned in a wrong direction. This occurs in ordinary cases of masturbation. As in masturbation, so in other forms of sexual depravity, the vice is more apt to become permanent if it begin early before the higher faculties have developed, and once the vicious habit of mind is definitely organised, development of appetite along the normal lines may fail to take place. Some such explanation as this seems more rational than the belief that an individual is born with the anatomical characteristics of one sex and the mental characteristics of another. Besides, it brings these cases into line with that form of sexual aberration with which we are most familiar, self-abuse. This view is also borne out by the fact that these cases are almost always complicated with it.

4 H. Ellis, *Studies in the Psychology of Sex. Vol. 1. Sexual Inversion*, 1897, London: The University Press, pp. 83–100 *passim*

A late Victorian literary figure, socialist and radical, Havelock Ellis (1859–1939) was the first British doctor to discuss female homosexuality at any length. This extract is from the first edition of *Sexual Inversion*, which became involved in a court case; the publisher was convicted of obscenity. Ellis added more material in later editions which were published in America.

It [homosexuality] is specially fostered by those employments which keep women in constant association not only by day but often at night also, without the company of men. This is, for instance, the case with the female servants in large hotels, among whom homosexual practices have been found very common. Laycock, many years ago, noted the prevalence of manifestations of this kind, which he regarded as hysterical, among seamstresses, lacemakers, etc., confined for long hours in close contact to one another in heated rooms. The circumstances under which numbers of young women are employed during the day in large shops and factories, and sleep in the establishment, two in a room or even two in a bed, are favourable to the development of homosexual practices.

In theatres this cause is associated with the general tendency for homosexuality to be connected with dramatic aptitude, a point to which I shall have to refer later on. I am indebted to a friend for the following note: 'Passionate friendships among girls, from the most innocent to the most elaborate excursions in the direction of Lesbos, are extremely common in theatres, both among actresses and, even more, among chorus and ballet girls. Here the pell-mell of the dressing-rooms, the wait of perhaps two hours between the performances, during which all the girls are cooped up, in a state of inaction and of excitement, in a few crowded dressing-rooms, affords every opportunity for the growth of this particular kind of sentiment. In most of the theatres there is a little circle of girls, somewhat avoided by the others, or themselves careless of further acquaintanceship, who profess the most unbounded devotion to one another. Most of these girls are equally ready to flirt with the opposite sex, but I know certain ones among them who will scarcely speak to a man, and who are never seen without their particular 'pal'

or 'chum', who, if she gets moved to another theatre, will come round and
wait for her friend at the stage-door. But here again it is but seldom that the
experience is carried very far. The fact is that the English girl, especially of
the lower and middle classes, whether she has lost her virtue or not, is
extremely fettered by conventional notions. Ignorance and habit are two
restraining influences from the carrying out of this particular kind of perversion to its logical conclusions. It is, therefore, among the upper ranks, alike
of society and of prostitution, that Lesbianism is most definitely to be met
with, for here we have much greater liberty of action, and much greater
freedom from prejudices.'

...

... In some cases, on the other hand, such relationships [passionate friend-
ships], especially when formed after school life, are fairly permanent. An
energetic emotional woman, not usually beautiful, will perhaps be devoted
to another who may have found some rather specialised life-work but who
may be very unpractical, and who has probably a very feeble sexual instinct;
she is grateful for her friend's devotion, but may not actively reciprocate it.
The actual specific sexual phenomena generated in such cases vary very
greatly. The emotion may be latent or unconscious; it may be all on one side;
it is often more or less recognised and shared. Such cases are on the border-
land of true sexual inversion, but they cannot be included within its region.
Sex in these relationships is scarcely the essential and fundamental element;
it is more or less subordinate and parasitic. There is often a semblance of a
sex relationship from the marked divergence of the friends in physical and
psychic qualities, and the nervous development of one or both the friends is
often slightly abnormal. We have to regard such relationships as hypertro-
phied friendships, the hypertrophy being due to unemployed sexual instinct.

...

A class of women to be first mentioned, a class in which homosexuality,
while fairly distinct, is only slightly marked, is formed by the women to
whom the actively inverted woman is most attracted. These women differ in
the first place from the normal or average woman in that they are not
repelled or disgusted by lover-like advances from persons of their own sex.
They are not usually attractive to the average man, though to this rule there
are many exceptions. Their faces may be plain or ill-made, but not seldom
they possess good figures, a point which is apt to carry more weight with
the inverted woman than beauty of face. Their sexual impulses are seldom
well marked, but they are of strongly affectionate nature. On the whole,
they are women who are not very robust and well-developed, physically or
nervously, and who are not well adapted for child-bearing, but who still
possess many excellent qualities, and they are always womanly. One may
perhaps say that they are the pick of the women whom the average man
would pass by. No doubt this is often the reason why they are open to homosexual advances, but I do not think it is the sole reason. So far as they may

be said to constitute a class, they seem to possess a genuine though not precisely sexual preference for women over men, and it is this coldness rather than lack of charm which often renders men rather indifferent to them.

The actively inverted woman differs from the woman of the class just mentioned in one fairly essential character: a more or less distinct trace of masculinity. She may not be, and frequently is not, what would be called a 'mannish' woman, for the latter may imitate men on grounds of taste and habit unconnected with sexual perversion, while in the inverted woman the masculine traits are part of an organic instinct which she by no means always wishes to accentuate. The inverted woman's masculine element may in the least degree consist only in the fact that she makes advances to the woman to whom she is attracted and treats all men in a cool, direct manner, which may not exclude comradeship, but which excludes every sexual relationship, whether of passion or merely of coquetry. As a rule the inverted woman feels absolute indifference towards men, and not seldom repulsion. And this feeling, as a rule, is instinctively reciprocated by men.

... Notwithstanding these characters, however, sexual inversion in a woman is as a rule not more obvious than in a man. At the same time, the inverted woman is not usually attractive to men. She herself generally feels the greatest indifference to men, and often cannot understand why a woman should love a man, though she easily understands why a man should love a woman. She shows, therefore, nothing of that sexual shyness and engaging air of weakness and dependence which are an invitation to men. ... While the inverted woman is cold, or at most comradely, in her bearing towards men, she may become shy and confused in the presence of attractive persons of her own sex, even unable to undress in their presence, and full of tender ardour for the woman whom she loves.

The passion finds expression in sleeping together, kissing and close embraces, with more or less sexual excitement, the orgasm sometimes occurring when one lies on the other's body; the extreme gratification is *cunnilingus* (*in lambendo lingua genitalis alterius*), sometimes called sapphism. There is no connection, as was once supposed, between sexual inversion in women and an enlarged clitoris, which has very seldom been found in such cases, and never, so far as I am aware, to an extent that would permit of its use in coitus with another woman.

The inverted woman is an enthusiastic admirer of feminine beauty, especially of the statuesque beauty of the body, unlike in this the normal woman whose sexual emotion is but faintly tinged by aesthetic feeling. In her sexual habits we rarely find the degree of promiscuity which is not uncommon among inverted men. I am inclined to agree with Moll that homosexual women love more faithfully and lastingly than homosexual men. ...

It has been stated by many observers who are able to speak with some authority – in America, in France, in Germany, in England – that homosexuality is increasing among women. It seems probable that this is true. There

are many influences in our civilisation to-day which encourage such manifestations. The modern movement of emancipation – the movement to obtain
the same rights and duties, the same freedom and responsibility, the same
education and the same work – must be regarded as, on the whole, a wholesome and inevitable movement. But it carries with it certain disadvantages.
It has involved an increase in feminine criminality and in feminine insanity,
which are being elevated towards the masculine standard. In connection
with these we can scarcely be surprised to find an increase in homosexuality
which has always been regarded as belonging to an allied, if not the same,
group of phenomena. Women are, very justly, coming to look upon knowledge and experience generally as their right as much as their brothers' right.
But when this doctrine is applied to the sexual sphere it finds certain limitations. Intimacies of any kind between young men and young women are as
much discouraged socially now as ever they were; as regards higher education, the mere association of the sexes in the lecture room or the laboratory
or the hospital is discouraged in England and in America. Marriage is
decaying, and while men are allowed freedom, the sexual field of women is
becoming restricted to trivial flirtation with the opposite sex, and to intimacy with their own sex; having been taught independence of men and
disdain for the old theory which placed women in the moated grange of the
home to sigh for a man who never comes, a tendency develops for women to
carry this independence still further and to find love where they find work. I
do not say that these unquestionable influences of modern movements can
directly cause sexual inversion, though they may indirectly, in so far as they
promote hereditary neurosis; but they develop the germs of it, and they
probably cause a spurious imitation. This spurious imitation is due to the
fact that the congenital anomaly occurs with special frequency in women of
high intelligence who, voluntarily or involuntarily, influence others.

5 C.G. Seligmann, 'Sexual Inversion Among Primitive Races', *The Alienist and Neurologist*, Vol. 23, No. 1, 1902, pp. 11–13

Following an important expedition to New Guinea in 1898, Seligmann (1873–1940)
became one of the leading anthropologists of his day, and was later appointed professor
of anthropology at the London School of Economics.

But few details of sexual inversion and perversion are known among savages,
and it is commonly and tacitly assumed that abnormalities of the sexual
instinct are the concomitants of oriental luxury or advanced civilisation.

. . .

A somewhat different condition of things prevails among the Tupi: a
Brazilian tribe in a low stage of civilisation to whom Lomonaco has devoted

considerable attention. While noting that sodomy was prevalent in almost every local tribe, and that a class of men were met with whose function it was to lend themselves to the practice, he states that among the Tupi many women took no husbands, devoting themselves for the whole of their lives to perpetual chastity, and quotes Gandavo to the effect that there are some women among those who decide to be chaste who will not consent to know men even under threats of death. They wear their hair cut in the same fashion as the males, go to war with their bows and arrows, and take part in the chase. They frequent the company of men and each one of them has a woman who waits on her, to whom she says she is married and 'with whom she communicates and converses like man and wife.' It seems probable that here, among a people addicted to sodomy and in whom there is no strong feeling against homo-sexual relations, there is an element of true congenital inversion similar to that present in the sporadic cases among Papuans to be immediately described.

6 S. Freud, 'Female Sexuality', in *On Sexuality, Freud Library Vol.* 7, 1979 [1905], Harmondsworth: Penguin, pp. 374–6

The founding father of psychoanalysis, Freud (1856–1939) developed his ideas about lesbianism further in a later essay, 'The Psychogenesis of a Case of Female Homosexuality' (1920).

First of all, there can be no doubt that the bisexuality, which is present, as we believe, in the innate disposition of human beings, comes to the fore much more clearly in women than in men. A man, after all, has only one leading sexual zone, one sexual organ, whereas a woman has two: the vagina – the female organ proper – and the clitoris, which is analogous to the male organ. We believe we are justified in assuming that for many years the vagina is virtually non-existent and possibly does not produce sensations until puberty. ... In women, therefore, the main genital occurrences of childhood must take place in relation to the clitoris. Their sexual life is regularly divided into two phases, of which the first has a masculine char- acter, while only the second is specifically feminine. Thus in female development there is a process of transition from the one phase to the other, to which there is nothing analogous in the male. A further complication arises from the fact that the clitoris, with its virile character, continues to function in later female sexual life in a manner which is very variable and which is certainly not yet satisfactorily understood. ...

Parallel with this first great difference there is the other, concerned with the finding of the object. In the case of a male, his mother becomes his first love-object as a result of her feeding him and looking after him, and she remains so until she is replaced by someone who resembles her or is derived from her. A female's first object, too, must be her mother: the primary conditions for a choice of object are, of course, the same for all children. But at the end of her development, her father – a man – should have become her new love-object. In other words, to the change in her own sex there must correspond a change in the sex of her object. The new problems that now require investigating are in what way this change takes place, how radically or how incompletely it is carried out, and what the different possibilities are which present themselves in the course of this development.

. . .

Quite different are the effects of the castration complex in the female. She acknowledges the fact of her castration, and with it, too, the superiority of the male and her own inferiority; but she rebels against this unwelcome state of affairs. From this divided attitude three lines of development open up. The first leads to a general revulsion from sexuality. The little girl, frightened by the comparison with boys, grows dissatisfied with her clitoris, and gives up her phallic activity and with it her sexuality in general as well as a good part of her masculinity in other fields. The second line leads her to cling with defiant self-assertiveness to her threatened masculinity. To an incredibly late age she clings to the hope of getting a penis some time. That hope becomes her life's aim; and the phantasy of being a man in spite of everything often persists as a formative factor over long periods. This 'masculinity complex' in women can also result in a manifest homosexual choice of object. Only if her development follows the third, very circuitous, path does she reach the final normal female attitude, in which she takes her father as her object and so finds her way to the feminine form of the Oedipus complex. Thus in women the Oedipus complex is the end-result of a fairly lengthy development. It is not destroyed, but created, by the influence of castration; it escapes the strongly hostile influences which, in the male, have a destructive effect on it, and indeed it is all too often not surmounted by the female at all.

7 E. Carpenter, *Love's Coming-of-Age*, 1915 [1906], London: Methuen, pp. 114–34 *passim*

The work of Edward Carpenter (1844–1929), utopian socialist and himself homosexual, was widely read in the years before World War I. This chapter on same-sex love had previously been privately published in 1895.

The intermediate sex

In late years (and since the arrival of the New Woman amongst us) many things in the relation of men and women to each other have altered, or at any rate become clearer. The growing sense of equality in habits and customs – university studies, art, music, politics, the bicycle, etc. – all these things have brought about a *rapprochement* between the sexes. ...

We all know women with a strong dash of the masculine temperament, and we all know men whose almost feminine sensibility and intuition seem to belie their bodily form. Nature, it might appear, in mixing the elements which go to compose each individual, does not always keep her two groups of ingredients – which represent the two sexes – properly apart, but often throws them crosswise in a somewhat baffling manner, now this way and now that; yet wisely, we must think – for if a severe distinction of elements were always maintained, the two sexes would soon drift into far latitudes and absolutely cease to understand each other. As it is, there are some remarkable and (we think) indispensable types of character, in whom there is such a union of balance of the feminine and masculine qualities that these people become to a great extent the interpreters of men and women to each other.

...

More than thirty years ago, however, an Austrian writer, K.H. Ulrichs, drew attention in a series of pamphlets (*Memnon*, *Ara Spei*, *Inclusa*, etc.) to the existence of a class of people who strongly illustrate the above remarks, and with whom specially this paper is concerned. He pointed out that there were people born in such a position – as it were on the dividing line between the sexes – that while belonging distinctly to one sex as far as their bodies are concerned they may be said to belong *mentally* and *emotionally* to the other; that there were men, for instance, who might be described as of feminine soul enclosed in a male body (*anima muliebris in corpore virili inclusa*), or in other cases, women whose definition would be just the reverse. And he maintained that this doubleness of nature was to a great extent proved by the special direction of their love-sentiment. For in such cases, as indeed might be expected, the (apparently) masculine person instead of forming a love-union with a female tended to contract romantic friendships with one of his own sex; while the apparently feminine would, instead of marrying in the usual way, devote herself to the love of another feminine.

People of this kind (i.e., having this special variation of the love-sentiment) he called Urnings; and though we are not obliged to accept his theory about the crosswise connexion between 'soul' and 'body,' since at best these words are somewhat vague and indefinite; yet his work was important because it was one of the first attempts, in modern times, to recognise the existence of what might be called an Intermediate sex, and to give at any rate *some* explanation of it.

...

Contrary to the general impression, one of the first points that emerges from this study is that 'Urnings,' or Uranians, are by no means so very rare; but that they form, beneath the surface of society, a large class. It remains difficult, however, to get an exact statement of their numbers. ...

In the second place it emerges (also contrary to the general impression) that men and women of the exclusive Uranian type are by no means necessarily morbid in any way – unless, indeed, their peculiar temperament be pronounced in itself morbid. Formerly it was assumed, as a matter of course, that the type was merely a result of disease and degeneration; but now with the examination of the actual facts it appears that, on the contrary, many are fine, healthy specimens of their sex, muscular and well-developed in body, of powerful brain, high standard of conduct, and with nothing abnormal or morbid of any kind observable in their physical structure or constitution.

... It is also worth noticing that it is now acknowledged that even in the most healthy cases the special affectional temperament of the 'Intermediate' is, as a rule, ineradicable; so much so that when (as in not a few instances) such men and women, from social or other considerations, have forced themselves to marry, and even have children, they have still not been able to overcome their own bias, or the leaning after all of their life-attachment to some friend of their own sex.

... It would be a great mistake to suppose that their attachments are necessarily sexual, or connected with sexual acts. On the contrary (as abundant evidence shows), they are often purely emotional in their character; and to confuse Uranians (as is so often done) with libertines having no law but curiosity in self-indulgence is to do them a great wrong. At the same time, it is evident that their special temperament may often cause them difficulty in regard to their sexual relations. Into this subject we need not now enter. But we may point out how hard it is, especially for the young among them, that a veil of complete silence should be drawn over the subject, leading to the most painful misunderstandings, and perversions and confusions of mind; and that there should be no hint of guidance; nor any recognition of the solitary and really serious inner struggles they may have to face! ... I have thought it might be advisable in this paper simply to give a few general characteristics of the Intermediate types.

As indicated then already, in bodily structure there is no point which will certainly distinguish the subjects of our discussion from ordinary men and women; but if we take the general mental characteristics it appears from almost universal testimony that the male tends to be of a rather gentle, emotional disposition – with defects, if such exist, in the direction of subtlety, evasiveness, timidity, vanity etc.; while the female is just the opposite – fiery, active, bold and truthful, with defects running to brusqueness and coarseness. Moreover, the mind of the former is generally intuitive and instinctive in its perceptions, with more or less of artistic feeling; while the mind of the latter is more logical, scientific, and precise than usual with the normal woman.

...

It appears that the loves of such women are often very intense, and (as also in the case of male Urnings) life-long. Both classes feel themselves blessed when they love happily. Nevertheless, to many of them it is a painful fact that – in consequence of their peculiar temperament – they are, though fond of children, not in a position to found a family.

We have so far limited ourselves to some very general characteristics of the Intermediate race. It may help to clear and fix our ideas if we now describe more in detail, first what may be called the extreme and exaggerated types of the race, and then the more normal and perfect types. By doing so we shall get a more definite and concrete view of our subject.

...

[A]s the extreme type of the homogenic female, we have a rather markedly aggressive person, of strong passions, masculine manners and movements, practical in the conduct of life, sensuous rather than sentimental in love, often untidy, and *outre* in attire; her figure muscular, her voice rather low in pitch; her dwelling-room decorated with sporting-scenes, pistols etc., and not without a suspicion of the fragrant weed in the atmosphere; while her love (generally to rather soft and feminine specimens of her own sex) is often a sort of furor, similar to the ordinary masculine love, and at times almost uncontrollable.

These are types which, on account of their salience, everyone will recognise more or less. ... But in reality, of course, these extreme developments are rare, and for the most part the temperament in question is embodied in men and women of quite normal and unsensational exterior. ... And it may be supposed that we may draw the same conclusion with regard to women of this class – namely, that the majority of them do not exhibit pronounced masculine habits.

...

To come now to the more normal and perfect specimens of the homogenic woman, we find a type in which the body is thoroughly feminine and gracious, with the rondure and fulness of the female form, and the continence and aptness of its movements, but in which the inner nature is to a great extent masculine; a temperament active, brave, originative, somewhat decisive, not too emotional; fond of outdoor life, of games and sports, of science, politics, or even business; good at organisation, and well-pleased with positions of responsibility, sometimes indeed making an excellent and generous leader. Such a woman, it is easily seen, from her special combination of qualities, is often fitted for remarkable work, in professional life, or as manageress of institutions, or even as ruler of a country. Her love goes out to younger and more feminine natures than her own; it is a powerful passion, almost of heroic type, and capable of inspiring to great deeds; and when held duly in leash may sometimes become an invaluable force in the teaching and training of girlhood, or in the creation of a school of thought or action among women. Many a Santa Clara, or abbess-founder of religious houses, has probably been a woman of this type; and in all times such women – not being bound to men by the ordinary ties – have been able to work the more freely for the interests of their sex, a cause to which their own temperament impels them to devote themselves *con amore*. ... Of the latter and more normal types it may be said that they exist, and have always existed, in considerable abundance, and from that circumstance alone there is a strong probability that they have their place and purpose. ...

The instinctive artistic nature of the male of this class, his sensitive spirit, his wavelike emotional temperament, combined with hardihood of intellect and body; and the frank, free nature of the female, her masculine independence and strength wedded to thoroughly feminine grace of form and manner; may be said to give them both, through their double nature, command of life in all its phases, and a certain freemasonry of the secrets of the two sexes which may well favour their function as reconcilers and interpreters. Certainly it is remarkable that some of the world's greatest leaders and artists have been dowered either wholly or in part with the Uranian temperament – as in the cases of Michel Angelo, Shakespeare, Marlowe, Alexander the Great, Julius Caesar, or, among women, Christine of Sweden, Sappho the poetess, and others.

8 F.W.S. Browne, *The Sexual Variety and Variability Among Women*, 1917, London: British Society for the Study of Sex Psychology

Stella Browne (1880–1955) was best known for her radical activism in campaigns for birth control and abortion, and her feminist views on women's sexuality. This essay was first given as a paper to the British Society for the Study of Sex Psychology in 1915.

Artificial or substitute homosexuality – as distinct from true inversion – is very widely diffused among women, as a result of the repression of normal gratification and the segregation of the sexes, which still largely obtains. It appears, I think, later in life than onanism; in the later twenties or thirties rather than in the teens. Sometimes its only direct manifestations are quite noncommittal and platonic; but even this incomplete and timid homosexuality can always be distinguished from true affectionate friendship between women, by its jealous, exacting and extravagant tone. Of course, when one of the partners in such an attachment is a real or congenital invert, it is at once much more serious and much more physical. The psychology of homogenic women has been much less studied than that of inverted men. Probably there are many varieties and subtleties of emotional fibre among them. Some very great authorities have believed that the inverted woman is more often bisexual – less exclusively attracted to other women – than the inverted man. This view needs very careful confirmation, but if true, it would prove the greater plasticity of women's sex-impulse. It has also been stated that the invert, man or woman, is drawn towards the normal types of their own sex. These and other points, should be elucidated by the Society's work. Certainly, the heterosexual woman of passionate but shy and sensitive nature, is often responsive to the inverted woman's advances, especially if she is erotically ignorant and inexperienced. Also many women of quite normally directed (heterosexual) inclinations, realise in mature life, when they have experienced passion, that the devoted admiration and friendship they felt for certain girl friends, had a real, though perfectly unconscious spark of desire in its exaltation and intensity; an unmistakable, indefinable note, which was absolutely lacking in many equally sincere and lasting friendships.

Neither artificial homosexuality nor prolonged auto-eroticism – to use Havelock Ellis' masterly phrase – prove *innate* morbidity. Careful observation and many confidences from members of my own sex, have convinced me that our maintenance of outworn traditions is manufacturing habitual auto-erotists and perverts, out of women who would instinctively prefer the love of a man, who would bring them sympathy and comprehension as well as desire. I repudiate all wish to slight or depreciate the love-life of the real homosexual; but it cannot be advisable to force the growth of that habit in heterosexual people. ...

9 B. Hollander, *The Psychology of Misconduct, Vice and Crime*, 1922, London: George Allen and Unwin Ltd, pp. 141, 144

Bernard Hollander had studied under Krafft-Ebing in Vienna and subsequently worked in London psychiatric hospitals. He wrote popular books on psychopathology and psychotherapy.

Sexual perverseness

Sexual inversion or homosexuality, i.e. sexual predilection for the same sex, is frequent both in males and females. Homosexual tendencies appear sometimes in early youth and adolescence, but do not persist when rightly guided by experience and education in the widest sense of these words. ...

Unsuspecting parents are little aware how common homosexuality is among women, and how many little girls get seduced to the practice. The female Lesbian pervert may also be divided into two classes: the woman who seeks other women in order to carry out upon them male actions, and frequently delights in imitating male attire and male habits; and the passive woman who accepts the ardent caresses of other females. I have known a fashionable girls' school in London to be closed in consequence of the discovery of the degrading and criminal habits of the head-mistress who for years had seduced one girl after another.

If a homosexual male or female will volunteer to come for treatment, there is hope for them; but of the dozens that have consulted me only very few came a second time and kept up their attendance.

10 A.C. Magian, *Sex Problems in Women*, 1922, London: William Heinemann (Medical Books) Ltd, pp. 4, 105–10

Magian was a gynaecologist and venereologist.

Psychically, man and woman are absolutely different, physically they are different also. Each is dependent upon the other, and each plays a different part in the life-history of the human species. Woman's part should be that of taking care of the home, developing the love instinct in herself and her natural mate, and bringing up her children. If she despises this part and prefers to adopt that which is usually considered to be the prerogative of the male, she will have to face the prospect of non-success and pay the price with a disordered mind and body. It is the experience of many gynaecologists and others that women who go to extremes in the way of 'independence' are frequently the subjects of sexual abnormalities or deficiencies, or have so peculiarly constituted a nervous system as to be led away by their imagination beyond the control of common sense and reason.

...

One condition which is difficult of explanation is homosexuality, where an apparently normally-formed healthy and intelligent female is attracted not by the opposite sex but by her own. Whilst inclined to regard this also as due to mental causes, it must be admitted that sometimes one can obtain no certain evidence of such, and that possibly the glands of internal secretion may be at fault or that in some way the sexual organs are abnormally constituted or defective. Proof of these conditions is naturally almost impossible, since both endocrinous glands and internal sexual organs are hidden from view during life and autopsies of such cases are scarcely ever obtainable.

It is important to remember that sexual impulses of all kinds are intimately connected with certain areas in the cortex of the brain. There is, in fact, a cerebral centre which controls these impulses and which is stimulated to activity both by mental impressions and by the action of nerves connected with the genital organs, the breasts and certain other parts of the body. It will thus be seen that if the cerebral centre is defective or difficult to arouse, or where the conducting tracts are defective or blocked in some way, sexual impulses may be entirely wanting or deficient or irregular.

In the young girl the cerebral sex-centre is more or less dormant unless it has been unnaturally stimulated; and in the elderly woman atrophy and disuse of the sexual organs put an end to peripheral stimuli, whilst the centre itself is also practically inactive. Apart from the natural influence of age, certain diseases and morbid states of the body produce a dulling of the centre and a failure in the conducting tracts. Thus, alcoholism, drug habits, sexual excesses, general weakness, obesity, diabetes, serious organic maladies and degenerative changes in the brain and spinal cord may all greatly diminish sexual desires. But in some instances these conditions, although diminishing normal sexual desires, tend to produce an inclination for abnormal forms of sexual gratification. This has been explained as due to irritation of the sexual centre produced by impoverished blood plus irregular nerve conduction. There is doubtless a good deal to be said in support of this view, but it will be understood that absolute proof is wanting and that it is nothing more than a theory.

Abnormal sexual impulses have also been associated with deficient development of the uterus and annexa, and many authorities attach considerable importance to this, and also to malformations, malpositions and chronic inflammatory states of both internal and external generative organs. The main source of sexual perversions, however, is the force of corrupt example upon weak-willed persons. It is improbable that these two factors are ever absent in a well-marked case, but it must be understood that 'example' is meant to include not only what is seen, but what is heard, read, or otherwise conveyed to the intelligence.

...

In cases of apparently true sexual perversion where the woman inclines only towards persons of her own sex, she is designated as homosexual (urnindes). Such women engage in various forms of abnormal practices with other females (Uranism, Tribadism, Lesbianism). Tribadism consists in mutual masturbation, or if the one woman has a sufficiently enlarged clitoris, in the introduction of this organ into the vagina of the other. The so-called Lesbian love is a lingual excitation of the vulva, and is supposed to have been practised in ancient times by the women of Lesbos – hence the name. Intercourse by means of an artificial phallus made to represent the male organ and attached by bands to the genital organs of the woman assuming the man's part, is a third form of obtaining sexual gratification which has been adopted. Very elaborate articles of this nature have been described, and it would appear that their use was common amongst the ancient Greeks, and that even at the present day specimens are not unobtainable in the large towns of various countries. Von Maschka describes an indiarubber apparatus resembling in shape and size the male penis and testicles: it could be filled with warm milk and the contents expressed by pressure so as to counterfeit an ejaculation. To the various forms of artificial penes the appellations of godemiches, dildoes, bijoux indiscrets, consolateurs, etc., were given.

...

A confirmed tribadist is a most dangerous member of society. She is capable of perverting any number of innocent young girls and even children. She herself is usually a neurasthenic individual, irresponsible, hysterical and often mentally deranged. When not belonging to the prostitute class, she forms violent attachments to the partner of her perverted pleasures, is maniacally jealous if any other woman or man comes between them and will stop at no crime to prevent her 'friend' from leaving her or marrying. She adopts a peculiar jargon to express the bodily and mental charms of her 'friend,' and generally behaves as though she were a young man violently in love with some beautiful and adorable woman. Balzac's novel *La Fille aux Yeux d'Or* deals with this kind of vice, and numerous other authors have referred to it in unequivocal terms. The whole subject is repugnant in the extreme to the normally minded individual, but it is certainly necessary that the practising physician and the lawyer should be well posted in the details of this particular form of sex perversion.

11 M. Stopes, *Enduring Passion*, 1928, Hogarth Press, pp. 29–31

Marie Stopes wrote a number of marital sex advice books following the huge success of *Married Love* (1918) and was the best known interwar advocate of birth control. While she strongly condemned lesbianism – below she gives a 'scientific' justification for its abnormality as a sexual practice – she herself had crushes on older women when in her twenties.

Another practical solution which some deprived women find is in Lesbian love with their own sex. The other, and quite correct, name for what is now so often euphemistically called Lesbian love is homosexual vice. It is so much practised nowadays, particularly by the 'independent' type of woman, that I run a risk of being attacked because I call the thing by its correct name. One of the physical results of such unnatural relations is the gradual accustoming of the system to reactions which are arrived at by a different process from that for which the parts were naturally formed. This tends to unfit women for real union. If a married woman does this unnatural thing she may find a growing disappointment in her husband and he may lose all natural power to play his proper part. ... No woman who values the peace of her home and the love of her husband should yield to the wiles of the Lesbian whatever the temptation to do so.

A very *very* few women have strong inborn tendencies of this type; most of those now indulging in the vice drifted into it lazily or out of curiosity and allowed themselves to be corrupted. This corruption spreads as an underground fire spreads in the peaty soil of a dry moorland. Men with an excess of the 'feminine' qualities and 'masculine' women are, by the inherent bias given to their emotions by their physical equipment, very liable to enter into some degree or other of the many possible relationships with their own accredited sex. They may marry and yet have disastrous homosexual entanglements. Phases of the problems raised by such people seem to me to call for recognition, yet they lead us away from the theme of this book into difficult realms. I do not want to discuss homosexuality. Nevertheless I do want people to understand what seems to me a vital scientific argument against it untinged with any of the old-fashioned objections now so often repudiated. The bedrock objection to it is surely that women can only *play* with each other and *cannot* in the very nature of things have natural union or supply each other with the seminal and prostatic secretions which they ought to have, and crave for unconsciously. The same applies to self-masturbation.

Hence, homosexual excitement does not really meet their need, for the physiological fact (I have never yet seen it clearly stated anywhere, but it is of the greatest importance in a consideration of this problem) that, apart from the kisses, endearment, flattery, and love-making from her husband, a woman's need and *hunger* for nourishment in sex union is a true physiological hunger to be satisfied only by the supplying of the actual molecular substances lacked by her system. Lesbian love, as the alternative, is NOT a real equivalent and merely soothes perhaps and satisfies no more than the surface nervous excitement. It does not, and by its nature it never can, supply the actual physiological nourishment, the chemical molecules produced by the accessory glandular systems of the male. These are supplied to the woman's system when the normal act of union is experienced, and the man's secretions are deposited in her body together with the semen.

12 L. Hutton, *The Single Woman and her Emotional Problems*, 1935, London: Bailliere, Tindall and Cox, pp. 40–3, 86–7, 91–2, 101–4, 105–6

Laura Hutton was a psychiatrist at the Tavistock Institute, and her work challenged both orthodox Freudianism and sexology. In her chapter on sexual inversion, Hutton discussed both 'congenital' and 'psychogenic' theories of lesbianism, and argued that at this stage of knowledge all theories must be tentative.

Emotional friendships

... When two women decide to set up house together, they lack all social support, and their proposal is of significance only to the friends themselves. There is, of course, no contract of mutual obligation; no sympathy, approval or even interest is expected. There is no social recognition at all. ... Such partnerships in living, then, get nothing comparable with the hopeful start of every normal marriage, although they may, and often do, represent what has been called the 'major relationship' of two women's lives. ...

To many, no doubt, it will seem almost grotesque to compare two women's decision to throw in their lot together with a marriage between a man and a woman, and it will be thought that one can only be referring to definitely homosexual women. To such women certainly the situation does *feel* comparable to marriage; but in these days many women are driven, consciously or unconsciously, by the circumstances of their lives and their need for some more personal contact and intimacy than their work provides, to set up house with a congenial friend, and it scarcely seems an exaggeration, in view of the inevitability and magnitude of the emotional task that such a partnership will have to tackle, to compare it with a marriage. No plea is being made here for the institution of anything like a marriage contract between women friends, or for a marriage ceremony! All that is intended is to suggest the part that total lack of sense of social sympathy and significance may play in the transitoriness of women's intimate friendships and partnerships.

...

Sex in women's friendships

... It has already been suggested that sexuality may play a part in an intimate friendship between two women without their being aware of the fact. This must very often be the case, especially when the two friends live together and are in constant physical association, neither of them having any natural or direct outlet for the sexual part of their natures. The results of such *unrecognised* sexual stimulation are bound to be unfortunate. Tension and irritability will follow, on a substratum of perplexity, resentment and vague guilty feeling, the last particularly if the sexual nature of the emotional-*cum*-physical excitement is dimly divined. The first prerequisite for the management of the sexual element in any friendship is its frank recognition and acceptance. Nor is it to be regarded with horror and disgust. It offers certainly a problem to be worked out with care, but it is not necessarily something to be eradicated, root and branch, without further consideration. Dr. Esther Harding has said in her book, *The Way of All Women* (and she also urges the frank discussion of the sexual element in women's friendships), ' ... love between women friends may find its expression in a more specifically sexual fashion which, however, cannot be considered perverted if their actions are motivated by love.' This surely suggests a sound general principle in considering the problem of sexual relations between women. ...

The physical aspect

... One must, however, also consider this question from the point of view of sexual morality. Here the criticism is likely to arise that any mutual sexual stimulation between women must be bad (quite apart from being perverse), because the sexual organs are being used purely for the purpose of pleasure, and without any connection with their biological purpose – that of reproduction. Here, it seems, we come ... to general principles of sexual morality common to both hetero- and homo-sexuality. It is absurd to say that all heterosexual caresses are intended to lead up to the act of procreation. Biologically it may be so, but in fact such an issue is the exception rather than the rule. The sexual act may be completed, but the impregnation of the woman is not thought of as its end, and more than probably means have been taken to prevent such a result. In heterosexual relations, that they should be the natural expression of *love* is the utmost that a morality of personal integrity (as distinct from social or conventional morality) demands, and this is surely the criterion that demands consideration in homosexual relations. ...

The social aspect

... [W]hat of the case of two mature women, with knowledge of life and of themselves, who may, in the course and development of an intimate friendship, come to sexual expression of their love for one another? Surely it may be left to them to work this out along their own lines, with mutual respect and consideration – reassured as to the physical harmlessness of genital caresses,* if they have the impulse to such, under the conditions described. As to the emotional aspect of this physical expression of love, one may be perhaps allowed even to suggest that nothing but good need come from such a relationship, providing guilt, anxiety and conflict are absent, and the only desire is to give pleasure and relief from tension, as an expression of love and tenderness. These are, one must emphasise, extremely stringent conditions, but in so far as the sexual relations in a friendship of this kind are the expression of such intentions they raise the masturbatory act from a purely auto-erotic, or at least self-centred, act to something more nearly approaching the normal use of sexual impulses, and they may thereby contribute, in a way that is entirely useful and constructive, to the solving of the problem of the unmarried woman's frustrated biological fulfilment. To say this (and to many people it will be already saying outrageously too much) is not by any means an attempt to give such sexual friendships a higher place in the solution of the problem of women's loneliness than friendships in which no such element enters or is dreamt of. As has been suggested, only women to some extent sexually inverted, or at least bi-sexually inclined, are likely to find their way to such a sexual expression of their love for one another. All that is intended is a suggestion that friendships between responsible women of the type just described – i.e., involving (perhaps only very occasionally) some sexual expression – may indeed play quite a useful part in society at the present day. It is said, moreover, in view of present-day conditions, where the surplus of women, and our marriage laws and customs, make it impossible for very large numbers of women to find their natural biological fulfilment. Such women have a difficult enough task in the adjustment of their emotional and physical natures. If some of them, being mature and responsible women, come to the solution of the problem which we have described, it may be that a society, whether it regards them with sympathy and respect or with horror and contempt, will ultimately benefit; but the benefit will be greater if the former rather than the latter attitude is adopted.

* Again the reservation may be made in regard to the use of any instrument, though it is not likely that the single-hearted impulse of love would prompt to such manipulations.

Sexual inversion

... It is only within recent years that the subject of sexual inversion or homosexuality has become a topic of frequent discussion in certain sections of society. At the present time references to it in novels and plays are indeed constantly made. So much so that one is asked if homosexuality is actually more common now than it was. I should say that the answer to this question is in the negative so far as homosexual tendency is concerned. What has happened, it seems to me, is that, with the recent growth of freedom and of thought in regard to sexual questions, homosexual tendencies are now more often recognised as such. A self-consciousness has appeared on the one hand in the victims of this abnormality, so that there are a larger number of conscious, and fewer 'innocent,' homosexuals than there were; and at the same time friendly couples of the same sex are now much more readily suspected of homosexual tendencies than would have been the case, say, twenty years ago.

13 C. Allen, *The Sexual Perversions and Abnormalities*, 1940, Oxford: Oxford University Press, pp. 124–6

Clifford Allen wrote several medical books on sexuality and psychology. He treated the case he described here while working at the Tavistock Clinic. In the late 1950s he was Consultant Psychiatrist to the Dreadnought Seamen's Hospital, Greenwich.

Case 3. A case of homosexuality, with neurotic symptoms in a woman

This case was that of a young woman aged 23 years. She complained of various hysterical symptoms – 'neuralgia' pains in the hip, abdominal pain, and backache. She had attacks of depression in which she found it was difficult to speak to others and noticed that there was a strong tendency *to fall in love with women* – particularly the women with whom she worked (she was a nursemaid). She felt hostile to the children placed in her care and was frequently unkind to them, although she was not sure why she behaved in this way. She had no gross glandular disease but did show a little fine down on her upper lip, such as one frequently finds in normal women.

Her family history was a bad one. Her father had been a drunkard and had injured one of her two brothers while drunk, and had been sentenced to imprisonment as a consequence. Her sister had had treatment for a neurosis.

The patient had had a number of homosexual attractions, including a nurse in hospital and fellow servants. Her personality showed some homosexual traits – she dressed in a somewhat severe masculine fashion and showed a quite exceptional wish to ride, and in order to indulge it had saved for many months to buy a riding outfit (she rode astride) and spent a week's wages on an hour's ride. She did not use cosmetics and was not fond of feminine pleasures.

Treatment lasted a year and she was seen twice weekly. It was found that she was trying to reproduce in her ordinary life the situation in which she found herself when a child. The children she had to take care of represented her brothers and sister (whom she had hated), but the woman for whom she felt such strong attraction represented not her mother but her father. Her mother and she had never loved, and she filled the patient with distrust and dislike. Fortunately this patient tended to 'dissociate', and while in a hypnoid state would produce memories which would have been otherwise inaccessible. She would go into this state a few minutes after treatment commenced at each session, and talk for a full hour without the analyst saying anything, so that suggestion was practically eliminated. Her speech was often childish and approximated to the period she was talking about – usually early childhood. She brought up intense emotion regarding her father and talked passionately of him for long periods at a time. This material suggested that her father when drunk had stirred her sexuality by touching her vagina and so on. She appeared to have her homosexuality based on a frank Oedipus situation and slowly swung round from homosexuality to heterosexuality. She did this by means of her male employers, whom she went out of her way to seduce and did have intercourse with one. She had a year's treatment, but at the end of it she found it very difficult to control her newly discovered heterosexuality and had liaisons with various men. In order to try to control this excessive sexuality she had a short course of treatment under another psychotherapist (the writer was unable to spare the time to treat her during this period). She finally married and has settled down more or less contentedly to married life.

This case is one of great interest. Here we have a girl who was strongly homosexual and who was converted to heterosexuality by the release of her deep attachment to her father. It would seem that the mechanism of her homosexuality was as follows: she was the eldest child and was exceptionally attached to her father, who was very fond of her when she was first born. On the other hand, she was exceptionally hostile and jealous of her mother and brothers and sisters whom she regarded as likely to deprive her of her father's affection. When her father returned from the War he had changed considerably and was drinking heavily. He was then unkind to her, and this increased the longing for his affection. As it was hopeless to obtain it from him, however, she tried to obtain it from other women as a substitute for him. Those women with whom she fell in love represented him, and it was impossible for her to mate with a man until this emotion had been dispelled and she was released from it. This emotion when it was released was so intense that it was not immediately easily controlled. The remarkable thing is the complete change which was brought about by the psychotherapy. This was only possible because she was driven on by her painful symptoms and shows clearly that the presence of painful symptoms gives one a much greater chance in curing a homosexual than if it is absent. Naturally enough these symptoms disappeared completely after treatment.

14 K. Walker, *The Physiology of Sex*, 1940, Harmondsworth: Penguin, pp. 144–5

Kenneth Walker (1882–1966) was a prominent urologist and a pioneer of sex education and marriage guidance.

Nor is the trafficker in woman-flesh the only factor in prostitution that must be dealt with. Poverty and poor conditions of living, slums, unemployment, drunkenness, and mental deficiency all tend to swell the unhappy army of prostitution. It is not from any innate wish of their own, but from necessity that most women enter this profession. Indeed, psychological investigation has shown that, far from being over-sexed, the majority of prostitutes are under-sexed. Many of them are even homosexual, with no feeling whatever for men. Winifred Richmond states that 'not infrequently a girl sex-delinquent is a girl struggling against homosexual tendencies, who chooses relations with boys as the lesser of two evils.' 'In an effort to assure herself of her normality she becomes promiscuous.'

15 A.L. Winner, 'Homosexuality in Women', *The Medical Press*, Vol. 218, No. 10 (No. 5652), 3 September 1947, pp. 219–20

One of the most distinguished medical women of her generation, Albertine Winner

(1907–1988) was chief woman doctor to the women's services during World War II, with special responsibility for the health of the ATS. After the war she became deputy chief medical officer at the Ministry of Health.

... Probably the psychological mechanism underlying male and female homosexuality is the same, though its manifestations are so different. In dealing with large numbers of Lesbians one of the most striking things is the recurrent traits of immaturity, mainly emotional, but showing themselves in many unexpected ways, that one meets in women of high intellectual or artistic development. This certainly bears out the view that the homosexual relation is an immature one, an arrest of normal sexual development at an adolescent stage.

There are, of course, two categories of female homosexuals, clinically quite distinct and probably aetiologically different. On the one hand you have the woman who tends to prefer the society of women, to have strong female friendships and only detached relations with men; there is every grade from the harmless and usually quite unconscious friendship to the real love affair with or without physical love-making, but the relationships are sincere, often extremely faithful and showing many of the finer attributes of normal heterosexual love without, of course, its final satisfaction in procreation. Such relationships are only anti-social in their sterilisation of two women and are otherwise harmful only to the individuals concerned. There is, however, a second and much more dangerous type, the promiscuous Lesbian who, passing quickly and lightly from affair to affair, usually with physical relations, may cause great harm and unhappiness. Such women are usually dominant and forceful personalities and may often seduce weaker and more pliable women who are otherwise perfectly normal heterosexuals. Some are psychopathic heterosexuals themselves (or rather, bisexuals) who, bored and dissatisfied with promiscuous and purely sensual relations with men, take to going with women in an effort to find novelty and satisfaction. It is with them that we find the grosser perversions and elaborate physical practices, not with the general run of Lesbians. Fortunately, they are rare birds and such cases, at any rate in this country, are relatively very rare.

This brings me to one of the surprising and little recognised characteristics of Lesbianism, at any rate as we see it to-day. The great majority of homosexual relations among women, including many of the true 'love affairs,' are not associated with anything that could be described as sexual intercourse. There may be a good deal of love-making, caressing, love-play, but mutual masturbation, any real attempt at producing orgasm, is not at all common. Whether this makes the condition better or worse from a moral and social point of view is not for a doctor to say, but it certainly helps from a psychological point of view as preventing the development of the guilt complexes that appear to occur so frequently in men. Many Lesbians, even if they realise what they are and the nature of their relationship, appear sincerely convinced that there is nothing wrong and that society has no right to condemn them.

Many anti-social activities practised by male homosexuals are almost unknown among women. Though the schoolgirl 'crush' is very common and may lead to the tragic situations described in 'Mädchen in Uniform' and 'Regiment of Women,' what may be described as the 'Choir-boy Syndrome' is practically non-existent. Little girls fortunately do not seem to have the attraction for their own sex that little boys do. From this, perhaps the most anti-social of all male homosexual perversions, women are mercifully exempt.

The comparative rarity of promiscuous Lesbianism results in another difference – the absence of prostitution. I believe in Berlin before the last war there were certain female prostitutes who specialised in women, but then vice in Berlin was on an entirely different scale from anywhere else. As far as I have been able to ascertain there are very few, if any, female prostitutes in London who go with women. Thus the second main anti-social activity of the male homosexual is also not associated with women. The reason lies almost certainly in the relatively small place actual physical relations takes with Lesbians. Love-making, which is the most important part, requires a partner who is lovable and likeable, qualities apparently unimportant to the promiscuous male.

From both the above characteristics comes the fact that Lesbianism was not an important problem in the Women's Services. The problem was dealt with in a very sensible way and every effort was made to avoid magnifying it, for gossip and scare-mongering are far more dangerous than the unfortunate Lesbians themselves. In one Service a wise and sensible memorandum was written by the then Senior Woman Medical Officer which was available as required. A certain number of minor cases arose of unwise friendships, most of which were dealt with by judicious posting of the culprits. A very small number indeed of serious cases came to light, mostly centring round a promiscuous psychopath, and, in the same Service, only some half-dozen women had to be discharged on these grounds out of nearly a quarter of a million who passed through our hands. This is a very remarkable record and I want to emphasise that it is not due to ignorance of the possibilities, though there certainly was a very sensible awareness of when action was and was not required.

These few notes are entirely derived from a non-psychiatric clinical practice which happened to include a considerable number of Lesbians, and from Service experience. I am fully aware that they represent an unorthodox point of view, quite different from that found in the standard works on sexual anomalies. But the authors of these works are invariably men, and I submit that the Lesbian seldom consults a man on these matters and never talks freely to him. One day a work on this subject must be written by a woman, after careful investigation and research. Meanwhile these remarks are offered very tentatively as a preliminary approach to the subject.

16 E. Chesser, *Sexual Behaviour, Normal and Abnormal,* 1949, London: Medical Publications Ltd, pp. ix, 164

Eustace Chesser (1902–1973), psychiatrist and social reformer, is best known for *Love Without Fear* (1941) and later books on sexual pleasure in marriage. He supported the decriminalisation of abortion and male homosexuality. This diatribe against women who repudiate motherhood can be seen in the context of post-war pro-natalism.

... Finally, this book has been written to provide an answer to the demands of the more extreme feminists who advocate a course which must inevitably set women at war with their own nature and which, indeed, cannot be carried to its logical conclusion unless women deliberately turn their backs upon their maternal instinct. ... The rejection of the maternal role is not included in the familiar lists of perversions which appear in the text-books – yet it is *the greatest perversion of all.*

Auto-matricidism: the maternal rejection pattern

Classifications of women

In the main, those who have made this unconscious decision may be placed in one or another of three categories, each large enough to contain many different individual emotional types.

Group (A) includes those who not only reject feminine attitudes but wish to adopt masculine attitudes and who may be lesbians.

Group (B) consists of those who repudiate their feminine sexuality, but go no further.

In Group (C) are the women who renounce anything and everything to do with the maternal role, yet in all other respects adopt feminine attitudes. There are many 'shadings' in this group.

Group A. The women in this group wish they were men. At an early stage of growth they tended to reject the feminine role. The mother-pattern, as seen through their infant eyes, seemed entirely unsatisfactory, with the result that they turned away from it and chose, instead, to model their lives so far as possible on that of their fathers. The group includes practising lesbians who adopt the active role, but it is not confined to lesbians.

Such women are naturally very sensitive to all that tends to reinforce their essentially masculine attitude, and they find much to strengthen their dislike of everything feminine, although in many cases they reach adulthood without realizing that their outlook is distinctly masculine. In adult life, however, they find themselves increasingly withdrawing from feminine pursuits and preferring masculine attitudes, so that sooner or later they usually come to realize that theirs is really a masculine outlook. Often they glory in this; but sometimes feelings of guilt or unworthiness cause them to strive to conceal their masculine outlook as far as possible.

17 British Medical Association, *Homosexuality and Prostitution, A Memorandum of Evidence Prepared by a Special Committee of the Council of the British Medical Association for Submission to the Departmental Committee on Homosexuality and Prostitution*, 1955, London: British Medical Association, pp. 18–19, 48–9

The section on female homosexuality of the BMA evidence to the Wolfenden Committee was drafted by a separate committee of women doctors from the Medical Women's Federation, only one of whom was on the main BMA Committee. The paragraphs on female homosexuality were much more positive than the discussion of male homosexuality, which was strongly associated with sex in public places.

Homosexuality in females

33. Some homosexuals desire to become mothers, and in some cases they marry in order to have children, although they are seldom able to obtain any pleasure from intercourse with their husbands. Conscious or unconscious homosexuality is one of the recognized causes of frigidity in married women. Female homosexuals do not appear to have any greater predisposition to neurotic or psychotic tendencies than the average heterosexual.

34. On the whole, homosexual women apparently feel no sense of guilt apart from what one might call social guilt. They do not feel that their preference for a member of their own sex is in any way immoral or wicked. Many homosexual relationships, however, do end in disaster, usually because one or both parties become jealous and possessive. In some cases one of the parties falls in love and marries, causing great unhappiness to the one who is left. On the other hand, members of the Committee of the Medical Women's Federation have personal knowledge of cases in which an active homosexual association has been a positive and constructive factor in the lives of the participants. They also know that some women of distinction, who have made a valuable contribution to the life of the community, have been practising homosexuals maintaining a faithful love relationship for many years. The promiscuous Lesbian, sometimes addicted to perverted physical practices, who delights in seducing and corrupting weaker members of her sex, is relatively rare.

35. The Committee of the Medical Women's Federation is unanimously agreed that the corruption of young girls is uncommon among women, who do not appear to find them sexually attractive.

36. Female homosexuality as a form of organized vice exists to a limited extent in most large cities. The promiscuous Lesbian who is often incapable of love plies her trade for money only, and it may be that she arrived at this stage after passing through one or more homosexual experiences which involved some sort of love relationship, and having drifted into this form of life she has degenerated into homosexual prostitution. There is, however, little actual knowledge on this point. Such women are not infrequently psychopaths, and many of them associate their homosexual practices with various sadistic and masochistic activities.

37. It is a surprising fact that there has been so little public or official condemnation of female homosexuality. Although there are references to it in the literature of the Church, the condemnation seems to have been less strong than in the case of male homosexuality. The secular law has not concerned itself with female homosexuality, perhaps because until relatively recent times woman was regarded in law as only the chattel of man. Moreover, homosexual practices among women seem never to have been regarded as constituting a social danger. The reasons for this may be that they were rare; that, owing to the fact that women do not find little girls attractive as sexual objects, there have been very few cases of seduction or violation of girl children by women; and that such homosexual practices as have occurred have arisen for the most part between consenting adults and have been carried out in private.

38. The Federation's Committee is strongly of the opinion that there is no case for legal interference with any form of female homosexuality. The negative attitude of the law throughout the ages appears fully justified by the known facts. Female homosexuality has never presented a very serious social problem. The very occasional break-up of a marriage, or the degrading behaviour of promiscuous Lesbians, can best be dealt with by social condemnation. The only danger foreseen is that homosexuality may be exalted by the foolish or vicious into a cult, and that could not be prevented by legal intervention.

...

125. *Treatment of Homosexual Women.* The Committee of the Medical Women's Federation writes: As regards treatment, we know of no evidence that any form of drug treatment is of any use in treating sex deviations of women, except in so far as allied conditions, such as drug addiction or poor general health, complicate a case. The proper approach appears to be indirect, through the avoidance of obvious errors in the bringing up of children, and the encouragement of social conditions favourable to the development of normal heterosexual love. Recognition of the undesirability (or as some believe, the essential wrongfulness) of this barren way of life is of major importance, for the adolescent may be pushed one way or another by external suggestion, as well as by an inward drive.

126 Psychiatric treatment may be of great benefit in early cases, but is

unlikely to cure the congenital or deeply rooted invert. Even where cure is improbable, however, a psychiatrist may be of great assistance in guiding the Lesbian to adjustment which will not injure others.

18 M. Schmideberg, 'Reality Therapy with Offenders', *British Journal of Delinquency*, Vol. 5, No. 2, April 1965, pp. 179–80

Case 7

Irene R. was the first delinquent patient I treated. I was then a psychoanalyst, though not an orthodox one, and I tried to apply analytic findings and give interpretations, though in a very modified manner. Irene was about thirty, the only daughter of a prim English middle-class family. She was a schizoid psychopathic with many quirks and peculiarities since childhood; after having had an illegitimate child at the age of sixteen she had become a prostitute. The result of my analytic treatment was that she became homosexual and that her occasional dishonesty consolidated into more serious lawbreaking and pathological querulousness. When she was charged before the court I succeeded in having her put on probation, for which she never forgave me. As soon as her period of probation lapsed she returned to prostitution.

This case taught me the danger of giving analytic interpretations, or indeed of dwelling on 'interesting' material. I have never since used an analytic approach, and have increasingly become more directive, having learned that controls and maturity must be developed and not the unconscious uncovered.

19 E. Bene, 'On the Genesis of Female Homosexuality', *The British Journal of Psychiatry*, Vol. 111, No. 478, September 1965, pp. 815–21

In this period, the first large-scale 'scientific' studies of lesbians began, taking as subjects women who were not already psychiatric patients. This development was dependent on the emergence of an organised lesbian sub-culture; these studies by Bene, Kenyon and Hopkins took their sample population from the membership of the Minorities Research Group. The usual method was to compare a group of lesbians with a group of heterosexual women to test out a range of psychological or physical hypotheses.

Summary

The present investigation was concerned with the question of how the childhood relations of homosexual women with their parents differ from those of heterosexual women. The sample consisted of 37 lesbians and 80 married women, and the investigation was carried out with the aid of a test which facilitates the recollection of early family feelings.

The results of the investigation show a far greater difference between the feelings the lesbians and the married women recalled about their fathers than between those recalled about their mothers. The lesbians were more often hostile towards and afraid of their fathers than were the married women, and they felt more often that their fathers were weak and incompetent. The results also point towards a relationship between the parents' wish for a son and the homosexuality of their daughter.

20 M.J. MacCulloch and M.P. Feldman, 'Aversion Therapy in Management of 43 Homosexuals', *British Medical Journal*, Vol. 2, 3 June 1967, pp. 594–7

It is often assumed by lesbian and gay historians that aversion therapy (particularly popular in the 1950s) was only carried out on gay men. This research report shows that it was also sometimes considered to be an appropriate treatment for lesbians. The patients in this study were treated at the Crumpsall Hospital, Manchester.

A wide variety of techniques have been used in the treatment of homosexuality. They include psychotherapy, psychoanalysis, hormones, and several types of aversion therapy. ... [A]pproximately one quarter at best of treated homosexual patients make a satisfactory response to treatment in that they display a noticeable change in the direction of their sexual preference and practice towards heterosexuality. ...

Treatment technique

... The aversive stimulus (unconditional stimulus) is provided by a 12-volt make/break induction coil and is controlled by a rheostat. About 24 stimulus presentations are used per session, and each session lasts for about 20 to 25 minutes. On average each patient receives 18 to 20 sessions of treatment. ...

Results

Forty-three patients are reported here. We offered treatment to all those who presented; no selection criteria other than the inevitable self-selection (two potential patients declined the offer) have been used. ... Two of the series were females, and were partners in a lesbian 'affair'; both were aged 18, and both completed treatment. All other patients were male homosexuals. ...

Sexual practices

... Both lesbian patients were practising heterosexual intercourse with a variety of partners. Neither patient found this pleasurable, and both felt a considerable degree of contempt for their male partners. ...

Results of treatment

... The two lesbian patients had made a very good improvement and neither displayed any homosexual fantasy, interest, or practice. One of them was still practising heterosexual intercourse; and, compared with her practice before treatment, she did so with great pleasure and a high regard for her partner, who was a relatively permanent one. The other lesbian patient no longer practised heterosexual intercourse but had a good heterosexual relationship with her partner, again a fairly stable one. ...

21 F.E. Kenyon, 'Physique and Physical Health of Female Homosexuals', *Journal of Neurology, Neurosurgery and Psychiatry*, Vol. 31, 1968, pp. 487–9

Method

An anonymous postal enquiry was instituted with the help of an organisation devoted to the interests of lesbians and having as one of its aims the furtherance of research. A random sample of 150 lesbians (roughly a third of the membership living in England) was sent a specially prepared questionnaire, the Maudsley Personality Inventory (M.P.I.), and the Cornell Medical Index Health Questionnaire (C.M.I.). Another organisation of married women, formed to assist in social services, was used as a control group of normal heterosexual women, and similarly investigated. ...

Results

Physical measurements

All subjects were asked to give their height (without shoes and in feet and inches), weight (in stones, pounds and ounces in indoor clothes), bust (in inches), waist (in inches) and hips (in inches). ... The three measurements which significantly distinguish lesbians from controls are weight, waist, and bust. Lesbians are heavier, with bigger busts and waists. They are less tall than controls (although the difference is not significant, it nearly reaches the 5% level), but have slightly but not significantly bigger hips.

Medical history

... More lesbians (61%) than controls (53.6%) had had operations, but this difference is not significant. The frequency distribution shows an interesting contrast between appendicectomy and gynaecological operations, with almost exactly opposite proportions – that is, 21% and 12% for lesbians, and 10% and 21% for controls, respectively. Other contrasts are not so striking, but with the general tendency for lesbians to have proportionately more operations of all kinds, except gynaecological.

Menstrual history

... It is noteworthy that 35% of controls, but only 24.4% lesbians, reported feeling tense premenstrually. Combining the categories 'nervous' and 'anxious' $x^2 = 40.33$; $P < 0.05$, which is significant. Subjects were next asked 'In general, do you at all resent having periods?' This gave a highly significant difference in that 51.2% lesbians answered 'Yes' but only 14.6% controls ($x^2 = 23.94$; $P < .001$). ... As a matter of general interest, the sex of the subjects' usual general practitioner was asked for, to see if more lesbians would in fact register with female doctors. This was found to be the case, as 19.5% of the lesbians and 9.8% of the controls had a female practitioner – a significant difference. ...

22 J. Hopkins, 'The Lesbian Personality', *The British Journal of Psychiatry*, Vol. 115, No. 529, December 1969, pp. 1433–6

... It is the purpose of this study to describe 'the lesbian personality' with more accuracy and objectivity than has been attempted hitherto. This paper presents the hypothesis that there are no personality factors, either primary or second order factors as observed on Cattell's 16 P.F. Test, which will be statistically significantly different between the lesbian and heterosexual groups. ...

The subjects for this study consisted of two groups of women, 24 lesbians and 24 heterosexual women. ...

... [A] good, descriptive generic term for the average lesbian would be 'independent'. Furthermore, the scores show lesbians to be more reserved, more dominant, more bohemian and more self-sufficient. The fact that the lesbian group is significantly different on Factor III, alert poise, which is suggestive of a resilient personality, is considered another finding of importance, again one which suggests a less vulnerable personality than the traditional 'neurotic' label might have suggested. ...

... The following terms are suggested as appropriately descriptive of the lesbian personality in comparison to her heterosexual female counterpart:

1 More independent
2 More resilient
3 More reserved
4 More dominant
5 More bohemian
6 More self-sufficient
7 More composed.

4

EDUCATION

INTRODUCTION

The experience of the crush – overwhelming love and obsession for another girl or woman – has always been a widespread youthful female experience, not restricted to those women who may later come to call themselves lesbian. In contrast to the comparative lack of ordinary language to describe adult lesbian love, there has been a wide variety of common or slang terms for these adolescent feelings – crush, rave, gonage ('gone on'), pash, g.p. (grand passion). Some were specific to one school, while others were in much wider use.

Historians of lesbianism have taken seriously this form of love between women. While not all girls who experience schoolgirl crushes grow out of them, many look back wistfully from later heterosexual marriage to the power of these feelings. It has been argued that this experience of love needs controlling by a society keen to impose compulsory heterosexuality (Faraday 1989, Auchmuty 1992).

The arena of education has been a particular site for social anxiety about lesbianism, and therefore for the projection and policing of love between women. This fear can be identified from at least the late nineteenth century, and may have reached its height in the interwar years. But schools still remain potent places for concern about female homosexuality; witness the passing of Section 28 of the Local Government Act 1988 and subsequent debates about abolishing it. The constant reiteration of disquiet in text after text reflects the significance attributed to the period of adolescence in modern British society and changing notions of how to manage it. Puberty is seen as a crucial time for the young woman to receive a class and gender-appropriate education and training for her future adult roles: a heterosexual future of marriage and motherhood. Anxiety about the meaning of intense friendships between girls, and the powerful disruptive challenge of teenage girls' love for older girls or schoolteachers was expressed in this context. Teachers were supposed to be role models, teaching correct behaviour as well as academic subjects, but this authority was part of their appeal as objects of desire and was both reinforced and subverted by crushes.

The focus of attention in these commentaries is sometimes on the girl's crush, and sometimes on the sexuality of the women teachers. Much of the material about crushes in girls' schools comes from contemporary commentators concerned about the long-term effects on girls, writing on how to manage these powerful emotions, and sometimes about the effects of spinster and lesbian teachers on girls' sexuality. The writers, who were often headteachers them-selves, reflected and utilised a variety of discourses. There was a well-established nineteenth-century debate about the emotional significance of crushes and how to contain their disruptive nature, which was later joined by a variety of medical and psychological approaches discussing them in more sexu-alised terms. These sources coalesce around particular issues – how to control contagious raves at all-girls schools, the malevolent effects of 'vampire' women teachers corrupting girls, and the debate around how co-education could restore a healthy and natural heterosexual ethos in schools.

There are also a number of sources written by women describing their youthful crushes; how they were carried on, the responses of peers and teachers, the power and pleasure of the feelings evoked. The dynamics, conduct and rituals of homoerotic friendships – the meaning of symbolic gifts and services, the nego-tiation of the power relations of the participants – have been explored in detail (Vicinus 1991, Edwards 1995). Many of the sources are accounts by adult women of their being attracted as schoolgirls to other women. Those writing in the 1920s and 1930s, and sometimes looking back over several decades, use or refer to the various psychological discourses discussed above. However while the language of sexuality may have been helpful to describe the power and intensity of these love relationships, the authors often engage with psychological discourses from a critical perspective. They emphasise the seriousness and profundity of their feelings, sometimes stressing that later (heterosexual) love affairs did not match the intensity and satisfaction provided by youthful crushes and friendships. These women felt obliged to comment on the healthiness or otherwise of crushes; psychological discourses were evidently powerful enough to provoke a need to respond. Discussing their girlhood passions with hindsight, however, women often use a sophisticated vocabulary to justify and defend their love, rather than to support notions about its dangers.

One consequence of the developing medical discourses about sexuality, evident by the 1920s, was the sexualisation of girls' adolescence. A considerable number of advisory publications appeared, written by doctors, psychologists and others especially for the benefit of educationalists and youth workers. The focus of these was how to understand and manage the development of adolescent sexuality as part of a heterosexual career, as Tinkler puts it (Tinkler 1995). This shift has stimulated a number of historical debates and problems. Vicinus sees this newer discourse which emphasised girls' behaviour as sexual and psycho-logical, as running alongside the existing perspective of crushes as emotional, for quite some time; the medical discourse only gradually came to replace the older perspective. The process by which female friendships and crushes came to be pathologised and seen as dangerous occurred gradually in the years before and after World War I (Vicinus 1991).

Attacks on crushes and on the negative effects of all-girls' schools did not occur simply as a consequence of new pathologising medical discourses. It has also been argued that these attacks were part of an anti-feminist backlash against women's increased independence and power. The reformed girls' schools were already seen by some in the late nineteenth century as dangerous hotbeds of women's emancipation and as a challenge to patriarchy, encouraging young women to seek university entrance and careers rather than marriage, and as nurseries of the suffrage movement (Dyhouse 1981). Concern about raves simply provided another instance of how they were alleged to distort true femininity. After World War I, which raised further anxieties about the masculinisation of women and their marriage prospects, anti-feminist commentators picked up medical discourses to add further weight to their attacks on institutions such as girls' schools which symbolised women's independence (Beddoe 1989).

The issue of schoolgirl crushes also became closely entangled in two wider educational concerns of the interwar period; anxiety about the influence of the spinster teacher, and the debate over co-education. There was already a nineteenth-century stereotype of the governess as a masculine woman, with fears expressed that she might steal girls' trust and affection away from their mothers. This concern deepened, as girls were increasingly educated away from home and family in day or boarding schools (Faraday 1989, Vicinus 1991). It was in the late nineteenth and early twentieth centuries that the role of the professional woman teacher became well established. Due to a widespread marriage bar, the majority of women teachers, especially those in secondary schools, were single women. In the context of new ideas about female sexuality, the challenge of the suffrage movement and the subsequent backlash against feminism, spinster teachers were increasingly considered to be an unhealthy influence in girls' schools. They were represented as undersexed and bitter – thwarted in woman's true desire for marriage and motherhood – who would teach their pupils feminist ideals and independence, and encourage them to hate men and avoid marriage. By the 1920s and 30s, one strand of this stigmatisation of spinster teachers had developed into full-blown allegations of lesbian corruption. This also reflects the social fears surrounding this group of professional economically independent women; the lesbian label was partly a way of marking the boundary and undesirability of women's power and autonomy (Oram 1989, 1996).

One solution increasingly suggested by progressive educationalists after World War I was to expand co-education. This would address the problems of unhealthy crushes in girls' schools and the challenge of feminist teachers' emphasis on their pupils' economic and social independence. Mixed schooling, it was argued, would create a more 'natural' environment to foster co-operation instead of competition between the sexes, i.e. prepare girls more effectively for marriage and motherhood (Faraday 1989, Auchmuty 1992).

Fiction was also a site for the expression and circulation of changing attitudes towards the schoolgirl crush. In adult fiction, raves in schools and colleges were often portrayed positively up to about the 1920s. Faraday's survey of interwar lesbian fiction showed that the most popular occupation for the lesbian character was teaching and that girls' schools were a common setting. Anti-lesbian portrayals of the insidious influence of adult women over girls associated lesbianism with a craving for power, with the older partner usurping the mother's role (Faraday 1985).

In fiction written for girls, Tinkler suggests that censorship was already underway in the period after World War I. In schoolgirl magazines, girls' friendships were presented as close but not sentimental, and crushes were very rare after 1920. She argues that the editorial staff on girls' magazines were likely to be particularly sensitive to contemporary anti-lesbianism (Tinkler 1995). Publishers of schoolgirl stories responded less rapidly to current concerns about love between women. Close friendships and crushes were a common element in schoolgirl series, such as Brent-Dyer's Chalet school series, Blyton's Mallory Towers, and Oxenham's Abbey Girls books and were often a crucial part of the plot. Auchmuty argues that love between adult women as well as between girls was openly and unselfconsciously described in these books from the 1900s to the 1930s. These stories describe girls and women kissing and sharing beds, discussing the feelings and dynamics of their relationships at length, and taking a homoerotic pleasure in each other's appearance. From the 1930s, however, these descriptions of intense feeling between women fade, to be replaced by greater emphasis on heterosexuality and marriage, a process that she links to *The Well of Loneliness* trial and wider awareness of ideas about lesbianism. By the 1950s, reprints of some of these books even censored what by then had become sexually suggestive scenes between women (Auchmuty 1992).

The considerable body of source material, giving different perspectives on love between women in the world of education, is testament to the anxieties it provoked. But it also indicates that this was a common, and even sometimes acceptable setting for lesbian desire.

1 L.H.M. Soulsby, *Stray Thoughts for Girls*, 1893, James Parker & Co., pp. 164–8

When she wrote this book Lucy Soulsby was Head Mistress of Oxford High School.

Friendship and love

Nothing excites so much laughter and hard speaking in the world as 'schoolgirl friendships;' as often as not they are found among older people, but school-girls have given a name to this particular kind of folly, so it behoves school-girls to keep clear of it, and to deprive the name of its point.

... Have you ever had some violent friendship – or laughed at it in others, – which meant running in and out of each other's houses at all hours – being inseparable – quoting your friend, till your brothers exclaimed at her very name – and making all your family feel that they ranked nowhere in comparison with her? In this matter of home and friends conflicting, I quite see the point of view of some: – 'My family don't give me the sympathy and help that my friend does – they always tease or scold if I come to them in a difficulty, and yet they are vexed and jealous, when I find a friend who can and will help.'

I do not say: Cut yourself off from your friend, – she is sent by God to help you; but: – Remember to feel for your Mother; – see how natural and loving her jealousy is, and spare it by constant tact – instead of being a martyr, feel that it is *she* and not *you* who is ill-used. And in all ways, never let outside affections interfere with home ones. It is the great difference between them, that outside self-chosen affections burn all the stronger for repression and self-restraint; while home ones burn stronger for each act of attention to them and expression of them, e.g. postponing a visit to a friend for a walk with a brother will make both loves stronger, and *vice versa*, – and your friendship will last all the longer because you consume your own smoke. ... Friendships are God-given ties, when they are real, but insepa-rable ones are mostly only follies; – anyhow, family ties are the most God-given of all, and friendship should help us to fulfil family claims better, instead of making us neglect them. The best test of whether your love for an outside person is of the right kind, is, does it make you pleasanter at home?

2 H. Ellis, *Studies In The Psychology Of Sex, Vol. 1, Sexual Inversion*, London: The University Press, 1897, pp. 82–5

With girls, as with boys, it is in the school, at the evolution of puberty, that homosexuality first shows itself. It may originate either peripherally or centrally. In the first case two children perhaps when close to each other in bed, more or less unintentionally generate in each other a certain amount of sexual irritation, which they foster by mutual touching and kissing. This is a spurious kind of homosexuality; it is merely the often precocious play of the normal instinct, and has no necessary relation to true sexual inversion. In the girl who is congenitally predisposed to homosexuality it will continue and develop; in the majority it will be forgotten as quickly as possible, not without shame, in the presence of the normal object of sexual love. ...

...

The cases in which the source is central, rather than peripheral, neverthe-less merge into the foregoing, with no clear line of demarcation. In such cases a school girl or young woman forms an ardent attachment for another girl, probably somewhat older than herself, often a school-fellow, sometimes her school-mistress, upon whom she will lavish an astonishing amount of affection and devotion. This affection may or may not be returned; usually the return consists of a gracious acceptance of the affectionate services. The girl who expends this wealth of devotion is surcharged with emotion, but she is often unconscious of or ignorant of the sexual impulse, and she seeks for no form of sexual satisfaction. Kissing and the privilege of sleeping with the friend are, however, sought, and at such times it often happens that even the comparatively unresponsive friend feels more or less definite sexual emotion (pudendal turgescence with secretion of mucus and involuntary twitching of the neighbouring muscles), though little or no attention may be paid to this phenomenon, and in the common ignorance of girls concerning sex matters it may not be understood. In some cases there is an attempt, either instinctive or intentional, to develop the sexual feeling by close embraces and kissing. This rudimentary kind of homosexual relationship is, I believe, more common among girls than among boys, and for this there are several reasons: (1) A boy more often has some acquaintance with sexual phenomena and would frequently regard such a relationship as unmanly; (2) the girl has a stronger need of affection and self-devotion to another person than a boy has; (3) she has not, under our existing social conditions which compel young women to hold the opposite sex at arm's length, the same opportunities of finding an outlet for her sexual emotions; while (4) conventional propriety recognises a considerable degree of physical intimacy between girls, thus at once encouraging and cloaking the manifestations of homosexuality.

These passionate friendships, of a more or less unconsciously sexual character, are certainly common. It frequently happens that a period during which a young woman falls in love at a distance with some young man of her acquaintance alternates with periods of intimate attachment to a friend of her own sex. No congenital inversion is usually involved.

3 K. Tynan, *Twenty-five Years: Reminiscences*, 1913, Smith, Elder & Co., p. 57

Katharine Tynan, Irish poet, attended the school at the Siena Convent in Drogheda, in the early 1870s.

We had our little passions, sometimes for a nun, sometimes for each other. The nuns had a convention of discouraging these special adorations. I am sure they really delighted in them. Mine was a passion for an elder girl about to become a nun. She was going to the convent at Lisbon, which gave my passion the poignancy of impending separation. She was a rosy-cheeked, dark-eyed girl, with burnished black hair, which at one temple showed a strand of white. As her departure was close at hand she was not exactly in the school life and she came and went a good deal, as she was preparing her convent trousseau. I used to cry a great deal at night because she was going away, and she used to come and comfort me. I knew her footstep in the corridor and I used to feel faint with love when she came. Once, on a dark winter morning, washing in cold water as was our ascetic custom, and groping my way by candle-light, I was told she had come back the night before. At first I thought it was too good to be true and suspected a trick. When I was persuaded of its truth, what was it that turned the January morning to June and made the chilly dark rose-coloured and shining? In the dark corridor on the way to Mass, as we passed the warm kitchen, delightful on a cold winter morning, she came behind me and kissed me. Oh, rapture! oh, delight! oh, ecstasy! Was there anything in more mature passions quite as good?

4 P. Blanchard, *The Case of the Adolescent Girl, A Book for Teachers, Parents and Guardians*, Kegan Paul, Trench, Trubner & Co., 1921, pp. 136–9

Phyllis Blanchard was based at Clark University in Massachusetts, USA, but her book was published in Britain with a preface by the British doctor Mary Scharlieb. It was one of the first texts to apply psychological ideas to the adolescent girl. Her discussion drew on a whole range (indeed mish-mash!) of theories and sources in psychology and psychoanalysis. The following section is drawn from Chapter 5, 'Pathological Manifestations of Libido in Adolescent Girls'.

One of the passing perversions of the libido among adolescent girls is the fixation of the affections on members of the same sex, and apparent indifference or even aversion to male companionship. In extremely pathological cases, this tendency may involve gross physical manifestations; but generally it is a very high and noble sentiment, and is to be censored only as it prevents an ultimate transference of the affections to their more natural object.

Ambivalent forms of the Oedipus complex, in which the mother has been idealized and the father disliked or feared, is one factor which helps in this turning of the affections to other girls or older women; a distaste for the marital relationship caused by the teaching that it is degrading or the impression that it involves suffering and pain is a second motive, while finally, the domination by a power complex may incite a dislike of yielding to the domineering influence of the male, when some degree of passing affection can be obtained through the worship of other girls, whose attitude at the same time gratifies the longing for power.

Moreover, there are certain conditions in the social life of our times which tend to favour the development of this unhappy trend in the adolescent girl. There is a growing antagonism to the masculine double moral standard and general attitude toward women on the part of girls who have accepted the feminist philosophy which makes them unwilling to venture into matrimony with the average man whom they meet. The newly aroused ambition of woman for a life work of her own other than wifehood and motherhood is another powerful force impelling her to hesitate before entering upon a relationship which will in all probability thwart such desires. With the denial of an outlet for her sex impulses in marriage, however, comes the degrading temptation to substitute unconventional relationships. This proceeding becomes all the easier with the existence of a comparatively large number of women, who approximate to some extent the traditional male characteristics of aggression and enterprise.

5 C. Dane, *The Woman's Side*, 1926, Herbert Jenkins Ltd, pp. 53–65

Under the name of Clemence Dane, Winifred Ashton (1888–1965) first followed a career as an actress and later turned to writing, producing popular plays and novels. Before writing her first novel, the anti-lesbian *Regiment of Women* (1917), she taught for a time in a girls' school.

Chapter 5. *'A problem in education'*

... [This is] one of the oldest and most puzzling problems in existence – the problem of emotional attachments between members of the same sex.

... We know, of course, that the problem is an old one, that in one form or another it has engaged the attention of thinking men and women since the days of Plato. But the use and abuse of friendship between man and man, and woman and woman, is only indirectly under discussion here. The reader is concerned with this problem as it propounds itself in the schools, and in the schools, perhaps significantly, it has no name, it is only recognised by a slang phrase. In the American girls' schools it is 'a crush'. Over here it is known as a 'G.P.' or as 'being keen on' someone. In Germany they call it *Schwärmerei*, an elastic word that covers 'hysteria, enthusiasm, hero-worship, dreaminess, fanaticism, extravagant devotion, exaltation, visionary raving, bees about to swarm, dissipation and ecstasy.'

The words stand also for the queer fact that girls of thirteen and onward, at day-schools and still more at boarding-schools, not only form normal and wholesome friendships with children of their own age, but that they are easily moved to a sort of hero-worship for an older girl or woman which, not always, but very often develops into a wild, unbalanced passion of affection that directly affects their health and happiness and indirectly their whole future. To put it crudely, a girl, before she is either physically or mentally ripe for it, sometimes falls in love, goes through all the nerve-shattering emotions proper to such a state of mind, and suffers even more than an older woman in the same situation because she has no idea of what is the matter with her, and because there is no possibility of her affection being satisfactorily returned.

... [It] can be proved that the problem presents itself first at the time when a child is physically becoming a woman, when in some countries, and in our own not so long ago, she would be already betrothed, if not married: that the similar problem in boys' schools is unquestionably due to that cause: and that, mentally at least, the experience is practically identical with the ill-starred love affairs of later life.

And by acknowledging that sex is at the root of the trouble we at least clear the ground: we at least admit that all these boys and girls, instead of being 'silly' or 'abnormal' or 'wicked', or whatever we choose to call it, are following as well as civilisation will let them the laws of their being. They are with Nature, not against her, and if things go wrong they must in common justice be considered, not knaves and fools, but victims ...

... [T]he present system of education does not render it impossible for a morbid and selfish woman to amuse herself and gratify her love of excitement by playing on this tendency to exaggerated hero-worship in the children and mistresses under her care. Such women do exist. It is to be hoped that they are rare; but they do exist. I have myself come across such types and I have been told, not by hysterical schoolgirls but by sober head-mistresses of many years' experience, stories enough of such women. I quote one of them –

'I have known at least four of these vampire women in my own experience, and have heard of many others. Two belong to my school and college days, the other two to my days as head-mistress, and both have been sent packing. I am responsible for over eighty boarders, so you may imagine I feel pretty strongly about this sort of love-making.'

That is the attitude, I think, of nearly all our head-mistresses: in fact, they so drastically disapprove that they often defeat their own excellent intentions. A principal of a school once told me that she considered the outcry upon this subject exaggerated, and that in all her experience she had never seen anything really disturbing. 'But, of course,' she said, 'when I see the beginning of any such silliness I suppress it at once. I don't give it a chance. I stamp it out ruthlessly.'

I know she does. Yet I could have told her that one of the worst cases I ever came across did happen at her own school. There was one of those charming young women there, with nothing at all of the vampire in her nature, but who, nevertheless, had a disastrous effect upon her pupils. She over-excited them. There was at one time a 'craze' for her: that was a fashion, harmless enough on the whole. But with several girls, though few guessed it, it was more than a fashion. Long after the craze was over, in fact for nearly three years, they lived in an almost inconceivable state of tension and excitement and jealousy. One, certainly, was naturally hysterical, but the others were perfectly normal, pleasant girls: and I shall not easily forget the extreme resentment and bitterness with which one of them, some years later, spoke, not of the mistress concerned, but of the fact that she had been allowed to get into such a state, that it had been possible for her to be subjected to such an experience. She seemed to feel that her whole capacity for happiness and suffering had been blunted by it. She said – 'It was torment, and I only pray that I never have to go through such a hell again.' This, let us remember, in a school where the head-mistress ruthlessly suppressed anything of the kind.

6 M. Stopes, *Sex and the Young*, 1926, Gill Publishing Co., pp. 45, 48–9, 53–6

Two children whatever their age and sex should never be permitted to use the water closet together, and any child who is observed to spend a long time in the water closet should be carefully watched.

... The head mistress is less likely to have this particular danger [homosexuality] to face in an acute form among her girls, unless it is introduced by a Lesbian mistress. As a rule, however, even a practising Lesbian would be less likely to go to extreme physical lengths with a girl pupil, and would probably stop at the mental damage and injury indicated on p. 54 et seq.

Chapter 5. 'The head teacher's problems'

It is customary (although there are exceptions in this country) for the teaching staff of a school or college to be of the same sex as the pupils. This results, particularly in girls' schools, in the congregation of a number of young people in the charge of a number of unmarried persons of their own sex. This is generally accepted as being natural and right. I hold it to be fundamentally wrong.

All teaching staffs should contain as high a percentage as possible of married teachers. The teaching profession should be pre-eminently one in which marriage should be a legitimate anticipation, and should not truncate the career either of the woman or the man teacher who marries. ...

...

On the other hand, where the staff are all unmarried I fear I am not pessimistic in saying there is increasingly the risk that there may be one or other member whose sex manifestations are not natural, and who is partly or completely homo-sexual. Such a one may have a social conscience well enough developed to restrict the expressions of abnormal feeling to an adult partner, but, on the other hand, it is not unknown (although it is generally completely hushed up) that such an individual may corrupt young pupils under his or her charge. As in all else human, the degrees of variability in this feature range widely. There are those who are merely slightly erotic and almost hysterically affectionate to another member of their own sex: those who develop a passion for one of their own sex without any physical manifestations: those indulging in intense and repeated physical experiences with a member of their own sex. Some form a mutual attachment lasting faithfully for many years; others are fickle and desirous to corrupt ever fresh young lives.

Such perverts are not so rare as normal wholesome people would like to believe, and now act as though they did believe them to be. My own observations have led me regretfully to the opinion that there are few large institutions in which one or more of the first two types may not be found. I have watched the career for years of a pair of the third type. Before the permanent attachment was formed the elder of these teachers was a great danger to the junior pupils in school and injured a number of adolescent girls.

...

One of the signs which should undoubtedly warn every head mistress to be alert about a member of the staff is a too eager and too fervid popularity among the pupils. Any mistress who has a love-sick following, which she encourages instead of cooling off, should be watched most carefully and a wise Head will distinguish between this sickly and unwholesome 'rage' and the jolly open, healthy popularity which is the natural reward of every true and well-balanced teacher.

Deplorable as such a type may be in a girls' school, it is even more disastrous among boys. With girls the corruption is chiefly mental and evanescent, and even if Sapphoism is practised, detrimental as it may be, it does not so profoundly injure the girl's physique as the corresponding physical side of homo-sexual manifestations may affect the young boy or lad.

7 L.M. Faithfull, *You and I, Saturday Talks at Cheltenham*, 1927, Chatto & Windus, pp. 118–21

The talks published in this book had been given by Lilian Faithfull when she was Principal of the Ladies College, Cheltenham. These talks, on a range of topics including Boys and Girls, Slang, Honour, Honesty, Pain and Suffering, Conversation, How to make and keep a Friend etc., were given to the Upper School on Saturday mornings after prayers, and the girls were encouraged to write in to her with their comments afterwards. In this chapter, on 'Real and Counterfeit Friendships', Faithfull made a strong distinction between raves and true friendships, commenting perceptively on the power of raves, and warned against obsessive long-term devotions, terming them sentimental and neurotic. This talk elicited many letters from pupils.

Comments

I learn from various letters that I am quite wrong in stating that a girl is limited to one rave at once. It seems that you can have as many as seventeen, and that at any rate three is quite usual! We must be talking of different things. For experiences that you can duplicate over and over again like this are perfectly futile, – without meaning or value in your life. This absurd kind of rave is just a matter of fashion, and you adopt it because you want to be in the fashion. But it is distinctly mischievous, and you must be warned against it, and urged to give it up. It will give you a habit of spurious forced emotion, which is exceedingly silly, and which you may find that you cannot get rid of easily. Indulgence in these false emotions may be the prelude to flirtation later on.

A good many anonymous letters have described the writer's symptoms in some detail; and in most instances it is clearly a case of hero-worship and not of rave. A really honest devotion to someone of fine character, who is however rather remote from you, is healthy and natural. Its influence may be altogether good, if the person who experiences it has perception delicate enough to know that her feeling must be purged of everything silly to be worthy of so fine an object. We miss a great incentive in life if we have no capacity for hero-worship. To have lost the faculty of being roused to enthusiasm by any great person, living or dead, in literature, art, history or politics, is to be insensible to nobility of character, and to forego much that helps, and that acts as inspiration.

Indignant protests have come in against the statement that raving is the fashion here, the writers being generally anxious to clear their own houses from the imputation. I am quite sure that the seniors in each house do their very best to put it down: and it can be seen from the letters that in many cases elder girls treat the younger ones very sensibly. But they must, as some writers point out, beware of teasing as a remedy. Here we are talking quite generally and we can afford to laugh at a joke about the whole subject. But when you are dealing with a 'patient', so to speak, you must remember that she is in a very sensitive state emotionally: and teasing is a doubtful and dangerous remedy. This is particularly true of a shy person, and you will never cure her folly by alluding to it openly; you will only increase the strain. Of course if the rave is only a pose, and costs nothing, you may do well to ridicule it.

If you should be in the awkward position of being raved upon, you must try to bring it to an end. Do not play with the conditions, encouraging one day and snubbing the next. It is very easy to be inconsistent in this way, when your own happiness is not at all involved; but it is harmful as well as cruel. The fact is we are all apt to enjoy the exercise of power in this direction. You must examine yourselves carefully, and ask whether you want this state of things or not. Otherwise it is so easy to encourage it at the beginning, especially if you are flattered, and then to get irritable, annoyed and even revolted as it goes on. That is not fair. If you are not ready for a real equal friendship with the other person, you must set your face against any relationship at all. Be quite firm, repulse all advances, give no encouragement. Your severe treatment must be carried out persistently.

But as a rule the sufferer must cure herself; it is rarely possible for anyone else to say the right thing, or suggest the right attitude. A girl who had been a very bad case for about three years told me that nothing that was ever said to her in various exhortations affected her at all; but she believed that if the utter waste involved in the whole episode had been pointed out, she would have been cured much sooner, instead of having to wait until it came to an end simply by a strict policy of neglect on the other side. If she had realised, she said, how her energy, faculties, mind and heart were being wasted, so that she was no good to herself or anyone else, and rapidly losing all self respect, she would have stopped.

8 *The Manchester Guardian*, 7 September 1932, p. 3

Schoolgirl's suicide

Teacher's evidence

Questioned on letters

The inquest ... at which correspondence between a 15-year-old schoolgirl and her teacher had been mentioned was concluded at Croydon yesterday, the jury finding that the girl, Kathleen Humphreys, of Lodge Road, West Croydon, who was found dead from gas poisoning, had committed suicide while of unsound mind.

A rider was added to the verdict in the following terms:– 'With regard to the letters, we do not think the teacher had any ulterior motive in writing them, but we consider them a little indiscreet as from teacher to pupil.' The Coroner expressed his agreement with this.

At the previous hearing the girl's mother stated that her daughter corresponded with a teacher at the school she attended in St. James's Road, Croydon. She became agitated when no letters arrived.

Mr. Morey (the coroner) recalled how the girl's mother found the letters, and, not liking their tone, said that her daughter was not to correspond with the teacher. The girl was upset.

Miss Winifred Lee, the teacher, was called and gave her address as

Lullington Road, Anerley. She told the Coroner that she could not remember how many letters she had written, but perhaps it might have been about a dozen. The girl was one of two who were her special favourites.

Made heroine of teacher

The Coroner: She made rather a heroine of you? – I think she did.

The Coroner: Can you explain why she should blush and get so embarrassed when her mother found the letters? – Everyone at school had found her highly strung, and other teachers said she blushed when they spoke to her.

The Coroner then read another letter which began by saying it was very late, and continued that after what had been said that evening she felt that she must write. 'What does that relate to?' he asked. 'Some remark she had passed?'

Miss Lee: She said she liked me better than she liked her mother.

The Coroner then quoted from the letter: 'Your feelings for me and for your mother cannot be contrasted. They stand on two different planes. ... I can never approach the position your mother holds in your life. It must needs be that other loves come into our lives. Think of David and Jonathan. In some special cases we must love one another especially. We are to be classed as special ones.'

The Coroner: What does that mean? – Just that we were extremely fond of one another and friends.

The Coroner: But, you see, you were in the position of teacher and mistress, and you are twenty years older than she was. Do you think it a proper thing to have written to this girl? – Yes, I think so.

The Coroner was reading a third letter, when he said that if Mr. Wilberforce Jackson (representing Miss Lee) objected to the letters being read he must say so.

Mr. Jackson: I only want to know what the object is. If it is to clear up the parents' difficulty it would have been better done privately. But if there is any question for the jury to consider as to whether the letters had anything to do with the girl's death, or whether Miss Lee was deserving of censure, I agree that they should be read.

The Coroner: This witness has been summoned at the special request of Mr. Humphreys. On the second point, if the jury feel that the letters are deserving of censure they will, no doubt, say so.

The father observed that he could not see why his daughter should be so fond of Miss Lee, considering that she was not with Miss Lee the whole of her time. She had no more to do with Miss Lee than with other teachers.

Mr. Jackson (to Miss Lee): Did you at any time, either by actions or words, do anything in any way to upset this girl's affection to her parents? –

No. One of my letters to her says that anything she had from me I hoped would help her in her life.

Head mistress's view

Miss Margaret Wood, head mistress of the school to which the girl went, was asked by the Coroner if she knew of the existence of correspondence in this case. Miss Wood replied that she knew nothing about it previously. He handed the second letter to Miss Wood and said: 'Remembering the position of a mistress and pupil, and the difference between the ages, is that a letter which would have met with your approval had you seen it before it was sent?'

Miss Wood, after reading the letter, replied: 'I think it is a thing I cannot enter into. I do not know how much the child loved Miss Lee, but it is a usual thing for a child to love a mistress.'

The Coroner: You see nothing wrong in it, and you would have approved it? – I think so.

There is no doubt that Miss Lee is eminently satisfactory as a school mistress? – I have seen absolutely nothing to object to at the school at all. I have been there four and a half years, and Miss Lee has been there ten years.

The foreman of the jury pointed out that in the letters was 'a big strain of religion running through,' and asked Miss Wood if Miss Lee was 'a very religious person.'

Miss Wood: I don't consider her more so than ordinarily.

Summing up, the Coroner said: 'We all know that when we were at school we had got heroes, and girls, I suppose, had got heroines. It might be a boy in an older class. Sometimes it goes on into older life. You may remember the play 'Journey's End,' in which a boy named Raleigh has a hero in another class called Stanhope, and later in life they meet in France. Of course, that is only fiction, but it is a very good example of what does occur in real life. That may well have been the position of this young girl and Miss Lee. There is no doubt about the fact that she was extremely fond of her.'

9 M. Chadwick, *Adolescent Girlhood*, 1932, George Allen & Unwin, pp. 223, 243–6, 250–7

Mary Chadwick was a psychologist based at the Tavistock Clinic. She had published an earlier book on child development. In this book, the aim of which was to discuss 'the more everyday problems of the girl at home and at school', she took a more sophisticated approach than some contemporary texts, using psychoanalytic theory to discuss different kinds of schoolgirl crushes, in terms of identification, and the mother–child relationship.

... This is one of the reasons why the adolescent girl so eagerly seeks in her phantasies, if she is too shy to do so in reality, a substitute mother-image, the foster-mother or lost mother of the fairy-tale phantasy, to whom she can confide her troubles and ideals without running the risk of being laughed at.

It is this longing for a new mother which will often be one of the foundations of that difficult state of affairs which we recognise frequently among many of the older girls at school in relation to their teachers, commonly known as the crush or G.P. The girls, because of their age, are only too ready to fall headlong into it; many of the mistresses, too, because of their age or temperament, are just as willing to receive the devotion of the girls as they are to give it. Both gain a great deal of emotional gratification from the exchange, but whether it is a healthy outlet for either in the long run we must leave for further discussion in the next chapter, when we examine the causes and effects of adolescent friendships.

...

We will be ready to admit that girls who are absorbed in the stress of a violent adolescent friendship, either with a girl of the same age, a little older, or with a mature woman, find it difficult to carry on the ordinary affairs of their daily life. Their school work deteriorates. They are unable to concentrate upon their former outside interests. They will cease to care for their old friends or relations. Everything else fades out, or is pushed into the background until the blaze of this fierce passion has burnt itself out. Often the girl suffers extremely from her failure to gain the response she desires. Yet it can be so exacting as to be impossible to attain, or to be long continued. The girl, then, feeling bitterly disappointed and disillusioned, breaks off the friendship in anger. She may often fall into a severe depression for some time, with a nervous breakdown of some kind terminating the episode.

How far these relationships go, and what actual expressions of love gratification the participants allow themselves, naturally varies according to the degree of freedom possessed by each for deriving satisfaction from different forms of sexual requirements and love-play connected with the several component instincts. They may only want to kiss each other, look at each other's bodies, or to be looked at, touch one another, tickle or stroke each other. They may indulge in various ways of causing one another pain, following the dictates of the sadistic impulse, or may procure pleasure from various more direct forms of mutual or one-sided masturbatory acts. This question of type of gratification chosen will depend upon the particular wishes of one or both of the individuals concerned.

...

But some of the most important friendships of adolescence, which provide very serious problems, are those which arise between the young girl and the older one, or again with the mature woman. On the one hand, it will represent an elder sister identification; on the other, the ideal mother,

who is not the mother of childhood, connected in the girl's mind with memories of early threats and punishments, loves, hatreds, and jealousies.
...

The adolescent finds some woman attracts her because of her appearance, intellect, manners, or general *savoir-faire*. She seems to be so sure of herself. She has arrived where the girl hopes to come some day. Other people admire her too, and show themselves equally anxious to be with her, because of some quality she possesses. She has had what the girl envies most of all – experience of life. She has read books, seen things and places; has numbered among her friends interesting people who sound so exciting when she tells the girl about them. She seems to have, in short, all that the girl feels she lacks, but wishes so ardently to have. Some girls may become jealous and hate her for this superiority to themselves in this wealth of attainment, but others fall under her spell and love her for it instead, only really happy when they can be near her. They will seek to do little services for her, take her small presents, often costing much more than they can actually afford, offerings of flowers and the like, and do their best to model themselves upon the same pattern.

Now, what the ultimate results of this infatuation will be depends upon what sort of woman she is to whom the girl has attached herself, and what she wants from this unequal friendship. We will frequently notice that she is a type exactly opposite to that of the girl's own mother. ...

10 *Daily Herald,* 5 September 1935

This extract is from the report of an education conference at which Dr Williams was a speaker.

Dr Williams had dealt with the effect on the temperament of the ductless glands, and said that games such as hockey and lacrosse develop that part of the suprarenal gland which presides over the combative element of a person's character. 'You cannot confine the desire and aptitude for combat to cricket and football,' he said. 'They inevitably appear in the whole character, and what was originally a gentle, feminine girl becomes harsh and bellicose in all relations to life. The women who have the responsibility of teaching these girls are, many of them themselves embittered, sexless or homosexual hoydens who try to mould the girls into their own pattern.' 'And far too often they succeed.' Dr Williams declared that girls who have no desire to play combative games are cajoled and coerced into taking part by 'these thin-lipped, flat-chested, sadistic creatures.'

11 R.K. Davies, *Four Miss Pinkertons*, 1936, Williams & Norgate Ltd, pp. 35–6, 72–5, 78–80

This is an autobiographical account of schooldays at Roedean at the end of the nine-teenth century. The author had just arrived at Roedean, and was sitting in the prep room writing her first letter home, as other girls were preparing for the Saturday evening festiv-ities. She immediately succumbed to a crush. This account strongly justifies the validity of such feelings of love, and condemns the clumsy treatment of crushes.

The majority of the house seemed to be collected here, but my attention was all for Stella. She was perfect – tall, with broad shoulders, and a slender waist, encircled by the white webbing belt, much effected by the 'bloods' of the school, though it scarcely showed beneath the blouse of her games dress. The colour of her eyes didn't strike me then, but I noticed her sleepy, rather drawling voice, and her beautifully curved mouth. Her hair, of a dark flaming red, was plaited into the inevitable pigtail.

... She had noticed that I was looking at her! She was crossing the gym towards me. Already it was beginning to resound with a gay waltz tune, played by one of the junior music mistresses, with her head almost turned back to front to see whether people were beginning to dance. How she pounded the piano! And my heart was beginning to pound too, for why was Stella Hitchcock smiling, why did she stride over the slippery floor, bearing down upon me? 'Will you have this dance?' Her arm was round my waist, her firm hand on my back, I was whirled off, hardly knowing where I went or what I did. ... Then the music stopped, I heard 'Thank you very much', and the wonderful moment was over.

...

I suppose it was on one ordinary weekday towards the end of my first year that we were startled by a mysterious announcement on the notice-board. The whole school, with the exception of the prefects, was summoned to appear in the Great Hall after supper! This happened so seldom that there was something almost uncanny about it, in fact to the knowledge of most of us, it had never happened at all. We were inclined to shiver in our shoes, for that a 'jaw' of heroic dimensions was forthcoming we never doubted. We had been doing something frightful and were about to be called to account for it, and the whole school was implicated. Well, if it were so the whole school would share the blame, and that would not be so bad. Perhaps it was even a little exciting. We stiffened our backs.

Eight o'clock found us duly marshalled in our 'forms', as we always lined up for morning prayers, apprehensive perhaps, but a thousand times more curious. What *could* be going to happen? But when Gertrude Johnson mounted the platform and faced us, I think we all sympathized with her to the extent of being sorry for having committed some crime that had brought her there. She informed us quickly enough, and surely it was the most extraordinary announcement that one young girl ever made to a gathering of her kind.

When I look back on that evening the whole affair seems next to unbelievable. Of course this was before psychology as such, came into fashion. I speak of a time when the words 'repression' and 'complex' had scarcely come into the language in the sense in which they are employed now. ... Still it did argue a good deal of *naïveté* on the part of Miss Vaughan and her confederates that such a task as this should have been entrusted to a creature, who, however gallant, was, after all, nothing but a schoolgirl. Of course Gertrude Johnson never suspected that she was meddling with a subject nearly related to the central problem of all existence, she did not dream that sex had anything to do with our emotional alarms and excursions, and perhaps her ignorance was less dangerous to us than the so-called knowledge of the 'modern' girl might have been. She obviously suffered, for she was no exhibitionist. But she was a very brave girl, and she stood foursquare and told us what she thought of us. ...

She did not speak for long. It would not have been like Gertrude if she had, but when she was finished ears tingled and cheeks were scarlet. When I dared to raise my eyes to look at the neck in front of me I saw that it was as burning as my own. She knew how people talked, she heard them whisper '*Isn't* SHE sweet? Look out, SHE's coming!' and fly to open doors for their idols, and fling themselves on the floor, two at a time, to take off their cricket pads in the boot-room. What did we think of ourselves now we had it put straight before us? Wasn't it ludicrous, wasn't it revolting? She had come to tell us it must stop. There must be no more of this – this sickening *nonsense* at Sutton Weald. The school itself was getting a name for it, and had we ever thought how bad it was for the school? (I don't suppose it had ever occurred to her that it was bad for *us*, except in so far that we were the school.) But for the sake of the SCHOOL she flayed us alive, for myself I felt raw and bleeding, though I could not be sure of her effect on others as I could not bring myself to look at any face. Towards the end she adopted a kinder tone, and there her straight wholesome instincts brought her very near the right remedy. There was to be no more of this putrid furtive 'thing', but real friendship was to take its place. Idolaters and idols were to be on frank, happy terms together, 'they' would see to that, she knew, and the new order was to begin at once. (Poor Gertrude, she was an optimist!) As for us, we were to think well over what she had said, and she trusted to our honour to stamp out the shameful business for ever, for the sake of the SCHOOL. Else we were unworthy of Sutton Weald! Gertrude stopped quite suddenly, ran down the platform steps, passed quickly along one side of the hall, and disappeared. We were left standing in our forms, a hundred startled shivering children, afraid to face ourselves, afraid to glance at one another in that darkening hall.

...

There was a knock at my door. 'Come in.' I quavered, and lay flat. Stella was very tall, about the tallest person in our house, so though it was nearly pitch dark I could just make out that a long figure was leaning over me.

'Well, Rachel?'

'Yes, Stella?'

She sat down on my bed. I think she put her arm round me. The New Friendliness! This was how it was to begin!

'You heard what Gertrude said in the Great Hall to-night?'

'Yes, Stella.'

'And don't you think you've been very silly?'

'Yes.'

'And will you promise never to be again?'

'Yes, Stella.'

'That's right. You and I must be proper friends you know.'

'Yes, Stella.'

'Well, good-night.'

'Good-night, Stella. Stella –'

'Yes?'

'May I still go on making your bed, please?'

'Yes – if you like.'

'Oh thanks – *awfully*!'

Then she kissed me. It was not cold or official, but then it never had been. I remember her face pressed against mine for quite a long time, longer than usual. Probably she meant it. She had found me lying in the dark, and must have felt sorry for me, anyhow for the moment, and had let herself go. Then she got up, said 'good-night, Rachel' again in her lovely lazy voice, and went away.

As for me, I lay still, but I felt as if I were in a cloak of rapture, looking down at my past wretchedness as if it had been a filthy old garment that had slipped, a grey mass, to my feet. I wanted to lie awake all night and hug my bliss, but that evening's strain had been more exhausting than I knew, and I must have gone to sleep very soon. Next morning I heard that, in obedience to Gertrude Johnson's request, all the 'gonees' had been round to call on their various 'gonages' on the previous night.

... It was better that the old enthusiasm and devotions should go on than that brutality should have been used to destroy them. To my knowledge nobody ever attempted to kill them again.

12 A.S. Neill, *Hearts Not Heads in the School*, 1945, Herbert Jenkins Ltd, pp. 78–9

Neill was famous for his work as headteacher at Summerhill, a co-educational public school renowned for its liberalism.

'Sex and the future schools'

The school of tomorrow will be co-educational. Our segregated schools are clearly wrong in that they separate boys and girls from the opposite sex in an unnatural and dangerous way. ... The segregated school is fundamentally a funk hole made by parents and teachers who fear sex and too often hate it. They are ready to face the evil that youthful sex, when denied a natural outlet, tends to become homosexual, apparently thinking that, of the two, homosexuality is less objectional than heterosexuality. The conspiracy of silence about homosexual practices at public schools is a well-preserved one, and only a fraction of public school products will admit that homosexual affairs took place in their schooldays. Just as silent is the conspiracy to hide the fact that boarding-school girls get passions on bigger girls and mistresses, a fact that must throw some light on the prevalence of frigidity among many middle- and upper-class women. If a woman is unconsciously seeking love from a schoolmistress, she cannot be much of a wife or mistress to a mere man.

13 J. Macalister Brew, 'How The Mind Works', *Club News*, January 1945, p. 2

Josephine Macalister Brew was an influential youth leader in the 1940s and 1950s. She wrote powerfully about the importance of informal education in books and articles. She was a frequent contributor to *Club News*, the journal of the National Association of Girls' Clubs and Mixed Clubs. In the extract there is a separation of crushes, as a stage of sexual development, from homosexuality as a separate issue. The latter appears to have a sexual expression, the former only intense feelings.

V. Sex development in adolescence

... In the next stage of development, there is an increasing interest in the *same* sex. ... The girl usually becomes interested in older girls or women whom she *knows*, since her interest is always much more personal. For her, at this period, the complete ideal of what a woman should be, may be found in the P.T. instructor or in some essentially motherly type of woman whom she knows. These interests are familiar to us all, and whilst many people seem to think there is something rather touching in the boy's hero-worship, they are apt to be rather more unkind in attitude towards the girl with her crushes or G.P.'s or whatever may be the familiar slang for her hero-worship.

We must never forget that these idealised first loves are a very tender emotional experience, and we should never commit the unforgiveable sin of laughing at them on the one hand and wallowing in them on the other.

Much could be written about the duty of the Club leader, whether it be man or woman, to handle such delicate young love as tactfully and as sympathetically as possible, without in any way encouraging it. If young adults are cruelly hurt during this phase of their emotional development, it may have very serious repercussions on their later love life, so serious maybe, that they will never be able to realise to the full, complete love and happiness with someone of the other sex.

Often during this period in which boys and girls are interested in their own sex, instead of these attachments to older persons they develop a very close friendship with someone of their own age. We are all familiar with the type of girl in the Club world who says, 'I'll do it if my friend does' and with the boy who is always telling you what 'the fellow he knows at work' says about this, that and the other. Here again you have a violent friendship which is very touching in its loyalty and which one need not concern oneself with very much, provided that one of the two people concerned in the friendship does not suddenly become conscious of power over the other. As a rule, except for watching it carefully and sympathetically, there is no need for interference.

...

Many people get worried about various difficulties, such as masturbation and homo-sexuality. On the whole there is no need for the average person to be concerned with this unduly; both things are evidences of incomplete stages of development. In some cases, it is true that they block the natural development of the individual and this is partly the reason for the disapproval, both religious and social, with which they have always been regarded. For most people, both boys and girls, masturbation and homo-sexuality is a phase through which they may pass and has no deep significance. If, however, a Club leader is worried about either of these things it is always advisable to take expert advice. There is no problem of which it is more true that a little knowledge can be a dangerous thing.

14 J. Newsom, *The Education of Girls*, 1948, Faber & Faber, p. 149

John Newsom was an influential educationalist in the post-war years.

Teachers in girls' schools then should be for the most part attractive women who, even if unmarried, look as though they could have married if they had liked. Some of them should be married and others should not; for only too many of their pupils will need examples of successful spinsterhood. The woman who is unhappily married should be kept out of the schools, for she is apt to be bitter and resentful. So, incidentally, should the man who has made a mess of his married life. Such tragedies are often due to major failures in adjustment and development, and they produce states of mind which are both infectious and undesirable.

The same thing is true of persons with strong homo-sexual impulses – or perhaps it would be better to say, persons in whom their homo-sexual impulses have distorted their attitude towards the opposite sex. They should not be in a position to influence children over the age of eleven. Between eleven and fourteen feelings of love and admiration are normally directed upon persons of one's own sex. If children of this age take for their models adults who have not progressed beyond this stage, or who have reverted to it, they may themselves become incapable of healthy growth. After fourteen, when the emotions should be taking a hetero-sexual direction, the companionship of the abnormal is stultifying. This danger exists in spite of complete self-control on the part of such models, and even when they are unconscious of their own abnormal state. It is greatest in girls' schools because, contrary to the general belief, the effects of homo-sexuality are even more serious in women than in men.

15 M. Fleming, *Adolescence, Its Social Psychology*, 1948, Routledge & Kegan Paul (2nd edition 1963), p. 235

This text book would have been read by teachers in training.

'Adolescents with problems'

Adolescent sex difficulties deserving of the name are also found among those whose home life has been lacking in satisfaction of the basic human needs. Prostitutes and sexual perverts (when case studies are made of their history) are, for the most part, individuals from broken homes, from family groups where mother or father was unduly possessive, or from homes where the children were unwanted. Homosexual perversions also reach the dimensions of a problem chiefly in the artificial segregation of single-sex establishments; and on evidence such as this, the promiscuity of the prostitute, the unattached student in Bohemia or the less-intelligent soldier in a foreign land is now believed to have its origin in loneliness and lack of social interests rather than in strong sexuality. It is paralleled by the longing for approval of the adolescent girl who has had no father to pay her attentions and no satisfactory home life with opportunities for joyous sharing in many activities.

Present-day treatment of such difficulties is turning, therefore, to an interpretation based upon the safeguards of a social interest which can be developed by competent organisation of group friendlinesses rather than to an acceptance of the older viewpoint that 'it is as difficult for some individuals to escape the hands of the law as it is for them to add one cubit to their stature'.

An extension of wholesome heterosexual contacts in genuinely co-educational day schools or clubs is now known to be more efficacious as an aid to healthy maturing than the violent exercise formerly advocated for boys or the parental whippings administered to girls. In this connection also it is coming to be believed that wiser situational treatment can reduce many of the problems of adolescent behaviour.

16 J. Hemming, *Problems of Adolescent Girls*, 1960, Heinemann, pp. 76–9

This was the report of an academic study of 3,259 letters sent to a girls' weekly magazine between 1953 and 1955.

1   615 – friendship (girl–girl) (16.5%)
2   492 – friendship (girl–boy) (13.2%)
3   367 – anxieties about personal deportment (9.8%)
4   242 – crushes on older girls or adults (6.5% of total)

'The beginning of love'

The crush relationship

The 242 problems on crush relationships, coming from all over Great Britain, and from girls of ages eleven to fifteen years, in general confirm the findings of previous research. 'Some of the Grand Passions cause great unrest', writes Professor Valentine; 'the girls act like fond, doting lovers – kissing the book lent to them by a beloved mistress, walking up and down the road past the house where the loved one lives.' This kind of passionate involvement emerges from a majority of the crush letters. 'I have taken a very great liking to one of our mistresses and I think she knows this', writes one fourteen-year-old girl. 'I keep on thinking about her even when I am working. What should I do to stop myself thinking about her too much?'

Intense feeling is often expressed: 'At school we have a young mistress who takes geography and games, for nearly two years I have loved her. I am leaving school in one week and I know I will simply go mad or pine to death over her. My parents say that I will soon forget her when I start working but I know that I won't. I have hundreds of photos of her and my snapshot album is nearly full of her. Whenever I have a spare moment I always dash to her classroom, I am always at her side.'

Another girl writes: 'There is a young lady at my school whom I like very much. In fact, I love her. I want to see her all the time. I think about her all day and at night, and when I see her I feel funny and I want to cry. I should like to tell the teacher how I feel but I am too scared. Please help me, but don't tell me to forget her. I can't. I have felt like this about her for about a year now.' Sometimes two friends share a passionate regard for a teacher. 'Both my friend and myself are deeply in love with a teacher', one girl writes. 'She is about ten years older than we are. We cannot sleep for thinking about her. Our work is being affected because nearly everything reminds us of her.'

Crushes on senior girls are mentioned in the correspondence about as frequently as crushes on mistresses. A thirteen-year old girl states: 'I have a crush on another girl at school, I find it is interfering with my lessons, and all I can do is talk about her which makes people cross. I try to forget about her but I can't.' Another writes: 'I love our head girl. I wish she were my sister.'

Occasionally a letter describes a passionate regard for a girl of about the same age as the writer:

> There is a girl in my form at school who is four months younger than myself, yet I would do anything for her. I like her more than anyone else in the world. At night I dream about her. One night I dreamt that I was dying and was delirious and that this girl only could break the fever. I've had more dreams similar to that. Please do not think I am insane or that I do not get enough sleep. I am thirteen. We are just friends, she does not know that I like her so much. Can you tell me what this is caused by and if possible why I am like this.

... This letter shows, as do many others, that a crush is much more than a passing fancy. It may persist for a long time as an important element in a girl's emotional life. ...

The correspondence leaves the strong impression that the crush relationship is not accepted or understood in many of the schools from which the queries come. The girls complain of being ridiculed by their companions or, sometimes, treated coldly and fobbed off by the objects of their admiration. No doubt it is embarrassing to be pursued by a pathetic young adorer, but better understanding of what was going on could convert these awkward relationships into formative experiences. The letters even give some evidence of attempts to obliterate crushes by punitive means. 'At our school', writes one correspondent, 'we have crushes on the senior girls. Our headmistress says this is a waste of time and degrading to our characters. She is trying to stamp out this "stupidity" by forbidding us various privileges until it stops. I am very attached to a senior and do not feel I could give her up.'

A number of letters are received from the seniors themselves who, amid the general misunderstanding and embarrassment, find it beyond their powers to adjust to the attentions of juniors who admire them: 'I am a Sixth Form prefect. In the Third Form are two girls who have developed a passion for me. Everywhere I go I see them. I am becoming so embarrassed I must do something, but what?' Thus, we appear to have the curious situation in Britain that what is now known to be an inevitable stage of emotional development for many adolescents is, in some schools, treated as foolish, ridiculous or wrong. It follows that adolescents who are caught up in a crush relationship may have their perplexities increased by a sense of guilt about their feelings and by lack of understanding upon the part of those to whom they should be able to turn for support and guidance.

17 H. Richardson, *Adolescent Girls in Approved Schools*, 1969, Routledge & Kegan Paul, p. 50

Staff did not hide from the problems of homosexuality. They were aware of the 'crushes' girls had for members of staff, which could drive the girl to excesses of showing off and jealousy, and which were generally handled with sympathy and realism (avoiding, for instance, situations where compromise was possible). They were aware of 'crushes' on other girls, and recognized the exaggerated male or female hair styles or gait or other gestures involved. They were alert to the possibility of bed-sharing, but avoided drawing attention (or those who were wise did) in a shocked way, since this would have made the practice more interesting – just as they had to appear only mildly interested if a mentally defective girl stole the electric light fuses, while endeavouring to stop her through this very 'disinterest'. They believed the problem of homosexuality was kept within safety limits in the school.

5

LAW

INTRODUCTION

Legal discourses concerning lesbianism in nineteenth-century and twentieth-century Britain are both highly complex and under-researched. Historical analysis of the legal position of the lesbian is in its infancy. Few sources for lesbianism and the law have been identified to date, but this may reflect the absence of research as much as any actual paucity of evidence. In this chapter we have presented a variety of types of source. Some are official reports of the law-making processes in parliament and the law-keeping of the courts which provide a way into dominant legal discourses. Newspaper articles can show how legal parameters regarding lesbian sexuality were understood and represented to a wider public. There is also evidence of how the female worlds created by the legal system – for example reformatories and prisons – were important settings for lesbian sub-cultures.

The gender difference manifested in the legal treatment of homosexuality is one of the most striking features reiterated by historians. The sexual activities of women, men and children have always been a powerful focus for legal intervention in Britain. Yet while sexual activities between men have repeatedly been debated and dealt with punitively, sex between women has been given scant attention. Church authorities in England had acknowledged and castigated homosexual behaviour in women from as early as the seventh century but there was a singular absence of interest in the subject in the burgeoning civil legal systems over the following centuries. It is understandable then that Lord Alfred Douglas, whose lover Oscar Wilde had met with such harsh punishment by the judiciary in 1895, should rail against the unequal treatment of men and women with regard to their homosexual activities:

> Perhaps you are not aware that 'Lesbianism' exists to any extent in London, but I can assure you that it does, and though of course I cannot mention names, I could point out to you half a dozen

women in society or among actresses who would be considered as 'dangerous' to young girls as Oscar Wilde will I suppose henceforth be considered to boys.

(Montgomery Hyde 1972: 170)

Names were not named and the evidence that exists for the nineteenth century suggests that consideration of lesbian activities was largely absent from the criminal law. Faderman notes finding only a dozen cases where women were accused of lesbianism in court before the twentieth century (1985). In 1921 parliament debated the possible criminalising of lesbianism and while this was mooted again in 1937 and in 1956 it never took place. It was, however, effectively illegal under British military law until 1999 (Crane 1982).

While male homosexuality emerged forcefully and highly visibly in areas of the law, the existence of lesbian behaviour has largely been denied or, if it must be acknowledged, has been seen as a rare and exotic oddity. Thus there is little reason for the legislature to consider it. A persistent representation in twentieth-century legal discourse is that lesbianism is an evil that requires regulation and, if possible, eradication. But here the possibility of its incidence increasing, by virtue of the attention given to it, has persistently served to mute any discussion of it. This has led historians to argue that the denial and censorship of lesbianism is the strategy through which the law has sought to control love between women (Faraday 1985, 1988).

Historians have suggested that the law has been an important means of social regulation of women's behaviour generally, while also acting as a means of resistance (Smart 1992). Although the mechanisms appear to be less overt, it may also be worth considering whether this dynamic comes into play for lesbians. The sources below provide evidence to show that, while not controlled directly by the law, lesbianism has entered the legislature and courts in relation to a number of issues during the past two centuries. One issue is the way lesbianism was feared and perceived to undermine heterosexual marriage. The charge of fraud, for women passing as men in order to marry, was a theme illustrated in Chapter 1. The question of whether lesbianism should be grounds for divorce repeatedly surfaces in both legal and medical literature. Less explicitly, the issue of sex between women as indecency appears within these debates and cases. These concerns come together, particularly in the twentieth century, in the processes and justifications for the censorship of material referring to lesbianism, e.g. books and plays, on the grounds of obscenity. But women have also used the law themselves, to challenge slander and libels on their character through imputations of lesbianism. This again has served to bring the idea before the courts and often into the public domain through press reporting.

A valuable early source that illustrates how allegations of lesbianism might powerfully regulate women's relationships with each other is the case of Woods and Pirie v Gordon in 1810. This has been seen as a significant event in lesbian history (Faderman 1985, Moore 1992, Donoghue 1993). Marianne Woods and

Jane Pirie complained that their school near Edinburgh was ruined after the removal of Lady Gordon's granddaughter Jane Cumming and the subsequent rapid withdrawal of all the other pupils. Lady Gordon's counsel countered that she was 'credibly informed and verily believed that the pursuers had been guilty of indecent and criminal practices'. Both the trial and Lady Gordon's appeal to the House of Lords vindicated the women. But the accusations are discussed with forthright and searching inquiry and the exhaustive documentation (there are over a thousand pages of trial transcripts and related papers) raises many important issues concerning both the limits of the law in relation to female behaviour and contemporary attitudes.

During the nineteenth century, lesbianism was rarely discussed in the legal system. The cryptic insinuations in the reporting of the divorce case of Codrington v Codrington in 1864 have been carefully investigated for evidence of lesbianism by Vicinus (1997). It remains unclear whether lesbianism was involved, but the case is nevertheless important because the silences it reveals certainly admit the possibility of a knowledge of lesbianism, not only amongst the participants in the legal process, but amongst the readership of *The Times* and other newspapers where it was extensively reported. Edwards' (1981) argument that the lack of legal recognition of lesbianism reflects the nineteenth-century belief in the sexual passivity and invisibility of women is convincing, although the law's considerable focus on prostitutes should be remembered.

In the twentieth century, however, as our sources suggest, there was greater overt legal discussion of lesbianism. While the law never directly prohibited sexual relations between women, it increasingly came to correlate such activity with criminal indecency and lesbianism became more firmly linked with immorality. In the World War I period there were a number of important judicial and legislative events. Lesbianism was a key issue in the well-publicised libel case brought by Maud Allan in 1918, even though it was reported in very coded form in the press (Bland 1998). This was soon followed by Radclyffe Hall's successful 1920 slander case, also brought to defend herself against charges of immorality with another woman. By 1921, when attempts were made to include lesbianism within the criminal law, the topic had begun to be openly aired in the courts. Doan hypothesises that this attempted criminalisation of female homosexuality may have been a move to intimidate the Women Police Service, a feminist group led by lesbians who were trying to establish their powers as an independent women's police force (Doan 1997, 1998b).

As divorce became more common in the 1930s and 1940s (Smart 1996), lesbianism was mentioned from time to time as a cause of marriage breakdown. Despite its growing significance in the legal system, sex between women continued to be treated apart from sex between men. In 1957 the Royal Commission on Homosexual Offences and Prostitution again resisted attempts to equate it with male homosexuality and claimed it 'found no case in which a female has been convicted of an act with another female which exhibits the libidinous features that characterise sexual acts between males' (Edwards 1981: 45).

While the Wolfenden Committee had a powerful role in shaping male homosexual identities, practices and social relations, it left lesbianism to be dealt with by social censure rather than direct legal methods (Moran 1995).

In contrast to the muted presence of lesbianism in the courts, the creative worlds of literature, art, theatre, cinema, television and radio frequently depicted the lesbian and were legally censored for so doing. The study of censorship and obscenity in the nineteenth and twentieth centuries reveals changing attitudes to lesbianism in the workings of the law that merit further attention. Publishers were sometimes dissuaded by the Home Office, prior to publication, from launching books which had explicit lesbian content, and other novels and plays, as well as the famous *The Well of Loneliness*, were suppressed or prosecuted for obscenity between the wars (Faraday 1985, Sidhe 2000). While lesbianism as such was not necessarily the principal concern of the censors, it might be seen as connected to those issues that were: sexual immorality, male homosexuality, blasphemy and national security. Indeed as lesbianism became a clearer concept during the twentieth century, it was also increasingly associated with a semi-criminal under-world of violence, murder and sexual depravity generally.

While the sources below provide plentiful material for discussing the motives of the legislature and the multiple discourses informing the courts, a far more detailed examination of local records and of specific cases across the social class spectrum is needed before we can move beyond speculation about the historical relationship between the lesbian and the law.

1 Miss Marianne Woods and Miss Jane Pirie against Dame Helen Cumming Gordon, 1975 [1810], New York: Arno Press

In 1809 two schoolteachers, running their own small private boarding school near Edinburgh sued Dame Helen Cumming Gordon for defamation. Dame Gordon's 16-year-old Anglo-Indian granddaughter was a pupil at the school. Her accounts of activities there persuaded her grandmother that the teachers, Marianne Woods and Jane Pirie, had engaged in 'improper and criminal activity' with each other. The women were ruined by the lengthy trials and legal wranglings that followed.

... The following Statement is made on the part of Lady Cumming Gordon, the defender.

The defender's granddaughter, Miss Jane Cumming, was born in India and placed, in early infancy, in one of the most respectable boarding-schools in Calcutta. At the age of seven years, she was sent to this country, and has since resided with the defender, except for about (blank) years, during which she was boarded with Miss Charles at Elgin, who had been previously governess in the defender's family, and who had educated all the defender's daughters.

In 1810, Miss Cumming, who is now sixteen years of age, was entrusted to the care of the pursuers, who had recently before set up a boarding-school at Drumiheugh, and in whose success the defender was much interested, the sister of Miss Pirie having been governess in her daughter Lady Dunbar's family.

The young ladies at the boarding-school slept chiefly in two apartments; in one of which Miss Pirie slept and in the other Miss Woods. Miss Cumming was Miss Pirie's bedfellow.

The defender left Edinburgh, for the summer, on the 1st of May 1810. After she went away, Miss Cumming was often disturbed, during the night, by Miss Pirie conversing with Miss Woods, who came into bed with them; and these conversations were attended with strange noises and shakings of the bed.

One night Miss Cumming was awaked by Miss Pirie speaking to Miss Woods. Miss Pirie was at that time in bed, and Miss Woods was standing beside it, and they were kissing each other. Miss Pirie said 'O, do it darling!' Miss Pirie answered, 'Not to-night, it would awake Miss Cumming'. This raised Cumming's curiosity, who lay awake but pretended to be asleep. In a little Miss Woods came into bed, upon which Miss Cumming felt Miss Pirie put down her hand, and lift up her shift, so that Miss Cumming felt her naked skin. Miss Woods then lay above Miss Pirie; and when in that situation said 'I would like better to have some one above me.' Miss Woods then put down her hand, and they made a noise, which was a wet kind of noise, attended with a shaking of the bed. Miss Cumming, being disgusted, could lie no longer without speaking, and said twice, 'Oh Miss Pirie,' before the latter answered. At last Miss Pirie said, as if newly awake, 'What?' Miss Cumming said 'What shakes the bed?' Miss Pirie replied 'Nothing,' and covered herself with the bed-clothes.

Miss Cumming lay awake for a long time, complaining she could not sleep. Miss Pirie desired her two or three times to turn her face to the wall, and try to sleep; and Miss Pirie at last having turned herself, said, 'Now you must turn, as I have turned;' and she covered Miss Cumming with the bed-clothes. Then Miss Woods went out of bed, and when she had reached her own door might not be heard by Miss Cumming, who, however did hear it. In a little Miss Woods was heard to cough, when Miss Pirie said, 'Oh this is Miss Woods coughing, and I must go to her, poor soul;' and she went.

Next morning Miss Cumming told what had happened, to Miss M— a young lady of sixteen years of age, who slept with Miss Woods; and Miss M — informed Miss Cumming, that a few nights before, Miss Pirie had been in Miss Woods' bed, and she had observed the same motions, and the same shaking of the bed which Miss Cumming had described.

Another night Miss Cumming was awaked with a noise and motions as before described: at that time Miss Woods was lying above Miss Pirie and Miss Pirie said, 'Oh you are hurting me.'

Another time, when in the same situation, Miss Cumming felt them take up their shifts, and Miss Pirie said, 'Oh you are in the wrong place!' Miss Woods said, 'I know.' Miss Pirie said, 'Why do you do it then?' Miss Woods said, 'For fun.'

Another night Miss Cumming heard Miss Woods say to Miss Pirie, when in the same situation, 'Am I hurting you?' Miss Pirie said, 'No;' upon which Miss Woods continued the motions, and when about to go away, said, 'Good night, darling, good night, I think I have put you in a fair way to sleep.' To this Miss Pirie replied, 'No;' and Miss Woods again continued.

...

Miss Woods, as before mentioned slept with Miss M—. One night Miss M— was awaked by a noise in the bed, and day-light coming in, she perceived that Miss Pirie was also in the bed. She could not understand what they were doing; but the bed was shaking and Miss Pirie was lying above Miss Woods, and lay there a long time.

Miss M—'s family coming to town, she told what had happened to a nurse, adding, that she felt very disagreeable, and did not know what to do. Upon this the nurse said, 'Oh Miss! that's dreadful, if you are sure of that; do you know they are worse than beasts, and deserve to be burned; if it ever happens again tell me, and speak out, and let them know you notice it.'

In the course of the following week, Miss Pirie one night came again to Miss Woods' bed, and the same scene was repeated. Miss M— coughed to show that she was awake; upon which Miss Woods also began to cough, and desired Miss M—to fetch her some water from the dressing-room, which Miss M—did, and as she was returning, she saw Miss Pirie rush out of the room.

A servant-maid in the house repeatedly saw Miss Woods and Miss Pirie in improper situations, and using indecent familiarities with each other.

The morning after Miss M— was first disturbed, as before related, she rose earlier than usual, and was first in the school-room. The maid alluded to was doing up the room, to whom Miss M— said that she had slept ill, and had a dreadful night. The maid understood her at once, and said, laughing, 'It is a pity they cannot get a man, but that they will never get.' Two or three of the oldest girls came down soon after, and all joined in speaking of what had happened. The maid informed them, that one day going to seek for something wanted for the house, she found both the drawing-room doors locked, and looking through the key-hole, she saw Miss Woods and Miss Pirie lying on the sofa in an improper manner.

One morning after this, the maid came to the school-room door, and told some of the girls that she had just caught Miss Woods and Miss Pirie in the very act, having gone in on them abruptly. She said that Miss Pirie leaped out of bed immediately, half dressed, and that Miss Woods hid herself under the bed-clothes. When she had told this, she said, 'When I come in with the kettle at breakfast, notice what like their faces are.' When she did so, the young ladies observed that they avoided looking at her, and that Miss Pirie appeared much agitated.

The maid often said they were brutes, and worse than brutes, nasty brutes; and before the girls, she put out her tongue at them.

The Saturday after Miss M— had first disclosed the matter to the nurse, she had another interview with her, when she mentioned that Miss Pirie had been again in the bed, and the scene had been repeated which she before witnessed. The nurse asked her if any other person had seen them behaving in the same manner, and she said that Miss Cumming had been frequently disturbed, as above related. The nurse advised Miss M— to let it be known, that it might be put a stop to, and said, 'Surely, Miss Pirie must be a man.'

Miss Cumming and Miss M— are young ladies of the most unexceptionable character, enjoying the confidence and esteem of numerous respectable connections and friends. It will be proved, if thought necessary, that the pursuers themselves, before the detection of their own unhappy misconduct, uniformly spoke of both in terms of the warmest approbation.

2 'Not Fit to Marry', *The News of the World*, 24 January 1915, p. 5

Not fit to marry

Wife with 'platonic' views

Strange union between artist and actress

[Report from the Divorce Court]
... The husband, Mr Nigel Bruce Severn, an artist living in Kensington, desired to have his marriage annulled with Mrs Agnes Severn, otherwise Mickerin, otherwise de Llana, a Roumanian and an actress. An extraordinary story was outlined. ...

Before the wedding respondent suggested that her friend, a Miss Elstob, an actress, then living with her at Edward-square Cottages, Kensington, should continue to live with them after the marriage. Petitioner consented ...

Some time before the marriage ceremony respondent suggested that it should be a platonic union. ... On the wedding day petitioner and his wife went to Windsor for the day ... and that night respondent slept in a room with her lady friend, petitioner sleeping at his wife's cottage, as had been previously arranged. They lived in the same house for a fortnight, respondent all the while declining to be more than a wife except in name. ...

On the day he left the house petitioner admitted that there was a violent quarrel. She told him to get out, but he never threatened to 'ruin' her by going to all her friends. ...

Mrs Severn, a dark, handsome lady, declared that when petitioner asked her to marry him she said she was not in love with him, and did not think it proper to marry a man she was not in love with. What finally induced her to marry was because petitioner said they could assist each other in their careers, and they could be 'friends.' 'He always understood I could not live with anyone I did not love, because I considered it immoral,' asserted Mrs. Severn. ...

Miss Clare Elstob, an actress, and Mrs. Severn's friend, corroborated that lady as to the alleged arrangement before the marriage. ...

'I think the whole thing perfectly scandalous,' added the judge. 'I cannot express words too strongly of the position taken up by this lady. If her views are as she says, she ought never to have married ... ' A decree of nullity of the marriage was pronounced.

3 'Vision of Salome', *The News of the World*, 2 June 1918, pp. 3–4

Maud Allen (1873–1956), a well-known dancer, brought an action for libel in 1918, after she was accused of being a lesbian in an article with the heading 'Cult of the Clitoris'. The trial was widely reported, though details were heavily censored. The defence sought to discredit her in a number of ways and suggested that understanding the meaning of the word 'clitoris' was itself proof of lesbianism. Maud Allan lost her case.

Vision of Salome

Honour of a famous dancer impugned

Sensational disclosures in amazing trial

The first of the three indictments – that relating to the alleged libel on Miss Allan – recited that Mr Billing maliciously published on Feb 16 a false and defamatory libel concerning her in the form of a paragraph in a newspaper called 'Vigilante' (conducted by Mr Billing), meaning that Maud Allan was a lewd, unchaste, and immoral woman and was about to give private performances of an obscene and indecent character, so designed as to foster and encourage unnatural practices among women, and that the said Maud Allan associated herself with persons addicted to unnatural practices. The paragraph in question ... appeared under a heading that is unprintable. ...

...

In 1918 it occurred to Mr Grein, who was connected with the Independent Theatre ... to produce the play of 'Salome', which was written by the extraordinary, perverted genius Oscar Wilde. Miss Allan was invited to take part in the performance. ...

The defence argued that Maud Allan shared the 'hereditary vice' which had led her brother to murder.

Mr Billing: I deeply regret it, my lord, but I shall have to call evidence to prove the exact influence that that case has to bear generally on sexual perversion. ... The case referred to in that book. I shall have to call evidence that the vices referred to in that book are hereditary. ...

Mr Billing (To witness [Maud Allan]): Was your brother executed in San Francisco for murdering two young girls and outraging them? – Miss Allan (to the judge): I do not know whether that question is absolutely admissible in its entirety. ...

The defence also emphasised the friendship between Allan and Margot Asquith (wife of the Prime Minister), who was rumoured to be a lesbian.

... [Billing to Maud Allan] Did you go to Downing-street? – I did. – Did you dance? – No. – Did you see Mrs Asquith there? – Naturally, when I was her guest. – Have you met her anywhere else? – Yes. – Has she ever been in your dressing-room at the Palace? – Never. – You would recognise her, of course? – I have eyes. ...

Billing later called Dr Arthur Cooke as a witness, who gave his views on Mr Grein, the producer of Salome.

I next noticed the way in which he replied to questions. The language he used was most extraordinary ... – What language do you describe that as? – The language which is generally used by homosexualists. – Witness added that sexual perverts referred to physical acts of the senses as 'spiritual, poetic, beautiful, and pure love.' ... The play, 'Salome', he considered, was full of homosexual inclinations. ... Witness was aware from his own knowledge that there were many moral perverts in England.

4 A.T. Fitzroy, *Despised and Rejected*, 1988 [1918], GMP Publishers Ltd, pp. 217–21

A.T. Fitzroy was the pseudonym of Rose Allatini, a prolific popular novelist. The novel, which was prosecuted and banned, concerns the relationship between a conscientious objector, Dennis and his woman friend, Antoinette. Here they discuss their feelings for their own sex.

'What was it,' hesitatingly she spoke, choosing her words with care, so that he might not divine her ignorance, 'what was it, that time at Amberhurst, that showed you?'

'My child, the way you looked at that woman, was quite enough.'

Hester ... So that was it!

'You were in love with her, weren't you?'

'Yes ... '

'And there had been others, hadn't there? Other women?'

'Yes – Oh, yes.' Rapidly she cast her mind over those school-girl passions of her early youth – Miss Prescot – Natasha – passing flickers of emotion aroused here and there by the beauty or attraction of women she had met in hotels abroad – finally Hester. ... This, then, was the taint of which he spoke; the taint that they shared, he and she. Only whereas he had always striven against these tendencies in himself, in herself she had never regarded them as abnormal. It had seemed disappointing, but not in the least unnatural, that all her passionate longings should have been awakened by women, instead of by members of the opposite sex.

'And you were thinking of them, weren't you, when you said you'd known what the real thing was like?'

'Yes ... ' This, at all events, was the truth.

'You've never known it with a man, have you?'

'Never, Dennis.' ... Never until now.

'I've known it, once, with one of my own sex ... that was a long time ago. It was terrible ... and rather wonderful, but it had to be beaten down, and beaten down again, and the scar has never quite healed.'

She stole a glance at him, as he strode along at her side, a furrow between his deep-set eyes. A wave of burning tenderness and longing came over her. It was a shame that he should have to suffer so horribly from the consciousness of his abnormality, while her own had never caused her the slightest uneasiness. ...

'It's a case of "like to like" with us.' He had given his order for dinner and they faced each other across the narrow table. 'And because there's a certain amount of the masculine element in you, and of the feminine element in me, we both have to suffer in the same way.'

She felt suddenly compelled to honesty. 'I haven't suffered – because I didn't quite realise ... about myself.'

'And I've made you realise ...? Oh, I'm sorry.'

'Don't be sorry,' she implored, 'I should have had to know sooner or later.' And she was glad that it was he who had made her realise. ... glad. ...

'Yes,' he assented, 'of course you would. Not much peace of oblivion for people like us. Not much happiness either, so far as I can see. Not when one always has to fight and watch and take care, and pay the penalty for having instincts that aren't like other people's.'

Yet she had been happy, blissfully happy during her brief passion for Hester. She had not fought nor watched nor taken care, for she had never realised the need of doing either. She felt as if she had not been justified in being happy, as if it were unfair to him that she should have escaped paying the penalty. But in future she would not escape. Suffering must inevitably accompany realisation. Again she was glad: for by suffering shared, she would earn the right to stand by him in his loneliness.

5 'A Pernicious Book', *The Times*, 27 September 1918

A pernicious book

Publishers charged under defence regulations

C.W. DANIEL (LIMITED), Tudor-street, and MR. CHARLES WILLIAM DANIEL, a director of that company, were summoned at the Mansion House yesterday for making statements in a book entitled 'Despised and Rejected' likely to prejudice the recruiting, training and discipline of persons in his Majesty's forces. The defendant Mr. Daniel said they pleaded 'Not guilty.' As he had been ill since the summonses were served, he had not been able to instruct a solicitor, and he applied for an adjournment.

Sir Richard Muir for the prosecution, said that the defendant had admitted that he was the publisher of the book, but said he did not accept responsibility for the statements made in it. The book was of a most pernicious character. It seemed to be written to exploit two ideas – one of them in relation to sexual matters and the other to put at their very highest the views of those who objected to military service of any kind including non-combatant service. To make the doctrines so put forward more acceptable, the person into whose mouth they were put was the hero, and where they were not personally uttered by him they were uttered by his friends and fellow-thinkers, including a young woman. The hero was a member of a family all of whom were normal; he alone was abnormal. In one passage it was said: – 'lasting peace can never be obtained by war because war only breeds war.' There was a reference in the book to a new recruiting poster which said in effect that this country was not worth fighting for; while of tribunals it was stated, 'You will find them consisting for the most part of beefy, sanctimonious old men.'

It was stated that the book was written by Miss Rose Allatini, whose *nom de plume* was 'A.T. Fitzroy'; 1,012 copies had been printed and 677 sold.

Colonel Lord Chichester, of the Adjutant-General's Department, War Office, said that in his opinion there were statements in the book likely to interfere with recruiting and discipline.

The hearing was adjourned.

6 Parliamentary Debates (House of Commons), Criminal Law Amendment Bill, 4 August 1921, para. 1799–1806

Criminal Law Amendment Bill [Lords]

As amended (in the Standing Committee), considered.

New clause – (Acts of indecency by females)

Any act of gross indecency between female persons shall be a misdemeanour and punishable in the same manner as any such act committed by male persons under ... the Criminal Law Amendment Act, 1885. – [Mr. Macquisten.]

Brought up, and read the First time.

Mr. MACQUISTEN: I beg to move, 'That the Clause be read a Second time.'

The Clause has been put down by the hon. members for the Hartlepools (Mr. Howard Gritten) and Upton (Sir E. Wild), as well as myself. It is one which, I think, is long overdue in the criminal code of this country. I have had professional experience of very calamitous and sad cases due to gross practices indulged in of the kind specified in the Criminal Law Amendment Act, and which are referred to in my Amendment. These moral weaknesses date back to the very origin of history, and when they grow and become prevalent in any nation or in any country, it is the beginning of the nation's downfall. The falling away of feminine morality was to a large extent the cause of the destruction of the early Grecian civilisation, and still more the cause of the downfall of the Roman Empire. One cannot in a public assembly go into the details; it is more a matter for medical science and for neurologists; but all lawyers who have had criminal and divorce practice know that there is in modern social life an undercurrent of dreadful degradation, unchecked and uninterfered with. I believe that if the sanction – that is to say, the punishment – of the law were imposed upon it, it would go a long way to check it, and I believe that it would be possible to do a great deal in that way to eradicate it. Neurologists will tell you how largely the spread of the use of cocaine and other drugs is due to the dreadful nerve deterioration which besets many of the idle part of our population. In the course of my experience I have seen happy homes wrecked in this way. Only tonight I was speaking with a man whom I have known for a comparatively short time, and who told me how his home had been ruined by the wiles of one abandoned female, who had pursued his wife, and later some other misconduct happened with a male person which enabled him to get a divorce. But for that he would have been shackled for life to that abandoned person who had forgotten all the dictates of Nature and morality. I do not wish to speak on the matter at any length. I know that to many Members of this House the mere idea of the suggestion of such a thing is entirely novel:

they have never heard of it. But those who have had to engage either in medical or in legal practice know that every now and again one comes across these horrors, and I believe that the time has come when seeing that we are going to make an alteration in the law to deal with a question of morality with which it is necessary to deal, this matter, on account of its civil and sociological effects, this horrid grossness of homosexual immorality should also be grappled with. This is the far more deep-seated evil and it is only right that this House, which has the care of the law and to a large extent the morals of the people, should consider it to be its duty to do its best to stamp out an evil which is capable of sapping the highest and the best in civilisation.

Major FARQUHARSON: I do not desire to detain the House, but on behalf of those who are promoting this Bill I am very pleased to accept this proposed new Clause.

Colonel WEDGWOOD: I cannot believe that the House will really pass this Clause. In the first place, it is a beastly subject and it is being better advertised by the moving of this Clause than in any other way. ...

Sir E. WILD: . . . I can quite understand that many Members of this House, whose good fortune it is not to have to know about these things, may hesitate to believe that such things do take place. If they were to consult any neurologist, any great doctor who deals with nervous diseases, they would be told that this is a very prevalent practice. I have the authority of one of the greatest of our nerve specialists – I do not wish to mention names – who has told me with his own lips that not a week passes that some unfortunate girl does not confess to him that she owes the breakdown of her nerves to the fact that she has been tampered with by a member of her own sex. I wrote to him with regard to this Debate, and he says:

'It would be difficult to recite the various forms of malpractices between women, as it would be impossible to recite them in the House. If you wish for these it would be best to obtain a copy of Krafft-Ebing 'Psychopathia Sexualis,' or Havelock Ellis's work on sexual malpractices. My own feeling is simply to refer to the Lesbian love practices between women, which are common knowledge.'

I think that is enough. We do not want to pollute the House with details of these abominations. I have consulted many asylum doctors, and they assure me that the asylums are largely peopled by nymphomaniacs and people who indulge in this vice. I have also consulted the criminologists, and they say that these practices take place. I have here copy of a report, if anyone cares to read it, of a case at the Central Criminal Court before an eminent judge two or three years ago, in which a witness stated on oath that this practice had taken place between her and an elder woman. If you consult chief officers of police you will find the same thing. In one case I was told of a case similar to the one told to the House by my hon. and learned Friend (Mr. Macquisten), where a man said the whole of his married life was ruined because his wife had been taken from him by a young woman. It is idle to deny, although I will not say the vice is rampant in society, that there are people in society who are guilty of it.

In regard to the only valid argument of my hon. and gallant Friend, I admit that the difficulty of proof in these cases exists as in cases of the vice between men; but you do get evidence sometimes from a comparatively innocent party and sometimes through the intervention of the police. Surely it is fair to assume and say that if it be proved as it is proved, to the satisfaction of the House that this vice exists, it should not have immunity from punishment because it is difficult to prove. The other argument used was that of blackmail. There is always a danger in all this legislation against sexual vice that there may be blackmail. At the same time, it is a very big order at this time of day to say that, because there may be blackmail you are not to punish vice when it can be proved to exist. This vice does exist and it saps the fundamental institutions of society. In the first place it stops child-birth, because it is well-known fact that any woman who indulges in this vice will have nothing whatever to do with the other sex. It debauches young girls and it introduces neurasthenia and insanity. Anybody who is really interested in the punishment of vice would desire that the law should be clothed with power which can only be exercised if there be proper proof to put down a vice that must tend to cause our race to decline.

Lieut.-Colonel MOORE-BRABAZON: I am glad that this Clause has had a certain amount of discussion, though it required some moral courage to join in it. But I want to know whether the Clause is going to do good or harm. We must remember that on this subject we are not dealing with crime at all. We are dealing with abnormalities of the brain, and we have got to look on all these cases from that point of view. We want to decide whether it is wise to deal with mental cases in the Law Courts. If we do so, and are to go on logical lines, we should soon be introducing Measures into this House to give penal servitude for life to the hermaphrodite. In this case we are not trying to inculcate a fear of punishment. That already exists in society to-day, because the pervert is undoubtedly despised and shunned by all grades of society. There are only three ways of dealing with perverts. The first is the death sentence. That has been tried in old times, and, though drastic, it does do what is required – that is, stamp them out. The second is to look upon them frankly as lunatics, and lock them up for the rest of their lives. This is a very satisfactory way also. It gets rid of them. The third way is to leave them entirely alone, not notice them, not advertise them. That is the method that has been adopted in England for many hundred years, and I believe that it is the best method now, because these cases are self-exterminating. They are examples of ultra-civilisation, but they have the merit of exterminating themselves, and consequently they do not spread or do very much harm to society at large. There is this last reason why I would urge the House to leave this question alone and drop this Clause. To adopt a Clause of this kind would do harm by introducing into the minds of perfectly innocent people the most revolting thoughts and because of that I ask the introducers of this Clause to withdraw it.

Question put. 'That the Clause be read a Second time'.
The House divided: Ayes 148; Noes 53.

7 'Douglas-Pennant Case', *The Manchester Guardian*, 3 July 1931

After dismissal from her post as Commandant of the Women's Royal Air Force, Violet Douglas-Pennant rallied enough support to take her case to the House of Lords but failed to receive any satisfactory explanation. When, years later, allegations of lesbianism were finally revealed as the reason for her dismissal, she found she had no recourse to justice.

Douglas-Pennant case

The alleged charge

Protest meeting

(From our London Staff.)
Fleet Street, Thursday
A meeting for adults only, at which it had been stated that startling disclosures would be made, about the Douglas-Pennant case, was held to-night in the Central Hall, Westminster ...

Dr. Norwood said that for nearly thirteen years Miss Douglas-Pennant had borne the odium of dismissal on an unstated charge, which was much harder to bear than the odium of a charge that had been stated. She had been summarily dismissed from her position as Commandant of the Women's Royal Air Force, but the cause of her dismissal had never been known either to her or to the public. This was a national question, he said, for if such a thing were allowed to happen without protest serious things would happen to the nation.

'I do not suppose there is very much malevolence at the root of this case,' he continued, 'but I do feel assured there is a tragic mistake, and I see no reason why when human beings make a mistake they should not admit it, even if they belonged to the Government. We demand that the cause for this act shall be made public.'

Mr. J. J. Edwards criticised the findings of the House of Lords Committee and then made the disclosure of which the audience had been waiting.

At long last

'At long last,' he said, 'the charges that were made against Miss Douglas-Pennant and which brought about her dismissal are known. She was accused of being immoral with women, in other words, of being a Sapphist. That was the startling information that led the people concerned to agree among themselves in order to throw dust in the eyes of the public that it should be said she was accused of inefficiency.'

When that information was given to Lord Weir he was so shocked that he lost all sense of reason, and without any inquiry or investigation immediately gave orders through General Sir Sefton Brancker that Miss Douglas-Pennant should be dismissed from the corps in which up to that moment she had been commandant.

Mr Edwards said that the evidence of this charge was contained in documents sworn before a commissioner for oaths. 'Now that you know what the charges are,' he continued, 'you will find no difficulty in understanding the mystery surrounding this case. The charges were made by well-known people, and were authenticated in the manner I have mentioned.'

A Voice: 'Name?'

Brigadier General Blakeney said they had heard the vile accusation made against Miss Douglas-Pennant. 'In the East we know,' he said 'that such charges are sometimes made. It is not necessary to formulate them. It is done by the old method of whispered drives, as was done in this case.'.. He hoped the people of this country would compel the legislation to right the foul wrong.

8 Kerr v Kennedy, 1 All ER (1942) 412

In this case the judge decided the imputation of lesbianism in a woman was an imputation of unchastity. Damages of £300 and costs were awarded to the plaintiff for this 'very grave slander'.

Action for damages for an alleged slander. The plaintiff in the course of certain remarks alleged that the defendant said of the plaintiff: 'She used to live with other women. She is a lesbian.' The gist of the words complained of was that they imputed that the plaintiff was a female homosexual. ...

It is contended for the defendant that an imputation of lesbianism is not an imputation of unchastity within the Slander of Women Act, 1891, the argument being that the word 'unchastity' in the Act is limited to unchastity between a woman and a man and excludes immorality between persons of the same sex. ...

... the true approach to the construction of 'unchastity' seems to me to appear when the question is put, what imputations on a woman *qua* woman, in the sphere of sexual morality are grave enough to be actionable without proof of pecuniary loss, or so likely to cause pecuniary loss as not to call for such proof? Can any distinction be drawn on this basis between imputation of adultery and fornication on the one hand, and of unnatural relations with other women on the other – except that the latter are, if anything, more wounding, more likely to excite abhorrence on the part of average reasonable people, more likely to spoil the victim's prospect of marriage than the former?

In my view, no such distinction can be drawn: nor does it seem to me sense to say of a woman: 'She is a notorious lesbian, but she is perfectly chaste.' In the absence of any judicial guidance or authority as to the meaning of unchaste or chaste in this connection, dictionaries can be consulted and their definitions have been cited in this case. Almost all under the term 'unchastity' include 'impurity', 'lasciviousness,' and the like. Can anyone doubt that lesbianism is covered by such terms? In my view the imputation of lesbianism is an imputation of unchastity under the Act, and the legal objection of the defendant fails.

9 P. Epps, 'A Preliminary Survey of 300 Female Delinquents in Borstal Institutions', *British Journal of Delinquency*, Vol. 1, No. 3, 1951, pp. 187–97

Phyllis Epps reported on a survey of 300 girls aged between 16 and 23 committed to Borstal Institutions by courts in England, Wales and Northern Ireland between April 1948 and April 1950.

Emotional instability, noted in a marked degree in 27.6% of this series, is almost as big a problem as contamination. It appears to lead to two types of difficult behaviour. The first is concerned with the aggressive drive. ...

The second type of difficult behaviour, found particularly in unstable cases, is concerned with the sexual drive. True homosexuality seldom presents itself as a problem in this age group, but bisexuality, or a regression to the adolescent homosexual phase, due to the exclusively female environment, leads, in the unstable, to somewhat unhealthy erotic behaviour.

The problem presented by this emotional instability, can be considerably diminished by a less repressive regime, as in an 'open' or 'semi-open' Institution, where difficulties of social adaptation assume less exaggerated forms.

10 'The Case of Margaret Allen' in R. Huggett and P. Berry, *Daughters of Cain*, 1956, George Allen & Unwin, pp. 191–2, 209

On 12 January 1949 42-year-old Margaret Allen was hanged for the murder of Nancy Chadwick whom she had battered to death.

To the doctors who examined her, to the Home Office officials who advised the Home Secretary, to Mr. Chuter Ede who made the final decision of life or death, perhaps the most unfavourable and repellent feature in the case history of Margaret Allen was her homosexuality. There is an instinctive hostility to any divergence from the heterosexual pattern of behaviour, but in spite of this Margaret Allen made little attempt to conceal the fact that she was a lesbian whose natural sexual impulses were directed towards other women. She was the assertive, extremely masculine type of lesbian and perhaps this prompted her to an honesty seldom found amongst either male or female homosexuals. To the people of Bacup and Rawtenstall who had known her nearly all her life it merely characterised her as strange and eccentric, and it was only after the murder of Mrs. Chadwick that it assumed a more ominous and sinister importance.

She preferred to be called 'Bill' to Margaret, but was better known in the Rossendale Valley as Maggie Smith. In appearance she was certainly more like a man than a woman, dressed in jacket and trousers, with close-cropped hair, and although little more than five-feet tall she had the sturdy, tough build of many men. She told people with a sense of pride and justification that she had worked as a labourer, which seemed both reasonable and believable. To herself she was a man – a man except for an accident of birth.

...

It is regrettable that the greater part of what we know about the homosexual comes to us from unsavoury court cases, or a brief encounter with one unpleasant individual, and that our attitude should largely be based upon a spontaneous tendency to censure and condemn a way of life alien to our own.

...

It was largely the effects of being a lesbian that led to the circumstances in which 'Bill' Allen murdered Mrs. Chadwick and her masculine nature made it possible for her to use violence. If she had been a woman, with a woman's instincts, she would have lashed Mrs. Chadwick with her tongue or thrown the nearest piece of crockery, but she would have struck her with nothing more lethal than the back of her hand. All her life 'Bill' Allen possessed this masculine temperament and when roused to anger she fought with her fists like a man. It is not difficult to imagine that in a moment of heated temper she could hit Mrs. Chadwick on the head with a hammer lying beside her.

...

The prison authorities refused to let 'Bill' Allen see Annie Cook alone; they declined to alter the date fixed for her execution. At nine o'clock on January 12th Annie fulfilled the promise she made to 'Bill' Allen on her last visit, and stood at the corner of Bacup Road and Kay Street where they had so often met. She leant weeping against a wall as her sister tried to comfort her. In Strangeways Gaol seventeen miles away 'Bill' Allen had discarded her masculine clothes for the first time for more than a decade. She was led out to die wearing a striped prison dress and with the Chaplain praying God to have mercy on her soul, where society had none.

11 Letter to *Arena Three*, Vol. 5, Nos 5/6, March 1968, p. 13

Thirty seven years ago I knew Margaret Allen, who in January, 1949, was hanged for being a lesbian, and I weep for her every January.

The murder she committed was an insane one. But for the intolerance of her deviance, she would have been reprieved. The petition for her reprieve was circulated in an area of 60,000 population: it received 361 signatures, most of them by cripples and elderly people who remembered her as the kindest bus conductress on the route. Only a few weeks ago I had evidence of the fact that to this day this intolerance of her memory continues..

I remember her as a happy, laughing tomboy of 21. It is for me peculiarly horrible to know that 'public opinion' first succeeded in driving her insane, then in ensuring her extermination, and is still largely unchanged in that locality ...

Mr F.L. (London)

12 Spicer v Spicer (Ryan intervening) 3 All ER (1954) 208

In this case Judge Karminski granted the husband a decree nisi, finding the cruelty he alleged had been proved.

Divorce – Cruelty – Wife's cruelty – Lesbianism alleged – Persistent friendship with other woman – Injury to husband's health.

The husband petitioned for divorce on the ground of the wife's cruelty, alleging that she had formed an unnatural relationship with the intervener by reason whereof he had been compelled to leave the matrimonial home, and that although the parties became reconciled the wife resumed and, despite his pleas to her, continued the unnatural relationship. The unnatural relationship was alleged to be lesbianism. Both the wife and the intervener denied any unnatural relationship. During the hearing of the suit the wife while maintaining her denial stated that she would submit to a finding that her admitted persistent friendship with the intervener had amounted to cruelty.

HELD: the wife, having admittedly formed an affection for another woman such as to give her husband grave cause for anxiety as to the precise nature of that association, persisted in that association against the husband's entreaties; in so doing she had, on the evidence, occasioned the husband actual physical injury as well as a reasonable apprehension of future injury to his health, and the husband was entitled to the decree which he sought; and, there being no finding of any physical relationship between the wife and the intervener, the intervener would be dismissed from the suit. ...

KARMINSKI, J.: I think I can deal with this case on the evidence before me as it stands. I emphasise the words 'as it stands', because I have not heard yet the evidence of the intervener, who was at all times, I understand, denying the charges of lesbian practices between herself and the wife, and was prepared to go into the witness-box and deny them on oath. Counsel for the wife has indicated that the case alleged by the husband against the wife is cruelty. I have had a good deal of evidence that the wife admittedly formed for another woman an affection of such a kind as to give her husband grave cause for anxiety as to the precise nature of that association. More important still, when his suspicions were aroused and he was anxious, and properly anxious, that she should discontinue that association, she persisted in it against his entreaties and against his best endeavours. In so doing I am satisfied beyond any doubt whatsoever that she occasioned him actual physical injury as well as a reasonable apprehension of future injury to his health should her conduct continue. There was medical evidence before me from a doctor which left no doubt in my mind as to the injury and the extent of the injury.

So far as the precise nature of the association between the wife and the intervener is concerned, I make no finding, nor is it necessary for me, as I see it, so to do. I bear in mind once more the important fact that not only has the wife denied any physical association, and has denied it on oath, but that the intervener has taken an active part in the suit in the sense that she intervened, instructed counsel on her behalf and has pursued her denials up to this moment, and still maintains them. That being so I want to make it absolutely clear that in finding cruelty proved I am making no finding of any physical relationship between the wife and the intervener. On the extensive evidence before me, however, I have no doubt that I can and ought to find that the cruelty alleged in the petition has been proved. I, therefore, pronounce a decree nisi.

13 *Report of the Royal Commission on Marriage and Divorce, 1951–55*, 1956, HMSO, pp. 30–1

Lesbianism

The intention of witnesses who suggested that lesbianism should be a specific ground of divorce was to provide a remedy for a husband in circumstances similar to those in which a wife would have a remedy on the ground of sodomy. Lesbianism is merely a synonym for female homosexuality. In the case of both men and women homosexuality may range from feelings of affection which find no physical expression to some physical and emotional equivalent for normal sexual intercourse. Sodomy is a particular physical relationship. It might seem reasonable to put men and women on the same footing by making lesbianism a separate ground of divorce if the existence of a physical relationship analogous to sodomy could be proved. We do not think that this would in practice achieve what the witnesses have in mind. Apart from the difficulty of getting a workable definition, the difficulty of proof would be so much greater than in the case of sodomy as to make the provision of such a remedy virtually worthless. On the other hand, unless the ground were precisely defined, it would be open to a wide and uncertain interpretation and might lead to a divorce being granted against a wife when, in similar circumstances, relief would not be available against a husband practising homosexuality. Accordingly, we do not recommend that lesbianism, however manifested, should be made a separate ground of divorce.

In England, unnatural practices with other women persisted in by a wife throughout the marriage (with neglect of her home and child) have been held to amount to cruelty where her husband's health was affected. In a recent case, the court was prepared to go rather further, and to accept as cruelty persistence by a wife, to the detriment of her husband's health, in an intimate relationship with another woman, although there was no proof of unnatural practices.

14 J. Buxton and M. Turner, *Gate Fever*, 1962, The Cresset Press, pp. 114–16

Jane Buxton and Margaret Turner were involved in CND demonstrations and imprisoned in Holloway in 1960. They explained in the preface of their book that it comprised the letters they would have liked to have written to friends outside Holloway Prison. The extract from this letter from Margaret Turner to another friend gives some glimpses of lesbian affairs and rituals within the all-female environment.

Cell D. 4/5.
3 August 1960

Dear Constance,
... Some more of my discoveries on the yards are Lesbian love letters, written on lavatory paper and for some reason carelessly discarded and only half torn up. I've seen enough of them to realise what they are and they all seem to me rather sad. I have been surprised at the amount of open homosexuality there is here. Girls quite often boast of being Lesbian and I'm never quite sure how much of it is a sort of bravado and wishing to be in the fashion, just as some girls at my old school told everyone they had a 'pash' on such and such a mistress or prefect because they thought it was the done thing.

Most of the declared homosexuals that I have spoke to are long-term prisoners. Some of them have children outside but they seem to have lost touch entirely with their previous life and drifted into these affairs with other girls. From all accounts there are affairs between prisoners and officers but it's hard to see how these can be countenanced. On K Wing, where prisoners sleep two to a room the authorities have to be careful to split dangerous friendships. A rather hard-bitten fellow-prisoner asked me about K Wing when I was living there and said it must be nice in the married quarters! The officers too seem to regard the problem with a detached cynicism. When one of the girls on K Wing brushed her hair back in a boyish style she was asked by the officer if she was turning or had she turned! Cropped hair styles and boyish names are the danger signals here of course, and if a girl adopts a boy's name the other prisoners are often forbidden to use it.

I don't know if any help is given to girls with this problem. In theory homosexuality is condemned but it looks as though a blind eye is often turned. One of the girls I have spoken to told me that when she had tried to discuss it with one of the Assistant Governors she had been told that it wasn't very healthy, was it – and there the subject was left. I don't suppose that sort of comment is very helpful. This particular girl is in here indefinitely on a murder charge and I don't suppose there's much hope of her changing her ideas as long as she is in here. By the time she is out it will presumably be too late.

15 Lord Chamberlain's Papers, Correspondence, Memorandum of 26 March 1965 from the Assistant Comptroller to the Lord Chamberlain concerning *The Killing of Sister George*

In 1965 the play, by Frank Marcus, was a smash hit in London and later on Broadway.

'The Killing of Sister George'

Fletcher read this play first and was not sure about it so suggested a second opinion. I therefore asked Heriot to read it, and he does NOT recommend it for licence.

I have read the play, and I am not so sure. I entirely see Heriot's point of view vis-à-vis Osborne's play, but there is nothing really in the action of the play that would corrupt. It is clear that the two principal characters are Lesbians – and there are many oblique and sometimes direct references to this fact. For the record I have listed them. One sees them dressed as men for this party, but not the party itself (as in Osborne's play) nor do we see them in bed.

Therefore I am not convinced that a licence should be withheld. On the other hand it may be dangerous to let through a play with this theme. It does not offend me anything like as much as 'Dingo' for example.

There is no great hurry to decide, so I would be grateful if you would read the play – or would you like an opinion from Hill first?

A note on the memorandum written by the Lord Chancellor

After discussion with A/C and the two readers I have decided to licence the play without cuts.

PART III

MAKING LESBIANISM IN CULTURE

6

THE WELL OF LONELINESS

INTRODUCTION

The final part of this book opens with a case study of *The Well of Loneliness*. The previous chapter presented a range of evidence on lesbianism and the law. Here, one case which explicitly addressed lesbianism is considered in detail. In the late 1920s a novel, *The Well of Loneliness*, was prosecuted for obscenity and banned. The sources presented here indicate the range of ways in which the case was greeted. Some are rooted in the discourses illustrated in the first two parts; others suggest newly emerging responses to lesbianism. The increased awareness generated by the trial contributed to making lesbianism a more widely recognised cultural concept in twentieth-century Britain. The final two chapters of the book illustrate this process.

In the spring of 1928 Marguerite Radclyffe Hall, an established writer with four successful novels and a growing literary reputation, completed *The Well of Loneliness*. The novel's subject is the life of Stephen Gordon, a woman who believes 'the loneliest place in the world is the no-man's land of sex'. Lesbianism was not a new subject for the British novel in the late twenties (Faraday 1985). Had they sought for fictional representations over the previous decade readers might have found episodes in *Despised and Rejected* (1918), *A Regiment of Women* (1917), *The Tortoiseshell Cat* (1925), *The Hotel* (1927) and *Dusty Answer* (1928). *The Well of Loneliness* was different however. Its appearance has been seen by historians as representing a turning point in the understanding of lesbian sexuality and 'the great British public's introduction to lesbianism' (Hamer 1996: 84). Historians have examined its author's intentions, its subject matter and its reception and it has been argued that it was seminal in the development of a modern lesbian identity. While there is some danger in reifying the novel, consideration of its content and reception do raise a number of debates for lesbian history.

The novel's author was a striking public figure: a wealthy lesbian moving in upper-middle-class social and literary circles. Her life has prompted a number of biographies (Troubridge 1961, Dickson 1975, Baker 1985, Cline 1997, Souhami 1988). Born in 1880, from 1917 Radclyffe Hall, or John as she preferred to be called, lived with her partner Una Troubridge. The couple's public personae in the 1920s was striking. With their shingled hair, tailored suits and monocles they epitomised the modern independent woman and their physical appearance has been extensively analysed by historians (Rolley 1990, Doan 1998a). But it was Hall's novel that has taken centre stage in discussions of emerging lesbian identities. The book was polemical, written from 'a deep sense of duty', and with its sympathetic preface by Havelock Ellis and its strong Christian tone it explicitly demanded its readers to be the medical, moral and, most significantly, social arbiters in contemporary society's treatment of lesbians. While some analyses have tended to focus on Stephen's character and its supposed similarities to Hall herself, the novel also depicts wider aspects of lesbianism; childhood and adolescent sexuality, social ostracism, social class differences, the lesbian sub-culture of Valerie Seymour's Paris salon, the women's community of World War I ambulance drivers, and Stephen's relationships with the three women she loves.

It has been argued that the novel's depiction of its heroine as the mannnish lesbian already developed by the sexologists over the three proceeding decades may have led to the stereotyping stigmatisation of lesbian relationships in Britain, in direct opposition to Hall's intentions (Faderman 1981, Jeffreys 1985, Vicinus 1994), and that its representation of a female 'sexual invert' sexualised the hitherto asexual 'New Woman' (Newton 1991). Other writers have suggested that Stephen is not a lesbian, but that her inversion is more closely related to a transsexual or transgender identity (Ormrod 1984, Prosser 1998b).

In early August 1928 the book was published by Jonathan Cape. Within weeks the novel and its author had moved to public prominence when a virulent attack appeared in the *Sunday Express* of 19 August. By Tuesday the Home Secretary, Sir William Joynson-Hicks, had written to Cape demanding the book's withdrawal from circulation. The publishers, as owners of the published copies of the book, were prosecuted under the Obscene Publications Act, 1857. As the author, Hall could not be directly represented in the case nor summoned to give evidence. Given the book's subject matter, its discussion in the emotive tirade by James Douglas in the *Sunday Express*, and its submission to a notoriously censorious Home Secretary, its prosecution was almost ensured. The intention of the Obscene Publications Act was to protect audiences from material that might 'deprave and corrupt' them. The subsequent trial made the book a literary cause célèbre. Among the many witnesses prepared to defend it, but not in the event allowed to testify, were prominent literary figures including Virginia Woolf, A.P. Herbert, Rudyard Kipling, Rose Macaulay and E.M. Forster. Despite the emphasis in the literary journals on the case's significance in terms of literary freedoms and the novel's literary merits, the trial can also be seen as a public forum for the contemporary discussion of relationships between women.

Hall's hope that via the novel the woman invert's plight would reach a wider public was gratified. Ironically the publicity surrounding its censorship ensured its wide circulation and it was further publicised when debated in a range of journals and magazines. While censored by the authorities in Britain it did not suffer a similar fate abroad. It sold well in both France and the United States, where its attempted prosecution failed. The book's apologia for lesbians as 'congenital inverts' was not accepted uncritically by contemporaries; indeed the plot itself presents alternative readings, and the nature versus nurture debate was prominent in contemporary evaluations as it has been in subsequent analyses (Hennegan 1991, Griffin 1993).

Whatever their impact was on the specific understanding of lesbian sexuality, the novel and the trial's significance in widening the understanding of sexuality and of women generally needs to be assessed. Ingram (1986, 1989), for example, has argued that the working of the obscenity laws against *The Well of Loneliness*, and other banned books in the period, silenced the oppositional depiction of lesbians as non-mothers, as women who would not reproduce patriarchy. Some heterosexual contemporaries used the novel as a vehicle to promote their own views of sexuality and of lesbianism in particular. Characterisations varied from pleas for Christian compassion for those few unfortunates with, in Stephen Gordon's words, the 'mark of Cain' to cruel parody of the lesbian in an illustrated mock heroic poem 'The Sink of Solitude'.

Lesbians themselves were not Hall's desired primary audience yet at the time many lesbians wrote to Hall thanking her for her book; others, like Violet Trefusis, hated it. The responses of lesbians are a key element in assessing the book's resonance with the self-identity of contemporary and later lesbians (Faderman 1981, O'Rourke 1989). Ruehl (1982) and others (Weeks 1981, Dollimore 1991) have argued that *The Well of Loneliness* was important not because it cemented a single model of lesbianism grounded in a medical discourse, but because its very depiction of such a model created the space to challenge, debate and posit alternative lesbianisms. Similarly the indications that the book had an impact on the perceptions of all close friendships between women have begun to be explored (Johnson 1989).

The Well of Loneliness was not legally available in Britain until 1949 yet from its original publication it was regarded as 'the British lesbian novel'. The following selection of source materials indicates its abiding power as a catalyst for examining lesbian sensibility.

1 V. Brittain, 'New Fiction. Facing Facts', *Time and Tide*, Vol. 9, No. 32, 10 August 1928, pp. 765–6

New fiction. Facing facts

by VERA BRITTAIN

The Well of Loneliness. Radclyffe Hall. (Cape. 15s.)

...

Miss Radclyffe Hall's important, sincere and very moving study demands consideration from two different standpoints. In the first place, it is presented as a novel, and is therefore open to criticism as a work of imagination, a creative effort which challenges comparison with other examples of fiction. In the second place it is a plea, passionate, yet admirably restrained and never offensive, for the extension of social toleration, compassion and recognition to the biologically abnormal woman, who, because she possesses the tastes and instincts of a man, is too often undeservedly treated as a moral pariah.

...

It may be said at once that The Well of Loneliness can only strengthen the belief of all honest and courageous persons that there is no problem which is not better frankly stated than concealed. Persecution and disgusted ostracism have never solved any difficulty in the world, and they certainly do not make the position of the female invert less bitter to herself or less dangerous to others. Miss Hall's dignified challenge, presenting without sentimentality or compunction the dreadful poignancy of ineradicable emotions, in comparison with which the emotions of normal men and women seem so clear and uncomplicated, certainly convinces us that women of the type of Stephen Gordon, in so far as their abnormality is inherent and not merely the unnecessary cult of exotic erotics, deserve the fullest consideration and compassion from all who are fortunate enough to have escaped one of Nature's cruellest dispensations.

The book, however, raises and never satisfactorily answers another question – the question as to how far the characteristics of Stephen Gordon are physiological and how far they are psychological. Probably only an expert biologist could satisfactorily resolve such a difficulty. It certainly seems likely that a problem of this type must be intensified by the exaggeration of sex differences which has been peculiarly marked in certain ages of the world, and to which the English middle classes of the eighteenth and nineteenth centuries were particularly prone. Miss Hall appears to take for granted that this over-emphasis of sex characteristics is part of the correct education of the normal human being; she therefore makes her 'normal' woman clinging and 'feminine' to exasperation and even describes the attitudes towards love as 'an end in itself' as being a necessary attribute to true womanhood. Many readers will know too many happy wives and mothers for whom it is not, to take on trust Miss Hall's selection of the qualities essential to one sex or the other.

This confusion between what is 'male' or 'female' and what is merely human in our complex make-up, persists throughout the book. We feel that, in describing the supposedly sinister predilections of the child Stephen Gordon, much ado is often made about nothing; so many of them appear to be the quite usual preferences of any vigorous young female who happens to possess more vitality and intelligence than her fellows. ... This is not to deny that the problem described by Miss Hall does exist in a grave and urgent form, and that her presentation of it deserves the serious attention of all students of social questions. ...

2 'A Book that must be Suppressed', *The Sunday Express*, 19 August 1928

The Well of Loneliness (Jonathan Cape, 15s. net) by Miss Radclyffe Hall, is a novel. The publishers state that it 'handles very skilfully a psychological problem which needs to be understood in view of its growing importance'.

'In England hitherto,' they admit, 'the subject has not been treated frankly outside the regions of scientific text-books, but that its social consequences qualify a broader and more general treatment is likely to be the opinion of thoughtful and cultured people.'

They declare that they 'have been deeply impressed by this study'; they have felt that such a book should not be lost to those who may be willing and able to understand and appreciate it. They believe that the author has treated the subject in such a way as to combine perfect frankness and sincerity with delicacy and deep psychological insight.

Uncompromising

In his prefatory 'Commentary', Mr Havelock Ellis says: 'I have read The Well of Loneliness with great interest because – apart from its fine qualities as a novel – it possesses a notable psychological and sociological significance.

So far as I know, it is the first English novel which presents, in a completely faithful and uncompromising form, one particular aspect of sexual life as it exists among us to-day.

The relation of certain people – who, while different from their fellow human beings, are sometimes of the highest character and the finest aptitudes – to the often hostile society in which they move presents difficult and still unsolved problems.

The poignant situations which thus arise are here set forth so vividly, and yet with such complete absence of offence, that we must place Radclyffe Hall's book on a high level of distinction.'

That is the defence and justification of what I regard as an intolerable outrage – the first outrage of the kind in the annals of English fiction.

The defence is wholly unconvincing. The justification absolutely fails.

In order to prevent the contamination and corruption of English fiction it is the duty of the critic to make it impossible for any other novelist to repeat this outrage. I say deliberately that this novel is not fit to be sold by any bookseller or to be borrowed from any library.

Bravado

Its theme is utterly inadmissible in the novel, because the novel is read by people of all ages, by young women and young men as well as by older women and older men. Therefore, many things that are discussed in scientific text-books cannot decently be discussed in a work of fiction offered to the general reader.

I am well aware that sexual inversion and perversion are horrors which exist among us today. They flaunt themselves in public places with increasing effrontery and more insolently provocative bravado. The decadent apostles of the most hideous and loathsome vices no longer conceal their degeneracy and their degradation.

They seem to imagine that there is no limit to the patience of the English people. They appear to revel in their defiance of public opinion. They do not shun publicity. On the contrary, they seek it, and they take a delight in their flamboyant notoriety. The consequence is that this pestilence is devastating the younger generation. It is wrecking young lives. It is defiling young souls.

The plague

I have seen the plague stalking shamelessly through great social assemblies. I have heard it whispered about by young men and young women who do not and cannot grasp its unutterable putrefaction. Both aspects of it are thrust upon healthy and innocent minds. The contagion cannot be escaped. It pervades our social life.

Perhaps it is a blessing in disguise or a curse in disguise that this novel forces upon our society a disagreeable task which it has hitherto shirked, the task of cleaning itself from the leprosy of these lepers, and making the air clean and wholesome once more.

I agree with Mr Havelock Ellis that this novel is 'uncompromising'. That is why criticism cannot compromise with it. The challenge is direct. It must be taken up courageously, and the fight must be fought to the finish. If our bookshops and our libraries are to be polluted by fiction dealing with this undiscussable subject, at least let us know where we are going.

I know that the battle has been lost in France and Germany, but it has not yet been lost in England, and I do not believe that it will be lost. The English people are slow to rise in their wrath and strike down the armies of evil, but when they are aroused they show no mercy, and they give no quarter to those who exploit their tolerance and their indulgence.

No defence

It is no use to say that the novel possesses 'fine qualities', or that its author is an 'accomplished' artist. It is no defence to say that the author is sincere, or that she is frank, or that there is delicacy in her art.

The answer is that the adroitness and cleverness of the book intensifies its moral danger. It is a deductive and insidious piece of special pleading designed to display perverted decadence as a martyrdom inflicted upon these outcasts by a cruel society. It flings a veil of sentiment over their depravity. It even suggests that their self-made debasement is unavoidable, because they cannot save themselves.

This terrible doctrine may commend itself to certain schools of pseudo-scientific thought, but it cannot be reconciled with the Christian religion or with the Christian doctrine of free-will. Therefore, it must be fought to the bitter end by the Christian Churches. This is the radical difference between paganism and Christianity.

If Christianity does not destroy this doctrine, then this doctrine will destroy it, together with the civilisation which it has built on the ruins of paganism. These moral derelicts are not cursed from their birth. Their downfall is caused by their own act and their own will. They are damned because they choose to be damned, not because they are doomed from the beginning.

It is meet and right to pity them, but we must also pity their victims. We must protect our children against their specious fallacies and sophistries. Therefore, we must banish their propaganda from our bookshops and our libraries.

I would rather give a healthy boy or a healthy girl a phial of prussic acid than this novel. Poison kills the body, but moral poison kills the soul.

What, then, is to be done? The book must at once be withdrawn. I hope the author and the publishers will realise that they have made a grave mistake, and will without delay do all in their power to repair it.

If they hesitate to do so, the book must be suppressed by process of law. I observe that the Irish Free State Government have published the text of their Censorship of Publications Bill. It proposes to establish a Censorship Board of five, four of whom must agree before any publication is placed on the Black List.

Complaints must come through recognised associations, not from individual citizens.

It may be that the establishment of a similar Censorship Board will be found necessary in this country as well as in Ireland. But our existing law is sufficient, if it be properly administered. Therefore, I appeal to the Home Secretary to set the law in motion. He should instruct the Director of Public Prosecutions to consider whether The Well of Loneliness is fit for circulation, and, if not, to take action to prevent its being further circulated.

Finally, let me warn our novelists and our men of letters that literature as well as morality is in peril. Fiction of this type is an injury to good literature. It makes the profession of literature fall into disrepute. Literature has not yet recovered from the harm done to it by the Oscar Wilde scandal. It should keep its house in order.

3 Letter from Vita Sackville-West to Virginia Woolf, 31 August 1928, in L. DeSalvo and M. Leaska (eds), *The Letters of Vita Sackville-West to Virginia Woolf*, 1992, London: Virago, pp. 296–7

Manger-strasse II
Potsdam
August 1928
…

I feel very violently about *The Well of Loneliness*. Not on account of what you call my proclivities; not because I think it is a good book; but really on principle. (I think of writing to Jix suggesting that he should suppress Shakespeare's Sonnets.) Because, you see, even if the W. of L. had been a good book, – even if it had been a great book, a real masterpiece, – the result would have been the same. And that is intolerable. I really have no words to say how indignant I am. Is Leonard really going to get up a protest? or is it fizzling out? (What a conceited ass the woman must be.) Don't let it fizzle out. If you got Arnold Bennett and suchlike, it would be bound to make an impression. (Avoid Shaw, though.) I nearly blew up over the various articles in the *New Statesman*. Personally, I should like to renounce my nationality, as a gesture; but I don't want to become a German, even though I did go to a revue last night in which two ravishing young women sing a frankly Lesbian song.

4 'The Well of Loneliness Decision', *Time and Tide*, Vol. 9, No. 27, 23 November 1928, pp. 1124–5

'The Well of Loneliness' decision

'The decision of Sir Charles Biron with regard to The Well of Loneliness is,' says Mr. James Douglas, 'far more than a victory for the Sunday Express. It is a victory for good literature.' A victory for the Sunday Express the decision undoubtedly is; whether it is a victory for good literature, or for that matter, whether it is in the interests of society, we take leave to doubt.

It is arguable that The Well of Loneliness itself is neither a very wholesome book nor particularly good literature. Indeed, we should not be concerned to suggest that it is. It deals with a distasteful form of excess – and it handles its theme sentimentally, which is as distasteful a method of handling it as could well be found. Moreover, although there is not one word in the book which comes under the commonly accepted (which differs considerably from the legal) definition of obscenity, it does, in our view, show a certain morbidity as well as sentimentality in the treatment of its subject. At the same time it is obviously a book written with a purpose – if, as it appears to us, a mistaken purpose – and it is impossible to withhold a mead of admiration from Miss Radclyffe Hall for the courage she has shown in publishing it.

Mr. James Douglas's achievement

A society which came to have an intense, morbid interest in specialised and 'unnatural' forms of lust, or indeed in any form of lust, would be in an unhealthy state, and we should regret to see the public absorbed in reading or our writers absorbed in writing books dealing with such subjects. But what in fact, has been the result of the campaign against The Well of Loneliness? Obviously, as several of our correspondents point out, to increase public interest in it to a phenomenal extent. Rumour has it that the first result of Mr. James Douglas's article last August was that several hundred extra copies of The Well of Loneliness were immediately ordered by leading libraries. It is true that these copies have since been withdrawn from circulation, but it is also true that as a result of the protracted discussion on the whole subject there is scarcely an intelligent reader in the country who can fail to be aware of the subject which the book discusses, or who has not, as a result of the campaign, had his mind turned to consideration of that subject, whilst we are told that the booksellers in Paris and New York are doing a roaring trade. Between them, the Sunday Express, the Home Secretary and one of our Stipendiary Magistrates have succeeded, it would appear, in creating a world best-seller. It is a remarkable achievement. But is it exactly what they want?

The attitude of youth

The plea that such books are bad for youth seems to us a particularly bad one. Children whilst still in the schoolroom can, as one of our correspondents points out this week, be better protected by their own parents than by the law. Whilst young people once out of the schoolroom, always full of what Professor Gilbert Murray calls 'the normal and healthy reaction of youth against age' take a quite especially vivid interest in anything that they are told not to read. It may indeed be said that the interest of normal healthy youth in vicious and unwholesome matters is almost exactly proportioned to the amount of trouble which its elders take to keep such matters from it. Who can fail to realise, for example, that amongst the first results of the suppression of The Well of Loneliness will be that surreptitiously obtained copies of that work will circulate immediately through every one of our Universities and will be devoured with avidity by many a student who, if it had pursued its normal unsuppressed course, could on no account have been persuaded in the course of a busy term to find time to wade through its five-hundred pages.

The need for a free press

But even if it had been possible to secure the withdrawal of the book without bringing about that very concentration of the public mind on the subject with which it deals, which it has been the avowed object of Mr. James Douglas, Sir William Joynson-Hicks and Sir Chartres Biron to avoid, it would in our view have been a mistake to suppress it.

The fact is that whilst there is much to be said for keeping our streets and shop windows clean from pornographic postcards (whose object is clearly merely commercial) any laws which are stretched beyond this point, however specious the arguments on their behalf, are against the public interest. We cannot allow our literature to be purged of all books which are unsuitable for leaving upon the nursery table. It has been frequently and correctly pointed out that in that case we should deprive ourselves of Shakespeare, the Bible – and Mr. Bernard Shaw. It is true that if we reject the nursery table test we shall find the national bookshelves provided not only with Shaw and Shakespeare, but also with a certain number of books which will appear to many of us – perhaps to most of us – to be calculated to do more harm than good. The result of allowing a free press is that some things are published which contemporary opinion holds – and sometimes rightly holds – to be unwholesome and even vicious. Just as the result of allowing free speech is that every Sunday a number of Hyde Park orators make statements of which the mass of the general public heartily disapproves. But we have learnt to believe in free speech and (pace Mr. James Douglas, Sir William Joynson-Hicks and Sir Chartres Biron) we must learn – or re-learn – to believe in a free press.

5 Letter from Virginia Woolf to Roger Fry, 16 October 1928 in N. Nicolson and J. Trautmann (eds), *Leave the Letters Till We're Dead. The Letters of Virginia Woolf*, 1980, London: The Hogarth Press, Vol VI: 1936–1941, pp. 523–4

Tuesday 16th Oct. [1928]

... Noel Coward was rather interesting. He says the English theatre is so degraded that he will not produce any serious work for her in future. He says the middle classes make his life a burden. Old women in Gloucester write and abuse him for immorality. Lord Cromer can force him to leave out any sentence, or ban the whole play. He says they are infinitely more civilised in America and Berlin. So he is off to produce his plays in New York. There he makes £1000 a week, and he can say what he likes. Leonard, Morgan [Forster] and I have all got to appear in Court in defence of Miss Radcliffe Hall's Sapphistic novel [The Well of Loneliness, 1928] – which is so pure, so sweet, so sentimental, than none of us can read it – But you will be surprised to hear that the railwaymen who were ordered by the Customs to remove 500 copies of the book from the ship at Dover (it is being published in France) were so indignant at the injustice of the Law that they sent Radcliffe Hall a letter of sympathy! You must admit that the English are odd.

I am sending you my new book [Orlando] (this reads very professional) chiefly because I took the liberty of mentioning you in the preface. It is a joke, and therefore of course is being taken as a serious historical study, or allegory.

6 'Condemned Novel. Appeal to Sessions', *The Times*, 15 December 1928, p. 4

Court decision

The Bench retired, and after an absence of less than 10 minutes the Chairman (Sir Robert Wallace, K.C.) announced that the appeal would be dismissed with costs.

In delivering this decision the Chairman said that the book was admittedly neither a scientific nor a medical book; it was a novel addressed to the general public which read novels. The opinion of the Court was unanimous. The definition which had been accepted for 60 years as to what was the test in regard to these books was whether the tendency of the matter was to deprave and corrupt those whose lives were open to such immoral influences and into whose hands a publication of this sort might fall. There were plenty of people who would be neither depraved nor corrupted by reading a book like this. But it was to those whose minds were open to such immoral influences that he referred. The character of the book could not be gathered from the reading of isolated passages. The book must be taken as a whole. The view of the Court was that the book was a very subtle book. It was one which was insinuating and probably much more dangerous because of that fact.

Proceeding, the Chairman said: – 'In the view of the Court, it is a most dangerous and corrupting book. It is a book the general tendency of which would be to corrupt the minds of the general body of those who may read it. It is a book which, if it does not commend unnatural practices, certainly condones them, and suggests that those guilty of them should not receive the consequences they deserve to suffer. Put in a word, the view of this Court is that this is a disgusting book when properly read. It is an obscene book, and a book prejudicial to the morals of the community. In our view the order made by the magistrate is perfectly correct, and the appeal must be dismissed with costs.'

7 'Miss Radclyffe Hall's Appeal', *The Woman's Leader*, 21 December 1928, p. 354

The Well of Loneliness

Madam, – Many points of view have been aired, in the Press and in conversation, regarding Miss Radclyffe Hall's book, The Well of Loneliness. Sometimes it is the subject which is condemned, sometimes the treatment of it; the existence of the problem has been denied, the exaggeration of it attacked; the whole thing has been decried in the interest of another type of women's friendship, in the interests of public morality, decency, and a thousand precious causes to which it bears no particular relation. I appeal to the critical fairmindedness of your paper to allow me to put forward another point of view.

I am not concerned, nor is Miss Radclyffe Hall, with the woman or man who seeks primarily physical excitement through so-called unnatural vice, prostitution, or by any form of indulgence open to human ingenuity. Nor am I concerned with the specific 'invert' with whom Miss Radclyffe Hall deals, for wherever she exists – and it is dangerous to classify – she is only part of a much greater phenomenon which ought to claim the attention of every thinking woman.

There are thousands of women, independent, vigorous, capable, temperamentally rich and mentally alert, who are restless, hampered, frustrated, warped, according to their various degrees, because they are denied a proper emotional life. They have a mental outlet, a growing economic, social and political outlet, but they have no emotional outlet. Marriage, for a variety of reasons, has been denied to them. But they are not physical or physiological or pathological abnormalities. They ask, what any man in their position would probably have obtained for himself, the emotional satisfaction of an intimate affection and the assured spiritual and social companionship of a home. The physical side of it in many women's cases plays a very insignificant part; it would be developed, no doubt, in marriage, it is sublimated out of it – in any case it is relatively unimportant. Their yearning is the multiple and complicated need of a complex human being. They could find it, most of them, with equal success through man or woman – many of them, out of human disappointment turn to dogs, for something of that companionship they could not find elsewhere.

Thousands of women are conscious of this need. Equally, thousands of women have satisfied it in an intimate relationship with another woman, the degree and experience of which must always vary with the temperaments and character of the people concerned. But just as there is a physical sympathy which has no connection whatever with sexual excitement, so there is innate in human beings a need of intimacy and an instinct of appropriation – shown in the most legitimate relationships – which is wholly psychological.

That this kind of thing must be a matter for social conscience except in its broad aspects, is a moot point. The wise person of any sex and in any relationship has probably learnt that restraint is the very shape of life, as of art.

But I do hope that no woman will allow the magisterial condemnation of The Well of Loneliness to shorten her courage – and she will need much – in pursuing for herself honestly, wisely, and generously that life which will bring her real contentment.

CRIPICUS

8 M. Royden, 'Well of Loneliness', *The Guildhouse Monthly*, Vol. 3, No. 26, April 1929, pp. 94–5, 98–101

'Well of Loneliness'

Maude Royden

[Sermon given] At the Guildhouse, Sunday evening, February 17, 1929.
Lessons: Matt. xxv. 14–29.
'The Sermon in the Hospital,' E. Hamilton King.
I am not going to speak to-night about the book called 'The Well of Loneliness' which was during my absence abroad published here and then banned, but about the subject of that book. I do not suppose Miss Radclyffe-Hall desired the kind of advertisement that has been given to the book, but since it happened, and since the book has, largely in consequence of that advertisement, been very widely read, I feel bound to say that I find it difficult to understand why an official who permits the publication of books so filthy that it soils the mind to read them, and the production of plays in which everything that is connected with sex is degraded, in which marriage and adultery alike are treated as though they were rather a nasty joke, should have fastened on this particular book as being unfit for us to read. I do not desire that those other books or plays should be suppressed; I have no faith at all in that way of dealing with evil. It is better to concentrate our efforts on trying to be interested in something that is good than to take a short cut to virtue by repressing what is evil. But if there is to be censorship, why was this book chosen? I wish publicly to state that I honour the woman who wrote it, alike for her courage and her understanding; that I find her as just as she is merciful and as merciful as she is just; that her book seems to me to be altogether on the side of what is normal and right; and I do not understand how anyone can read that book patiently from start to finish, and not see that that is the conclusion of the matter.

These, however, are not reasons why I should preach about this book or on this subject. My reasons are these. The book is being very widely read. It is being widely read by members of this congregation, and by the younger members, who perhaps of all the people of my congregation are most – I will not say most dear to my heart, for all my congregation are dear – but most near to my conscience. And I have found that the advice frequently given by well-meaning, but almost incredibly ignorant people on this subject, is often tragic in its effect, not only on the lives of the abnormal but on the lives of others, normal or capable of becoming so.

What then is my subject? It is the fact that between people of the same sex friendship sometimes reaches a pitch of intensity which longs for physical contact, and for those intimacies and caresses which are normally only desired and only given between people of opposite sex. I do not say this love is more profound than any other kind of love, for the love of parents for their children, sometimes of brothers and sisters, sometimes of a more normal type of friendship, is sometimes quite as profound as the love of lovers. It may be, even in the life of a perfectly normal person, that the love of children is his – or more commonly her – ruling passion. But, even so, it has a different quality from sex-love; and it is this quality which sometimes exists between men for each other, and women for each other, and which creates the difficulties I speak of to-night.

If to some of you this 'passionate friendship' seems quite incomprehensible and unreal, I ask you nevertheless to accept the fact that it does exist. It is not even a new thing; it is not a consequence of the unnatural excitement and loneliness of the war and post-war periods.

. . .

I am going to assume to-night that what I call the 'true' invert, the person who cannot be altered either by psychologists or physiologists does actually exist. His abnormality is not due to delayed or even arrested development: it is inherent and incurable. Whence do they come? 'God made us,' they reply: 'what is he going to do with us?' . . .

Consider – the invert can have no children and no home in our sense of the word. His love, which seems to him as sacred as yours and mine, must seem to the world horrible. He creates no new centre of life from which life comes into the world. There is no pull outward again when he turns inwards: the rhythm of creation is broken. When two lovers, a man and a woman, meet in marriage, their love turns into itself but it creates something which draws them out again. The act of creation creates new life, and the parents' love is drawn out as the lovers' love was drawn in, and there is present the infolding and unfolding, the great and wonderful rhythm which runs through all life. But to the invert's love, this is impossible. The rhythm is broken. Love turns inwards and is locked there. The biological failure to create is paralleled by a spiritual failure. Need it be so, some of you ask? Cannot the love of the invert for his own sex, for her own sex, even though it be expressed physically, result in a spiritual creation? I do not think so. If it is to result in spiritual creation, it must be kept on a spiritual plane. If it yields to the desire for physical expression, it becomes spiritually valueless. Love is sacred – yes, all love is sacred. Let us never forget that. But love is naturally creative and sterile love is a contradiction in terms. It is the function of love to create, just as it is the function of hatred to destroy, for love is the very principle of creation, and to ask 'Why did God create?' is to ask a question without meaning. He creates because it is the nature of love to create. But when the invert argues that his love also may create spiritually, I think he falls into a fallacy; it creates spiritually only by the hard necessity of remaining a spiritual passion. I know the happiness that comes of a loneliness that is broken at last seems to release, and for a time there is a sense of being satisfied; but that is all. Such love does not turn outwards to the creation of life, and it remains a secret.

...

I submit that the invert should accept the fact of his own nature and consequent suffering, and not try to escape it. This is the kind of thing I am ashamed to say, knowing how often I have sought and seek to escape pain. Have we not all tried to escape from suffering and loneliness? If I dare to say to the invert, 'you must not try to escape,' it is because I am certain that in one sense you cannot escape altogether. But if you accept your suffering, you will find that you are one of a great company. The form of your suffering is lonely, but the fact of your suffering is common, for all whose lives are worth living suffer – all of them. You will find yourself not alone in the deepest sense, for this great company of sufferers becomes to you more than a company; it is a communion, a communion of the deepest of human experiences. The experience of a pain that you accept and do not try to escape makes you one of that great host of martyrs, prophets and saints, in whose hearts there is always a cross. In this communion your loneliness is transcended. ...

9 Letter from Radclyffe Hall to Maude Royden, 3 January 1930, Agnes Maude Royden Papers, Fawcett Library

Jan 3 – 1930 – from The Mermaid, Rye, Sussex.

Dear Miss Royden

I want very much to offer you my congratulations upon the honour which you have just received. And may I take this opportunity of telling you how much your support of 'The Well of Loneliness' has meant to its author during the past months of government persecution. I wrote the book in order to help a very much misunderstood and therefore unfortunate section of society, and to feel that a leader of thought like yourself had extended to me your understanding was, and still is, a source of strength and encouragement – thank you.

Yours sincerely,
Radclyffe Hall.

10 E. Mannin, *Impressions and Confessions*, 1936, Penguin, pp. 231–5

I admire Radclyffe Hall's courage tremendously. I had expected to find her despairing and embittered, but she is not even in despair about the puritanism of this country, as so many of us are; she contends that we are not really puritanical at all; merely hypocritical. She was too conscious of the great waves of sympathy flowing out to her from all directions during *The Well of Loneliness* case to become bitter about the ridiculous affair – even though it meant the destruction of two years' conscientious hard work and the sale of her beautiful house. She feels now that she has said all she has to say on the subject with which she dealt in that book, but she told me that if ever the time comes when she feels she has anything to add to it, she will have no hesitation in adding to it!

11 M. Renault, Afterword to *Friendly Young Ladies*, 1984 [1938], London: Virago, p. 281

In 1938, I was staying with a friend [Julie Mullard, her partner] in the small hotel of a French fishing village, somewhere near Hardelot. I think it was in Boulogne that we picked up a copy of *The Well of Loneliness*, then still banned in England. It was a thick, pale brown paperback, a collector's edition I expect today, but too bulky to have a chance at customs, so we left it behind. Every morning, before getting up and starting for the beach, we used to read it with the coffee and croissants, accompanied by what now strikes me as rather heartless laughter. It is a fact however that we both found it irresistibly funny. It had been out ten years, which is a long time in terms of conventions; but it does, I still think, carry an impermissible allowance of self-pity, and its earnest humourlessness invites irreverence. Solemn, dead-pan earnest descriptions of Mary knitting stockings for Stephen – and when there was real silk! – and mending her 'masculine underwear' (what can it have been? It was long before briefs; perhaps Wolsey combinations) are passages I can still not read with entire gravity.

12 G. Holmes, *In Love With Life*, 1944, Hollis & Carter, p. 136

Fussy provincial Edwardian parents gladly consigned their daughters clamouring for art, musical and other careers to the care of young women friends or aunts or cousins – anything provided that it was female and no goings-on with men were allowed. And then came the 'Well of Loneliness', that rather dull novel, so disappointingly lacking in detail. And oh the vicarages and country houses who felt their peace of mind forever poisoned as they contemplated Daphne, Pamela, Joan and Margery all living together with unthinkable consequences. Unthinkable is just about the right word!

Ordinary people who prate of homosexuality haven't the remotest idea what they are talking about, don't know that real homosexuality is an extremely rare thing. And, above all, don't know that it's completely suitable and natural for all human beings to form deep and tender attachments, permanent or passing, irrespective of age or sex – and rather unnatural if they don't.

13 A. Jivani, *It's Not Unusual. A History of Lesbian and Gay Britain in the Twentieth Century*, 1997, London: Michael O'Mara Books Ltd, p. 40

[quote from Barbara Bell]
It was a revelation, I thought well, I must join this club, I'm all for this – sounded like just what I was wanting and needing. ... Now of course I've got one on my shelf ... but then it was so secret, you'd pass it in a paper bag to somebody if you wanted to give it to them.

14 Hall Carpenter Archives Lesbian Oral History Group, *Inventing Ourselves. Lesbian Life Stories*, 1989, London: Routledge, pp. 49–50

Diane Chapman

It was when it was re-issued as a Falcon – 1949 – I think I was twenty-one when I read it. I saw it in George's bookshop in Bristol and I walked round it and I thought, 'It's no good, I've got to have it', even though it was thirty shillings. So I bought it. I had a dentist's appointment and I was kept waiting for an hour and a half so by the time I got into his chair and read about a third of the book and then I went home to my digs and sat there glued for the rest of the evening. I was shattered. I thought, 'This is me; this is what it's all about.' I wept copiously; I went about in a daze. I remember these terrible feelings that Stephen has and her frustrations because she's not a man and she loves a woman. All her finest feelings, all her love, everything is just dirty and desecrated and she can't talk about it and it's secret and I thought, 'yes, this is me.' But of course it also sold me the idea that all lesbians were masculine and tall and handsome and Stephenish and, of course, I should have looked at myself and realized I wasn't any of these things. I didn't think of lesbians as being ordinary women. I thought, 'There are some women who feel themselves to be men inside, and are therefore attracted to women.' What I didn't ask myself was, 'What about the women on the other side; what are they?'

I thought I was a lesbian but then I thought that it was ridiculous and awful and every book on psychology I ever read (and I had a stack of those blue Pelicans) told me that it was immature and that I should really get my act together and reconcile myself to my femininity and find myself a good man and have children. And so I thought, I must simply get on with being a normal woman. Which I tried to do without very much success. And of course in those days you didn't walk round with cropped hair and trousers, not unless you wanted to be pointed out in the street. I wore ordinary women's clothes. I never felt remotely attracted to men, but in those days, for any woman to be home by herself on a Saturday night or with another woman friend, was a stigma of the utmost failure. You were sexually unattractive and for a woman to be sexually unattractive was the kiss of death. It still is.

15 S. Neild and R. Pearson, *Women Like Us*, 1992, The Women's Press, pp. 127–39 *passim*

Dorothy Dickinson-Barrow was born in the Caribbean in 1934 and moved to London in 1957.

... When I was about thirteen or fourteen Radclyffe Hall's book, *The Well of Loneliness*, came out. I presume a lot of women of my age found it as their Holy Bible, or something like that. When you read that, it gave you some identity about what it was you were feeling. I really realised there was some labelling then, to who I was. And that was important, that 'Gosh'! For the first time I knew what liking women was, what this feeling you are getting was all about. I think the thing that attracted me to the book was the picture of Radclyffe Hall. And I used to fancy myself looking like this woman, you know, with the cravat and white shirt and tie. You had to keep this book a secret you see because it was banned from publication.

Recalling the early 1950s in Jamaica.

In those days, I think most of us lived in two worlds. One world was for one's family and one's community, and the other world was very private, where you met with your friends, you had your dinner parties. And you dressed accordingly: to suit your family, to suit society. But at home in the evenings, you dressed in slacks. And you'd even imitate my mentor, which was to dress in cravats – dinner wear, tails, making sure your shirt, the blouses you wore had cufflinks, and various things like that. Then as I got older, I can remember starting to smoke pipes or cigars. So there was a pseudo-imitation of your mentor, who was Radclyffe Hall in those days. There was an external behaviour and an internal behaviour, which was in private. That was the pattern, I think, for a lot of people.

Dorothy moved to England. In the early 1960s, after marriage and children, she fell in love with a married woman.

About that time I met another woman. I can remember her sitting down on the floor in her living room talking in this lateral way about books, and Radclyffe Hall came up. And she'd read her! And I can remember how the spark flew between us and that was the beginning of the first relationship I could really label as a sexual one. She was the sort of person who gave me meaning to what it was all about.

16 R. O'Rourke, *Reflecting on the Well Of Loneliness*, 1989, London: Routledge, pp. 117–42

Who reads The Well of Loneliness?

My mother gave it to me to read on a long bus ride. She said it was the first book about lesbians. I still don't fully understand her motivation.

(Read in 1959, aged 14)

In 1930 – I was at school in Paris, but extremely shy. I did manage to get myself to Adrienne Monnier's bookshop – circled timidly about, browsing – but could not find the courage to request the book ... in the first year of my married life, and pregnant, I came upon a copy – without even looking for it – in the within-walking-distance Public Library.

(Read in 1930, aged 19)

The most important things were 1) simply that the book existed and 2) it suggested that somewhere I might find a community, if only a small and beleaguered one – someday.

(Read in 1946, aged 15)

I knew little about other lesbians and it made me feel less lonely. I found the book well written and I enjoyed it as a novel per se.

(Read in 1955, aged 26)

At the time I found it wonderful and I think the romance was useful, uplifting, showed the possibility of lesbianism – But I didn't want to be a martyr, live in a twilight world. ... But it did give me sense of a cause which did actually spur me a bit.

(Read in 1964, aged 14)

Useful in that 'I was not alone' – harmful in that I went through a butch phase, acting a role I didn't really feel; I also thought the outlook seemed grim – went heterosexual for many years until the women's movement made all okay.

(Read in 1965, aged 17)

At the time in the 1950s I couldn't identify with the short-back-and-sides, male-suited identity of being a lesbian. Although I was having my first lesbian affair, I felt I wasn't a lesbian.

(Read in 1953, aged 27)

I think it was Stephen's character that gave the book its impact – not because she was masculine; but because she was innocent, guileless, honest. She wasn't devious, as lesbians are supposed to be by nature. That may be why I believed in the book in spite of my own better judgement and why it has survived.

(Read in 1965, aged 17)

I suppose I abstracted the sexual romance and the urgent plea for tolerance from it. I wrote in my diary at the time – or two years after perhaps? – about democracy and the rights of minorities. So it was a political book for me as well as erotic.

(Read in 1964, aged 14)

7

SOCIAL PERCEPTIONS

INTRODUCTION

The trial of *The Well of Loneliness* was not the only way the general public became increasingly familiar with the idea of lesbianism. This chapter brings together sources that reflect the creation of this modern sexual category in popular discourses; the broadening social awareness of lesbianism in the twentieth century, and the variety of responses to it.

In the nineteenth century there was only limited circulation of specific terms to describe love between women (sapphist, tommy, lesbian), but from the 1920s the concept of lesbianism became more clearly defined, and was more widely shared as a part of social knowledge. New cultural understandings of love between women were one aspect of changing ideas about female sexuality generally; from the nineteenth-century idea that respectable women were without passion through to the encouragement of women's sexual pleasure as part of modern marriage (Hall 2000). As the twentieth century progressed, discussion of lesbianism increased and widened in scope, moving from the specialised audiences of professional discourses and the imagined world of fiction and pornography, to encompass a wider reading, viewing and listening public via journalism and other forms of popular writing. The process of repeated naming of lesbianism in the popular press and a widening variety of media spread the concept until it became social knowledge at a popular level.

We still know little about which sections of society were first conversant with the idea of lesbianism, and which groups remained ignorant for longest. Debates have centred on how quickly the idea of lesbianism entered popular consciousness, and on the relative significance of particular discourses and events in facilitating this. In the 1980s historians argued that professional discourses, especially the medical discourses of sexology at the turn of the century, along with the publicity surrounding *The Well of Loneliness* trial were translated into an increased public awareness of lesbianism. They suggested that this had a fairly rapid (and negative) effect on public perceptions. It was argued that from the

1920s there was greater suspicion of female friendships as having, and hiding, a lesbian sexual component, and that by the 1940s, for example, depictions of love between women in girls' fiction, previously seen as innocent, were censored (Jeffreys 1985, Lesbian History Group 1989, Auchmuty 1992). Further research and discussion in the 1990s suggested that the process of lesbianism becoming a recognised cultural category was rather more prolonged and uneven. Bland and Doan have shown that sexology had little purchase even in the professional circles of law and parliament in the 1920s, although other kinds of knowledge about lesbianism were patchily apparent (Bland 1998, Doan 1998b). Some groups, for example those in intellectual or artistic circles, may have acquired knowledge of lesbianism more quickly than others. We need further research on what kinds of information about lesbian sexuality were available from journalistic reporting of court cases and social issues. Stereotypes of lesbians as women from certain class positions, or from artistic, criminal or urban milieux, were developing, but was it a relationship which could also be imagined for ordinary women in rural or suburban areas? The creation of lesbianism as social knowledge requires much more investigation.

The social commentaries in this chapter can be divided into two broad types of source. First, there are fairly lengthy treatments, by journalists and other popular writers, of lesbianism as a social issue and usually as a social problem. Here the lesbian is frequently depicted as disrupting tranquil social life and conventions, for example by seducing young women or destroying marriages. Some of this literature offers advice to the (presumed heterosexual) reader in the recognition of and appropriate responses to lesbianism. These writers probably saw themselves as liberal for daring to discuss such a difficult and taboo topic, but their approach was almost invariably negative until the end of the 1960s. Most of these examples of middlebrow journalism were aimed at the suburban middle class, although the extent of its readership is difficult to gauge. Journalism reflects social attitudes, and changing sexual values and knowledge, better than the professional commentaries quoted in the previous section. It also indicates what is sayable or censored. But these sources can only show what prurient journalists and popular writers believed was appropriate for their readers, rather than the real extent of knowledge of lesbianism among the general public. Even when extracts quote ordinary people, these are chosen and controlled by the author to make a point.

Secondly, there is the published research of academics writing in a wide range of disciplines in the social sciences and arts. The academic and pseudo-academic treatment of lesbianism would have reached a number of discrete and small audiences and was invariably limited in its scope. It was not until the closing decades of the twentieth century that British academics, in any discipline, focused sustained research on the lesbian. Until the 1960s, whatever the type of social commentary, lesbianism rarely emerged as a subject in its own right. Instead it appeared as part of wider considerations of women in specific historical and cultural settings. Themes which were associated with lesbianism, and which remained remarkably consistent over the century, include the linking of lesbianism with man-hating and feminism; criminality; fears of social decline and of urban danger.

Donoghue (1993) has argued that some knowledge of lesbian culture existed throughout the eighteenth century and later in various genres of published literature and in women's networks. Some of the sources in our first two chapters on cross-dressing and romantic friendship suggest occasional social unease about mannish women and close attachments between women. But for much of the nineteenth century it appears that the idea of sex between women was ambivalent, imprecise and muted, and there is insufficient evidence to judge how widely known it was. The roving scholars of Victorian anthropology were charting the lesbian sexual behaviour of women in many non-European societies but any explicit discussion of lesbianism in Britain was largely to be found in either the professional discourses of sexology, medicine and education or in fiction and pornography. There was probably some private awareness of lesbian sexuality in the mid nineteenth century. Vicinus's fascinating study of the Codrington divorce case of 1864 illustrates how silences and the absence of categorising can nevertheless suggest lesbian intimacy (Vicinus 1997). From the late nineteenth century, increasing economic independence for women, combined with the classificatory discourses of sexology and the growth of feminism, contributed to public commentary on the New Woman. New Woman couples, especially those who were vocally anti-marriage, may well have suggested the possibility of sex between women, though this connection was rarely made explicit (Gowing 1997, Kent 1999: 248).

World War I is often credited with enhancing social awareness of lesbianism. The blurring of gender lines as women took over some male roles, the masculine image of women in the uniforms of the auxiliary services, and the challenge to conventional sexual morality led to fears about the prevalance of both male and female homosexuality (Hamer 1996, Kent 1999). The supposed emancipation of women, politically and in employment, together with the new boyish fashions of the 1920s, have led some historians to suggest there was increased concern about women's sexual perversion. But others have argued that masculine clothing was not associated with lesbianism until after the trial of *The Well of Loneliness* in 1928 (Doan 1998a). It seems that mannishness in women was only read as lesbianism in some circumstances before the mid twentieth century. While sexologists had noted that many lesbians were involved in the suffrage movement, it was only in the 1920s and 1930s that this link was made more widely in the public domain following publications by writers such as Arabella Kenealy, who blamed the women's movement for making women masculine and abnormal (Kenealy 1920, Weeks 1977, Doan 1998a).

The 1921 parliamentary debates about criminalising lesbianism threw up a number of themes which persisted in social commentaries through the following decades. In the debates it was said that sex between women was a vice known by two groups of professional men – medical doctors and those working in the law (police, criminal lawyers and divorce lawyers). The association of lesbianism with crime was also made in the popular press and literature. Lesbians were implicitly or explicitly associated with other allegedly degenerate activities such as drug-taking, prostitution, alcoholism and racial mixing, and thought to inhabit the same shady underworld of nightclubs, and particular cafés. The literature commenting on these dangerous sub-cultures of urban life, particularly in London, frequently features immorality as a strong narrative thread, and the lesbian figures prominent in the lurid dramatisations of the city have their roots in nineteenth-century visions of the terrifying metropolis (Walkowitz 1993). Here the links between conventional fictional representations of lesbianism, for example of the beautiful but cold lesbian vampire, merge with the purported documenting of real city life. The representations of older lesbians preying on innocent girls, and breaking up happy marriages, also connected to a broader contemporary panic about population decline. Lesbianism might lead to the rejection of marriage and childbirth and the ultimate destruction of civilisation.

Tracking the sources for evidence of shifts from social ignorance of lesbianism to general knowledge is difficult, but a change in its treatment is indicated in the 1940s and 1950s. In the 1921 parliamentary debate it was said that even many MPs had no knowledge of this vice, let alone most respectable women. By the 1940s all-female work environments away from home, such as the women's services, provided young women with greater sexual knowledge, and probably led to increased awareness of lesbianism, as well as opportunities for lesbian relationships. By then the term 'lesbian' was more commonly used. Social commentators offered a variety of clues to spot the lesbian, especially a tailored style of dress and the enjoyment of masculine social freedoms. When discussing female couples a tolerant but pitying tone was adopted. Lesbians were becoming a recognisable social type.

The 1940s and 1950s saw commentators increasingly turn outwards to open up public debates about appropriate social attitudes towards, and sanctions to control, homosexuality, including lesbianism. Liberal journalists began to discuss lesbianism in much greater depth in the 1960s, again as part of wider debates on sexual morality and the position of women. By this time, knowledge of lesbianism seems to have been taken for granted. Much of this journalism and social research continued to see lesbianism as a social problem: the term 'misfit' with its semi-psychological connotations was frequently used. But in this period there was also much more detailed discussion of lesbian social worlds. These were presented more dispassionately in newspapers and magazines, and on radio and television. The complexities of lesbian relationships and straightforward, non-prurient accounts of lesbian sexual practice also appeared towards the end of the 'permissive sixties'.

1 S. Hicks, *Difficulties: {An Attempt to Help}*, 1922, London: Duckworth and Co., pp. 260–1

Seymour Hicks (1871–1949) was a well-known actor-manager. He wrote and produced 64 plays and a number of books. This was a more elaborate version of a book called *If I were your Father*. It was dedicated to 'every young man but especially to Britishers and their American cousins'.

And not only from the male rover is it your duty to protect your wife. There are many strange types of women abroad to-day who may desire her, and who are just as great pests to society as the male degenerates who consort only with their fellows. That your wife would indignantly dismiss them I have no doubt, for, thank God, the world is peopled by a great majority of clean-minded, lovely women, but knowing that these wretches have multiplied immoderately of late, all I can say to you is that the moment you are aware that there is one of them who is trying to become a *persona grata* in your home – and they are as easy of recognition as blight on a rose – show her the door and bang it with no uncertainty, for these kind are more dangerous than all the men who attack your household put together. The male, however subtle, will be to your observant eyes obvious in his objective, and you will be able to challenge his behaviour with no degree of uncertainty, but a woman who seeks your wife is difficult to demand an explanation from, as her caresses may have as an excuse 'sympathetic femininity,' and you may hesitate to label her a Lesbian. But if you are uneasy, better to be brutal and make a mistake than have the innocent to whom you are devoted subjected to the advances of a wretch of this kind, who, if she succeeds, will wreck your home more thoroughly than you can imagine. Therefore in your early married life watch the women who approach your wife if anything more closely than you do the pleasant men who are not your friends.

2 T. Croft, *The Cloven Hoof. A Study of Contemporary London Vices*, 1932, London: Denis Archer, pp. 79–84

Croft believed that vice had increased since the war. The book was in part 'an attempt to counteract that too phlegmatic, too self-satisfied point of view of the Englishman'. Lesbianism was discussed alongside male homosexuality, prostitution, drug-taking, white slave traffic, pornography, alcoholism, gambling and the occult.

A more frequent cause is that strange state of mind which falls like a cloud on the senses of a woman during and after pregnancy, when, repelled or disturbed by the approach of a man, she desires only the caressing proximity of some fond member of her own sex. It is purely pathological but almost invariable, and in some cases sexual friendships which have sprung up at such a time between women have long outlasted the period, and occasionally resulted in their subjects becoming completely perverted.

Again, in the menopause, in that queer psychological twilight of middle age, which has no parallel in male development, there is often a tendency in a woman to become aggressively Lesbian. Such tendencies, though frequently repressed, have been known to turn in the years following, into the full ugliness of perversion in a person of late middle-age, and have caused women, who till then had been normal wives and mothers, to assume all the outward marks of the pervert.

But all such cases belong to a pathological consideration of the subject, such as I have no intention of making. We are concerned here, not objectively, with Lesbianism as a practice, but with its manifestations as a vice, and, more particularly, with those manifestations as they affect the life of London. To those scientifically interested in the subject there are a good many channels of information open – the works of Mr. Havelock Ellis deal fully with it.

Whether or not it is per se a vice, one fact is certain, that is that it can be one, and frequently in fact, is – especially among the conscious, separate, clearly-defined homosexual women whose lives are as distinct from the normal as those of homosexual men.

Here again there are differences. Conscious and practising Lesbians are not, as a class, as esoteric and organised as male urnings. The type is not so pronounced. But just as homosexual men affect a certain type of dress – the floppy, highly-coloured and feminine, so Lesbians wear clothes which are as a rule of set outline, neatly tailored and masculine.

One sees frequently among them the tailored coat and skirt, high collar, and man's tie. They wear too, very often, a man's wristlet watch, and, in place of jewellery, a signet ring. There are only about five modistes in London who specialise in this type of clothing and are patronised by Lesbians, and they are all expensive, charging as much as twenty-two guineas for a coat and skirt, and three guineas for a shirt. The result is that the few conscious Lesbians among the poorer classes rarely indulge in a specialised form of dress, since such costumes are the one style of clothing most difficult to imitate successfully at a low figure.

Until quite recently, in fact, the 'aware' type of Lesbian seemed only to exist among two classes, the well-to-do and sophisticated, and the highly educated and philosophical. It is only of recent years that servant girls and shop assistants, fully conscious of the peculiarities of their own natures, have begun openly to discuss it, and to imitate in manner, and even occasionally in dress, the more prosperous. But the cult is certainly beginning to spread among them, and a number of such girls, under the impression, perhaps, that it is chic and modern, at any rate to know about it, have grown intensely curious in the matter.

But in any case women of this type are often distinguishable by outward characteristics other than dress. The voice, both in male and female, is astonishingly often an indication. In the man, homosexuality makes the voice sometimes high-pitched and feminine, with a noticeable hiss on the 'S' sound, sometimes peculiarly deep and melodious, but always it gives to it that curious coquettish intonation which is not easily describable, but once heard, is never forgotten. In the female it does not always add a manly note – occasionally the voice is quite shrill – but always it produces an unusual intonation which is somehow crude and animal.

Just as in men, as we have seen, homosexuality has propagated or been concurrent with artistic and other achievement of a very high order, so with women, from Sappho downwards. And just as beside this with the male has gone a great deal of charlatanism and pretension, so with the female – perhaps, indeed, more so. For Lesbian women seem nearly always to imagine themselves creative or intellectual and have made the most febrile attempts to prove it.

There have been a number of them, in the last few years, publishing extremely second-rate stuff of an obviously Lesbian nature, nearly always abroad, and the motive, it seems to me, is nearly always a desire for self-advertisement. In conversation, too, their intellectual pretentiousness is formidable; they are downright, even bombastic, to the point of bad taste.

It is strange how much of that pretentiousness runs to literature in one form or another. Not only do they write, but are not infrequently prodigious collectors of books. I know of two very valuable private libraries owned by Lesbians, both of which have large pornographic sections, and one of them is unique, I believe, for the number and variety of its books on subjects connected with this practice.

As for actual contacts between women of this sort and homosexual men, these are of a kind both unexpected and interesting. Socially, they seem to seek each other, and at several of the night clubs of the more degenerate kind, they may be seen in company with well-known urnings.

It is, perhaps, because they have in common the fact of their outcast or chosen – according to the way they look at it – state. But it is also because the society of degenerates and semi-degenerates in London exists as a society, and claims for its own the vicious of whatever stamp. There are a few fixed stars in it, names which recur wherever a few of such people gather, and they are of all types – drug-takers, uteromaniacs, perverts, alcoholists. They depend for society on others, and in the meeting-places of these people one is thrown with the vicious of every cult. Which accounts for the frequency with which one sees men and women homosexualists together.

But they have actual sexual connections, as well. There have been frequent cases of marriage between them, in recent years, and not always marriages of convenience. That they actually form physical alliances may be explained, perhaps, by the fact that each, grown by the habits of promiscuity, past reserve of any sort, past any kind of modesty or control, may begin such alliances in the form of experiment, without there existing the least sexual attraction on either side. It is possible for such things to come about among people who have indulged most appetites to the full, merely in an attempt to investigate another possible source of pleasure. In other words, at a purely mental urging. This, I maintain, could only come about between abnormal people. For sexual desire is literally the only power strong enough to break down the high barriers of reserve between the average man and woman.

Among the poorer types, too, one has seen lately a growing kindred between male and female homosexuals. In the teashops and cafés described in the last chapter, Lesbians may be seen with groups of urnings, and also at their parties. There are very few exclusively Lesbian rendezvous in London, only one tea-place being famous for it.

Curiously enough the feminist movement seems to have had little or no relationship with this vice, either in its inauguration, or since. Nor do feminine sporting circles by any means attract it as they are occasionally supposed to do. Homosexual women are given chiefly to the more conspicuous and egotistic forms of sport – automobile racing, speed-boat racing, flying. They are not infrequently mechanically inclined, and are thus attracted by these diversions.

These notes on the outward characteristics and habits of homosexual women are sketchy and inclined to generalisation; but it is impossible to speak of them as one can for their male counterparts, for they are very much more individual both in their behaviour and appearance. It is easier, perhaps, to speak of their habits as a consciously vicious section of London society.

3 Mrs C. Chesterton, *Women of the London Underworld*, 1938, London: Readers Library Publishing Co. Ltd, pp. 72–4

Mrs Cecil Chesterton (Ada Jones) was founder of the Cecil Homes for homeless women and girls in London. Her accounts of women's involvement in crime were based on her 'adventures' when visiting lodging houses, casual wards, restaurants and night-clubs in the capital.

There is a side of life in these unhealthy centres which plays a significant and sinister part in the demoralization of the young girl. You will find in the more expensive ill-run night club a type of woman expensively dressed, well groomed, of early middle age and with a curiously unsexed look about them. They may have a mannish suggestion about their dress, or they may be feminine and fluffy in appearance. But male attention leaves them unmoved, though the sight of a pretty girl with a soft complexion and the look of genuine inexperience brings a light to their eyes. This type of woman is on the look-out for companions of her own sex. Abnormal desires in the sex direction can always be gratified – given money and opportunity

— and an appetite for abnormality can readily be satisfied in many night clubs in that quarter. It may often happen that the girl selected is utterly unsuspicious of what the older woman is after, and readily accepts an invitation to dinner, the theatre, or to a social evening. The advance in such a case is insidious, and the more ingenuous the girl the more difficult for her to distinguish between the evidences of a natural affection, and those of an unhealthy desire. Once a girl is debauched in this manner it is difficult for her to regain a normal view of sex. She is spoiled.

There are, we know, those who by inheritance are unhappily deterred from normal sex relations. But for the most part these take their own ways of dealing with their problem. They are not often found on the prowl for the young and innocent. It is rather those women who, vitiated by excess of all description, look for untasted experiences who are to be dreaded.

I have known girls who, warned by anxious relatives of the dangers of making acquaintance with strangers who may be white slavers, have quite innocently accepted friendly advances from women of whom they have not the least knowledge. Sometimes the sequel is quite harmless. Sometimes it has other conclusions. As a matter of fact, wealthy women of abnormal tastes do not often seek recreation from chance encounters in the street, or other public places.

It is at the gateways to the underworld, fascinating little café bars, dance clubs, feverish centres of excitement and emotional stimuli that you will find them.

Emotionally speaking, once such an association is formed it is very difficult to induce a young girl to break it. Women of this type are very often brilliant intellectually with a power of fascination difficult for a young thing to resist. Extravagantly lavish, the older woman will endow her protégé with jewels, dresses, surround her with every kind of luxury. Sometimes the association drags on for years, long past the period when a girl might hope for marriage or a natural attachment for a man. It happens, however, quite often that the connection is violently ruptured. The woman meets another more attractive girl and the former possessor of her interest and caresses is flung off. Deprived of all contentment with normality, her nerves wrecked, with a ravaged mind and body, the abandoned one may either take to drugs and drink, or an even worse fate — transfer herself to a fresh protectress.

4 'London's Night Club Pests Fear Police Clean Up', *The People*, 9 July 1939, p. 17

London's night club pests fear police clean up

Dens that should be closed

London's shady night-resort proprietors, the suave racketeers who charge twenty-five shillings a bottle for the doubtful privilege of drinking whisky or gin in badly ventilated cellars, are perturbed.

They fear that Recorder Sir Gerald Dodson's outspoken attack on night-club life at the close of the Mayfair men's Old Bailey trial last week may herald a widespread 'clean up.'

The Recorder said that one day public opinion might drive out of existence such places as night clubs. His acid comments have caused a good deal of uneasiness in a host of undesirable haunts in the Soho and Piccadilly area. ...

They flourish by the score in dingy side-streets, alley-ways, cellars and basements between Oxford-st. and Charing Cross, moving their headquarters so frequently that in twelve months one man may open six different premises with different names.

It's only the name that changes. The surroundings are always the same – a dimly lit room – they keep the lights low to hide the dirty walls – a few dusty and wilting palms to add 'glamour,' and a handful of semi-drunks going through the motions of dancing on a tiny patch of linoleum. ...

Rouged men

I could take you to three different dens almost next door to one another in the same alley that should be closed immediately. One caters for blond and rouged young men and Eton-cropped women; the second for coloured men and women of low repute; and the third for a gang of criminals with convictions ranging from blackmail to drug peddling.

5 E. Blyton, *Five on a Treasure Island*, 1942, Hodder and Stoughton, pp. 15–16

George, the girl who wants to be a boy, appears in all the 'Famous Five' stories. Here she is introduced for the first time. On the one hand this shows that to be a tomboy was acceptable for girls; on the other it suggests the possibility of a self-presentation outside the bounds of conventional femininity for the younger reader exploring her own sexuality.

Chapter 2. The strange cousin

... 'Where's Georgina?' asked Anne, looking round for her unknown cousin.

'Oh, the naughty girl! I told her to wait in the garden for you,' said her aunt. 'Now she's gone off somewhere. I must tell you, children, you may find George a bit difficult at first – she's always been one on her own, you know. And at first she may not like you being here. But you mustn't take any notice of that – she'll be all right in a short time. I was very glad for George's sake that you were able to come. She badly needs other children to play with.'

'Do you call her "George"?' asked Anne, in surprise. 'I thought her name was Georgina.'

'So it is,' said her aunt. 'But George hates being a girl, and we have to call her George, as if she was a boy. The naughty girl won't answer if we call her Georgina.'

The children thought that Georgina sounded rather exciting. They wished she would come. But she didn't ...

Later that evening Anne wakes to find George in the bed opposite her.

'I say ! Are you Georgina?'

The child in the opposite bed sat up and looked across at Anne. She had very short curly hair, almost as short as a boy's. Her face was burnt a dark-brown with the sun, and her very blue eyes looked as bright as forget-me-nots in her face. But her mouth was rather sulky, and she had a frown like her father's.

'No', she said. 'I'm not Georgina.'

'Oh!' said Anne, in surprise. 'Then who are you?'

'I'm George,' said the girl. 'I shall only answer if you call me George. I hate being a girl. I won't be. I don't like doing the things that girls do. I like doing the things that boys do. I can climb better than any boy, and swim faster too. I can sail a boat as well as any fisher-boy on this coast. You're to call me George. Then I'll speak to you. But I shan't if you don't.'

'Oh!' said Anne, thinking that her new cousin was most extraordinary. 'All right! I don't care what I call you. George is a nice name I think. I don't much like Georgina. Anyway, you look like a boy.'

'Do I really?' said George, the frown leaving her face for a moment. 'Mother was awfully cross with me when I cut my hair short. I had hair all round my neck; it was awful.'

6 Mass Observation, *The Pub and the People. A Worktown Study*, 1943, London: Victor Gollancz Ltd, pp. 184–5

Mass Observation was a pioneering social research organisation operating from the late 1930s to the 1950s. This Mass Observation study was carried out in 1937–1939 in Bolton. The extract is from the chapter on 'Drinking'.

The landlords of some pubs refuse to serve pints in the parlour. Women do not drink pints – the story of a woman who used to do so bears out these points: it is a discussion in the parlour of a small beer house, among a number of women, some of whom are drunk.

Discussion about a lesbian woman. They concentrate *like hell* to try and remember her name. After four minutes working on it and puzzling, one remembers it, and there is joy all round and the name is reiterated again and again. The following remarks were made about her:

'She be dead and buried now.'

'The worst thing about her is neither woman or man.'

''er and Emily lived together.'

'She was rather on the vulgar side.'

'She was very dirty spoke though.'

'She'd stand up at fire.' (This mentioned twice.)

'She'd rather have a pint than a gill.'

Undoubtedly, the pint mug is associated with labourers, men drinking in dirty working clothes, and old chaps who spit a lot and smoke cheap twist.

7 J. McCrindle and S. Rowbotham (eds), *Dutiful Daughters: Women Talk about Their Lives*, 1979, Harmondsworth: Penguin, pp. 142–3

Jean Mormont recalled meeting lesbians during her wartime work in the Auxiliary Territorial Services (ATS), the women's branch of the army.

You meet all kinds of girls [laughs] – yes, I've met all sorts, you know. That's why I think it is a good life, because I'd never really been able to mix before that, and you meet people from all walks of life. I even got some shocks and all, you know, because I met some people, and you met girls I've never … I never knew what a lesbian was, and I met some girls in there, and it used to puzzle me, I couldn't make it out, you know, till I was told like, you know, by the other girls, what it was all about. I thought to myself, well, you're learning all the time, and I thought to myself, good job me mother don't know. [Laughs.] After the girls told me what it was all about, they used to lay on the bed there cuddling one another, and I thought to myself, that's funny, you know. [Laughs.] Yes, they do, they do. You know after a while you just don't take any notice of it. It's their way of life and that's it. They don't interfere with you, or they don't try it on me, I didn't mind. [Laughs.]

8 L. Fairfield, 'Homosexuality in Women', *Medico-Legal Journal*, Vol. 15. No. 1, 1947, pp. 18–20, 22–3

At its meeting on 23 January 1947 the Medico-Legal Society discussed 'The Sociological Aspects of Homosexuality'. There were two women contributors. Letitia Fairfield was qualified as a barrister as well as in medicine. She served as a doctor in both World Wars I and II, and was a senior medical officer to the London County Council until 1948. She presented this paper and Helena Normanton (the first woman barrister to be made a KC), contributed to the discussion. The President's comment probably refers to Seymour Hicks' book *Difficulties*.

I propose in the few minutes at my disposal to deal mainly with this subject as it affects women and children, those being the aspects which have come to my notice in my professional life. One may begin, however, by answering the question which the President has posed on the attitude of society to the whole matter. Many discussions on homosexuality are gravely vitiated by a failure to realize that it is impossible to help the homosexual without a clear preliminary agreement that (a) society is right in condemning homosexual activities, and (b) is justified in supporting this condemnation – in the case of persistent offenders of responsible age – by the usual sanctions of social ostracism and legal penalties.

Omitting the specifically Christian arguments, it would appear obvious that society cannot afford to come to terms with a way of life which diverts into sterile channels the very force upon which its continued existence depends. If permitted as a recognized substitute for normal heterosexual love, homosexuality could not be limited to an isolated class. It would soon demonstrate the truth of Kant's principle of universality as a test of virtue, for the more it was practised the more disastrous it would be to any community.

Nor would such toleration be likely to achieve the result which the advocates of a 'modern attitude' suggest it would produce, i.e., the happiness of individuals. A homosexual cult may provide an immediate gratification or desire, but it leads to frustration and inferiority feelings, to bitter emotional disappointments and jealousies no less poignant than those experienced in heterosexual love and without its consolations and hopes of fruition. Some of the saddest tragedies I have seen were episodes of this kind, when women have drifted into a partnership with a woman friend (often quite unconscious of its homosexual nature) which has grown deeper and more exclusive as the years have gone by. Often the younger woman wishes ultimately to marry and the older woman is left with a terrible sense of desertion and frustration. Another type of tragedy familiar to practitioners in the divorce courts occurs when a 'hangover' from a previous Lesbian friendship makes a happy marriage impossible.

It is the illumination thrown by the teachings of Freud and others of the psycho-analytic school on homosexuality which supplies the strongest argument for demanding that the attitude of society should not only be clearly defined but supported by sanctions. If perverted love were wholly or solely a mental abnormality or disease, it could be tolerated with greater impunity, or treated on entirely medical lines, for there would be no fear of spread to 'normal' persons. If it were in fact a mental disease, it would be a self-limited condition. But homosexual desires are common to nearly everyone at some stage of growth; as Freud expresses it, homosexuality is a fixation at an early stage of infantile sexuality due to a variety of causes, some inherent and some environmental. To put it in another way, human beings by their very nature are susceptible and not immune to homosexual influences. It is therefore only good sense to protect them from exposure to infection.

Thus, an atmosphere of toleration would inevitably mean that children would be tempted to exploit their perverse attraction for certain adults, that adults would be tempted to use their power over children; and adolescents, especially those who shrink from the alarming problems of adult life, would be tempted to seek a retreat into a childish phase of emotional life.

I have stressed the possibilities of corruption of the young more than those of shock, although, with all respect to certain psychologists, the risk of grave shock is not negligible. It is probably true that – contrary to popular belief – shock from homosexual advances or assaults is greater even in adolescence than in childhood, and the deplorable effect may extend into adult life.

Discussion

{Mrs Helena Normanton}

She did not desire to discuss that aspect any further, but she wanted to touch on the matter which her friend, Dr. Letitia Fairfield, had already spoken about, namely, homosexuality among women. Dr. Fairfield had said that the law could not touch Lesbianism. If she was dealing with the infatuation of schoolgirls, very likely not, but there was a very crude manifestation of Lesbianism between women which the law ought to touch, particularly the Continental forms of it which were increasing in London at this moment. An attempt was made to bring this within the law when the House of Commons was discussing the Criminal Law Amendment Act of 1922. In that debate a male Member of Parliament suggested that it was unjust to punish the man guilty of an unnatural offence and not to punish the woman, whereupon Lady Astor said that that was all nonsense, because there was nothing of the sort between women. But the matter concealed obvious injustices. A woman might divorce her husband if he committed unnatural offences with other men, but her husband had no remedy if she committed unnatural offences with other women. In spite of what Lady Astor said on that occasion such cases did occur between women, and there were now cases in which actually Lesbianism between women was being promoted by men and run as a source of profit. There were houses in some of the most expensive and aristocratic quarters in London where an enormous amount of money was being earned in this way and the law could not touch the people concerned.

The PRESIDENT, in closing the discussion, said that he thought they would all agree that they had listened to some most interesting and important speeches. It seemed to him clear that this problem of homosexuality could not rightly be judged in any monopolist spirit. There were so many factors with which lawyers and doctors had severally to deal and there were many angles of approach. He did not know whether there was any theatrical manager in the audience that evening, but he remembered some twenty-five or thirty years ago a theatrical manager, whose name was highly respected by everybody in this country, writing a book which took the form of letters to his son. One of those letters was on getting married, and this theatrical manager, clearly writing from his own experience, told his son not to pay any attention to flirtations of his wife with other men but to watch the women with whom she associated, whether they were young or old. That touched upon an aspect of the matter mentioned by Mrs. Normanton.

He thought that the discussion would help to crystallize their views on this subject.

9 S. de Beauvoir, *The Second Sex*, 1972 [1953], Harmondsworth: Penguin, pp. 441–4

Simone de Beauvoir's classic work on women was published in France in 1949 and in Britain in 1953. In it she devoted a chapter to the lesbian and, while doom-laden, it does explicitly present lesbianism as a rational choice for some women in a male-dominated world.

If such amours are often stormy, it is also true that they are ordinarily carried on under more threatening conditions than are heterosexual affairs. They are condemned by a society with which they can hardly be integrated success-fully. The woman who assumes the virile role – through her nature, her situation, or her strength of passion will regret not giving her loved one a normal and respectable life, not being able to marry her; and she will reproach herself for leading her friend into questionable ways: such are the sentiments that Radclyffe Hall attributes to her heroine in *The Well of Loneliness*. This remorse is manifested in a morbid anxiety and especially in a torturing jealousy. The passive or less deeply smitten partner, on her side, will in fact suffer from the weight of social censure; she will believe herself degraded, perverted, frustrated, she will feel resentment against the woman who brings all this upon her. It may happen that one of the two women wants to have a child; if so, she can sadly resign herself to her sterility, or the two can adopt a child, or the one who longs for maternity can appeal to a man; the child may serve to unite them more firmly, or it may be a new source of friction.

What gives homosexual women a masculine cast is not their erotic life, which, on the contrary, confines them to a feminine universe; it is rather the whole group of responsibilities they are forced to assume because they dispense with men. Their situation is the reverse of the courtesan's, for she sometimes takes on a virile character from living among men – as did Ninon de Lenclos – but still depends upon them. The peculiar atmosphere that surrounds lesbians comes from the contrast between the gynaeceum-like climate of their private lives and the masculine freedom of their public existence. They act like men in a world without men. Woman by herself, apart from man, seems somewhat unusual; it is not true that men respect women; they respect one another through their women – wives, mistresses, or the prostitutes they pimp for. Without masculine protection woman is helpless before a superior caste that is aggressive, sneeringly amused, or hostile. As an erotic 'perversion', feminine homosexuality may elicit a smile; but as implying a mode of life, it arouses contempt or scandalized disapproval. If there is a good deal of aggressiveness and affectation in the attitude of lesbians, it is because there is no way in which they can live naturally in their situation: being natural implies being unselfconscious, not picturing one's acts to oneself; but the attitude of other people constantly directs the lesbian's attention upon herself. She can go her own way in calm indifference only when she is old enough or backed by considerable social prestige.

It is difficult to state with certainty, for example, whether the lesbian commonly dresses in mannish fashion by preference or as a defence reaction. Certainly it is often a matter of spontaneous choice. Nothing is less natural than to dress in feminine fashion; no doubt masculine garb is artificial also, but it is simpler and more convenient being intended to facilitate rather than to hinder activity; George Sand wore male clothing; in her last book, *Moi*, Thyde Monnier confessed her preference for trousers; every active woman likes low heels and sturdy materials. The significance of woman's attire is evident: it is decoration, and to be decorated means to be offered. The heterosexual feminists were formerly as intransigent in this matter as the lesbian; declining to make themselves into merchandise, offered for sale, they affected severe tailor-made suits and felt hats; elaborate low-neck gowns seemed to them symbolical of the social order they were fighting. Today they have succeeded in gaining the reality, and so in their eyes the symbol is of less importance. But it remains important for the lesbian to the extent that she must still assert her claim. It may happen also that severe dress is more becoming to her, if physical traits have motivated her choice of lesbianism.

It should be pointed out, further, that one function of finery is to gratify woman's tactile sensuousness; but the lesbian disdains the appeal of velvet and silk: like Sandor she enjoys them on her friend or her friend's body itself may take their place. For similarly, also, the lesbian often likes to drink alcohol, smoke strong tobacco, use rough language, take violent exercise: in her eroticism she gets enough feminine sweetness, and by way of contrast she enjoys a climate that is not so mild. Thus she may come to enjoy the company of men.

But here a new factor is involved: that is the relation – often arduous – which she sustains with men. A woman fully assured in her virile powers will want only men as friends and companions; but assurance will hardly be found in any woman who does not have interests in common with them, who – in business, activities, or art – does not work and find success like a man. When Gertrude entertained friends, she conversed only with the men and left to Alice Toklas the duty of talking with the ladies.* But towards women the strongly virile female homosexual will take an ambivalent attitude: she feels contempt for them, but with them she suffers from an inferiority complex both as woman and as man. She fears that to them she will seem at once a defective woman and an incomplete man, and this leads her to affect a haughty superiority or to show towards them – like Stekel's transvestite – a sadistic aggressiveness.

But such cases are rather rare. Most lesbians, as we have seen, reticently avoid men: in them, as in the frigid woman, there is a feeling of resentment, timidity, pride; they do not feel truly men's peers; to their feminine resentment is added a masculine inferiority complex; men are rivals better equipped to seduce, possess, and retain their prey; they detest the 'defilement' to which men subject woman. They are incensed also to see men holding social advantages and to feel that they are the stronger: it is a burning humiliation to be unable to fight with a rival, to know that he is capable of knocking you down with a blow of his fist. This complicated hostility is one of the reasons that impels certain female homosexuals to make themselves conspicuous; they flock together; they form clubs of a sort to show that they have no more need of men socially than sexually. From this the descent is easy to empty bragging and all the play-acting that springs from insincerity. The lesbian plays first at being a man; then even being a lesbian becomes a game; masculine clothing, at first a disguise, becomes a uniform; and under the pretext of escaping male oppression, woman becomes enslaved to the character she plays; wishing not to be confined in woman's situation, she is imprisoned in that of the lesbian. Nothing gives a darker impression of narrow-mindedness and of mutilation than these groups of emancipated women. It should be added that many women declare themselves to be homosexuals only through self-interested compliance: they adopt lesbianism only with their growing awareness of its equivocal allurements, hoping moreover to entice such men as may like 'vicious' women. These noisy zealots – who are obviously the most noticeable of the lesbians – help to cast discredit upon what common opinion regards as a vice and as a pose.

The truth is that homosexuality is no more a perversion deliberately indulged in than it is a curse of fate. It is an attitude *chosen in a certain situation* – that is, at once motivated and freely adopted. No one of the factors that mark the subject in connection with this choice – physiological conditions, psychological history, social circumstances – is the determining element, though they all contribute to its explanation. It is one way, among others, in which woman solves the problems posed by her condition in general, by her erotic situation in particular. Like all human behaviour, homosexuality leads to make-believe, disequilibrium, frustration, lies, or, on the contrary, it becomes the source of rewarding experiences, in accordance with its manner of expression in actual living – whether in bad faith, laziness, and falsity, or in lucidity, generosity, and freedom.

* A heterosexual woman who believes – or can convince herself – that her merits enable her to transcend sexual differences will easily take the same attitude. So it was with Mme de Staël.

10 V. Musgrave, 'Women Outside the Law', *The Twentieth Century*, Vol. 164, No. 978, August 1958, pp. 178–84

In a special issue of *The Twentieth Century* on women, Victor Musgrave, the director of Gallery One, was invited to write about his knowledge of prostitution in response to thirteen questions posed by the editor. The tenth question asked simply 'Lesbianism?'

There's undoubtedly a latent lesbian streak in many prostitutes. They spend an inordinate amount of time gossiping among themselves, and will frequently sit apart from the men in groups in the clubs. But the proportion of active Lesbians is very small. Some of the girls have experimented briefly and tentatively, but they quickly return to men, if they ever left them. I know of only a handful of permanent Lesbian relationships among the girls. The bond between them is rather that of the feminine concord of a society outside the law.

11 D. Rowe, 'A Quick Look at Lesbians', *The Twentieth Century*, Winter 1962–3, pp. 67–72 *passim*

This article was introduced as follows: 'Male homosexuals are persecuted in Britain, and their problems have been exhaustively discussed. Yet the problems – and the dangers – of feminine homosexuality have been curiously ignored. In the belief that it ought to be taken seriously and understood, we asked several experienced journalists to investigate. Two drew a blank. The third supplied an introductory report on some aspects of this misty, unmapped world.' It was the publication of this article that prompted the founding of the Minorities Research Group.

'The homosexual wants to be accepted by society for what he is, particularly the male homosexual. It's not so difficult for a woman. You can always be a female homosexual in this country, as long as you breed dogs, or keep a cake-shop. ... '

The speaker was a professional woman, a confessed homosexual (like many of the franker kind, she does not like the word Lesbian). A woman with a highly developed, if slightly eccentric social conscience, she gives a good deal of thought to the position of homosexuals in society, although her main preoccupation is her campaign for a cause which concerns society in a more general way. In talking to me about her own homosexuality she combined a sense of bravado with occasional hints of a sense of deprivation. One price she pays is that her intense idealism over what she wants for the world is overlaid with the shabby cynicism of the social misfit, and of course where people are concerned her deep loyalties are often hopelessly misplaced. She says: 'The only reason why I don't shout my homosexuality from the roof-tops is that I want my campaign to be accepted. Sometimes I have fantasies about being given some kind of decoration – yes, like being made a Dame or something – and announcing when I accept it that I am a homo-sexual.' She went on to ask me if as a heterosexual woman I felt any revulsion for her. Be honest, she said. I threw discretion to the winds in favour of caution, and told her honestly that I did. I saw that it was the answer she had hoped for.

The kennels and tea-shoppe atmosphere of English Lesbianism (laced with occasional spicy whiffs from the green room) makes even people who might be most affected by it (parents, social workers) casual about its conse-quences. It is hardly taken seriously, if it is noticed at all, because to all appearances it is practised cosily, within the law. At least Lesbians are not hounded around the country as male homosexuals are; they are not classified with such finicky distinctions in the criminal records. Women homosexuals only appear in the statistics in a specialized category of 'indecent assault of a woman by a woman'. But, as the Wolfenden Committee discovered, a woman who was helping a man in this enterprise would qualify (at the last annual round-up the number was three).

Public awareness, though, of male homosexuality, even in the form of persecution or natural disgust, is beginning to put parents on their guard against the emotional traps which turn boys into inverts, against all-male institutions such as prisons and the public schools. But the possibilities hardly ever occur to most parents of girls; although it is from their relation-ships – according to psychological theory – that Lesbianism springs. Dr S., a woman doctor who specializes in marriage guidance and has a long experi-ence of treating psychosexual problems, talked to me about women patients who are frigid because they have latent homosexual tendencies. She said that they were almost without exception women who in adolescence had failed to become emotionally involved with their fathers. This was often because the father was the weaker partner (or because the mother made out that he was), a poor provider, or an alcoholic. The girl's emotions had become fixed on the mother, she rejected men and sought other mother-figures, felt guilt about heterosexual relations, etc. etc. 'Even if the father is a criminal,' said Dr S., 'it is better for the girl to fall in love with him at about 15. At 17 she can see him for what he is ... '

Family troubles certainly played their part in the lives of some of the Lesbians who agreed to talk to me. J. C., for instance, has been having homosexual love affairs since she was eighteen (she is now in her middle thirties). The only guilt she feels is about some of the women she had seduced. She says that at eighteen she could have attracted any man she wanted (this seems quite likely), and often set out to prove this, but in the event was repelled by men. Her father left her mother during the second world war when she was eight for an American woman he had met while serving in the RAF. She was brought up by a mother and grandmother. Her father was only allowed to come to the house to see her if he used the side-entrance. Another woman who talked to me, D. F., is married with two sons. Her husband has now left her. She does not seem to connect this with her own vague homosexual relations: the main importance of them to her is that they put her into the 'artistic' set. She started having them after a chance meeting at a hotel in Eastbourne. Her mother committed suicide when she was sixteen: she bitterly resented her father, especially having to leave school to look after him.

12 *Towards A Quaker View Of Sex*, 1964, Revised Edition, London: Friends Home Service Committee, pp. 37–40

This essay by 'a group of Friends' was presented as an unofficial contribution to contemporary debates on homosexuality and promiscuity. First published in 1963, it aroused widespread interest and ran to six impressions before the second edition was published in 1964.

Homosexuality is probably as common in women as it is in men. Although with girls today heterosexual social relationships start early, the early adolescent phase may still be a time of passionate friendships and of an adoration of an older girl or woman. Close physical contact is common: girls will dance together, share a bed, or walk arm in arm, often without any strong emotional feeling. Many women continue to attach themselves to others of their own sex beyond the phase of adolescence, but owing to their nature and to society's different attitude, homosexuality in women takes forms differing from those in men. Female homosexuality is free from the legal, and to a large extent from the social, sanctions which are so important in the problems of male homosexuals. Analysis of the two forms, their differences and similarities, may therefore suggest what might happen if these sanctions were to be modified for men.

Any personal relationship between two people carries a sexual element, the nature of which will depend upon the balance of the male and female in each of the two personalities. A friendship between two individuals, one predominantly male and the other predominantly female, as with the normal man and woman, is different from one between two men in whom maleness predominates or between two women in whom femaleness predominates. In the first case the relationship is enriched by the stimulus of two very different mental patterns, in the second and third the richness lies in the freedom of a common background of thought process. A man, however, will sometimes enjoy in a woman a vigour of mind which he regards as masculine and the woman will equally welcome in a man an intuitive sympathy and tenderness which she regards as feminine. Similarly, at moments in a friendship between men, one may show 'feminine' tenderness and care for the other and between women one may show 'masculine dominance'. (The latter is not always easily distinguishable from maternal dominance). These simple facts, though rarely formulated, are widely accepted and none would criticize a marriage, or a friendship between two persons of the same sex, in which they appear.

Society's criticism begins when the female element in a man or the male element in a woman is permanently and overtly dominant, a criticism which is almost as much directed against a married couple where the woman 'wears the trousers', as in a relationship between two members of the same sex which has a homosexual element. Social structure has a further influence on this type of situation however, since there is a strong feeling of condemnation of two persons of the same sex so linked that neither is likely to marry, a condemnation based on a conviction, which is probably socially valuable, that marriage and the procreation of children is a major responsibility of members of society.

Such criticism is far less violent against homosexual relations between women than those between men, and the reasons for this tolerance merit examination:

1   Maternal tenderness in a woman, expressing itself in kisses and embraces, is socially acceptable and it is probably for this reason that society is neither offended nor disturbed by seeing two women of any age or of very different ages kissing and embracing in public, nor by seeing two little girls or young women going about hand in hand, arm in arm, or with their arms round each others' waists.
2   The giving of maternal tenderness is so profound a need in a woman that much of the satisfaction from caresses between women will be of this kind. Society values this need in a woman and calls upon it freely, and there is considerable tolerance of its expression.
3   A very large number of women involved in homosexual relationships would frankly admit that they would prefer or are looking forward to a heterosexual one. The adolescent girl adoring an older woman or more

closely involved with a contemporary would usually reject indignantly the idea that this precludes or replaces the male lover or husband and family to which she looks forward. The pair of middle-aged women, which society on the whole views with such tolerance, often have heterosexual experiences behind them or have been deprived of marriage, as by death or by an unhappy love affair, and thankfully find comfort, consolation and happiness in each other without in any way minimizing the value of the experiences they have had or missed. Even pairs of younger women of marriageable age – the types of female homosexuality on which society looks more askance – are often at least apparently seeking male society with a view to finding husbands. This acceptance of heterosexuality as good and desirable makes for tolerance of female homosexual pairs by society.

4   Tolerance of the pair of older women, in this country at least, probably developed when it was socially unacceptable for a single woman to live alone and it was therefore taken for granted that two single women should set up house together. This tolerance was probably reinforced in this century by the long period following World War I when there was a large surplus of women.

5   It should be emphasized that two women have often lived together in a companionship which replaces many aspects of the companionship of married life and yet in which few if any caresses are exchanged – probably true of some male partnerships as well. It is recognized that such partnerships between older women, with or without physical expression, can form a useful unit in society, each partner pursuing her avocations the better for the strength of the companionship and tenderness she finds at home, and the pair together able to offer a generous and welcome hospitality.

This is the positive side. Before considering the effect which a comparably more tolerant attitude in society would have on male homosexual relationships, it is necessary to examine the negative, and to see whether what is harmful and regrettable in female homosexuality has the same form or is similar in origin to what is harmful in homosexuality among men.

The first and most conspicuous feature is that female homosexuality is often associated with deep unhappiness. In the young girl unhappiness is probably at the minimum when the object of adoration is remote, but may even then become deeply disturbing if the emotion is so dominant that it throws life entirely out of proportion. An adolescent girl is probably more likely to be subject to this kind of disturbance than is a boy, since her emotions have often developed faster than her intellect, and she has no other dominant interest to distract her such as sport, engine-spotting or the constant care of a bicycle.

When in early adult life the relationship is more intimate, many of the features already noted as harmfully characteristic of male homosexuals may again be present: we find again the restless jealousy, possessiveness, and the torments of changing partnerships. These are often associated with an overt or unacknowledged sense of guilt or of resentment at being involved in what is not giving full satisfaction. This fact is probably far more important than would ever be acknowledged by the partners and, while some homosexuals are accurate when they say they do not want heterosexual relationships, many more, in their determined proclamations of this, are in fact doing violence to fuller impulses, which they are unable to perceive. The sense of guilt may at times be stronger in a young girl than in a man because she cannot, if she is at all feminine, escape the feeling of frustration at thus avoiding motherhood.

The same tensions and frustrations occur in unhappy partnerships of later life. The emotional strains, the deep bitterness arising from a continued search to find in another woman the satisfaction that only a man could give, produce the twisted embittered woman, only too familiar to psychiatrists. She may become cut off from society by her own self-absorption, for in such a situation self-absorption is dominant. She is a menace to her friends and colleagues and spreads unhappiness wherever she goes. Society is rightly critical and wrongly unsympathetic – yet sympathy is hard to give, for it is demanded on false grounds and when offered is often fiercely rejected.

This is the picture, then, of the positive and negative in female homosexuality. What can be deduced from it as to the possible course of male homosexuality if legal restrictions were removed and moral ostracism diminished? The most conspicuous feature that appears to be missing altogether from female homosexuality, even with the freedom which society allows it, is the brief contact of a purely or almost purely physical nature which is so characteristic of a certain section of male homosexual society. This is probably inherent in the different nature of the physical sexual responses of a man and a woman. It seems easier for most men than for most women to have physical relations without emotional involvement with the partner. The experience is thus phallus-centred and produces excitement without deep commitment. In heterosexual life a man may have fleeting affairs with other women without of necessity betraying his emotional fidelity towards his wife; in homosexual relationships he may be forever changing the partner. Women, on the other hand, are more often committed with the whole of their being; they are less likely to be genital-centred in their physical experience, but can achieve sexual satisfaction from various parts of the body. They are more personally involved, and more dependent on the partnership apart from physical contact. Women, therefore, will often try to work towards a lasting partnership, whether in marriage, in extra-marital love or in homosexual friendship.

13 M. McIntosh, 'Bent or Straight Mates – A Sociologist's Views', *Arena Three*, Vol. 1, No. 6, June 1964, pp. 4–6

The sociologist Mary McIntosh rejected the search for a monocausal explanation for lesbianism. In 1968 she wrote a highly influential paper 'The Homosexual Role' which developed the critique of sexology and psychology presented in this brief comment.

In her article, 'Bent or Straight Mates?' (January, 1964), DMC notes two common approaches to the problem of the causes of lesbianism. I should like to comment on her discussion of these, and to suggest that there is a third – and much more fruitful – approach.

The theory that homosexuality is an inborn characteristic or predisposition has a long history. On the one hand, there have been many largely unsuccessful attempts to find physical correlates of homosexuality; on the other, there have been equally vain attempts to establish homosexuality as an inborn characteristic that is independent of any physical or other measurable traits. In order to demonstrate the latter theory, it would be necessary to show either that it was inherited genetically, or that it could not be explained by anything that occurred after birth. It is impossible in practice to be sure that one has eliminated all alternative explanations, since they are infinite in number; but efforts have been made to examine the hypothesis of inheritance. These studies of one-egg and two-egg twins have so far proved inconclusive. Thus the evidence for the theory that homosexuality is an innate characteristic is at least as weak as that for the 'acquired neurosis' theory.

DMC admits that she presents the psychoanalytic approach in simple terms; but some of her criticisms of the approach apply only to her simplified account. She comments on the fact that both an inadequate relationship with the father, and an over-identification with the father, have been cited as causes of lesbianism. There is in fact no contradiction: both are examples of failure to make the proper relationship with the father thought to be necessary to learning the feminine role. Incidentally, it is quite possible that Radclyffe Hall over-identified with her father. This can occur even when there is little contact between the two, because in this context identification refers to a projected image, and not to the actual individual. A child may thus identify with an idealised image of the father; and indeed this image will be easier to maintain if the two are not very intimate.

One great disadvantage of psychoanalytic theories is that they are difficult to test, because they are theories, not about the effects of 'events occurring outside the individual', but about the effects on current behaviour of the individual's handling of past events. The evidence must therefore be sought in the unconscious; and one cannot expect to find a direct correlation between external events and behaviour. But, whether specific psychoanalytic explanations of lesbianism are true or not, the insights of this school have made it clear that it is impossible to divide the determinants of behaviour into internal and external factors. Growing up has been described as 'the process by which the outside gets inside'; what the individual is affects the way he reacts to a situation, and his reaction moulds the new individual who faces the next situation.

I suggest that both the theories outlined by DMC are too simple, and that we may expect the explanation of lesbianism to be at least as complicated as the explanation for the career a person takes up. In choosing a career, some innate characteristics, such as aptitudes, seem to play a part; but so do many factors in the person's life experience. There are familiar mechanisms which can be seen operating again and again. Once one path has been taken, for instance, it may be difficult to get back on to another. A child who is thought of as musical or intelligent, and encouraged along these lines, is more likely to develop his musicianship or his intellect. Young people choose an occupation from among those they have heard about and think they are eligible for on the basis of their tastes and ambitions, the availability of jobs, wages, prospects, and so on. They often try several before they find the one they finally settle for; some, or course, never stay at one thing, or else they change over late in life. Mechanisms similar to these are undoubtedly at work in making homosexuals; although the process is not so obvious since it does not take place within a formal system of exams and training, and open discussion.

Clearly this analogy cannot be taken very far. A person's sexual orientation appears to be much more firmly fixed – and, some psychiatrists would argue, fixed at a very early age – than their occupation, and it involves much more of their personality; some sexual patterns are socially condemned, and others approved. Nevertheless, the analogy indicates the kind of way in which theories could be formulated which would postulate homosexuality neither as a completely innate characteristic nor as a neurosis originating in early childhood. Simone de Beauvoir's theory is of this type: she claims that there is a typical situation for many women to which lesbianism is one typical response, but not the only one possible. This is perhaps a rather simple explanation of the type, but such a theory is more promising than any monocausal explanation. Its aims are not so grand, but it is more likely to achieve them.

DMC is concerned with examining the causes of lesbianism in order to shed light on what should be done about it. This is entirely appropriate, and in keeping with the aims of the MRG. We must beware, however, of choosing a theory of causation simply on the grounds of its apparent implications for action. For one thing, to do this is to be guilty of bad faith, of seeking justification for a moral standpoint that has already been decided upon. Anthony Storr says: 'All homosexuals have a vested interest in affirming that their condition is an inborn abnormality rather than the result of circumstances; for any other explanation is bound to imply a criticism either of themselves or of their families, and usually of both.' But – and this is the second objection to choosing a theory on those grounds – the moral implications of any theory are never beyond dispute. It is not true that 'any other explanation *is bound to imply* a criticism ... '. An explanation may be more appropriate to one line of action than to another, but the one never logically determines the other.

What is curious about DMC's argument is her assumption that *if* lesbianism is curable or preventable, *then*, as a value judgement, it should be cured, or prevented. There are two objections to this: the first is that it assumes lesbianism to be undesirable. The second is that it ignores the costs of cure or prevention, and especially the side-effects of interfering with family life. Even if it were universally agreed, and methods were known, lesbianism could not be banished as easily as septicaemia.

In any case, it would be perfectly consistent to hold both that lesbianism was brought about by events occurring after birth, and that it was not a bad thing requiring cure or prevention, for which the people involved, or those who brought them up, should be blamed.

Considering herself as the moral equivalent of the thalidomide baby is surely not the only way for a lesbian to remain at peace with her conscience.

14 N. Dunn, *Talking to Women*, 1965, London: Pan, pp. 43–4

In this extract from a book of conversations with women the author of *Up the Junction* is interviewing Kathy Collier, a 26-year-old worker in a butter factory. Kathy is a single parent with a ten-year-old son.

NELL: Your husband was your husband and that was it.

KATHY: That was it, yes. You were married and you were married.

NELL: You mean people didn't carry on much then?

KATHY: Well they did carry on but you didn't hear as much of it then as what you do now. As for Lesbians, my mum never heard of anything like that. Like just lately, you know? My mum never knew what it was.

NELL: Is there a lot about just lately, Lesbians?

KATHY: Oh there is more, yes. Definitely. I mean everywhere you go.

NELL: Do you see Lesbians in Battersea?

KATHY: Oh yes. There's lots in Battersea now. What about that girl who was in the pub and you said you'd like to sketch her one night, she was singing on the mike, that girl who was a prostitute. What about her? I mean she's married, got two kids, she's been married twice got two kids, she was on the game and she's turned Lesbian. Who'd ever believe that?

I was out the other night somewhere, I was sitting in the pictures and I was shocked, she was sitting down in front of me, kissing and cuddling with this –

NELL: With a girl?

KATHY: Yes. She could have been no more than twenty. Very very timid looking thing and she's a great big sort isn't she?

NELL: Isn't that amazing? They could get arrested, couldn't they, Kath?

KATHY: They can't apparently.

NELL: Can't they?

KATHY: No. She was in the show and everything, in the Cricketers.

NELL: They can kiss and cuddle with a girl and not get arrested? I didn't know that. I thought it was illegal.

KATHY: Lots of people don't know, do they, that they're girls, do they?

NELL: They're dressed like men?

KATHY: She dresses like a man and everything, you know.

NELL: Or could you see straight away she was a woman?

KATHY: I could, I could myself, I mean lots of people might not, some people are very stupid, like my mum for instance, you know what I mean? Or my dad like, we were in a pub and my dad didn't even know that somebody was like it. My dad didn't believe it, they're old-fashioned really, you see they didn't see it going on much in their time and they expect it's still the same. That's the thing.

NELL: Do you think people are born queers or Lesbians or do they just turn that way from bad influence?

KATHY: I think some are. Some it is born in them I think. Or some of them – with men – I think it's a lot to do with their mothers, say for instance the only child – you don't often find that – that it is the only child, it might be a big family, I know there's a big family of twelve kids and one of the roughest, one of the roughest fellows that you could ever wish to meet and he got three years' imprisonment.

15 'Lesbian London' in H. Davies (ed.), *The New London Spy: a Discreet Guide to the City's Pleasures*, 1966, London: Anthony Bond, pp. 231–8

The novelist Maureen Duffy (1933–) was the author of this description of the Gateways Club. As the House of Shades the club is also the setting for her novel *The Microcosm*, which was published in the same year.

It is Friday night. Down the Kings Road, past Chelsea Town Hall where the hip young things are already ascending and descending their own private Jacob's ladder to the lighted church windows of the ballroom.

Past His Clothes and Glebe Place, where the P.E.N. Club is raising deco-
rous martinis to a visiting Russian writer whose works have never appeared
in English. Then behind a dull green door and down the cellar steps where
the girls are gathering to inaugurate the week-end. This is the famous
Gateways Club. It has been in existence since the 'thirties and acquired its
present exclusive flavour during the war. A war which affected a class revo-
lution in lesbianism, as it did in so many other fields of English social life.
The equality of uniform khaki or blue lowered the barriers, letting in the
other ranks who refused to return to anonymity when the war was over.
They wanted to dance; they were willing to spend. The juke-box ousted the
piano and afternoon tea. The older members regret it, remembering the
panache of white flannels and blazers, with nostalgia for the days when to be
different was to be doubly different. 'They knew how to spend too,' one of
them said. 'All shorts and none of this lasting out half of bitter all evening.
I've seen money flow like water. Now it's just teddy-boys and typists.'

...

It is half-past-eight. There are already between twenty and thirty people
sitting on the padded benches along the walls, usually talking gossip about
friends not yet arrived or detailed accounts of the progress of the current
affair, stretching out their hands to the glasses on the small round tables,
waiting.

The juke-box is kept constantly fed but hardly anyone is ready to dance
yet. The two fruit machines swallow their quota of sixpences. Each new
arrival peers round defensively for her group though there are a few walkers
by themselves who stand on the edge of the dancefloor, coolly appraising.
Soon the numbers will grow to fifty and then a hundred and the serious
enjoyment of the evening will begin.

The room is low-ceilinged with a long bar at the back. The walls are
covered with frescos showing the life and characters of the club.

Until the recent repainting many of the war-time originals still surveyed
the floor under peaked caps or wearing baggy trousered suits. Portraits of
the proprietors smile down paternally through the subdued lighting and
heavy smoke pall.

By now the floor is rocking under the dancers' feet. The tunes are those
popular in the charts at the moment but there is a distinct preference for
songs to and about girls. Some catch on because they can be very equivocally
interpreted.

Lovers dance locked together to the slower records but the beat numbers
are the most popular because of the opportunities for display like the
dancing of cranes and for sheer physical response to rhythm. Neither partner
is committed except to the music.

The floor becomes so crowded that it is impossible to do anything more
than gyrate on the spot and by half-past-ten nearly two hundred people will

be packed between the bulging walls. Eyes smart and water in the smoke and a trip to the bar and back is an obstacle race with the prize a full glass.

There are few men and they are likely to be homosexual themselves. Mostly they simply stand and talk but sometimes they will dance with one of the girls, often a young butch in fly-front trousers and button-up shirt whose gestures are more obviously masculine than her partner's. At the other extreme are the femmes (pronounced as the first syllable in feminine), in their tight-skirted cocktail dresses, while in between lie infinite variations and degrees of masculinity.

...

The newcomer may find it difficult to get herself accepted into a group until she has been seen there two or three times and found people with similar interests or jobs. They will want to know if she is a scrounger or mixed up with the criminal world in which case she will probably drift away to one of the seedier little clubs in Notting Hill.

There is less mixing of the levels of society among female than among male homosexuals: teachers talk to other teachers, factory workers and petrol pump attendants clan together with lower-paid office workers and bus conductresses.

Jobs where slacks can be worn are popular because these as a rule involve less deception. Many girls work unsuspected in offices but, like their male counterparts, they must be careful to keep the two halves of their double life apart.

A lot of lesbians are professional women struggling against antifeminist discrimination and they are unlikely to visit the club, very often because their own difficulties make them intolerant of people whose intelligence does not match up to their own. Select dinner parties, evenings at the theatre are their social outlet. They do not want to be regarded as second-class citizens themselves and so avoid contact with people who are obviously this. For the same reason they avoid extremes of dress. They are closer to social acceptance; the others realise that they can never have it without a radical change in the whole attitude of society to women, particularly as semiskilled workers, as well as the more obvious acceptance of minority groups.

Most people come to the Gateways because they are looking for forms of amusement and chances of meeting partners equivalent to those they would find in the heterosexual world that their ex-school friends and neighbours now inhabit.

Dance halls are out since although women do dance together in public they do not do so exclusively or affectionately. Pubs are still often risky places for unaccompanied women, youth clubs are impossible. Dining out with the girlfriend is an expensive business and few women earn as much as men. Restaurants often bar women in slacks but a great number of homosexual women feel uncomfortable in anything else.

From time to time girls are beaten up but they don't as a rule complain to the police. They know that in a sense they are guilty of provocation simply by being themselves and they don't expect anyone else to sympathise.

At the clubs they can dance together and dress as they like with no need to pretend to like someone if they don't and no fear of difficult or ugly situations beyond their control.

Most of their friends will be homosexual so that they are spared embarrassing questions about marriage and boyfriends. Families pose a problem. Some people manage to tell their parents and remain on good terms with them but others either lead a double life, dressing up when they go home to visit and fending off questions as they arise, or drift away from their families altogether.

They come to London from the provinces and from all over the world. The Commonwealth provides a generous quota, principally of Australians and South Africans, who are looking for freedom from a basically pioneering culture where men are still men and women stay home and rock the cradle.

Like other young people who come to this country they are drawn to Bayswater, Notting Hill and South Kensington, because of the chances for flat-sharing and reducing expenses and because of the shifting cosmopolitan population which doesn't care what you are or how you dress as long as you add to the atmosphere of freedom and excitement.

There are Indians and Africans, girls from America and Italy, and there is a constant to and fro between the clubs of London and Paris. Holidays abroad are extremely popular, and many girls give up their jobs to travel au pair or to go hitch-hiking. Jobs are either taken very seriously as careers or picked up and dropped as a means of getting from day to day with enough for a room and the weekend's entertainment. Faces which have been missing for months suddenly reappear suntanned from Israel or Tangiers with hair raising tales to tell which are always good for a free drink.

New Year's Eve is the big night of the year when hundreds of members look in during the long evening and as many as possible jam the floor at midnight to see in the new year with its promise of new affairs that must surely last longer than the old, resolutions to drink less and work more, nostalgia for past failures. The end of an affair does not necessarily mean the end of a friendship. After the first bitterness is over people continue to see each other, and under the bursting balloons and thrown streamers old relationships are renewed on the level of affection.

The Gateways has thousands of members – membership is cheap at ten shillings a head – but fortunately they don't all try to get in at once. Many live outside London and rarely come up, but like to know it's there if they want it. The hard core live in London but all have their favourite nights. Friday and Sunday are usually full house with Saturday an unbelievable crush. Thursday and Wednesday have their following and a few people drop in at lunchtime for a quiet drink and talk.

The Gateways' only serious rival has been a club which recently moved to new premises in Westbourne Park. The clientele is slightly different: there are more tourists and more of the extreme transvestites, many of them from the women's barracks. There are also one or two after-hours drinking and coffee clubs in this district, mostly patronised by prostitutes and their girl-friends, who live on the fringes of the criminal world and are therefore more likely to be involved in fights and drug-taking.

...

Many of the girls have one or two friends among male homosexuals and they often make up groups to visit the boys' clubs or pubs. Two of the most popular where there is often a good sprinkling of the girls are one in Battersea, a mainly working-class pub with two-piece band and soloists from the audience, and one in Notting Hill which caters for the more sophisticated. These relationships are of mutual benefit. They borrow each other's partners when they want to impress the outside world at the firm's dinner and dance or at a family wedding or birthday party, and they also provide a link with the opposite sex in however modified a form.

Language is another common factor. The terms 'gay' and 'queer' for themselves are used by both male and female as is 'butch' for a masculine type of either sex. The rest of the world are 'normals' or 'heteros', sometimes but not often 'straight'. 'Drag' for clothes of the opposite sex is used by both and also 'camp' for anyone whose behaviour or appearance is obviously homosexual in an effeminate way. No parallels exist however for 'trade' and 'rent' since there is no prostitution among the girls themselves. 'Who pays for what they can get for free?' as one put it. Sometimes they imitate the boys' gestures and accents in fun but it is laughing with them, not against them.

Recent expressions from the American Beats have become current via the drug and pop world. 'Scene' is probably the most popular but 'hooked' and 'hung up' to describe a relationship are coming up fast. The term 'lesbian' itself is universally detested and hardly ever used except when quoting an outsider. They themselves prefer to be known in formal terms as female homosexuals or colloquially as 'the girls' or 'gay girls'.

...

You will need a member to sign you in, a few shillings for a couple of drinks, a fashionable rig, preferably from John Michaels or one of the men's boutiques in the King's Road, and then you are ready to dance the evening through or mark the variations in dress and character from the dark-suited butch in the corner to Little Lord Fauntleroy in velveteen jacket and ruffles.

The public are much more knowledgeable about lesbianism than they used to be, as anyone knows who has listened to an audience at the National Film Theatre howling its way through an oldie. But acceptance is a long way away. Two women together, particularly if they are young and one has a masculine air or style of dress, are quickly recognized and remarked upon.

So a club like the Gateways is not only the best place. For most people, there is nowhere else to go.

16 N. Timms, *Rootless in the City*, 1968, London: The Bedford Square Press, pp. 36–8

Noel Timms was a lecturer in the Department of Social Science and Administration of the London School of Economics. This book described and assessed a project set up in 1962 to help rootless girls in London. Of the 80 girls involved half believed they were lesbians.

The day centre

Each of the community service volunteers was asked to make a written comment on some aspect of the work. The following extract from one of these indicates the kinds of strain experienced by the volunteers and their reactions to them:

'I had only been at the centre a few days and my mind was still full of terrifying though totally unrealistic, images of hypodermic syringes and homosexuality, when there was a telephone call announcing that one of our girls, accompanied by a "butch lesbian" was on her way to see us. The word "butch" conjured up in my mind grotesque images of a huge masculine girl. The "butch" turned out to be a slim tall, gentle girl of twenty-two. It was obvious from her build that she was a girl, though her disappointment was marked whenever this was made known to her.

'I suppose that because my environment up to the time of joining the centre had not included drugs, lesbians, and the kind of deprived girl we saw at the centre, I had no idea what to expect. Consequently I imagined the girls as phenomena rather than individuals. Most of them, as it turned out, had sweet natures and were very unhappy people desperate for help. The help they desperately needed was often the kind it seemed impossible to give.

'I remember one afternoon visiting two girls who at this time had a dingy flat in Olympia. With them were a number of other West-Enders, including a "butch" who talked to me. She seemed in a totally depressed state, and begged me to lend her money to bail her friend out of Holloway. She said this friend in prison did not love her, but she could not bear to see her unhappy over Christmas. She also said without this girl's love her own life was not worth living, but being afraid of suicide, she chose instead to take heroin. How could I get her off it?

'Thus one was presented with seemingly unreal and unknown situations, to which there appeared no solution. There arose in me just a feeling of helplessness.

'It was important to realise, however, that some of the girls reacted to your feeling of helplessness by making excessive demands. They seemed to know that your guilt, irrationally caused by being unable to solve their problems would make you more indulgent towards them. Sometimes one felt outraged because they took it for granted that we would provide them with things they wanted. Yet to some of them the centre was home, and like children they would make demands, as children can make on mothers. The homes some of them came from were so inadequate that they provided nothing. Sometimes a family would demand more of a girl than she was able to give and thus she could not see the balance being restored by the excessive demands she made on us. Those whose homes were better on the whole made smaller demands, or at least we saw less of them at the centre.'

17 S. McDermott, *Studies in Female Sexuality*, 1970, London: Odyssey Press, pp. 63–4, 66–70 *passim*

The monthly sex periodical *Forum* undertook a two-year study of British women to investigate female sexuality. The magazine's subscribers formed the bulk of the respondents and McDermott usually interviewed them in their own homes. Women's relationships with each other were discussed in Chapter 5 'Lesbianism and Deviation'.

A twenty-six-year-old West Indian girl, who had an isolated homosexual relationship, fell for the gentleness of love-making from another woman. 'We were introduced and she just liked me so it happened. She made love to me and I enjoyed it. I made love in response to her because I was fond of her. We made love every week for a few months and through this I came to the conclusion that women definitely have an understanding of one another's sexual needs. This girl was bi-sexual and I couldn't see either of us ending up as exclusively lesbian. I don't go out and look for girls but I suppose if I liked someone it could happen again. During love-making with my girl-friend I would always come to orgasm. She would kiss my genitals and that more or less automatically gave me an orgasm. We would kiss and I would respond to her. I think that I received more tenderness from her than I have ever had from any man. I think that men use women.'

... But there are other reasons which contribute to a larger public acceptance of lesbianism. ... The lesbian is less inclined to accentuate her homosexuality publicly by adopting masculine dress and habits. The 'camp' jargon and behaviour so often displayed as a defence mechanism by male homosexuals has no real parallel in the lesbian world. Even if a woman does adopt the short hair and tweed suit mode of dress she is still likely to be excused as she fits into either the role of the self-sufficient career woman who has been forced to veer towards masculinity to survive in the competitive male business world. Alternatively, the school-marm spinster in her brogues and floppy hat is considered more the eccentric of her community than as a sexual deviant and is regarded with benign amusement.

A lesbian is a woman and not a man – therefore in later life she may be more strongly drawn to a home and secure relationship. Lesbians embark on monogamous relationships with one another, more frequently and more successfully than male homosexuals. Because it is common for two women, widows, sisters, mother and daughter to live together as companions, they are not thought at all odd. Their relationship stands a better chance of survival than a similar relationship between two men because it is automatically accepted by the community and free from the strains of ostracism. In turn this liberates the lesbian from the necessity of short term relationships and promiscuity which heterosexuals tend to find so distasteful in the male homosexual. In many cases one of the partners may have a child, the result of a failed heterosexual marriage, and this contributes further to the public eye's vision of respectability.

On a day to day level women are allowed to display openly a physical closeness which, especially in Great Britain, is not permissible for men. Women kissing one another farewell or walking arm in arm is never considered offensive. The sight of women demonstrating affection has somehow come to appear more aesthetic than two men doing the same and this follows through to lovemaking. A woman as an individual has more aesthetic appeal than a man. It was pointed out to me that recently a whole national exhibition of photography was devoted to the subject of women. 'There would never be such an exhibition with the male form as its subject', said my informant. She added, 'You know, apart from the occasional film star, I never hear women referring to men as beautiful, they are more appreciative of other women as aesthetic objects because that is the way in which our whole culture regards women'. Thus the image of two men making love can never contain the aesthetic value inherent within a similar image of two women. For a number of men, and indeed for some women, the fantasy of two women making love is full of erotic appeal. It is evident from literature that the lesbian fantasy is popular among men. Excitement comes from the thought that women whom they equate with passivity can be autonomously active in sex; here is sex for pure pleasure, totally divorced from the reproductive function.

Because there is less prejudice against female homosexuality in comparison to male homosexuality, it does not follow that there is no prejudice nor that a female homosexual does not suffer from the problems of self-acceptance I mentioned previously. Some women are more able than others to adjust to their homosexuality, but there is inevitably a struggle involved in the full acceptance of the implications of homosexuality. A woman who arrives at the conclusion that she is almost exclusively homosexual must also arrive at the realisation that for her life will be quite different to that of the majority of women. She will not marry, she will not have children, she will be forced to support herself financially for the rest of her life, she will probably have to make a secret of her sexual orientation as far as employers, workmates and certain social contacts are concerned, the selection of sexual partners is limited and the chances of finding a secure and loving relationship in which sex plays its part are far less than those of the heterosexual.

Laura first became aware of her lesbian tendencies when she was quite young although she says that at the time she was not aware of the full significance of them. True to the traditional image, she was a tomboy and always felt much more attracted to girls than boys. She was thirteen when she embarked on her first affair with a girl five years older than herself. ...

... She gets on well with men and enjoys their company but feels no sexual desire for them whatsoever. She is ready for a permanently-based relationship with another woman but not to the extent that she would plunge into such a relationship indiscriminately.

She has found that married women will seek a lesbian partner through boredom. This boredom stems from two sources, boredom with their husbands as lovers and with empty afternoons after the housework is over. 'I would think that there are quite a large number of married women who have had lesbian relationships at some time or another. I have met quite a number who are having lesbian affairs despite their marriage. It is said of lesbianism that you can never break free of it and this is probably true. I know a woman who had a lesbian relationship before she got married and she was happily married for twelve years. She thought that it was all in the past. When she was forty-five she went to a party where she happened to see the other woman in the room and it was just like that – her marriage went completely on the rocks. She got divorced and went off to live with another woman. I think that if a woman has had lesbian experiences they will always crop up.'

Laura was appalled at the amount of ignorance which prevails concerning lesbian love-making and laughed at the general opinion that lesbians wield dildoes and strap artificial penises to themselves. 'It must be remembered that lesbians attach a great deal more importance to affection rather than just the actual physical side of sex. The sensuous touch of the body can sometimes be full of meaning. I have never met any lesbians who use artificial aids, such as dildoes. Any girl who wants another female doesn't want an imitation of a male. If they do, well let them go and get the real thing. It goes without saying that one woman knows another woman's body much better than a man and that she can work another woman up to a much higher state than a man can, simply because she possesses more control. As a woman you know exactly what will excite your partner. I once had an affair with a nymphomaniac. She was bi-sexual and loved sex. She told me that she had never had the same satisfaction from a man that she had had from me. Let's face it, a woman has a much greater control over a long period of time than a man and with someone as highly sexed as a nymphomaniac, this is important. Basically, I suppose lesbians are much more sensual than men –

that is, the play on the body and the nerves of the body is much greater than in the heterosexual relationship. A number of women have complained to me that the men, once they have had their orgasm, couldn't be less interested and nine times out of ten the woman is left unsatisfied. I realise that this is elementary, but it's amazing the number of men who are concerned solely with their own satisfaction. What most men are not aware of is that women's backs are particularly sensitive. The nerve centres are very sensitive, much more than the breasts which many men make such a fetish of. You can work up a woman to a tremendous pitch by caressing the body, gently, sensitively. There are of course many variations of the theme – other areas which excite women are the back of the knees and the thighs. Also, behind the ears and neck. It depends on the individual, but I would say that the average woman needs forty-five minutes of love play before she reaches her peak'.

8

IDENTITIES AND
NETWORKS

INTRODUCTION

The concept of lesbian identity carries with it many problems when applied to the past. Today's idea of lesbian identity – sexual desire for other women – as a conscious labelling of one's sense of self would have been a puzzling notion to most early-nineteenth-century women, and really only emerged fully during the twentieth century. That is to say, lesbian identity is a historically specific phenomenon.

Historians have posed questions about the gender and class nature of the notion of sexual identity. Identity implies a very modern Western liberal idea of the *individual* exercising control and agency in the way their life is lived and shaped; an opportunity possible mainly to men in the last two centuries. For women, a sense of self that emphasised connection to the family was paramount, even when sexual categories and identities became thinkable.

Is it feasible then to seek for lesbian-like subjectivities in the past or is this ahistorical and limiting? It is important to look for how women interpreted feelings of same-sex love and desire to themselves, and for any sense of whether they felt set apart from mainstream heterosexuality because of this. If we reject the idea of lesbian consciousness as anachronistic or too fluid, then we run into the danger that women's erotic choice for other women becomes invisible again (Freedman 1998).

This also begs larger theoretical questions of how people form their identities (Weeks 1985). As we suggested in the introduction to this book, we see lesbianism as sexual feeling, desire and love between women that is constructed in both a cultural and material social context which changes over time. The previous chapters have demonstrated the variety of professional and social commentaries which informed British cultures in this period and within which people might create meanings out of their own and others' behaviour. Access to this knowledge would have been considerably moderated by women's differing class and educational backgrounds. The emergence of lesbian identities, roles and subjectivities at particular historical moments depends on the material possibilities open to women; on the degree of economic independence they can muster within and away from the family, for example. Not least important is the individual woman's agency in the shaping of a sexual self in the context of (but also often despite) the social, cultural and economic circumstances of her life and times (Clark 1996). For example, the young woman drawn to the city to escape marriage and to look for other women like herself was creating a personal subjectivity perhaps even before she knew of lesbianism as a concept.

Women who loved women often needed to seek one another and this was a difficult undertaking when a lesbian identity was only partly formed and available. Were there lesbian networks comparable to the gay male sub-cultures documented by some historians? Sub-culture is a late-twentieth-century term that suggests more precise and public groupings for lesbians than we might expect to find in earlier periods. The notion of sub-cultures suggests – as well as a pre-existing idea of lesbian identity – particular styles of language, dress and behaviour and some shared signifiers to mark women who loved women out from heterosexual women. For example a specific haircut, or the finger on which a ring was worn, might signal a lesbian. Icons and role models (from Sappho to Dusty Springfield) might be identified and used to strengthen lesbian identity and solidarity. Specific meeting places might exist, and links made through specialist journals or coded communications in mainstream publications as sub-cultures became more established. We find some of these markers of a lesbian sub-culture by the middle of the twentieth century. But in earlier periods women did not necessarily have independent access to public space or the personal autonomy to build such sub-cultures. Historians have cautioned against looking for features which parallel urban gay sub-cultures of the late twentieth century (Gowing 1997). Instead we can re-read sources for more nebulous signs of lesbian *networks* (Auchmuty 1989).

Since it explores the changing subjectivities and networks of lesbians this chapter is the one which most strongly depicts lesbians speaking for themselves. Declarations of love between women may be found in Chapter 2, but conscious consideration of what that desire means for self-identity is harder to find. Women may have reflected on their position as lovers of women in letters, diaries or poems, but little of this has been preserved or published. The early-nineteenth-century diaries of Anne Lister are an important exception. In concentrating on printed – public – sources in this collection, the paucity of material for the nineteenth century, when a lesbian identity was very imprecise anyway, is not surprising. Where there was a cultural knowledge of sapphism or lesbianism and women recognised their sexual feelings as somehow transgressive, a wariness or self-censorship in writing might have been stimulated, and letters and diaries destroyed. When lesbian identities became more widely discussed and delineated after World War I, many middle-class women who had close erotic relationships with other women may have resisted conceptualising themselves as lesbian or homosexual, and emphasised other meanings for their relationships. For a range of reasons, then, women have been reticent about their loving relationships with other women. This has meant that autobiography with an explicit acknowledgement of lesbianism is rare and has also resulted in biographers obliterating women's central love relationships or transforming them into friend-ships of secondary importance (Lesbian History Group 1989, Whitelaw 1990, Stanley 1992).

Vicinus has emphasised 'the many roots from which the modern lesbian iden-tity has grown' (Vicinus 1989: 173). She drew attention to four forms that describe women's same-sex relationships in the nineteenth century: cross-dressing, romantic friendship, bi-sexuality and androgyny. These archetypes are to some extent useful for indicating arenas where we might seek evidence of lesbianism and also for understanding the ways in which women could create and recognise 'lesbian-like' identities for themselves in this period. These archetypes are layered and overlapping and each contributes in part to modern lesbian identities: the invert, femme, occasional lover of women and the mannish New Woman.

We can also speculate that lesbian networks in the past, as today, overlapped considerably with wider women's networks and cultures. There seems to have been little shared language of sapphism in Anne Lister's immediate provincial culture yet she understood her desires as sexual, and a number of women in her circle had same-sex relationships. She had to largely create her own methods for placing herself and for identifying other women who might share her feelings and practices (Clark 1996).

Faderman and Smith-Rosenburg discussed lesbian experience as part of nineteenth-century, white, middle-class female cultures, and stressed its accept-ability in that context. More recent work however, has questioned their non-sexual reading of these cultures, and indicated that there was a careful line of accept-ability for romantic friendship, and varying degrees of awareness of the transgressive nature of desires and passions for other women (Moore 1992).

Women's communities away from family restrictions, such as schools, hospi-tals, colleges and settlement houses, certainly provided opportunities for erotic ties between women (Vicinus 1985). Intense female friendships here were widely conceived of as being devoid of sexual connotations and thus usefully bolstered women's respectability. We find similar complexity within networks of feminists in the late nineteenth century and early twentieth century. Political consciousness sometimes created new kinds of sexual subjectivities, for example in rationales for marriage refusal and a preference for female company and friendship, but to what extent can the historian equate these with lesbian identity?

All these forms of lesbian identities continued into the early twentieth century, but for some women sexology – at least its more radical and sympathetic strands – could provide a new language for describing feelings and relationships between women. Other women might have rejected a lesbian label, however, if they perceived it as pathologising, and perhaps relied upon older interpretations of women's friendships; living together as spinster friends, for example.

In the twentieth century we see more self-conscious attempts to build sub-cultures around the idea of love and sex between women as an awareness of this possibility becomes more widespread. The printed sources reflecting this devel-opment become slightly more numerous. We have presented extracts from three journals which relate to different kinds of women's and lesbian cultures. The feminist *Freewoman* shows how Carpenter's idea of the Intermediate Sex, as a special category with which women might identify, was just beginning to circulate among metropolitan and bohemian circles, as do the letters written to Carpenter at this time (Bland 1995, Stanley 1992). The journal *Urania* demonstrates a very strong advocacy of passionate love relationships between women – although it either avoided or condemned what it named 'sexual perversion' (Oram 1998, Hamer 1996). It probably had a very limited readership, but its pages invoke many of the lesbian signifiers still familiar in early-twenty-first century Britain.

The magazine *Arena Three* emerged out of the debates of the 1950s and 1960s on homosexuality, 'permissiveness' and women's position. It was a political journal in that it sought to address the social problems of lesbians (now definitely categorised as a *sexual* identity) and to represent their views to a hostile or ignorant heterosexual world. It documented the existence of a lesbian sub-culture that was growing in confidence, colonising pubs and creating clubs and social groups. But it also documented the tensions of occupying a lesbian identity in the 1960s, featuring stories of self-censorship and unhappiness at work; difficulties in forming relationships that were exacerbated by isolation; self-hatred and generally negative encounters with the medical profession, particularly psychiatry. In articulating and discussing these tensions and difficulties, *Arena Three* can be seen as an important forerunner of both the women's and gay liberation movements.

1 H. Whitbread (ed.), *I Know My Own Heart. The Diaries of Anne Lister, 1791–1840*, 1988, London: Virago, pp. 268–71

In her diary Anne Lister recounted how she attempted to disguise her own sexuality from Miss Pickford while simultaneously trying to explore the nature of Miss Pickford's relationships with women.

Saturday, 26 July 1823

At 10 1/4, went into the stables. The plasterer there (Wm. Eden) painting a darkish drab – quite a wrong colour. Did not sufficiently fill up the worm-eaten holes in the wood. Staid there painting these parts over again myself til 12.40, then called in because Miss Pickford had called. ... She rather fought off on the subject of Miss Threlfall, then allowed, or rather, encouraged it a little, that I told her she coquetted on this subject, & she did not deny that perhaps she did do so; that my remark was not unjust. We had been talking about being whimmy. I said I believed the people here thought me so. She had heard this, & that I did not go to the Saltmarshes' as often as I used to do. I excused myself that I really had not time. I said I was more whimmy in speech & appearance than reality. We agreed there were some subjects one could not be whimmy upon. Not, for instance, in early-formed close connections. The tie was strong. Said Miss Pickford, 'I could not be so, for I know I could break [Miss] Threlfall's heart.' I took no notice of this but thought to myself, more than ever, what the connection between them must be. Miss Pickford has read the Sixth Satyr (sic) of Juvenal. She understands these matters enough.

Thursday, 31 July 1823

Took Miss Pickford into the stable. She thinks the alterations very good. At 8.40, set off to walk with her. ... Got on to the subject of Miss Threlfall. Went on & on. Talked of the classics, the scope of her reading, etc. & what I suspected, apologising & wrapping up my surmise very neatly till at last she owned the fact, adding 'You may change your mind if you please,' meaning give up her acquaintance or change my opinion of her if I felt inclined to do so, after the acknowledgement she had made. 'Ah', said [I], 'That is very unlike me. I am too philosophical. We were sent on this world to be happy. I do not see why we should not make ourselves as much so as we can in our own way.' Perhaps I am more liberal or lax than she expected & she merely replied 'My way cannot be that of many other people's.' Soon after this we parted. I mused on the result of our walk, wondering she let me go so far, & still more that she should confide the secret to me so readily. I told her it would not be safe to own it to anyone else, or suffer anyone to talk to her as I had done. I think she suspects me but I fought off, perhaps successfully, declaring I was, on some subjects, quite cold-blooded, quite a frog. She denied this but I persisted in that sort of way that perhaps she believed it. I shall always pursue this plan. I would not trust her as she does me for a great deal. It will be a famous subject for us & she owns she does not dislike it. I never met with such a woman before. I looked at her & felt oddish, but yet I did not dislike her. It was too dark to analyse each other's countenances & mine would have betrayed nothing. She will amuse me. I will treat her in her own way, that is, as I should treat a gentleman & this will suit her. She rather looks down, I think, on women in general. This is a foible I can manage well enough.

Friday, 1 August 1823

At 4, had the black horse, Caradoc, in the gig & drove to Skircoat Moor. Had not been there more than 1/4 hour when a car-man said a lady in black had just been inquiring which way I went & she was gone down by the free-school. I followed & soon overtook Miss Pickford. Took her into the gig & made George walk. ... Our subject, both driving & walking, was Miss Threlfall. I said I know she could not have made the confession if she had not supposed I understood the thing thoroughly. She answered, 'No, certainly.' I dilated on my knowing it from reading & speculation but nothing further. She was mistaken. 'No, no,' she said, 'It is not all theory.' I told her her inference was natural enough but not correct. Asked if she had heard any reports about me. I said I had only two very particular friends. Miss Norclifffe was out of the question from her manners, habit, etc., & the other, M—, was married which, of course, contradicted the thing altogether. Asked her which of them it could be of whom the report could be circulated. At last she said it was M—. I said I know the report & should not have cared about it had it not annoyed M—. For my own part I denied it, tho' Miss Pickford might not believe me. Yet, in fact, I had no objection to her doubting me for, had I had the inclination for such a thing, I should have pleased myself by trying &, could I have succeeded, I should have thought myself very clever & ingenious & that I must be very agreeable, but I must [say], really, Miss Pickford, it seemed, could make herself more agreeable than I could. I wished I had her secret. I dwelt a good deal on having had no opportunity, & the froggishness of my blood. She told me I said a great many things she did not at all believe. Whether she credits my denial of all practical knowledge, I cannot yet make out. However, I told her I admired the conduct of her confession & liked her ten thousand times more for having told me. She was the character I had long wished to meet with, to clear up my doubts whether such a one really existed nowadays. Said she was very agreeable. I just felt towards her as if she were a gentleman, & treated her as such. This seemed to suit very well.

2 Minnie Benson, 1871, retrospective diary quoted in B. Askwith, *Two Victorian Families*, 1971, Chatto and Windus, p. 138

From her schooldays Minnie Benson's life was marked by intense relationships with girls and women. On a visit to Wiesbaden in Germany the 26-year-old Minnie, wife of Edward White Benson and mother of five, fell in love with a Miss Hall. These extracts from her retrospective diary reveal the intensity of her passions for women.

Then I began to love Miss Hall – no wrong surely there – it was a complete fascination – partly my physical state – partly the continuous seeing of her – our exquisite walks. If I had loved God then *would* it have been so – could it be so now? I trust in god, NOT – Yet not one whit the less sweet need it be – I have learnt the consecration of friendship – gradually the bonds drew round – fascination possessed me then the other fault. Thou knowest I will not even write it – but, O God, forgive – *how* near we were to that.

(She later wrote of that time) I haven't gone and I can't fully into the way I wronged my dear ones here – I lost my head – and, blessed by Thy name O

Lord, I came to grief. The letter – ah! My husband's pain – what he bore, how lovingly, how quietly – our *talk* my wilful misery – my letter to her. Ah Lord, how blind thou allowedst me to get.

3 E. Simcox, 'Autobiography of a Shirtmaker', quoted by P. Johnson, 'Edith Simcox and Heterosexism: A Lesbian-Feminist Exploration' in Lesbian History Group, *Not a Passing Phase*, 1989, London: The Women's Press, pp. 55–76

Edith Simcox (1844–1901) was a feminist whose life was characterised by a wide variety of intellectual and political pursuits, including the co-founding of a women's shirt-making co-operative and learned contributions to prominent Victorian periodicals. She wrote a 170,000-word diary between 1876 and 1900. Much of this was concerned with her unrequited passion for her friend Marian Evans, the novelist George Eliot, whom she first met in 1872.

16 November 1878

I dream of new ways of wooing her – if I could feel that she was learning ways to know and love me more!

9 March 1880

I asked her to kiss me – let a trembling lover tell of the intense conscious-ness of the first deliberate touch of the dear one's lips, I returned the kiss to the lips that gave it and started to go – she waved me a farewell.

28 March 1880 – extract from an unsent letter

Do you see darling that I can only love you three lawful ways, idolatrously as Frater the Virgin Mary, in romance-wise as Petrarch, Laura, or with a child's fondness for the mother one leans on not withstanding the irreverence of one's longing to pet and take care of her. Sober friendship seems to make the ugliest claims to a kind of equality: friendship is a precious thing indeed but between friends I think if there is love at all it must be equal, and whichever way we take it, our relation is between unequals.

2 January 1881 – After Marian's death Edith compares herself with Maggie Tulliver, the heroine of The Mill on the Floss

My love for her has made her understand such temptations as Maggie's. ... I felt always that it was by no choice of mind that I was doomed to woo her only by trying ah how vainly! To be good! I must – I do try to be thankful for what I have had, to think of that rather than of what I never wanted. It *is* a blessing that what was abnormal in my passion caused no pain or grief to her – bore nothing worse than mere denial for me.

18 January 1881

Went yesterday to see Mrs Congreve. Learnt with a rush of pleasure that she had loved my darling lover-wise too – too much to repeat much of her words, but she told me how on seeing her again after an interval, her heart was palpitating so violently that to avoid a painful breaking down she forced herself into a calm that seemed cold.

28 June 1889

Is it my fault that every wholesome, natural, reasonable passion I have felt from the young ambition of the tomboy to the fierce worship of Her lover – is it my fault that all without exception have been choked off by a churlish fate and I hauled back upon the one inexhaustible gospel of Renunciation?

4 D. Campbell, 'The Woman Offender', *The Freewoman*, Vol. 1, No. 21, 11 April 1912, pp. 408–5

The Freewoman, published between November 1911 and October 1912, was an influential feminist paper despite its small circulation. Alongside articles on women's suffrage, employment and co-operative housekeeping, it conducted very open debates about sexuality, birth control, marriage and spinsterhood, printing a variety of perspectives. The journal did publish articles on homosexuality (or Uranianism) in its early months, but these were usually by and about men. Readers would have found a number of references to Edward Carpenter's *The Intermediate Sex*. There was very little mention of lesbianism; nevertheless this was the first time the subject was overtly referred to in the feminist press. This is an extract from an article discussing different types of prostitutes.

This woman is only a minor edition of a more fortunate sister ... who wants fleshy plays alternated with American rag-time and Parisian chansonettes, who occasionally likes a clear sky and a bountiful sun, but who usually prefers the white lights of night-time and the music of the Tziganes to that of the birds. It is among these that you find the intelligent, charming woman who has lost her interest in men, although naturally sensual. Here is the Trybade, the Lesbian. Perhaps the best poetic explanation of this passion is to be found in 'Les Chansons de Bilitis,' by Pierre Louys.

Stern scientists have said: 'Le Saphisme comporte bien moins de reverie ideale que l'homosexualité masculin.' This is Dr. Moreau's opinion, but it is representative.

5 'The Human Complex', *The Freewoman*, Vol. 1, No. 22, 18 April 1912, pp. 437–8

The middle-class writer of this letter and her sister were orphaned and left impoverished in their late teens.

MADAM,

...

It was then that I thought of sitting to lady artists as a model – not for the nude. We had moved to Chelsea by then, and that gave me the idea. I sent notes round to five or six ladies who had big studios, not too far off, and I enclosed my photo – a very flattering one, done by a theatrical photographer.

I got two answers. One was some way from Chelsea, in another artistic neighbourhood. I went there first, because the letter was so kind.

The lady I saw was a woman, whom I now judge to have been between thirty-five and forty, but she then gave me the impression of having left youth far behind. She was tall, rather flat in figure, with thick, dark hair, going grey, rather coarse and wiry, and brushed well back from her forehead; but her eyes were very fine, brown, and flashing.

She said she was delighted with my appearance; I was, in fact, just what she wanted, and she asked me my terms. I had no idea what I had to ask, so, seeing my hesitation, she fixed my services at half a crown an hour, and demanded if I would accept them. In the terrible state of our resources, I was only too glad to sit at these terms. This lady was most kind and considerate, and for six or seven weeks I sat to her for my head and shoulders. She invariably gave me luncheon, and, if I was sitting late, tea as well.

About this time my sister got a six weeks' engagement at Leeds, and I was left alone in our Chelsea lodging in the care of our landlady!

I told everything to my patroness – our sad, sordid little struggles, our hopes and fears for the future. I found out that she was a woman of considerable private means, without a relation living.

She was always envying me my youth, and praising me extravagantly, especially the beauty of my hair. My head was quite turned by all this foolish admiration, and somehow it made me uncomfortable too. But I was really merely an unsophisticated child, and my sister, though older, was not much better. We were woefully trusting and unsuspecting.

Knowing that I was now alone, my artist friend insisted on my coming to live with her at the studio, which had a bedroom and kitchen attached to it.

Without asking my sister, I joyfully accepted, thinking, poor child, no manner of harm. It is very difficult for me to say now what I found out about this unhappy creature. I only understood it when I was older, and when it was all too late. This rich, clever – for she was brilliantly clever – artistic woman was bi-sexual. On the third day of my stay at the studio I ran away. I was thoroughly frightened – too frightened and ashamed to mention my awful experience to anyone – and I left my box and all behind. This was sent after me directly; no message came with it. A fortnight later I went into the neighbourhood of the studio again. It was shut up and empty.

After a lapse of two years, I read an obituary notice of this same woman.

You may think this an abnormal case. Long after, when I was married – and widowed – I mentioned it to a doctor, the only living soul I breathed it to. He assured me that cases of this kind were enormously on the increase!

For heaven's sake, FREEWOMAN, try and break down this shameful and dangerous ignorance which people allow their unfortunate girls to remain in. I should never have written what I have if I didn't think good might come to others through knowing even of such a thing as this. I may add it has been an experience which has embittered my whole life.

MARAH.

April 9th, 1912.

6 'Frances Wilder' to Edward Carpenter, 25 October 1915, Carpenter Collection MS 386/262, Sheffield Public Library, Sheffield, South Yorkshire

Carpenter received many letters from men and women who had read his writings on sex.

I have recently read with much interest your book entitled The Intermediate Sex & it has lately dawned on me that I myself belong to that class & I write to ask if there is any way of getting in touch with others of the same temperament. I am a woman, 30 years of age & horribly lonely tho' I have a number of friends & acquaintances many of whom think quite a lot of me, but I unhappily feel quite out of touch with them. For about two years past I have longed intensely for a woman friend who would be to me more than anyone else in the world. I have on the wall in my room a little prayer (tho' I don't pray). It runs thus 'All day I have looked at the multitude & no eye met mine in understanding, no life touched mine in help, no hand clasped mine in fellowship. In a thousand companions I have felt no companionship; a myriad hearts go by but none stop to beat in time with my heart etc., etc., & I have wished in my loneliness that I believed in someone to whom I could pray that prayer which finishes – Thou who guidest souls through the chartless seas of life steer some woman's soul my way.'

I have for many years called myself a feminist but the average woman does not easily attract me; there always seems to be an indescribable barrier between them & myself. (I do hope this doesn't bore you, but I believe you are sympathetic.)

I might mention that I have been engaged to marry on two occasions. The first affair was in my early 20's. I liked the man a good deal & I suppose I thought I loved him but when the time came for him to talk of furniture & marriage I backed out. The thought of marriage & all that it meant repelled me & disgusted me. ...

But tho' I never have been in love with any man I have been very much in love with women. The first affair was at about 14 & lasted two years. I cared for this girl (who was my own age) very much more than she did for me. There was not the slightest physical (or rather sexual element in my love for her – & by the way I might mention that I personally never experienced any sex desire till I was about 28 – two years ago.)

At 17 I was again in love with a fellow member of a Bible class which I then attended tho' that love didn't last long as it happened at a time when I was throwing off the last shackles of orthodoxy & the unreasoning dogmatism & narrowness of thought & outlook & this girl soon lessened my admiration for her. And after that 12 years went by without my meeting anyone whom I liked enough to cultivate. I was 28 when I again fell in love with a girl about my own age. I made it my business to cultivate her but soon found that tho' she was quite friendly & admirable she cared less for me than I did for her. Often when alone with her I had a strong desire to caress & fondle her but I am naturally reserved & restrained & we never advanced further than the formal handshake. I had no sexual desire in connection with her & I couldn't quite understand my feelings toward her. I just concluded that I had somehow in my composition a dash of the masculine (I have been told more than once that I have a masculine mind & I know how much more reasoning & logical than the ordinary or even the so-called advanced woman). But my attachment for this girl was quite emotional – I loved to be with her – to hear her talk even tho' I seldom agreed with her. However one-sided attachments can't last long & I soon reasoned to myself that the best thing for my peace of mind was to consign her to a very much less important place in my thoughts – & shortly after I knew her she was transferred from London to Birmingham.

After she came into my life & went out of it I thought to myself that surely somewhere in the world there must be a woman who could fill the emptiness in my life if I could only find her – and in the early part of the year I voiced my need in a little pacifist & socialist paper asking if any lonely woman rebel would care to correspond with another.

I had about 16 answers, the first was from a girl or woman with whom I am at the present time in love she is rather younger than myself & has all the characteristics which I most admire in women. She is delightfully self-reliant, capable & humorous. It was she who introduced me to your book &

somehow made me realise that I was more closely related to the intermediate sex than I had hitherto imagined & she also I think (tho' I haven't questioned her on the subject is certainly not a normal female – she is much too nice!) When I think of her I have physical desire & should love above all things to be able to live with her & be as intimate as it is possible to be & I don't feel that this desire is at all immoral or degrading, it is not merely or chiefly physical desire – I can't bear the idea of losing her friendship even if the physical desire is never gratified & I don't for a moment expect it will be. I should be intensely grateful if I could just hold her hand & tell her how much I love her. This may look awfully stupid on paper, but it is very real to me. I feel there is nothing I wouldn't do for her that I could do.

I am afraid that the attachment is one-sided & I do so want to meet someone who could care for me as intensely as I care for this girl. I have recently started a correspondence with a woman (about 30) in Scotland. She has been living for the last 4 years with a woman friend & they are very much in love & their relationship is physical as well as spiritual. They are intensely happy & I quite envy them. I long more than I can say to love a woman completely & absolutely & to have that love returned. The world would say that a physical relationship between two of the same sex is an unspeakable crime.

But after a few weeks consideration I have come to the conclusion that this relationship can never be as degrading as the normal sex relationship can be & usually is. I know it is a big thing to say that the normal sex relationship of men & women is more degrading than the other, but it will be true wherever – so long as women are in economic slavery to men & I think you will agree.

...

It is possible that I shall have to leave my chances of meeting a kindred spirit to Fate or luck but I am hoping you may know of some society or channel through which I may meet my other half. One of the correspondents in the appendix of your books speaks of having associated with urani organized & otherwise.

I should be very grateful to have a line from ...

7 E. Smyth, *Streaks of Life*, 1921, Longmans and Co., pp. 173–4

Ethel Smyth, the composer and feminist, wrote a number of autobiographical volumes. Here she recalls visiting Germany in 1902.

But the most exciting of all the acquaintances I was privileged to make, thanks to Madame de Bulow if I except One who will appear in these pages later on – was the great Greek scholar and poet Herr von Wilamowitz-Moellendorff. About this time Professor Gilbert Murray had given non-classical scholars like myself an insight into Greek thought and poetry such as we had never hoped to obtain, and Wilamowitz's translations, which Madame de Bulow introduced me to, are quite as fine. Once I dined quietly with Wilamowitz, and he showed me an unknown poem of Sappho's, of the Faynum series, which he had just deciphered. Incidentally he informed me that in his opinion Sappho was the most maligned of women, that she was really a sort of High School Mistress, and the famous passions merely innocent 'Schwärmerei' between her and her pupils. Luckily it is open to those who have no Greek to reject this depressing reading of 'burning Sappho'.

8 M. Silvera, 'Man Royals And Sodomites: Some Thoughts on the Invisibility of Afro-Caribbean Lesbians', *Feminist Studies*, Vol. 18, No. 3, Fall 1992, pp. 521–32 *passim*

Silvera was born in Jamaica and spent her early years in Kingston. The first part of this extract is from a conversation with her grandmother.

Yes, there was a lot of women involved with women in Jamaica. I knew a lot of them when I was growing up in the country in the 1920s. I didn't really associate with them. Mind you, I was not rude to them. My mother wouldn't stand for any rudeness from any of her children to adults.

I remember a woman we use to call Miss Bibi. She lived next to us – her husband was a fisherman. I think he drowned before I was born. She had a little house that back onto the sea, the same as our house. She was quiet, always reading. That I remember about her because she use to go to the little public library at least four days out of the week. And she could talk. Anything you wanted to know, just ask miss bibi and she could tell you. She was mulatto woman, but poor. Anytime I had any school work that I didn't understand, I use to ask her. The only thing I remember though, we wasn't allowed in her house by my mother, so I use to talk to her outside, but she didn't seem to mind that. Some people use to think she was mad because she spent so much time alone. But I didn't think that because anything she help me with, I got a good mark on it in school.

She was colorful in her own way, but quiet, always alone, except when her friend come and visit her once a year for two weeks. Them times I didn't see Miss Bibi much because my mother told me I couldn't go and visit her. Sometimes I would see her in the market exchanging and bartering fresh fish for vegetables and fruits. I use to see her friend, too. She was a jet Black woman, always her hair tied in bright colored cloth, and she always had on big gold earrings. People use to say she lived on the other side of the island with her husband and children and she came to Port Maria once a year to visit Miss Bibi.

My mother and father were great storytellers and I learnt that from them, but is from Miss Bibi that I think I learnt to love reading so much as a child. It wasn't until I move to Kingston that I notice other women like Miss Bibi. ...

Let me tell you abut Jones. Do you remember her? Well she was the woman who lived the next yard over from us. She is the one who really turn me against people like that and why I fear so much for you to be involved in this ting. She was very loud. Very show-off. Always dressed in pants and man-shirt that she borrowed from her husband. Sometime she use to invite me over to her house, but I didn't go. She always had her hair in a bob haircut, always barefoot and tending to her garden and her fruit trees. She tried to get me involved in that kind of life, but I said no. At the time I remember, I needed some money to borrow and she lent me, later she told me I didn't have to pay her back, but to come over to her house and see the thing she had that was sweeter than what any man could offer me. I told her no and eventually paid her back the money. ...

We still continued to talk. It was hard not to like Jonesie – that's what everybody called her. She was open and easy to talk to. But still there was a fear in me about her. To me it seem like she was in a dead end with nowhere to go. I don't want that for you.

...

The next section is from a conversation with her mother.

Yes, I remember Miss Jones. She smoke a lot, drank a lot. In fact, she was an alcoholic. When I was in my teen she use to come over to our house – always on the veranda. I can't remember her sitting down – seems she was always standing up, smoking, drinking, and reminiscing. She constantly talked abut the past, about her life. And it was always women: young women she knew when she was a young woman, the fun they had together and how good she could make love to a woman. She would say to whoever was listening on the veranda, 'Dem girls I use to have sex with was shapely. You shoulda know me when I was younger, pretty, and shapely just like the 'oman dem I use to have as my 'oman.'

People use to tease her on the street, but not about being a lesbian or calling her sodomite. People use to tease her when she was drunk, because she would leave the rum-shop and stagger down the avenue to her house.

I remember the women she use to carry home, usually in the daytime. A lot of women from downtown, higglers and fish-women. She use to boast about knowing all kinds of women from Coronation market and her famil-iarity with them. She had a husband who lived with her and that served her as her greatest protection against other men taking steps with her. Not that anybody could easily take advantage of Miss Jones; she could stand up for herself. But having a husband did help. He was a very quiet, insular man.

He didn't talk to anyone on the street. He had no friends so it wasn't easy for anyone to come up to him and gossip about his wife.

No one could go to her house without being invited, but I wouldn't say she was a private person. She was a loner. She went to the rumshops alone, she drank alone, she staggered home alone. The only time I ever saw her with somebody were the times when she went of to the Coronation market or some other place downtown to find a woman and bring her home. The only times I remember her engaging in conversation with anybody was when she came over on the veranda to talk about her women and what they did in bed. That was all she let out about herself. There was nothing about how she was feeling, whether she was sad or depressed, lonely, happy. Nothing. She seemed to cover up all of that with her loudness and her vulgarness and her constant threat – which was all it was – to beat up anybody who troubled her or teased her when she was coming home from the rumshop.

Now Cherry Rose – do you remember her? She was a good friend of Aunt Marie and of Mama's. She was also a sodomite. She was loud too, but different from Miss Jones. She was much more outgoing. She was a barmaid and had lots of friends – both men and women. She also had the kind of personality that attracted people – very vivacious, always laughing, talking, and touching. She didn't have any children, but Gem did.

Do you remember Miss Gem? Well, she had children and she was also a barmaid. She also had lots of friends. She also had a man friend name Mickey, but that didn't matter because some women had their men and still had women they carried on with. The men usually didn't know what was going on, and seeing as these men just come and go and usually on their own time, they weren't around every day and night.

Miss Pearl was another one that was in that kind of thing. She was a dressmaker; she use to sew really good. Where Gem was light complexion, she was a very black black woman with deep dimples. Where Gem was a bit plump, Pearl was slim, but with big breasts and a big bottom. They were both pretty women.

I don't remember hearing that word sodomite a lot about them. It was whispered sometimes behind their backs but never in front of them and they were so alive and talkative that people were always around them.

The one woman I almost forgot was Miss Opal, a very quiet woman. She use to be friends with Miss Olive and was always out of her bar sitting down. I can't remember much about her except she didn't drink like Miss Jones and she wasn't vulgar. She was soft-spoken, a half-Chinese woman. Her mother was born in Hong Kong and her father was a black man. She could really bake. She use to supply shops with cakes and pastries.

So there were many of those kind of women around. But it wasn't broadcast.

9 *Urania*, No. 21, May–June 1920, p. 8

Behind the purdah

'Another phenomenon that I must not forget to speak of is the passionate love of one woman for another woman which is frequently found among us. It may be due to our being shut out for the greater part of the day from men, and being permitted to see women only. It is more than friendship, and takes on the line of platonic affection, and our scented sandal-boxes often contain love letters written by one woman to another. No harm results from it, and in a country where marriages are not the consequences of voluntary love, but develop into love often, though not always, human affection finds a safe vent in this manner. The husbands would no doubt be jealous of this innocent sentiment, if they knew of it; but they are generally ignorant, and we pass hours of rapturous joy in each other's company, and pine for the next meeting, and blame one another for the days of parting which we fondly imagine the coy beloved of our own sex has voluntarily inflicted on us to fan the flame of love, so that the impetuous moth may dash itself into immolation with greater zest. This, too, forms a frame-work for the joys and woes of the idle rich … '.

'Whispers from Behind the Purdah', *East and West*, December 1919.

10 *Urania*, Nos 51 and 52, May–August, 1925, p. 3

Mitylene

'So upon the wish we are in Hellas,
In the purple hills and it is summer,
The wind wanders through the groves of ilex;
There are sounds of birds and falling water;
The leaves whisper full of wind and shadow;
That red road in the ravine below us
Leads the travelling eye through fields of mallow,
Seeding grass and flame-bright oleander,
Down the meadowy country to the seaboard,
Where the breakers beat their crooning rhythms
On the yellow sand. That phantom city,
White and small against the purple distance,
With her looming walls and spars and towers
Gleaming in the sun is Mitylene.'

* * *

'Quickly,
Look before she passes that next corner!
Not so tall as you: an Oriental,
Slim and dark; the blue-black hair that crinkles,
Knotted at the neck; the smouldering crimson
Mounting through the cheek's transparent tawny;
And the earth-brown eyes that glow and darkle;
Sappho's very self! ...
AND THUS
'I LOVED thee, Atthis, in the long ago,
When the great oleanders were in flower
In the broad herded meadows full of sun.
And we would often at the fall of dusk
Wander together by the silver stream,
When the soft glass-beads were all wet with dew,
And purple-misted in the fading light,
And joy I knew and sorrow at thy voice
And the superb magnificence of love, –
The loneliness that saddens solitude,
And the sweet speech that makes it durable,
The bitter longing and the keen desire,
The sweet companionship through quiet days
In the slow ample beauty of the world,
And the unutterable glad release
Within the temple of the holy night.
O Atthis, how I loved thee long ago
In that fair perished summer by the sea!

Bliss Carmen

11 *Urania*, Nos 101 and 102, September–December, 1933, p. 1

One-hundred-and-one

Those responsible for the First number of URANIA can none of them have anticipated a Hundred and First. To carry on for ten years would have most likely constituted their utmost ambition. But it is eighteen years since we first began.

Our circulation has been a little over two hundred, as a rule. Our contents have provided a record of the feminist movement, of a rather unique sort. ...

Five or six addresses have requested us to discontinue sending them the paper. ... One or two of the Oxford 'Ladies' colleges surprised us by declining what Cambridge willingly accepts. And we had one very peppery letter from an unmarried lady whose eagle – (or shall we say, vulturine?) – eye detected untold horrors in our refined pages.

253

12 *Urania*, Nos 115 and 116, January–April 1936, p. 8

Geraldine Jewsbury

Geraldine Jewsbury enjoys a precarious immortality, clinging onto the skirts of the Carlyles. Her recent Life by Suzanne Howe cannot be said to do much to alter the picture presented of her by Annie Ireland. She wishes to tone down the impression given by the latter author: but how can we ignore the letters that evince what Suzanne Howe herself calls 'an authentic grand passion?' 'You [Jane Carlyle] will let me be yours and think of me as such, will you not?' 'I feel to love you more and more every day, and you will laugh, but I feel towards you much more like a lover than a female friend!' 'I have found you, and now I wonder how I ever lived without you.' 'You know I love you as nobody else can, and everything you do is right in my eyes.' 'Recollect that I am really in a bad way about you, and I think of you much more than if you were my lover. So God bless you, my dear love!' Jane confirms this: – 'Such mad, lover-like jealousy on the part of one woman to another, it had never entered my heart to conceive.' Indeed, 'I am as jealous as a Turk ... as jealous as a tiger,' wrote Geraldine. Jane tried to calm her by ridicule – 'I set the whole company into fits of laughter the other day by publicly saying to her after she had been flirting with a certain Mr. — that I wondered she should expect me to behave decently to her after she had for a whole evening been making love before my face to another man!' But ridicule had no effect. Still, it was very much to Jane's annoyance that Geraldine swore eternal friendship to the charming American, Charlotte Cushman, and wrote her fervently affectionate letters.

Geraldine glimpsed the reality of the matter when she wrote: – 'I believe we are touching on better days, when women will have a genuine, normal life of their own to lead. Women will be taught not to feel their destiny manqué if they remain single. They will be able to be friends and companions in a way they cannot be now. – I do not feel that either you or I are to be called failures. We are indications of a development of womanhood which as yet is not recognized. I regard myself as a faint indication, a rudiment, of the idea of certain higher qualities and possibilities that lie in women: and all the eccentricities and mistakes and miseries and absurdities I have made are only the consequences of an imperfect formation, an immature growth.'

We may leave it at that.

13 P. Noble, *Profiles and Personalities*, 1946, Brownlee, pp. 68–72

Mary Morris (1915–1988) was an artist and actress from the Fiji Islands who made her home in England. She studied at RADA and in 1936 formed her own repertory company, Stranger Players, in Oxted. Over four decades she appeared in dozens of interesting and frequently strong roles first in films but especially in radio and television. Described by one cinema historian as 'the incomparable, darkly brilliant and rooftop-shouting lesbian' (Bourne 1996: x) this is part of an assessment of her half a century earlier.

Her career has taken many curious turns since that time. Korda recalled her from Hollywood to appear in his 'Prison Without Bars,' and she has since been seen in 'The Thief of Baghdad,' 'Undercover', and 'Pimpernel Smith' (opposite the late Leslie Howard). But in recent years she has developed as a painter and, to an extent, her love of the stage has been sublimated in her work in the studio. Still under thirty, she is reckoned to be a considerable artist. Many filmgoers believe, however, that she has yet to receive a worthy screen opportunity, and could easily become one of the finest film actresses in Britain.

Living in an artist's studio in Notting Hill Gate, she has solved the furniture shortage by making most of the furniture with her own hands. Beds, chairs, table, dresser – all these were made by Mary and her friend, Cecilie Krog, daughter of the Norwegian playwright, who shares the flat with her. 'When I took over this flat I had been out of a job for nearly a year,' Mary says, 'so that I had to make my own furniture, mostly out of margarine boxes, or go without!' This frankness and lack of affectation marks all Mary's actions. She does not mind admitting that frequent spells of enforced rest have been the result of managers and agents declaring that she was too unusual a type to be a theatre success.

But in spite of this, and the fact that Mary has often been known to express herself with the same frankness on the subject of certain anomalies in the commercial theatre, this brown-eyed friendly girl, with the thick mop of dark hair and the delightful, tip-tilted nose, has managed to succeed in the theatre. Her ambitions are to play 'Saint Joan' in London again, and to act in Scandinavia. Already she has learned Norwegian, and in a year or two she plans to act on the Oslo stage.

Mary Morris does not fit easily into any category. Neither does she want to. She is distinctive, sometimes aggressive, Leftist, idealistic, sincere, talkative, talented, likeable. She loves the stage, but is not satisfied that the English theatre has reached the stature which opens up a vista of promise for youth and for real experiment. Her main interests, besides acting and painting – her studio walls are covered with her own oil and water colour portraits of her close friends – are walking, talking and reading plays. She is an Orson Welles fan, a chain smoker, likes wearing slacks and staying in bed until lunch.

14 L. Heron (ed.), *Truth Dare or Promise. Girls Growing Up in the Fifties*, 1985, London: Virago, pp. 146–7, 219

Born in 1948 and 1951 respectively Alison Hennegan and Gail Lewis recall their growing awareness of their feelings towards their own sex during the 1950s.

Alison Hennegan remembers the impact of her piano teacher.

... And battles long ago

My own teacher, a young unmarried woman, probably in her mid-twenties when I began my eleven years' pupillage with her, was very different. Tall – over six feet – she dressed always in beautifully hand-tailored clothes, all in the finest fabrics, all of them brand-new – and all of them at least thirty years out of date. This enigma – the mixture of care, obvious expense and seemingly unconscious eccentricity – I never solved (and, needless to say, I never dared to go to the source by asking her directly for an explanation).

She was one of the very few people I've ever met who truly merited the description 'androgynous'. She had thin, fine – but enormous – hands and feet, long legs, narrow hips, tiny breasts and closely cropped, glossy brown hair. And a face of quite remarkable beauty – the beauty of a shy but intelligent seventeen-year-old boy. She would, I realised later, have served as a perfect visual model for Stephen Gordon, the lesbian heroine of Radclyffe Hall's *The Well of Loneliness*.

Whether her sexuality was also that of Stephen Gordon, I never knew. But to me there was something deeply disturbing, compellingly attractive about the conflicting messages conveyed by that face and that body in those clothes. She was a pervasive influence and the archetype later for many an erotic fantasy. (Later still I wondered whether her seemingly flamboyant outmodedness was in fact just another version of the disguise which I had sought in fat and quick-tongued attack – and for the same reason.)

Gail Lewis recalls the sexual adventures with boys and girls of her primary school days.

From Deepest Kilburn

These sexual forays were not all so horrible. In particular I remember one time when I and another little black girl did some experimentation with each other, and that was highly enjoyable. But I do remember that afterwards I was terrified that our parents might find out and blame me. I was the older, and somehow I know this was even more unacceptable than what we did with the boys. It was an incident that was to haunt me for years as an adult. While I was struggling to 'come out' (a process that lasted literally years) I kept remembering it and would cite it as evidence of my genetic abnormality. Even after I 'came out' I couldn't tell anyone – I still harboured secret fears that it meant I was 'born' a lesbian. I only overcame it when I learned of more and more women, heterosexual and lesbian, who had similar experiences as children.

15 'How It Started', *Arena Three*, Vol. 1, No. 9, September1964, p. 2

The idea originally occurred to our present Editor after reading an article in *Twentieth Century* by Miss Dilys Rowe, entitled 'A Quick Look at the Lesbians', to start a magazine which would give the general public, and – perhaps even more important – Lesbians themselves, a fairer and more evenly balanced picture. In June 1963, an ally was found – Miss D.M.C. (whose name for professional reasons cannot be given in full). Shortly after this, Cynthia Reid and Julie Switsus joined as founder-members and towards the latter part of 1963, MRG and the magazine were a reality.

16 *Arena Three*, Vol. 2, No. 2, February 1965, p. 13

I am suffering from isolation. I've been chucked out of my job – though the reason wasn't given that I'm a lesbian – I was forced to resign. Bad as social ostracism is, I feel the lack of recognition in art – decent art that is – especially in writing, TV, theatre and cinema. Even when lesbian novels are published, the heroines seem to have wretched ends. It is so very cutting off from life and tends to make life unreal.

I watched the TV broadcast and was almost shocked to be actually seeing something so vitally applied to me – it was so unusual! I was delighted that the myth that lesbian loves never work, never last, was exploded. I've never read a chapter on lesbians in any trick-cycling book that didn't stress the fact that it doesn't work – and although I didn't believe them this subtly had its effect on me. I have not found the trick-cyclists much help, and in one case quite dreadfully bad. I came to the conclusion that they didn't know very much about it themselves.
Mary L. (Petersfield)

17 *Arena Three*, Vol. 2, No. 6, June 1965, p. 11

Dear Miss Langley,
We read with alarm yet another article in the Sunday Press concerning the activities of MRG. We think that too much publicity about your club's activities in the popular press is making it very difficult for two women to live together unnoticed, without being viewed with suspicion. My friend and I have lived together now for four years, during which time we have worked with normal people, who thought nothing unnatural about 2 women living together. Since these articles have been appearing in the Sunday press and on TV we have noticed an increasing (but Morbid) interest in our relationship with each other.

While we are in sympathy with the 'lonely lesbians' who's (sic) cause you have undertaken so avidly, you have caused lots of unhappiness and unnecessary embarrassment to those who do not wish to advertise their personal feelings towards each other. We are not ashamed of our love, but we do not wish to be the subject of curious speculations. By no means are we alone in this, many of our friends hold the same viewpoint. Therefore we beg you to be more discreet.

We are *not* 'against the law' and do not need to fight a cause for the general public to be educated. So please let sleeping dogs lies (sic).

Yours faithfully,

Miss A.M.A.J.

Miss T.H.

18 *Arena Three*, Vol. 2, No. 1, January 1965, p. 4

Many members and supporters of MRG have said that they would like to read in 'A3' some autobiographical accounts by people of differing backgrounds and experience ...

It was shortly before my nineteenth birthday that I discovered that I was a homosexual. The process of discovering, or of just facing up to, this fact about myself had been long and acutely painful, and had brought me very close to a nervous breakdown. I never went completely over the edge, which would almost have been easier for me, but hovered somewhere on the brink.

At 18 I had fallen very suddenly and very violently in love with a girl of my own age. Simultaneously, perhaps consequently, I began to suffer from an intense depression unparalleled in my experience. I was in such a state of continuous tension that I feared at any moment something would snap inside me and I would start to scream. My own company and the company of other people became an almost intolerable strain. I was completely in the dark as to what was happening inside me, and I was unable to communicate with anyone: I was sure that no one would understand, even if I could find words to express myself.

...

I remember distinctly when I first heard the word 'Lesbian'. A girl at the same art school said, in an intentionally audible whisper: 'Look at that girl over there. She's a Lesbian ... ' It didn't take me long, in spite of my deadlock with the dictionary, to find out what she had meant.

It was still a long time before I could apply the word to myself – there were still certain things that just couldn't happen to me – but at the same time, in another part of my mind, I think I already knew. I saw a book in Smith's – 'Homosexuality in Men and Women' – and tried to make myself go in and buy it. I couldn't. I saw, in anticipation, the knowing look on the assistant's face as she handed me the book. Next day I went again, and then again. Eventually I went in, picked it up, and handed it to the assistant. My hands were shaking and I had literally broken into a cold sweat. She wrapped it up nonchalantly and handed it back to me without a glance.

Under the chapter on the 'causes of Lesbianism' I read what I had tried not to believe, under Cause No. 3. 'Instead of loving her father she (the child) may hate him. This may be because he has rejected her. He may be a thoroughly undesirable character whom it is impossible to love. Or there may have been some traumatic experience in childhood ...'

Goes on to describe her father's rages and sadism towards the family, and her mother's naïve loyalty to him in an attempt to create the illusion of a happy family.

When I first fell in love with a girl I felt completely isolated. My affliction must be unique; it could arouse only horror and disgust in others. No-one I knew could possibly have the same sort of feelings. ...

By the second time, I at least had no illusions about myself. She seemed to like me, in a passive sort of way, and we became close friends. I was very happy, but also unsure of her; sooner or later I would lose her. This happened after I had known her for almost a year. She came round to see me one night; she thought it would be better, she said, if we saw less of each other in future. She was very sorry. She liked me very much; but she thought it would be better for both of us. ... She didn't look at me once while she was talking.

Eventually I went to a psychiatrist to find out if there was a 'cure' for my condition. There wasn't, of course. But he helped me a lot, chiefly though his sympathy. He forced me to describe the incident with my father. Once I had done this I felt strangely liberated.

When I was 20, I met John, and for the first time formed a real friendship with a man. When we eventually confessed to each other that we were both homosexuals we felt even closer than before. We had had the same problems, we could share the same jokes. Sometimes, realising that our relationship has raised us above the suspicion of being 'queer' we felt as if we had played some sort of joke on society. We were both painters, and encountered as much social pressure in these supposedly unconventional circles as elsewhere. There was a stigma attached to being frigid, impotent, or 'inexperienced'.

In my last year at art school, a sort of miracle happened. The girl I loved and who had left me told me that she was in love with me. We went to live in a decrepid old houseboat. We were ecstatically happy together and hardly tried to conceal it from our friends – but no one seemed to mind. Perhaps we had exceptionally nice friends.

It is now a year since we have been apart. John has asked me to marry him; she has asked me to live with her in London. I don't know. Sometimes I need her so much I can hardly bear the thought of living without her. But I don't know what would really be best for her. I suspect, though I don't want to believe it, that a man could give her more than I can. Even with all my love, I can't give her children, or the respect of other people, or the security that she deserves.

Perhaps I am just trying to kid myself, and I already know what I will have to do, sooner or later. ...

19 *Arena Three*, Vol. 2, No. 10, October 1965, p. 14

Views on the proposed Club: –

Mrs. S.N. (Surrey) – Premises either in or outside London. If Club is reasonably exclusive, willing to pay any fee demanded, a condition of membership to be reasonable wearing apparel.

Miss H.W. (London) suggests that people should come to the Club premises in skirts, and change into slacks, etc. if they wished after arrival.

Miss T.G. (Clapham) says: 'Let us have more cultural interests. If a club was considered don't let it be another Bull's Head or Gateways. It would appear we have collected half the latter club. Completely disillusioned.'

(Note: – The 'Gateways' is one of the longstanding London clubs – Ed.)

Miss H.B. would very much like to attend meetings etc. but, not knowing a soul, is far too shy to come alone, and so feels she is stuck!

20 *Arena Three*, Vol. 5, No. 5, May 1968, pp. 4–5

The new group

Hope for the Provinces

Spring, 1965

It all began in the Spring of 1965 in Knutsford, Cheshire. Some A3 readers who had been informed of the existence of other local readers agreed to meet together. By the winter the group's membership had risen from twelve to twenty-five A3 readers and their friends in the Manchester area.

Monthly meetings began to be held because of the size, now at a member's flat in Manchester. Eventually a pub room was hired for the 'Women's Poetry Meeting'!! These arrangements did not however, prove satisfactory, and the group soon reverted to flat meetings.

Summer, 1966

By summer, 1966 a pattern had formed of monthly meetings in a central flat when talking, gossiping, drinking and dancing took place. The numbers fluctuated at the twenty-five to thirty limit, which appeared to be saturation level. Most members were in the professional and middle-class brackets and seemed content with the exclusive society they had formed. Most had been A3 subscribers, but once within the security of the group tended to drop their subscriptions. The group offered a comfortable social existence for many of the members. Now two schools of opinion began to emerge, the 'passivists' and the 'activists'. The 'passivists' who thought they had got all they wanted out of A3 – enough friends and a social life – seemed content to leave it at that. The 'activists', bored by this pattern, wanted speakers and more activities.

1967

A skeleton committee was formed and early in 1967 a meeting with the first speaker was held. The group limped on, with a slow dribble of new members through faithful A3. It was soon after this that the difficulties of flat meetings for large numbers became increasingly obvious. Antagonisms developed between members, making the idea of an open meeting more difficult of acceptance by those with partisan views. The regularity of the meetings often placed an undue strain on one flat owner. The group was also divided by those desiring the 'party-time' meetings – the monotony of which made others discontented.

These ideas within a closed lesbian society provoked antagonisms that were threatening to break up the whole group. Dread of the entrance of the so-called 'roughs' – full drag females with undertones of hidden violence and blackmailing instincts – developed into a myth out of all proportion to reality. At this juncture, when the fears of this restricted provincial group threatened to overpower it, a breakthrough took place through the idealism and hard work of a few unquenchable individuals.

The club

The problem was approached by seeking to utilise the other resources available in the city – the men's clubs. Eventually an eminently respectable (!) men's club was found. The owner was not only enthusiastic about the idea of monthly lesbian meetings on his premises; he was quite happy for us to use the premises free of charge and to concede us membership of his club. His enthusiasm was a boost to the whole group.

Other backstage activity included many abortive attempts at advertising, informing members of activities, and the intention to form the 'NEW GROUP' with a constitution and a definite 'social activities' policy. In September, 1967, the first meeting was held at the Rockingham Club. Thirty members attended, and everyone – even the most cynical – was highly delighted with the premises. It was a new beginning.

1968 – a wider horizon

The group has gone from strength to strength. By March we had a constitution and an organising committee. We have liason (sic) with the 'North West Homosexual Law Reform Society' and have shared advertising with them. And we are also in touch with the 'Albany Trust', 'kenric' and 'Arena 3' staff. Our membership has doubled and morale is high. Speakers and entertainments are planned and the quarrels of the past are forgotten. Hope for the regional groups seems to lie in using all the available facilities, for men and women, in the area. Expansion can only take place at the local level through the initiative of local people.

G.J.

21 *Arena Three*, Vol. 5, No. 10, October 1968, pp. 4–5

The uncivil service

Lorna Gulston interviews Helen B. in Northern Ireland

A letter from Helen B. of County Down (writes Lorna Gulston) in 'A3' (July, 1968) told how she lost her job in the Civil Service: she had admitted to being of homosexual disposition. I asked if she would consent to being interviewed, and a record of our conversation follows: –

Q. How long had you been in the Civil Service when the trouble started, Helen?

A. About fifteen months.

Q. During those fifteen months did you ever to your knowledge give cause for complaint in your job – for instance, through bad timekeeping, carelessness, backchat to superiors, anything like that?

A. Definitely not.

Q. You're quite sure about that?

A. Positive. Nothing was brought up against me at the final interview except my being homosexual.

Q. What led up to this interview?

A. Well, I'd known since my schooldays that I was a Lesbian. I suppose I thought, as one is apt to, that I was the only one in the world. I wished I could talk it over with my parents. But I daren't – they'd go mad. Though I'd been fond of a few girls I'd never told them or shown my feelings openly. I'd even gone out with boys, so long as they kept the dates platonic.

By now it was getting me down and I was feeling really lonely and miserable. I must have looked it. One morning Miss A, an older woman who was well above me in rank although not my immediate superior, asked me kindly what was wrong.

I wouldn't tell her, but she kept on and on at me. Then, she seemed so genuinely motherly and kind, I just blurted out the truth. She didn't seem shocked or disgusted. She was most sympathetic. I felt a lot better, then, for having been able to tell someone.

In the office, too, there was a girl – in her late twenties, a divorcee – that I liked very much and became very fond of. She always spoke to me, and was friendly. As time went on, I couldn't resist writing her a letter, more or less saying how I felt.

Q. Was this letter in any way suggestive – or could it have been interpreted that way?

A. No, honestly it wasn't. It was rather a kind of schoolgirl crush effort. I just explained that I liked her a lot, and I hoped she liked me, and so on. Nothing more than that.

Q. Did she answer it, or comment on it?

A. No. She never even mentioned it. She just behaved in the same friendly way as before.

Q. Were you attracted to any of the other girls in the office? Did you make any affectionate moves towards anyone else?

A. No. I only liked Mrs. H. And other than writing her this letter, I made no move at all.

Q. Well, so what happened next?

A. One day the older woman, Miss A, ordered me to report to one of the departmental officials in his office. He started straight in, by saying: 'I've been hearing things about you.'

Then he said he had before him a letter that I had written. I didn't deny anything. I was so stunned I couldn't have thought of anything but the truth. Besides, I didn't feel ashamed of being a Lesbian. I knew I hadn't done anything wrong, either.

The D.O. was very grim. He had over two hundred women in his department, he said. He couldn't have anyone like me around. He wouldn't even let me explain fully about myself. He asked me to resign from the Civil Service.

Q. Did you not know that, if you'd taken a firm stand, he couldn't have forced you to resign? That you'd have been within your rights to refer the whole matter to the Civil Service Commission?

A. No. I had nobody to help me, at that time. I thought then that admitting to being a Lesbian was just the end, as far as the Civil Service was concerned.

Anyway, the D.O. told me, if I refused to resign, he'd make life impossible for me, and give me a bad report. I was established, but I was just ending my 'probation' period. I thought that a bad report now would mean I wouldn't be kept on, anyway.

I was terribly shocked, and at my wits' end. And I was terrified he'd let my parents know.

Q. So what did you do?

A. I just agreed to resign. He said if I did, they'd keep me on until I got another job.

22 *Arena Three*, Vol. 6, No. 5, May 1969, p. 3

The young homosexual

Last month we invited younger readers to write and tell us of their own experience ...

Miss J.S. (Birmingham)

I was glad to hear of your interest in young homosexual girls. I am one. I am 15½ now. I hope to get a job in electrical engineering, get some money, meet someone I could live with and 'settle down', so to speak. I am quite sure I am homosexual, and think it would help to meet others like myself.

In answer to the questions you published, I first became aware of a 'difference' from my school associates when I was 10 years old. I had felt different from all other people since about the age of 6. The difference I noticed when I was 10–11 was just a crush and generally fancying girls, which no-one else seemed to do. Of course, I called it 'love', of course, each one was 'different'.

When I was 12 I really got going. It didn't surprise me that no-one believed me each time, when every other day I came home saying, 'This is it!' or, 'This time it's the real thing!'

Some of my feelings, as I say, are just the average excitement of seeing good looking girls in miniskirts and so on, and many of my 'fixations' were crushes. There is one exception, the only real love of my life, and I drove the poor girl into hating me. (She is 'normal'.)

Naturally my parents don't know exactly how I feel. I think my father accepts it, and my mother is beginning to. Every now and then I get her to sit down, and try to explain my ultimate aims in life.

As for dating boys, I don't. It is entirely up to the person concerned whether they do or not. Whether one ought, or ought not to, just doesn't come into it. No-one 'ought' or 'ought not' to have to do anything.

One other thing I would like to say. I get enraged at some of the comments made in FREE SPEECH. The way I see it, people are people. We should all accept each other, regardless of colour, creed, class, shape, or sex.

I have made many suicide attempts and been in the psychiatric ward of a general hospital. I see a psychiatrist once a week and am a client of the Samaritans. There seems no hope for me. Are there any others in my age group who would be interested in starting a social club in Birmingham?

(Note: We publish the above letter in full because it makes perfectly clear that neither A3 nor any club or social group that at present exists can be of much practical help in dealing with the problems of many of those who write to us. This is the kind of letter that we forward to the Secretary of the M.R. Trust and do not normally publicise in A3. Ed.)

23 A. Jivani, *It's Not Unusual. A History of Lesbian and Gay Britain in the Twentieth Century*, 1997, London: Michael O'Mara Books Ltd, p. 50

Barbara Bell described signifiers of lesbianism which were current from the 1930s onwards.

You'd recognise the lesbians by ... their little finger rings. So you'd plenty of chances for making passes if you were standing on the Underground or waiting at a bus stop and there was always this lovely glance of recognition and it was a lovely warm feeling to think, well you weren't the only one – there were hundreds. And if you 'married' – you swore that you would be together forever – you would exchange rings and wear them on your third finger. ... It was a good idea. ... It's like wearing a badge. I wore a little finger ring until the last two years but my fingers have got so thin now I can't keep one on.

24 Brighton Ourstory Project, *Daring Hearts, Lesbian and Gay Lives of 50s and 60s Brighton*, 1992, Brighton, QueenSpark Books, *passim*

Aunties was a very well-known gay pub in Walsall. I was the only woman there. That was in 1959. They said if I came down to Brighton the streets were lined with girls. I could just have my choice, go anywhere I wanted, they were all over the place. And I thought, 'Well, let's go down there.'

(Gill, born 1934, p. 13)

I'd written to Marjorie Proops and it took three months for an answer. She wrote back saying, 'Don't worry, dear, you'll grow out of it' and I sat there and sobbed. I sobbed my heart out over that woman. There were two things that I'd written about. I think I'd said something like, 'I think I'm lesbian and also I don't like men near me, I don't like boys and I don't want physical contact with men ... ' and she'd dismissed me in this one line ... and I just felt like screaming, it was awful.

(Siobhan, born 1948, p. 19)

Margaret and I used to come down to Brighton, used to come to Brighton often, come early in the morning, bring a picnic, Margaret used to make a picnic, we used to sit up on the Downs. But we never went to the clubs, Margaret and I never went to the clubs, we used to go and have a drink or bring a picnic and sit on the front, or we used to go on the hills past St Dunstans and up on the green there, that was mostly where we went because I enjoyed being up on the hill and watching the cliffs and all that. We walked all along there, by Roedean. We used to say, 'Nancy Spain went to Roedean.' You felt a connection, you see, because you knew she was gay.

(Vera, born 1918, pp. 59–60)

Everything was fun then, really. You've got to remember that in the sixties, everything was new, wasn't it? Everything hadn't been done before and certainly, from the lesbian point of view, it was the start of a whole new era for lesbians to actually come out as being like that, more so than ever. But to do something as controversial as 'The Killing of Sister George' then – although now it seems very dated and quite amusing – it was very brave, actually, very brave. And brave for the people who were in it.

(Janice, born 1944, p. 88)

I had been to teacher training college in Birmingham, where I met a girl who was six months younger than I was – I'd just turned my twenty-first birthday – and she told her parents that we were gay. They got me kicked out of training college. They said, if I ever saw their daughter again, they'd have me through court. So I left training college and went to work in various factories.

Teaching was all I ever really wanted to do. So, three years after I moved to Brighton, I wrote round every single private school in Brighton and Hove and one accepted me as a supply teacher. I did that for two years, that was juniors. I've still got a reference from that school, wonderful reference; the headmaster gave me a superb reference, so I suppose I must have done well enough there.

But then, because I wasn't fully qualified, you could only do two years' supply teaching, so I applied to go back to college in Bognor Regis. I went along for the interview and the interview went well and I was so sure that I'd got a place because the principal came running down the road after me and said, 'By the way, if I can't find you a place on the college campus, are you prepared to live out?' I said, 'Yes, of course I will.' And I went back home to my girlfriend and said, 'Great, I'm in. I must be. He wouldn't have said that otherwise.' And yet a fortnight later, back came a letter saying that I hadn't been accepted. And of course, when I thought about it I realised there's a clearing house in London for teachers and my file must have had lesbian stamped all over it, so that was that. I knew I would never get into teaching then, so I didn't try again. It really messed my life up. I felt there wasn't anything else I could really do well.

(Sandie, p. 34)

The fashions of the early sixties used to be these enormous skirts with layers and layers of tulle petticoats that we used to spend hours dipping in starch and drying, hanging all around the kitchen and all over the place. Of course, in those days we never had cars, like young people seem to have willy-nilly today, we went everywhere by bus. We used to get on the bus and we used to have to sit on the side seat. You couldn't sit on the seat that faced front because they would crush your skirts, so you looked for a side seat. And when you sat down, the thing practically came up over your head because there was so much of it! And those tight elastic belts, clip belts round your waist, and quite low-fronted jumpers. That was the way I dressed as a fem then.

(Sandie, p. 53)

Our first visit to a club, I had a skirt on. I'd never had a pair of trousers on in my life, I'd always worn skirts. I sat there fascinated, the whole night. We were just outsiders, they didn't know us, we weren't dressed like them. Well, I took a good look at what was going on around me. I thought, 'Well, next time I come back, I'll have trousers on.' So during the week I went into a men's shop and bought a pair of trousers.

(Vicky, p. 53)

25 R. Manning, *A Time and a Tide*, 1971, Marion Boyers, pp. 136–7

The novelist and children's writer first published this autobiography under the pseudonym 'Sarah Davys'. It begins with her suicide attempt and charts her struggles as a lesbian who believed it necessary to keep her identity secret.

For a time I inhabited the fringes of the claustrophobic world of homosexuals, seedy, it seemed to me, hectic and endlessly malicious. Seedy because their sights were so low, their contacts so narrow. There was a deadly similarity in their basement flats, with the fake antiques, and the clutter of third-rate knick-knacks; dusty bookshelves filled with dog-eared copies of Mary Renault's novels, and unwashed whisky glasses; greasy sinks and unemptied garbina bags. Though one or two individuals had other standards, most of those I encountered lived within this self-imposed compound, their contacts with other human beings virtually confined to lesbian parties, lesbian meetings, lesbian clubs. Their major topic of conversation was the people in their own narrow circle: who had left whom, who was sleeping with whom, and – this cropped up over and over again – who was in hospital having a hysterectomy (the occupational disease of lesbians) and what was happening to her current girl friend. It is fair to qualify this by saying that the squalor, restlessness and malice of a lesbian club or group can all be found in a correspondingly narrow section of heterosexual society, golfing and bridge sets, for instance, the common rooms and canteens of school or university or commerce; in small-town circles and in professional groups. But such things seem to grow to suffocating proportions in a set that is not only small but also all-female, and in addition belligerent and convinced that every man's hand and society's collective hand is against them.

Nevertheless I admit freely that at first I was fascinated by this world, by the odd and rather unreal sense of freedom engendered in the initial stages of being 'inside the group'; by the pleasure of being admired and found attractive both physically and as a writer.

26 E. Wilson, 'Gayness and Liberalism' in *Hidden Agendas. Theory, Politics and Experience in the Women's Movement*, 1986, London: Tavistock, pp. 139–47 *passim*

When I first arrived [at Oxford University] I was shocked to discover that what most of the women wanted was marriage. I was really stunned by this, my brain being the only aspect of myself I'd ever been taught to respect or feel positive about; and also I'd somehow got hold of Simone de Beauvoir's book The Second Sex, and she did after all, whatever we think of her now, rightly argue the necessity for women to fight for economic independence. And in a way I was right – though what I wanted, not white tulle and wedding bells, but a vague, imaginary kind of success, to be on a par with the men, was no better. Anyway, I think it was really only possible to succeed in competition with the men if you, as a girl, had terrific self confidence and could succeed both as a man and as a sex object.

I told some of the women in my college that I thought I was a lesbian and was upset and humiliated when they reacted either by brushing it aside as a phase, or else by looking on me as neurotic rather than sinful. This attitude of 'you are sick' rather than 'you are wicked' was actually the more undermining of the two.

This is still the most usual attitude in society today. In this scheme of things the homosexual is an inferior being unable by reason of his or her hangups to achieve a relationship with a member of the opposite sex. A homosexual is to be pitied for he or she is less than the 'normal' man or women. As Anthony Storr, well-known psychiatrist and apologist for sexism, puts it: 'Lesbians do not know what they are really missing' (Storr 1964). This view lacks the positive strength of wickedness. I certainly felt I was ugly, awkward, wrong; but I was no longer magnificent and tortured ('Evil, be thou my good') just a squalid social casualty, victim of my socially embarrassing background. If only I'd had a Daddy, everything would have been okay.

...

When I did finally meet and start an affair with another woman I immediately became very dependent on her, because, believing as I did that homosexuals were all doomed to misery (since that is what you read in all books on the subject) a happy relationship was something to cling to as hard as you could.

Sexual typecasting

We entered the 'swinging sixties' together and became the 'white negroes' of a rather pleasure-seeking, but mildly political, group of academics in the Midlands. What she and I gave each other that was positive (and there was a lot) was always subtly distorted by our living in this liberal, heterosexual world. I did not, in the beginning, see her as male, but everyone else did, largely because she had a higher-status job than me. The men she worked with gave her recognition as an honorary man. She could fancy birds and drink pints, but I remained 'feminine'. Yet I still preferred women, or could only find a woman, so I was the woman's woman, which made me the lowest of the low. This world, where we imagined we were freed from the domination of men, was shot through with male assumptions and male values. And it was the men, I think, who liked our company; most of the wives and girl-friends either saw us as manless and therefore to be pitied, or else a special kind of rival and thus not to be trusted. But we were so grateful for being accepted that we never even noticed the price we were paying (and nor did anyone else, since there was certainly nothing deliberate or malicious about all of this).

This then was our place in the Permissive Society – to make our friends feel liberated and progressive by 'accepting' us, without their having to feel any challenge to their own sexual identities.

We had a second, separate social life centering on the 'gay scene' in London. There we were also typecast, as a stable couple, in a group in which stability was much prized; and here too we were pressured to play the roles of male and female, 'butch' and 'femme', even though in the class-conscious scene such role playing was much more open and exaggerated among working-class than among middle-class women; the more middle-class you were the more you emphasized equality and sharing – but only in the way 'straight' middle-class couples do. That was still the standard we measured ourselves against.

This scene too was drenched in liberalism. That is, we said it was OK for everyone to do their own thing; you could sleep with whom you wanted and you shouldn't really be jealous; a good relationship was an open relationship; you shouldn't make moral judgments about sexual behaviour – an extreme of liberalism that clashed violently with the wish to 'succeed' as a stable lesbian couple, and often led to hysterical exaggerations of feeling, while at the same time a kind of shallowness in a world from which children were almost wholly absent so that what is usually the material reason for fidelity was missing and gave an air of unreality to the scenes and dramas.

Many of us were obsessed with clothes and our image. There was one particular group of women who seemed to associate together on the basis of all being very rich and beautiful. They all had affairs with one another – a tiny, incestuous clique. I remember a party of theirs we went to in a Dolphin Square flat where there was no furniture at all except an enormous bed surrounded by mirrors and hundreds of bottles and jars of make-up and scent – just like something out of a movie.

...

Along with our friends we drifted towards Marxism as the 1960s wore on. This was to begin with a largely intellectual conviction, but when the women's movement arose we at first rejected it as petit bourgeois. This at least was what we said, but I think it must have been more a result of our feeling cut off from the experience of most women, cut off perhaps from ourselves as women. With the gay movement we did on the other hand immediately identify, and this led to great changes in our lives. We separated and formed new relationships and I was somehow freed to be politically active.

I think one reason for this was that in its beginnings the great, explosive, positive thing about gay liberation was the feeling that there were hundreds of homosexuals who were not afraid to assert their homosexuality. It no longer had to be discreetly hidden. That was a truly liberating experience, and although perhaps gay liberation was essentially a liberal movement, its slogans 'gay is good' and 'gay is proud' are important in challenging the oppression and repression of homosexuals. Gay people really are oppressed, although their oppression is a peculiar one since it rests partly on the possibility of always remaining hidden and invisible. This was the reason for the stress on 'coming out' in gay liberation.

The lesson to myself of my life during the 1960s is that I could be tolerated as a homosexual provided I could be stereotyped. That way I did not challenge society, by wanting for instance to bring up children. One of the Dolphin Square women I mentioned earlier did transgress this unwritten rule by privately adopting a baby. The welfare officer concerned discovered her lesbian relationship and it was only because the adoption was a private one and had already gone over more or less all the legal hurdles that it was not reversed, and indeed the welfare officer did try to bring a court action to do this.

...

I have experienced homosexuality as a romantic ideal, and as a prison. It is only during the past few years that I have been able even to begin to experience it as a form of freedom. I do not want lesbianism distorted into some kind of ideal in the women's movement or anywhere else. I simply want us all to fight to free ourselves so that we can apprehend our real feelings more fully, whether we are straight or gay.

BIBLIOGRAPHY

Alexander, Z. (1990) 'Let It Lie Upon The Table: The Status of Black Women's Biography in the UK', *Gender and History* 2, 1: 22–33.

Auchmuty, R. (1989) 'By Their Friends We Shall Know Them: The Lives and Networks of Some Women in North Lambeth, 1880–1940' in Lesbian History Group *Not a Passing Phase: Reclaiming Lesbians in History 1840–1985*, London: Women's Press.

—— (1992) *A World of Girls*, London: Women's Press.

Baker, M. (1985) *Our Three Selves: The Life of Radclyffe Hall*, London: Hamish Hamilton.

Beddoe, D. (1989) *Back to Home and Duty: Women Between the Wars, 1918–1939*, London: Pandora.

Bennett, J. (2000) ' "Lesbian-Like" and the Social History of Lesbianisms', *Journal of the History of Sexuality*, 9, 1–2: 1–24.

Bérubé, A. (1990) *Coming Out Under Fire. The History of Gay Men and Women in World War Two*, New York: The Free Press.

Bland, L. (1995) *Banishing the Beast: English Feminism and Sexual Morality 1885–1914*, London: Penguin.

—— (1998) 'Trial by Sexology?: Maud Allan, *Salome* and the "Cult of the Clitoris" Case' in L. Bland and L. Doan (eds) *Sexology in Culture: Labelling Bodies and Desires*, Cambridge: Polity.

Bland, L. and Doan, L. (eds) (1998a) *Sexology in Culture: Labelling Bodies and Desires*, Cambridge: Polity.

—— (1998b) *Sexology Uncensored: The Documents of Sexual Science*, Cambridge: Polity.

Bourne, S. (1996) *Brief Encounters: Lesbians and Gays in British Cinema 1930–1971*, London: Cassell.

Bratton, J. (1992) 'Irrational Dress' in V. Gardner and S. Rutherford (eds) *The New Woman and Her Sisters: Feminism and Theatre 1850–1914*, Hemel Hempstead: Harvester Wheatsheaf.

Brighton Ourstory Project (1992) *Daring Hearts: Lesbian and Gay Lives of 50s and 60s Brighton*, Brighton: Queenspark Books.

Bruley, S. (1999) *Women in Britain since 1900*, London: Macmillan.

Cant, B. (ed.) (1997) *Invented Identities? Lesbians and Gays Talk about Migration*, London: Cassell.

Cassidy, J. and Stewart-Park, A. (1977) *We're Here: Conversations with Lesbian Women*, London: Quartet.

Castle, T. (1993) *The Apparitional Lesbian. Female Homosexuality and Modern Culture*, New York: Columbia University Press.

Clark, A. (1987) 'Womanhood and Manhood in the Transition from Plebian to Working-Class Culture, London, 1780–1845', Ph.D. dissertation, Rutgers University.

—— (1995) *The Struggle for the Breeches: Gender and the Making of the British Working Class*, London: Rivers Oram.

—— (1996) 'Anne Lister's Construction of Lesbian Identity', *Journal of the History of Sexuality* 7: 23–50.

Cline, S. (1997) *Radclyffe Hall: A Woman Called John*, London: John Murray.

Collis, R. (1994) *Portraits to the Wall: Historic Lesbian Lives Unveiled*, London: Cassell.

—— (1997) *A Trouser-wearing Character. The Life and Times of Nancy Spain*, London: Cassell.

Crane, P. (1982) *Gays and the Law*, London: Pluto.

Davidoff, L. and Hall, C. (eds) (1987) *Family Fortunes: Men and Women of the English Middle Class 1780–1860*, London: Routledge.

Dekker, R. and van de Pol, L. (1989) *The Tradition of Female Transvestism in Early Modern Europe*, London: Macmillan.

Dickson, L. (1975) *Radclyffe Hall at the Well of Loneliness. A Sapphic Chronicle*, London: Collins.

Doan, L. (1997) ' "Gross Indecency Between Women": Policing Lesbians or Policing Lesbian Police?', *Social and Legal Studies* 6, 4: 533–51.

—— (1998a) 'Passing Fashions: Reading Female Masculinities in the 1920s', *Feminist Studies* 24, 3: 663–700.

—— (1998b) ' "Acts of Female Indecency": Sexology's Intervention in Legislating Lesbianism' in L. Bland and L. Doan (eds) *Sexology in Culture: Labelling Bodies and Desires*, Cambridge: Polity.

Dollimore, J. (1991) *Sexual Dissidence. Augustine to Wilde, Freud to Foucault*, Oxford: Clarendon Press.

Donoghue, E. (1993) *Passions Between Women: British Lesbian Culture 1668–1801*, London: Scarlet Press.

Dugaw, D. (1989) *Warrior Women and Popular Balladry 1650–1850*, Cambridge: Cambridge University Press.

Duggan, L. (1998) 'The Theory Wars, or, Who's Afraid of Judith Butler?', *Journal of Women's History* 10, 1: 9–19.

Dyhouse, C. (1981) *Girls Growing Up in Late Victorian and Edwardian England*, London: Routledge and Kegan Paul.

Edwards, E. (1995) 'Homoerotic Friendship and College Principals, 1880–1960', *Women's History Review* 4, 2: 149–61.

Edwards, S. (1981) *Female Sexuality and the Law*, Oxford: Martin Robertson.

Faderman, L. (1981) *Surpassing the Love of Men: Romantic Friendship and Love Between Women from the Renaissance to the Present*, London: Junction Books.

—— (1985) *Scotch Verdict*, London: Quartet.

—— (1994) *Chloe Plus Olivia – An Anthology Of Lesbian Literature From The Seventeenth Century To The Present*, London: Viking.

Faraday, A. (1985) 'Social Definitions of Lesbians in Britain, 1914–1939', unpublished Ph.D. thesis, University of Essex.

—— (1988) 'Lesbian Outlaws: Past Attempts to Legislate Against Lesbians', *Trouble and Strife* 13: 9–16.

—— (1989) 'Lessoning Lesbians: Girls' Schools, Coeducation and Anti-lesbianism Between the Wars' in C. Jones and P. Mahoney (eds) *Learning Our Lines: Sexuality and Social Control in Education*, London: The Women's Press.

Freedman, E.B. (1998) '"The Burning of Letters Continues": Elusive Identities and the Historical Construction of Sexuality', *Journal of Women's History* 9, 4: 181–200.

Garber, M. (1992) *Vested Interests: Cross-Dressing and Cultural Anxiety*, London: Routledge.

Glendinning, V. (1984) *Vita: The Life of V. Sackville-West*, London: Penguin.

Gowing, L. (1997) 'History' in A. Medhurst and S. Munt (eds), *Lesbian and Gay Studies: A Critical Introduction*, London: Cassell.

Grant, J. (ed.) (1996) *Women, Migration and Empire*, Stoke-on-Trent: Trentham Books.

Griffin, G. (1993) *Heavenly Love? Lesbian Images in Twentieth Century Women's Writing*, Manchester: Manchester University Press.

Halberstam, J. (1998) *Female Masculinity*, London: Duke University Press.

Hall, L. (1994) '"The English Have Hot Water Bottles": The Morganatic Marriage of Medicine and Sexology in Britain since William Acton' in R. Porter and M. Teich (eds) *Sexual Knowledge, Sexual Science: The History of Attitudes to Sexuality*, Cambridge: Cambridge University Press.

—— (1997) 'Heroes or Villains? Reconsidering British fin de siècle Sexology and its Impact', in L. Segal (ed.) *New Sexual Agendas*, London: Macmillan Press.

—— (2000) *Sex, Gender and Social Change in Britain Since 1880*, London: Macmillan Press.

Hall Carpenter Archives Lesbian Oral History Group (1989) *Inventing Ourselves: Lesbian Life Stories*, London: Routledge.

Hamer, E. (1996) *Britannia's Glory: A History of Twentieth-Century Lesbians*, London: Cassell.

Hansen, K. (1995) '"No Kisses Is Like Youres": An Erotic Friendship between Two African-American Women during the Mid-Nineteenth Century', *Gender and History* 7, 2: 153–82.

Harman, C. (1989) *Sylvia Townsend Warner. A Biography*, London: Chatto and Windus.

Hennegan, A. (1991) Introduction to R. Hall, *The Well of Loneliness*, London: Virago.

Heron, L. (ed.) (1985) *Truth, Dare or Promise. Girls Growing up in the Fifties*, London: Virago Press.

Hitchcock, T. (1997) *English Sexualities, 1700–1800*, London: Macmillan.

Holton, S. (1996) *Suffrage Days: Stories from the Women's Suffrage Movement*, London: Routledge.

Ingram, A. (1986) 'Un/reproductions: Estates of Banishment in English Fiction after the Great War' in M.L. Broe and A. Ingram (eds) *Women's Writing in Exile*, Chapel Hill, NC: University of North Carolina Press.

—— (1989) '"Unutterable Putrefaction" and "Foul Stuff": Two "Obscene" novels of the 1920s', *Women's Studies International Forum* 9: 341–54.

Jackson, M. (1994) *The Real Facts of Life: Feminism and the Politics of Sexuality c.1850–1940*, London: Taylor and Francis.

Jeffreys, S. (1985) *The Spinster and her Enemies: Feminism and Sexuality 1880–1930*, London: Pandora.

Jivani, A. (1997) *It's Not Unusual: A History of Lesbian and Gay Britain in the Twentieth Century*, London: Michael O'Mara Books.

Johnson, P. (1989) '"The Best Friend Whom Life has Given Me": Does Winifred Holtby Have a Place in Lesbian History?' in Lesbian History Group *Not a Passing Phase: Reclaiming Lesbians in History 1840–1985*, London: The Women's Press.

Kenealy, A. (1920) *Feminism and Sex-Extinction*, London: T. Fisher Unwin.

Kennedy, E. and Davis, M. (1993) *Boots of Leather, Slippers of Gold: The History of a Lesbian Community*, London: Routledge.

Kent, S.K. (1999) *Gender and Power in Britain, 1640–1990*, London: Routledge.

Laqueur, T. (1989) 'Amor Veneris, vel Dulcedo Appeletur' in M. Feher (ed.) *The Fragments for the History of the Human Body. Vol. III*, New York: Zone.

Lesbian History Group (1989) *Not a Passing Phase: Reclaiming Lesbians in History 1840–1985*, London: The Women's Press.

Liddington, J., (1994) *Presenting the Past. Anne Lister of Halifax 1791–1840*, Hebden Bridge, West Yorkshire: Pennine Press.

Mason, M. (1995) *The Making of Victorian Sexuality*, Oxford: Oxford University Press.

Mavor, E. (1973) *The Ladies of Llangollen*, Harmondsworth, Middlesex: Penguin.

Maxwell, W. (ed.) (1982) *Letters. Sylvia Townsend Warner*, London: Chatto and Windus.

Montgomery Hyde, H. (1972) *The Other Love. An Historical and Contemporary Survey of Homosexuality in Britain*, London: Mayflower.

Moore, L. (1992) '"Something More Tender Still Than Friendship": Romantic Friendship in Early-Nineteenth Century England', *Feminist Studies* 18: 499–520.

Moran, L.J. (1995) 'The Homosexualization of English Law' in D. Herman and C. Sychin (eds) *Legal Inversions. Lesbians, Gay Men and the Politics of Law*, Philadelphia: Temple University Press.

Moscucci, O. (1996) 'Clitoridectomy, Circumcision, and the Politics of Sexual Pleasure in Mid-Victorian Britain' in A. Miller and J. Adams (eds) *Sexualities in Victorian Britain*, Bloomington and Indianapolis: Indiana University Press.

Mulford, W. (1988) *This Narrow Place. Sylvia Townsend Warner and Valentine Ackland: Life, Letters and Politics, 1930–1951*, London: Pandora.

Neild, S. and Pearson, R. (1992) *Women Like Us*, London: Women's Press.

Nestle, J. (1987) *A Restricted Country*, London: Sheba.

Newton, E. (1991) 'The Mythic Mannish Lesbian: Radclyffe Hall and the New Woman' in M. Duberman, M. Vicinus and G. Chauncey (eds) *Hidden From History: Reclaiming the Gay and Lesbian Past*, London: Penguin.

—— (1993) *Cherry Grove, Fire Island: Sixty Years in America's First Gay and Lesbian Town*, Boston: Beacon Press.

Nicolson, N. (1973) *Portrait of a Marriage*, London: Weidenfeld and Nicolson.

Norton, R. (1992) *Mother Clap's Molly House: The Gay Subculture in England 1700–1830*, London: GMP.

O'Connor, N. and Ryan, J. (1993) *Wild Desires and Mistaken Identities: Lesbianism and Psychoanalysis*, London: Virago.

Oram, A. (1989) ' "Embittered, Sexless or Homosexual": Attacks on Spinster Teachers 1918–1939' in Lesbian History Group *Not a Passing Phase: Reclaiming Lesbians in History 1840–1985*, London: The Women's Press.

—— (1992) 'Repressed and Thwarted, or Bearer of the New World? The Spinster in Interwar Feminist Discourses', *Women's History Review* 1, 3: 413–34.

—— (1996) *Women Teachers and Feminist Politics*, Manchester: Manchester University Press.

—— (1997) ' "Friends", Feminists and Sexual Outlaws: Lesbianism and British History' in G. Griffin and S. Andermahr (eds), *Straight Studies Modified. Lesbian Inter ventions in the Academy*, London: Cassell.

—— (1998) ' "Sex is an Accident": Feminism, Science and the Radical Sexual Theory of *Urania*, 1915–40' in L. Bland and L. Doan (eds) *Sexology in Culture: Labelling Bodies and Desires*, Cambridge: Polity.

Ormrod, R. (1984) *Una Troubridge. The Friend of Radclyffe Hall*, London: Jonathan Cape.

O'Rourke, R. (1989) *Reflecting on The Well of Loneliness*, London: Routledge.

Oudshoorn, N. (1994) *Beyond The Natural Body: An Archeology Of Sex Hormones*, London: Routledge.

Porter, R. and Hall, L. (1995) *The Facts of Life: The Creation of Sexual Knowledge in Britain, 1650–1950*, London: Yale University Press.

Prosser, J. (1998a) 'Transsexuals and the Transsexologists: Inversion and the Emergence of Transsexual Subjectivity' in L. Bland and L. Doan (eds) *Sexology in Culture: Labelling Bodies and Desires*, Cambridge: Polity.

—— (1998b) *Second Skins: The Body Narratives of Transsexuality*, New York: Columbia University Press.

Purvis, J. (1992) 'Using Primary Sources When Researching Women's History from a Feminist Perspective', *Women's History Review* 1, 2: 273–306.

Rendall, J. (1989) 'Friendship and Politics: Barbara Leigh Smith Bodichon (1827–91) and Bessie Rayner Parkes (1829–1925)' in S. Mendus and J. Rendall (eds) *Sexuality and Subordination*, London: Routledge.

—— (1990) *Women in an Industrializing Society: England 1750–1880*, Oxford: Basil Blackwell.

Rich, A. (1980) 'Compulsory Heterosexuality and Lesbian Existence', *Signs* 5, 4: 631–60.

Rizzo, B. (1994) *Companions Without Vows. Relationships Among Eighteenth Century British Women*, Athens, Georgia: University of Georgia Press.

Rolley, K. (1990) 'Cutting a Dash: The Dress of Radclyffe Hall and Una Troubridge'. *Feminist Review* 35: 54–66.

—— (1991) 'The Lesbian Sixth Sense: Dress as an Expression and Communication of Lesbian Identity', *Feminist Arts News* 3, 5: 6–12.

Rose, J. (1977) *The Perfect Gentleman: The Remarkable Life of Dr James Miranda Barry*, London: Hutchinson.

Rowbotham, S. (1999) *A Century of Women: The History of Women in Britain and the United States*, London: Penguin.

Ruehl, S. (1982) 'Inverts and Experts: Radclyffe Hall and Lesbian Identity' in R. Brunt and C. Rowan (eds) *Feminism Culture and Politics*, London: Lawrence and Wishart.

Scott, J. (1986) 'Gender: A Useful Category of Historical Analysis', *American Historical Review* 91: 1,053–75.

—— (1991) 'The Evidence of Experience', *Critical Inquiry* 17: 773–97.

Shaw, M. (1999) *The Clear Stream. A Life of Winifred Holtby*, London: Virago.

Sidhe, W. (2000), 'The Creation of Heterosexual National Identity Through the Abjection of Banned Books, 1918–1939', unpublished paper.

Skinner, S. (1994) 'The House in Order, Lesbian Identity in the "Well of Loneliness" ', *Women's Studies – An Interdisciplinary Journal* 23: 19–33.

Smart, C. (ed.) (1992) *Regulating Womanhood: Historical Essays on Marriage, Motherhood and Sexuality*, London: Routledge.

—— (1996) 'Good Wives and Moral Lives: Marriage and Divorce 1937–51' in C. Gledhill and G. Swanson (eds) *Nationalising Femininity: Culture, Sexuality and British Cinema in the Second World War*, Manchester: Manchester University Press.

Smith-Rosenburg, C. (1975) 'The Female World of Love and Ritual: Relations Between Women in Nineteenth Century America', *Signs* 1, 1: 1–18.

Souhami, D. (1998) *The Trials of Radclyffe Hall*, London: Weidenfeld and Nicolson.

Stanley, L. (1992) 'Romantic Friendship? Some Issues in Researching Lesbian History and Biography', *Women's History Review* 1, 2: 193–216.

Stanley, L. and Morley, A. (1988) *The Life and Death of Emily Wilding Davison*, London: The Women's Press.

Straub, K. (1991) 'The Guilty Pleasures of Female Theatrical Cross-Dressing and the Autobiography of Charlotte Charke' in J. Epstein and K. Straub (eds) *Body Guards: The Cultural Politics of Gender Ambiguity*, London: Routledge.

Summerscale, K. (1998) *The Queen of Whale Cay*, London: Fourth Estate.

Sweetman, D. (1993) *Mary Renault. A Biography*, London: Pimlico.

Taverner, J. (1997) *Rebellion*, London: Onlywomen Press.

Tinkler, P. (1995) *Constructing Girlhood: Popular Magazines for Girls Growing Up in England, 1920–1950*, London: Taylor and Francis.

Townsend, C. (1996) ' "I Am the Woman for Spirit": A Working Woman's Gender Transgression in Victorian London' in A.H. Miller and J.E. Adams (eds) *Sexualities in Victorian Britain*, Bloomington and Indianapolis: Indiana University Press.

Traub, V. (1996) 'The Perversion of Lesbian Desire', *History Workshop Journal* 41: 23–49.

Troubridge, U. (1961) *The Life and Death of Radclyffe Hall*, London: Hammond and Hammond.

Trumbach, R (1991) 'London's Sapphists: From Three Sexes to Four Genders in the Making of Modern Culture' in J. Epstein and K. Straub (eds) *Body Guards: The Cultural Politics of Gender Ambiguity*, London: Routledge.

Vernon, J. (2000) ' "For Some Queer Reason ... " The Trials and Tribulations of Colonel Barker's Masquerade in Interwar Britain', *Signs* 26, 1: 37–62.

Vicinus, M. (1985) *Independent Women. Work and Community for Single Women, 1850–1920*, London: Virago.

—— (1989) ' "They Wonder to Which Sex I Belong": The Historical Roots of the Modern Lesbian Identity' in D. Altman, C. Vance, M. Vicinus, J. Weeks (eds) *Homosexuality, Which Homosexuality?,* London: Gay Men's Press.

—— (1991) 'Distance and Desire. English Boarding School Friendships' in M. Duberman, M. Vicinus and G. Chauncey (eds) *Hidden From History: Reclaiming the Lesbian and Gay Past*, London: Penguin.

—— (1994) 'Lesbian History: All Theory and No Facts or All Facts and No Theory?', *Radical History Review* 60: 57–75.

—— (1996) 'Turn of the Century Male Impersonation: Rewriting the Romance Plot' in A.H. Miller and J.E. Adams (eds) *Sexualities in Victorian Britain*, Bloomington and Indianapolis: Indiana University Press.

—— (1997) 'Lesbian Perversity and Victorian Marriage: The 1864 Codrington Divorce Trial', *Journal of British Studies* 36: 70–98.

Walkowitz, J. (1993) *City of Dreadful Delight. Narratives of Sexual Danger in Late Victorian London*, London: Virago.

Waters, S. (1998) *Tipping the Velvet*, London: Virago.

Weeks, J. (1977) *Coming Out. Homosexual Politics in Britain, from the Nineteenth Century to the Present*, London: Quartet.

—— (1981) *Sex, Politics and Society*, London: Longman.

—— (1985) *Sexuality and Its Discontents*, London: Routledge.

Weiss, A. (1993) *Vampires and Violets: Lesbians in Film*, New York: Penguin.

Wheelwright, J. (1989) *Amazons and Military Maids: Women Who Dressed as Men in the Pursuit of Life, Liberty and Happiness*, London: Pandora.

Whitbread, H. (ed.) (1988) *I Know My Own Heart. The Diaries of Anne Lister (1791–1840)*, London: Virago Press.

Whitelaw, L. (1990) *The Life and Rebellious Times of Cicely Hamilton*, London: The Women's Press.

Wilson, E. (1990) 'Deviant Dress', *Feminist Review* 35: 67–74.

INDEX